Y0-CCG-461

February, 1937

PRINTED IN THE
UNITED STATES OF AMERICA

OUT OF DOORS

A Guide to Nature

D. Warren Boyer

"My hand alone my work can do,
So I can fish and study too."

OUT OF DOO

A Guide to Nature

BY

PAUL B. MANN

ASSOCIATE IN EDUCATION
AMERICAN MUSEUM OF NATURAL HISTORY
SUPERVISOR OF SCIENCE, SENIOR HIGH SCHOOLS
CHAIRMAN OF STANDING COMMITTEE ON SCIENCE
NEW YORK CITY

AND

GEORGE T. HASTINGS

FACULTY MEMBER OF NATURE CAMP
PENNSYLVANIA STATE COLLEGE
HEAD OF DEPARTMENT OF BIOLOGY
THEODORE ROOSEVELT HIGH SCHOOL
NEW YORK CITY

NEW YORK
HENRY HOLT AND COMPANY

OUT OF DOORS

A Guide to Nature

D. Warren Boyer

"MY HAND ALONE MY WORK CAN DO,
SO I CAN FISH AND STUDY TOO."

PREFACE

For years many of the pedagogical attempts to develop an enjoyable and lasting response to nature have seemed to defeat their own ends. The subject has been conventionalized into nature *study* and the time allocated to it has been limited to the early school grades. Interest in nature, however, is not to be bound by formal treatment or by the segregation prescribed by a curriculum. Young people are keen to know and to do. Their class work in biology during school hours, their scouting and camping after school hours, and their innate curiosity at all times have sharpened their appreciation of the out of doors. They need, therefore, not a scientific tome of intense specialization, but a book which will be a friendly guide on their walks and in their camps; a book interpretative by text and illustration of the whole field of nature, yet small enough to be a handbook. Such a book the authors have endeavored to provide in *Out of Doors: A Guide to Nature.*

If success has been attained it is due in no small measure to those friends and associates who have given so freely of time and interest, who have criticized the manuscript, and who have aided in securing illustrations. For such valuable assistance the authors are especially indebted to Marjorie C. Coit, Director of the School Nature League, New York City; to William Hassler of the Department of Herpetology, American Museum of Natural History; Edith J. Hastings; Ruth Paul Mann; Oliver P. Medsger of Jersey City High School; John T. Nichols, Curator of Fishes, American Museum of Natural History; and Mervin E. Oakes, State Normal School, Fredonia, N. Y.

Credit for the copyrighted pictures is given beneath the illustrations themselves, and the authors are glad to express their special gratitude to Mr. Medsger and to the American Museum of Natural History for their generous contribution of photographs.

P. B. M.
G. T. H.

CONTENTS

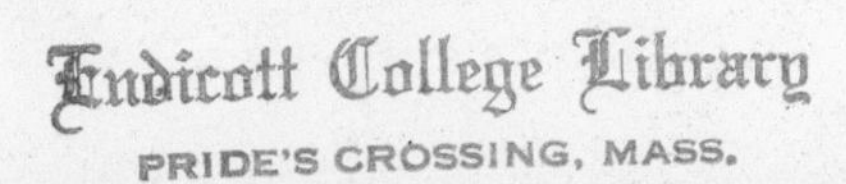

INTRODUCTION

THERE has been a great change from the time when the teaching of nature lore in schools was left to some substitute teacher and in camps entrusted to the least occupied counselor. Today nature study in elementary schools and biology in secondary schools call for talented and trained teachers while all good camps have nature counselors with nature work prominent in the camp program.

The increasing interest in the out of doors has evoked many books particularly for younger children, but no book has been written to meet the general needs of adolescents. This volume, happily entitled *Out of Doors: A Guide to Nature*, seems peculiarly adapted to young naturalists and would-be naturalists; it will also make a strong appeal to any adult. Its clear, graphic, yet simple language and carefully selected photographs and drawings will be a delight to every fortunate owner. Every field of outdoor science is included. When I was a boy I yearned for such a book as this.

The authors are among the best all-round naturalists of my acquaintance, with a splendid field and laboratory knowledge of the various phases of plant and animal life. Much of the information in the book is based on their personal experiences in the open and in summer camps. Each is also a practical teacher of biology at the head of the biology department of a large New York City high school. Each has served as president of the New York Association of Biology Teachers and in many other educational activities. From their long and rich experience they have incorporated in one volume the kind of nature material that will make this book invaluable to every teacher of biology and nature, to every camp director and nature counselor, and for every boy and girl a most attractive and useful interpreter of the out of doors.

OLIVER P. MEDSGER

OUT OF DOORS: A GUIDE TO NATURE

FOREWORD TO YOUNG PEOPLE

interest in nature be evoked by a friendly interpreter. To enter this domain with the seeing eye and the hearing ear is to find something new each hour. To remain is to become *nature-alized*, to become a citizen of nature, enlisted to discover facts, to think more clearly, and to enjoy life more fully. This is knowledge not procurable from libraries. You yourself must smell the dark earth and feel the touch of the night wind; you must taste the bark of young birches, see the wake of the swimming muskrat, and hear the whir of a startled partridge.

It is our hope that this book may be an interpreter, not only to enthusiastic young naturalists in country or city, but particularly to those who are starting their adventures in field and woodland. We want to lead you through a door opened on vistas of interest and beauty so that you may find joy and freedom in the out of doors. The breezes, the meadows, the sunrise, the fog, the moonlight, the varying smells, the sounds of bird or beast, the grass, the flowers, the ledge, and the stream are yours for the asking.

BIBLIOGRAPHY

BEARD, DAN CARTER, *Outdoor Handy Book.* Charles Scribner's Sons, 1912.

Practical suggestions for young people for camping and playing in the out of doors.

CADY, BERTHA CHAPMAN, *Guides to Nature Study.* Slingerland-Comstock Company, 1929–1931.

Excellent brief notes and directions for teachers and leaders.

CARR, WILLIAM, *The Stir of Nature.* Oxford University Press, 1930.

Short stories and descriptions of birds and animals, chiefly from the author's experience.

COMSTOCK, ANNA BOTSFORD, *Handbook of Nature Study*, 23d edition. Comstock Publishing Company, 1935.

Over 230 teacher's stories and lessons for nature teachers in the grades by the "mother" of nature study.

DOWNING, ELLIOT R., *A Field Book and Laboratory Guide in Biological Nature Study.* Longmans, Green and Company, 1918.

Directions for laboratory work and field studies, with keys to trees, weeds, and birds of the Chicago region.

—— *Our Living World.* Longmans, Green and Company, 1924.

An excellent biological text from an ecological point of view.

FULLER, RAYMOND T., *The Doorway to Nature.* John Day Company, Inc., 1931.

Outdoor narratives with descriptions of some common flowers and birds.

—— *Walk, Look, and Listen.* John Day Company, Inc., 1929.

Pleasant reading about what one may see in the out of doors.

GREEN, GEORGE REX, *Survey of Nature.* Slingerland-Comstock Company, 1929.

Just what the title suggests: short chapters on all types of living things, and on rocks, weather, and stars.

HEGNER, ROBERT WILHELM and JANE, *Parade of the Animal Kingdom.* The Macmillan Company, 1935.

A large and valuable reference book covering both vertebrates and invertebrates. Lavishly illustrated.

HOWES, P. G., *Backyard Exploration.* Doubleday, Doran and Company, Inc., 1927.

Beautifully illustrated accounts of some familiar forms of life.

MEDSGER, OLIVER P., *Nature Rambles — Spring,* 1931; *Summer, Autumn, Winter,* 1932. Frederick Warne and Company, Inc.

A set of four books, one for each season; informal and well-illustrated talks by a thorough naturalist about the things one finds on walks in fields, woods, mountains, and on the seashore.

MORGAN, ANN, *Field Book of Ponds and Streams.* G. P. Putnam's Sons, 1930.

A complete handbook of the life of ponds and streams, well illustrated.

NEEDHAM, JAMES G., *Natural History of the Farm.* American Viewpoint Society, Inc., 1931.

Written for boys and girls in the country by one of our foremost entomologists and naturalists.

PACK, A. N., and PALMER, E. L., *The Nature Almanac.* American Nature Association, 1931.

A survey of organized nature work in each state and suggestions for reading and study by months and grades, with references to *Nature Magazine.*

PALMER, E. LAWRENCE, *Field Book of Nature Study.* Slingerland-Comstock Company, 1929.

Tables, keys, life histories, outline drawings. A great amount of information in concise form.

—— *Camp and Field Notebook and Nature Series for the Grades.* Slingerland-Comstock Company.

A collection of outline drawings of birds, trees, flowers, and insects, and keys for most of these, all of which are sold separately or in sets. New items published frequently.

PEATTIE, DONALD CULROSS, *Almanac for Moderns.* G. P. Putnam's Sons, 1935.

—— *Green Laurels.* Simon and Schuster, 1936.

The lives and achievements of famous naturalists since the days of Aristotle. Beautifully told.

—— "Singing in the Wilderness," from *Essays on Famous Naturalists and Natural History.* G. P. Putnam's Sons.

An engrossing story of the pioneer bird-lover, Audubon.

VINAL, WILLIAM G., *Nature Guiding.* Slingerland-Comstock Company, 1926.

Directions for nature leaders and teachers with stories drawn from the author's wide experience in camps and schools.

WARD, HENSHAW, *Exploring the Universe.* Bobbs-Merrill Company, 1927.

Graphic and fascinating descriptions of "the incredible discoveries of recent science."

WILLIAMSON, H., *Salar the Salmon.* Ryerson Press, 1935.

A charmingly written story of the life of a salmon; fiction, but scientifically accurate.

GETTING ACQUAINTED WITH ANIMAL LIFE

Photograph by Mary C. Dickerson. *Courtesy of American Museum of Natural History*

SILENT SNOWS THAT SPEAK OF NIGHTLY QUESTS OF RABBITS AND OTHER FURRY FOLK.

CHAPTER I

FUR-BEARERS

The Mole had long wanted to make the acquaintance of the Badger. But whenever the Mole mentioned his wish to the Water Rat, he always found himself put off. "Badger hates Society," replied the Rat simply.[1]

— KENNETH GRAHAME

When people speak of an animal, they usually mean a four-footed, hair-covered creature, properly called a mammal. These creatures are all around us in the woods and fields but they usually avoid us so carefully that we are not even conscious of their presence. Dainty, white-footed mice may sometimes cross the path or may be seen peering down with their big bright eyes from a rafter; striped chipmunks may pick up scraps of food near the mess hall or even make a bold visit beneath our table, to scurry away at the slightest movement with tail erect; red or gray squirrels may be glimpsed in the trees; or woodchucks may be seen sitting up by their burrows in the open fields ready to dive in at any sign of danger; and sometimes a little brown rabbit scuttles across the trail ahead of us with his white tail-patch flashing. But there is little opportunity to study their habits, for most of them choose the nighttime to be about, largely to escape the unwelcome attention of man.

MICE. Of native mice, the most common are the white-footed or wood mouse, and the field or meadow mouse. Wood mice are very often found around camps, sometimes

[1] From *The Wind in the Willows* by Kenneth Grahame. Copyright by Charles Scribner's Sons.

causing considerable annoyance by their raids on the food supplies. A little larger than the common house mouse, they are fawn- or gray-colored above and white beneath,

FAMILIAR SMALL MAMMALS

These are among the most widespread and best known mammals.

with large ears. Very graceful little fellows they are and they can run along the side of a board wall or trip the beams as easily as any squirrel. They make their nests in hollow logs, in deserted birds' nests, or in cavities in the trees, often at a considerable height. About camp they seem to like corners in the buildings or boxes or drawers, where they gather a mass of soft material, dead leaves, and plant fibers; also, unfortunately, the stuffing from mattresses and pillows. If food is put out for them they will become as tame as chipmunks and let you study them. If a nest of half-grown young is found, they may be kept in a cage and will make good pets. In fact, young animals of almost any kind can be tamed, but wild animals should not be caged unless they can be cared for properly. It is against the law in most states to keep any wild fur-bearing animals unless a special permit is secured. Cages should be large enough to give ample room for moving about, with a box or shaded corner for a retreat.

Meadow mice (field mice) are as common as white-footed mice though not so large and lacking the grace of their woodland cousins. They are dark gray with short legs and tails, and with ears so small as to be almost hidden in the coarse fur. Their runways, little tunnels about an inch in diameter through the grass, if traced carefully will be found to lead to the entrance of the burrows, or perhaps to a summer nest in a little hollow or under a tuft of grass. Eating a great variety of plants and destroying the nests of bumble-bees, the meadow mice do a considerable amount of harm. Their numbers are kept in check by snakes, owls, and hawks. There are many species and varieties of meadow mice, all very much alike.

CHIPMUNKS. Chipmunks may often become quite tame if they are not frightened and if there are no cats or dogs about. Sometimes you see them at play, chasing each other around with a great rustling of dead leaves. Sometimes they will climb trees to gather nuts of which they seem especially fond. They will also eat wild berries and insects and at times catch and eat frogs. Unfortunately they destroy many birds' eggs and even the young birds. Bits of food put out for them will often bring them near the mess hall or kitchen, and they quickly learn where food is to be found. It is interesting to watch them fill their cheek pouches, then hurry off to their burrows to return in a few minutes for another load. Their burrows extend for some yards underground with many branches, and somewhere two feet or more below ground there is a nest cavity about a foot across, partly filled with bark fibers and leaves.

Courtesy of Oliver P. Medsger

A FAMILY OF YOUNG GRAY SQUIRRELS

Brought up on a doll's nursing bottle they became so tame that they would not leave when given their liberty.

SQUIRRELS. Relatives of the chipmunks and mice are the squirrels. In most regions the commonest are the red squirrels or chickarees. If seeds, nuts, or other food are left for them they soon learn where to come for it and may be encouraged to stay near by. Sometimes the red squirrels can be seen chasing each other up and down a tree or out among the branches; or one may sit on a branch and scold with his shrill, chattering cry. Interesting and attractive as he is, among nature lovers he is in disrepute because of his fondness for eggs and young birds as food. In this respect he is much worse than the chipmunk.

His larger cousin, the gray squirrel, is a less serious enemy of the birds, and like the chipmunk is tamed by protection and feeding. Often in the woods a squirrel's dining table may be found — a rock or stump on which he has opened many pine or spruce cones, or eaten out the seeds at the base of each part of the tulip tree fruit, leaving the waste parts scattered about.

Less often seen, though in many places not less numerous, are flying squirrels. They are nocturnal in habit, sleeping in their nests during the day. The nests are made of leaves or strips of bark, placed in hollows in trees, in bird boxes, about houses, or less often in forks of limbs or on top of old birds' nests.

RABBITS. Common to most regions of the United States are rabbits of several species, from the little cottontail of the East to the jack rabbit of the West. Sometimes they live in burrows dug by woodchucks or other animals, but often their only homes are the little hollows or "forms" in the grass or under the bushes. They are chiefly nocturnal, beginning to feed in the early evening. They eat a great variety of plants but are especially fond of such cultivated ones as cabbage and lettuce.

WOODCHUCKS. Woodchucks commonly live in open fields, where they make their burrows, digging out the soil and piling it up at the entrances. As the burrows frequently extend underground more than twenty feet, the piles of dirt are conspicuous. Their runways may often be traced for some distance through the grass to the feeding grounds. When surprised away from home they dash off to the burrows. If not too badly frightened they usually stop and sit up on the hillock beside the opening before plunging in. Go around to the upper side of the burrow after Mr. Chuck has gone in and lie quietly till he ventures out to explore. Considerable patience is required and the only reward is to catch a glimpse of his head as he cautiously comes up to reconnoiter. Being above him we have a chance to see him look in several directions before he spies us and drops out of sight again. Having fed on clover, grass, and weeds during the summer, in September or October he retires to sleep until early spring. According to the legends often believed by country boys, the woodchuck comes out of his burrow on February 2, ground-hog day, to look around. If the sun is shining and he sees his shadow he at once goes back to sleep for six weeks longer while cold weather continues, but if the day is cloudy, warm weather is at hand. Note the lament of James Whitcomb Riley's boy who had to chop wood:

Courtesy of Oliver P. Medsger

WOODCHUCK

Woodchucks hold their own despite the enmity of farmers.

> Nothin' ever made me madder
> Than fer Pap to stomp in, layin'
> On an extra fore-stick, sayin',
> "Grounhog's out and seed his shadder!" [1]

SKUNKS. Around most camps, skunks come at night to hunt for food. They are usually well behaved. Baby

[1] From *Green Fields and Running Brooks* by James Whitcomb Riley. Copyright by The Bobbs-Merrill Company. Reprinted by permission.

skunks make the best sort of pets, playful and affectionate, and as long as they are well treated will make no trouble for anyone. If there is a dog in camp, however, it would not be wise to try to keep a skunk. Secure in their ability to defend themselves, skunks show little fear of man or other animals. Farmers often object to them because of their fondness for eggs and young chickens, but away from

PORCUPINE

The quills are not only needle sharp but are barbed at the tip.

the barnyard they are valuable because they eat insects, rats, and mice.

PORCUPINES. As fearless as the skunk is the porcupine, armed with sharp quills. Porcupines have great appetites and are especially fond of the bark of pine, spruce, and other trees, but they particularly relish any wood that has the slightest trace of salt. Handles of paddles and oars receive enough salt from perspiring hands to be relished. Sometimes porcupines will gnaw through floors or sides of camp buildings. Though slow and stolid they are interesting, and much can be learned by watching them. Even a little first-hand observation would disprove the common superstition that porcupines shoot their quills. When alarmed they raise the quills so that the whole body bristles with them. If an enemy threatens they will slap with their tails, the quills easily coming loose as soon as they enter the flesh of the attacker. As they are backwardly barbed at the point, it is difficult to draw them out of the flesh and bad wounds result.

MUSKRATS. In swamps or along the shallow water of lake shores there can often be seen conical hillocks of grasses, cat-tail leaves, and brush, the homes of muskrats. Muskrats are the most valuable fur animals in our country, many million skins being used each year as furs, often passing under such trade names as "Hudson seal" or "river mink." While chiefly nocturnal they may frequently be seen swimming near their homes, especially in the late afternoon. In lakes or by streams where fresh-water mussels are found, look for piles of mussel shells — the mark of a place where the muskrat has brought his catch to eat. Besides shell fish, muskrats eat the stems and roots of water plants. Their living rooms are in the upper part of their houses, above water level, but the entrances are below water. Sometimes they make burrows into the river banks, leading from below low water up to a chamber or room where they live and where the young are born. Just as the English sparrow and starling, introduced here from their native countries, have become nuisances, so muskrats have become a nuisance in Bohemia where they were introduced in 1905 to lend interest to a nobleman's ponds.

BEAVERS. Even more interesting than the muskrat is the beaver. Exterminated in the eastern United States for their fur years ago, they have been re-introduced in many places from the West and have settled down and multiplied. If beaver dams and houses are near the camp, visit them in the early morning or late evening with a group small enough to insure quiet. If positions are taken near the dam, where the group can sit comfortably and half concealed, patience is almost sure to be rewarded by a sight of the beaver swimming about, perhaps carrying material for the dam, or cutting trees. If a small opening is made

Photograph by G. T. Hastings

ASPEN CUT BY A BEAVER

Tooth marks can be seen on both the trunk and the broad chips.

in the top of the dam (providing it is not illegal to do so), the beavers may be watched as they make repairs. From the dam, sticks can be secured that show the marks of beaver cutting at the ends and on the sides where the bark has been gnawed off. It is interesting to examine the stumps of cut trees to see how many kinds the beavers have been using for food. None of our animals is more interesting to study, and possibly none has had more stories that are not true told about him. But the fanciful stories of using their tails to carry mud for the dams, or as trowels, or of their intelligence in planning the size of lakes and the height the water is to be raised, are not so remarkable as the genuine skill they actually show in felling trees and making dams and houses.

DEER. In most forested areas deer are now increasing, due to the protection given them. Just the glimpse secured as they bound away, white tails erect, gives one a thrill, and to be able to watch them feed in the early morning or late afternoon is a real experience.

VIRGINIA DEER

As in other deer the buck only has antlers.

SHREWS. The smallest mammals of our region are the shrews — tiny little fellows with slender feet and legs, slender pointed heads with diminutive eyes and ears almost hidden in the thick fur. They hunt actively at night, remaining hidden during the day. Though rarely seen they are very common in old fields and in the edge of woods. You may come upon one when you turn over an old log or piece of bark, but you must be very quick if you would catch him as he scampers for shelter. The common shrew is grayish-brown or fawn-colored and has a tail about one-third the length of the body. The dark gray, heavier-bodied, short-tailed shrew has a tail less than one-fourth the length of the body. Most people take them for mice, although they are not closely related to mice. Mice are rodents; shrews are insectivores.

MOLES. Shrews are also mistaken for moles, which they resemble in the soft fur and small eyes, but they lack the broad front feet with which the moles dig their burrows. Probably everyone has seen the long ridges that are pushed up where the moles burrow close to the surface. These can often be followed for several hundred feet and are a source of annoyance to gardeners and owners of lawns, but of interest to nature lovers. Moles are so perfectly adapted to life underground that their eyes have nearly disappeared and they walk on the surface clumsily. Living largely on insects and worms they are useful animals, in addition to the fact that their soft, dense fur is prized by man.

COMMON MOLE

Though rarely seen, moles are very abundant in most parts of the country.

BATS. As the mole shows remarkable adaptations for life below ground, so the bat is equally well adapted for life in the air. The arms are very long and slender with fingers as long as the whole body. The thin skin stretched over the arms and fingers and extending back to the short legs and tail, makes powerful wings with which the bat skillfully zigzags through the air in the evening or at night, feeding on flying insects. Of the several kinds of bats in the Eastern States, the most common are the red bat, recognized by the reddish fur; the little brown bat seen about buildings; and the hoary bat which hangs up by day in trees. In the angles where the rafters join the roof in old barns or houses, bats can be found during the day. The baby bat is carried around clinging to the mother, in a fold of skin which makes a partial pouch. In the daytime bats are sometimes caught in the hands and can be kept in cages. They eat insects and bits of meat. Such active animals need much more room than a cage can furnish and should not be confined more than a few hours, if at all. The stories so often told and generally believed about bats becoming entangled in people's hair have no basis in fact. It is rather a sorry commentary on human intelligence to see the panic that often develops when a bat flutters into a tent or room and the violent efforts made to destroy it. It would be much better to watch it fly around, noting the sharp turns it makes and its skill in avoiding the walls and objects. In a short time, if not molested, it will make its way out as it entered and continue its beneficial work of destroying flies, mosquitoes, and other insects.

There are other animals living in our woods and fields — weasels, minks, opossums, raccoons, and foxes — but all so wary as to be seldom seen. Hunting for their tracks is more certain of results than hunting the animals themselves.

BIBLIOGRAPHY

Anthony, H. E., *Field Book of North American Mammals.* G. P. Putnam's Sons, 1928.

An excellent field book, well illustrated, with descriptions of all common forms.

Edge, Rosalie, *Finishing the Mammals.* Publication No. 59, 1936. Emergency Conservation Committee, 734 Lexington Avenue, New York City. May be obtained free.

HORNADAY, WILLIAM T., *American Natural History.* Charles Scribner's Sons, 1914.

A very valuable book for reference describing all the families and most of the genera of vertebrates.

NELSON, E. W., *Wild Animals of North America.* National Geographic Society, 1918.

Beautiful illustrations by Fuertes with interesting descriptions; also many animal tracks illustrated.

PAULI, G. W., *Dictionary of Furs.* Paw-Lee Jeffries Company, Educational Publicity Service, Davenport, Iowa, 1925.

A small and inexpensive booklet giving interesting information about furs.

SCOTT, W. B., *History of Land Mammals in the Western Hemisphere.* The Macmillan Company, 1913.

A rather technical account of the geological history of mammals.

STONE, W., and CRAM, W. E., *American Animals.* Doubleday, Doran and Company, Inc., 1905.

A popular account of the mammals of America. Many illustrations, some in color, with interesting notes and comments.

CHAPTER II

TRACKS AND CASTS

The cat does not show its claws in the track. In walking, the hind foot is set exactly in the track of the front foot; this perfect register offers many advantages and makes for a silent tread. The track of the cat will probably be noticed more than that of any other animal, owing to the large numbers of them in every locality.[1]

— Ernest Thompson Seton

We are often able to study animals from their tracks when direct observation is impossible. The ideal condition for observing tracks is when there is a light snow on the ground. This gives a complete record of an animal's activities. One may follow such a trail for some distance, seeing where the animal stopped to feed or reconnoiter, or perhaps where it hid from some enemy or dashed off in fright. There is a great opportunity for scientific conjectures as to the causes of variations in the trail. Such practice is one of the best checks on our knowledge of animal habits and behavior.

Observing Tracks. In summer the best we can do is to look for the fragments of the record in some patch of dust along the roadside, or in moist sand or mud near a lake or stream. It may pay to wet and smooth off a stretch of the lake shore in the afternoon; then next morning try to find what animals were there and what they were doing. If moist sand or ashes or fine dust is spread

[1] Copyright by the *National Geographic Magazine*. Reprinted by permission.

over the ground in the evening in some strategic place around the kitchen or mess hall, animals are likely to leave their autographs during the night.

The trail made by a caterpillar may frequently be found along a dusty road; perhaps we may find the tracks of a

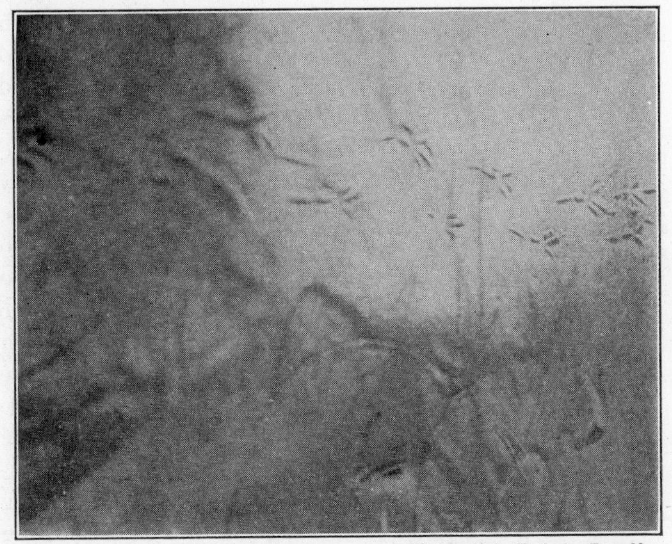

Photograph by Katherine Fernald

TRACKS IN THE SAND

A shore bird hunted here for food.

crow wandering up the same road in its constant search for food, the impressions of the four toes clearly marked, with little lines showing where the claws were dragged a bit at the beginning of a step. If the crow overtakes the caterpillar, only one set of tracks will go on from the point of meeting! To hunt for tracks and to see how much can be deciphered from them makes an interesting objective on a hike.

RECORDING TRACKS. In any serious study of animal tracks, careful sketches should be made, natural size or drawn to scale, of both right and left, front and back feet. If the details in the tracks are not all clear, several may be compared and the details lacking in one supplied from another. Use a pencil or twig to measure the length and breadth of the track. The drawing should show all details, such as the pad of the foot and the toes and claws if they can be seen.

THE CROW AND THE CATERPILLAR

Can you tell where the crow met the caterpillar, and also where the crow took flight?

After making sketches to show the form and size of the tracks, make a series of small drawings to scale of a succession of tracks to show their arrangement and the proportionate distance between them. This series will show the direction the animal was going; whether, if a bird, it hopped like a robin or walked like a crow; whether the animal was running or walking (the difference showing in the distance between the footprints); whether it ran like a dog or fox, putting one foot ahead of the other, or bounded like a rabbit with the hind feet striking the ground ahead of and outside of the front feet. These and many other characteristics of animals can be noted in their tracks.

Deer tracks are usually clear-cut, the sharp hoofs sinking for some distance into sand or soft soil. The raccoon and skunk walk flat-footed, the heel of the hind feet showing plainly; while mice, squirrels, dogs, and cats walk on their toes, making impressions of the toes and pads. With cats

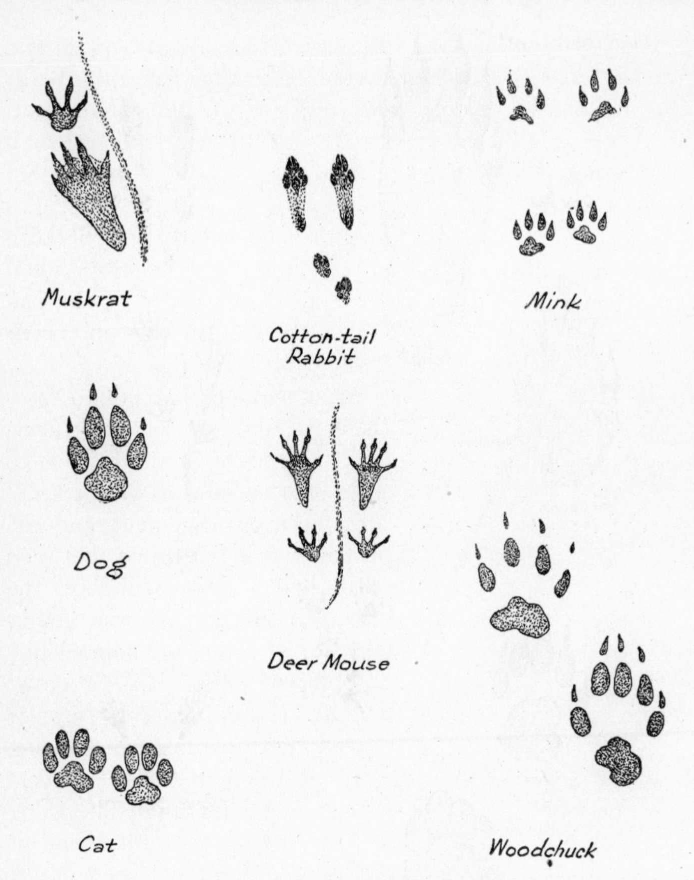

TRACKS OF COMMON ANIMALS

Note the marks made by the dragging tails of the muskrat and the deer mouse.

and their relatives, the claws are sheathed when walking so they do not show in the tracks, but with most other animals the claw marks show plainly. With most animals the tracks of the front feet show only four toes while all five toes of the hind feet leave impressions. Each time

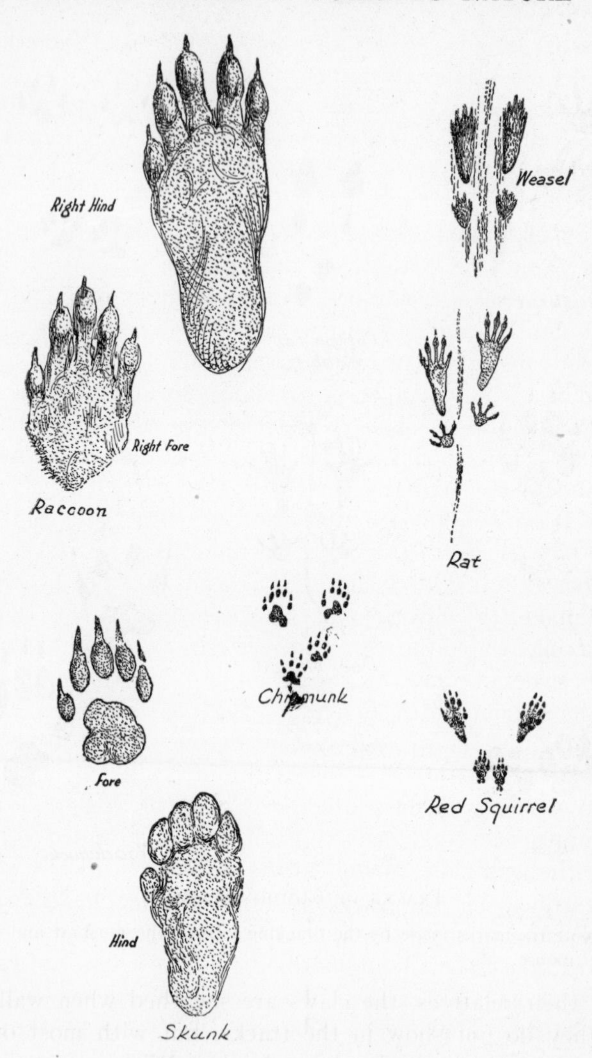

TRACKS OF COMMON ANIMALS

The weasel and the rat also have dragging tails which leave marks.

tracks are noted, new details may be found and something more learned about the animal that made them.

The illustration of the crow's walk along the road gives an idea of the sort of record that can be made. A notebook of such drawings makes a valuable collection.

The most fascinating method of making permanent records of animal tracks is the making of plaster casts. These cannot be made from footprints in the dust or soft snow but very accurate ones can be secured from those in moist sand or mud. The necessary equipment consists of two tin cans of one or two quarts capacity, strips of cardboard or a band of copper or tin about one and a half inches wide and eighteen inches or more long, a stick for stirring, a small can of talcum powder or a can of light automobile oil, and plaster of Paris, which may be carried in a third can. If cans of different sizes are used, the plaster and talcum powder may be put in the innermost can and the cardboard rolled and slipped between two of the cans. This makes the outfit compact for carrying.

Having located the tracks and selected the one that shows the best detail, dust the ground around it with the talcum powder or pour a little oil over it. It is possible, however, to get good results without talcum or oil. Then place the strip of cardboard or tin around the track like a fence, either pushing it down into the ground, or making a wall of mud or sand against it. Care should be taken not to have the wall close enough to the track to distort it when the cardboard is pushed down. Now mix the plaster in one of the cans, pouring the water from the other can and stirring till you have a liquid of about the consistency of thick pea soup, no thinner than is necessary in order to have it pour easily. That means somewhat less than half as much water as plaster. If the plaster is too thin, it will take a long time to harden and may crack as it dries. If too thick, it will be difficult to pour and will not fill in the details of the

Photographs by G. T. Hastings

STEPS IN MAKING A CAST

Above, the track is sprinkled with talcum and the collar ready. In the center the collar is in place; below, it is being filled with plaster.

track. Enough plaster can be mixed at one time to make three or four casts if the tracks are close together and are all prepared. In general, the quicker the plaster can be poured the better. After it once begins to harden it cannot be poured, nor can it be mixed up again with water and used.

Let the cast stand twenty minutes or more till hard, then remove the pasteboard or metal fence and lift up the cast with whatever mud or sand adheres. Do not clean off the soil at once but let the cast harden for some hours. Then it can be brushed off. The casts may be carried home in the cans. Put a little paper, soft moss, or dry leaves between them for protection against breakage.

These casts are negatives, the reverse of the actual impression. When cleaned up they should have the name and date written on the back. If positives are not to be made from them, they may be painted or varnished. In painting, a darker shade may be used for the track than for the background. A convenient way to keep a collection of casts of tracks is in flat trays or shallow boxes. In exhibiting them they can be placed on a table with the name and the place where they were secured. Pictures of the kind of animal that made them placed beside them or on the wall in back of them make the exhibit more interesting.

If a positive is desired it may easily be made from the negative, unless this is in very high relief with much overhang. Tracks made in soft mud are often so deep that the negative stands up very high and it is difficult to make a positive without injuring the negative. The face of the negative should be thoroughly covered with vaseline or oil to prevent the plaster of the positive from adhering to it. Place the negative on a work table or on the floor, then around the edges make a wall of cardboard, held in place with plasteline, or make the wall entirely of a ribbon of plasteline, making sure that the wall is higher than the highest part of the negative. Now mix plaster of Paris as before and pour over the negative. When thoroughly hardened remove the wall. In most cases positive and negative will appear to be firmly joined. If some of the plaster

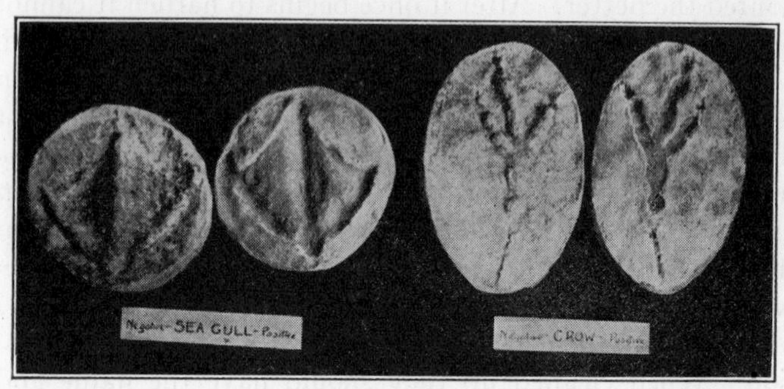

Photograph by G. T. Hastings

CASTS OF BIRD TRACKS

The negatives are at the left, the positives at the right.

has run down over the sides of the negative, shave this off with a knife. If the positive does not now lift off easily, insert the point of the knife blade between the two to loosen them. However if the negative was well coated with vaseline or talcum this should be unnecessary.

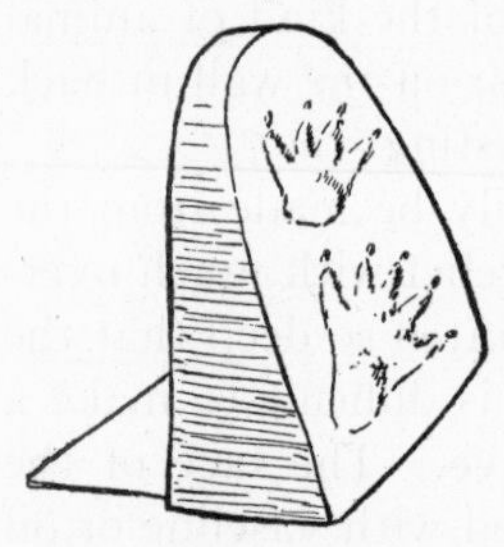

A BOOK END OF PLASTER

The tracks are those of a raccoon.

Numerous positives can be made from one negative, so that if several are making collections of tracks all may have copies. The casts will appear to better advantage if painted — the track itself a dark gray or brown with the rest a lighter shade. Casts can be utilized to make attractive paper weights and book ends. For book ends make a wall around the negative from 3 to 4 inches high at what is to be the base of the finished book end, tapering to $1\frac{1}{2}$ or 2 inches on the opposite side.

Elevate the top ends slightly so that the top of the wall is level and pour in the plaster. After the plaster has hardened and the wall has been removed, the sides may be smoothed with a pocket knife or a wood rasp. To make the book end of the illustration, a piece of tin, cut and painted with some enamel paint, may be placed in the plaster after it is poured and before it hardens.

If the cast is to be hung on the wall a loop of string should be set in the plaster before it hardens. Take a piece of string three or four inches long and tie a knot in each end. Press these ends into the plaster (soon after it is poured) at the side which is to be the top, making a loop half an inch long. If the loop is placed in the back just below the top it can be entirely concealed.

Leaf Prints. Plaster casts of leaves may also be made, but as leaves can be so easily pressed and mounted, or "printed," it is rather useless to make casts except for the interest there is in the process. A leaf may be laid in a plate and the plaster poured over it. When the plaster is hard the leaf is lifted off, leaving its impression in the plaster. Better prints can be made with the leaf in relief by using plasteline instead of plaster for the negative. Roll out a piece of plasteline — a piece of broom handle makes a good roller — till smooth and larger than the leaf to be used. If the roller is moistened, plasteline will not adhere. Put the leaf lower side down on the plasteline, roll it so that it sinks in, then lift the leaf off, make a wall of plasteline about ½ inch high around the impression and pour in the plaster of Paris. If the leaf impression of the finished positive is painted green and the background of some other color, the effect will be that of a natural leaf lying on the plaster.

Another use of plaster is in mounting rock specimens. If rings or rectangles of cardboard are set into plasteline bases and plaster poured into these, the specimens, with the best sides up, can be set in, and when the plaster hardens the name or other important information can be written on the smooth edges. If rings of uniform size are used, the effect will be attractive.

An ingenious person will originate many other uses of casts.

BIBLIOGRAPHY

BRUNNER, JOSEPH, *Tracks and Tracking*. The Macmillan Company, 1909.

A small volume written especially for hunters, with descriptions and drawings of the tracks of game animals.

ROSSELL, LEONARD, *Tracks and Trails*. The Macmillan Company, 1928.

A book for Boy Scouts on tracking and trailing with directions for making casts of tracks and for photographing animals and birds.

CHAPTER III

FEATHERED FLIERS

Oriole questing,
Where are you nesting?

High where the glowing
Elm boughs are blowing.

Wandering Phoebe
Where may your tree be?

Up where the fountain
Bursts from the mountain.[1]

— ARTHUR GUITERMAN

Birds' inimitable songs, and the grace with which they wing their way through the impalpable air have endeared them always to humanity. We realize our loss when they depart on their southern migration in the fall, and we anticipate their arrival in the spring, watching with eagerness for the first fox sparrow or robin, harbingers of renewed life.

STRUCTURAL DEVELOPMENT. Birds betray a probable ancestral relationship to reptiles in the possession of scales on the shanks of their legs and on their toes, and in the development of their feathers which apparently start out to become scales. Their eggs are also somewhat alike. The earliest birds, as shown by fossils, had teeth in the bill like most reptiles, and in addition possessed a long, lizard-like tail, so there seems considerable justification for regarding the bird, at least in descent, as a sort of glorified, flying reptile.

For flight the bird has a stream-line body, feathers over-

[1] From "Nesting Time" by Arthur Guiterman. Copyright by E. P. Dutton and Company, Inc.

SOME COMMON BIRDS

lapping toward the rear, extraordinarily good vision involving an extra protection in a third eyelid or nictitating membrane, tail for steering, wings, and a curious forward extension of the breast bone called the keel, to which the great operating muscles of the wings are attached. In addition, the bones of the back and spinal column are joined in a more or less solid structure, giving rigidity to the body during flight. Some birds are considered to have been modified in structure from their flying ancestors, and with the degeneration and practical disappearance of the keel, and an increase in the size of the body, such birds have become flightless. They include the ostrich, rhea, cassowary, etc. Could you give any reasons for the probability that our domestic fowls are losing the ability to fly?

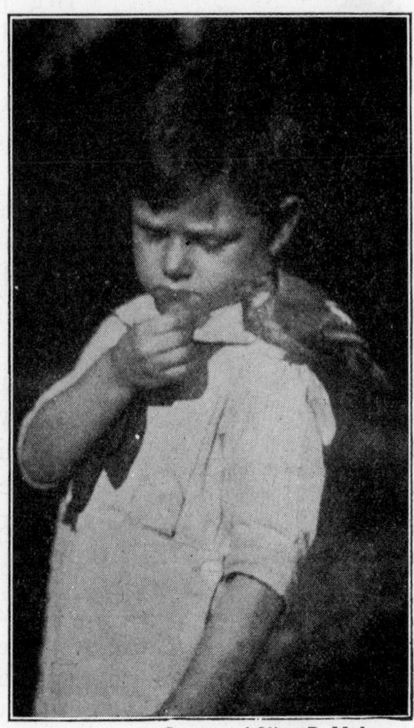

Courtesy of Oliver P. Medsger

GETTING ACQUAINTED

The young blue jay shows no fear of the boy who feeds him.

Birds are probably the most active animals in existence, since their energy is available through the oxidation of relatively more food than most animals consume. The temperature of birds is the highest of any animal, ranging from 102° to 112° F. The necessity for large quantities of oxygen is met by an interesting extension of the respiratory tract into the hollow bones, and, in addition to the usual pair of lungs, the inclusion of nine large air sacs. Because an increased amount of oxidation is so important to a bird, breathing is very rapid, but it would be useless without the circulatory system. This carries the oxygen to the cells — chiefly muscles — and transports to the excretory organs the wastes resulting from oxidation. For this purpose the bird has a four-chambered heart as efficient as that of mammals, working, however, at a much higher rate. The heart beat of a small bird is several hundred pulsations per minute.

A FLYING HAWK

The food of birds varies considerably so that an artificial grouping of birds can be constructed based on their types of food, as follows:

Birds of Prey....	Hawks, owls, vultures
Scavengers......	Gulls, sandpipers, cormorants, buzzards
Seed Eaters	Sparrows, finches, cross-bills, grosbeaks
Insect Eaters....	Woodpeckers, warblers, swallows, chimney swifts, nighthawks, flycatchers
Nectar Eaters ...	Humming birds

In their evolution, birds have lost their teeth, so the bills — and to a lesser extent the feet — of necessity become paramount in importance as aids in food-getting. To that end these structures present a variety of adaptations, many of which may be observed on any bird walk.

BIRDS OF PREY. The hawk, which spirals in the sky above us, is a member of the first group — the birds of prey, which have strongly-hooked upper bills or mandibles, valuable not only in carrying but in tearing animal food. The farmer's boy is sure he is after his chickens, but for once his nature lore is at fault. None of the high-soaring hawks should be blamed for chicken killing. Practically 90 per cent of hawks and owls are beneficial to us, their food consisting of mice, rats, and other rodents, besides hosts of injurious insects and some frogs and toads. Their curved claws or talons are long, sharp, and as strong as steel hooks. One of the authors saw an owl put its claws completely through the hand of a man who was offering the bird some meat. In the case of the owls, their feathered legs aid somewhat in producing a noiseless flight.

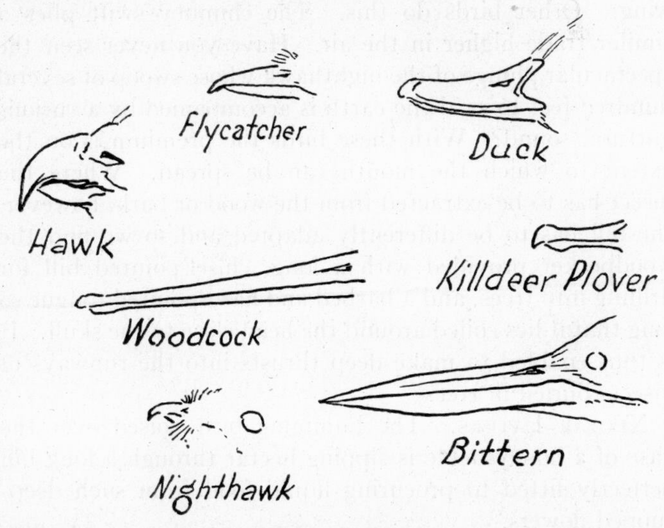

Types of Bills

Scavengers. There are so many scavengers that no particular type of bill can be looked for here.

Seed Eaters. Look closely at the next English sparrow you see (any other sparrow will do) and you will see how short and thick his bill is. This stout bill is typical of most of the seed eaters, and is especially adapted for tearing apart husks and dry fruits and for obtaining the contents from seeds. However, some seed-eating birds, like the parrots and parrakeets, have a bill even more hooked than that of the birds of prey.

INSECT EATERS. Most of the smaller birds which you will see in bushes and trees are insect eaters. Their bills are generally slender and sometimes hooked as is the case of the flycatchers. These characteristics are apparent with a good field glass. You have seen swallows darting everywhere — especially just over the tops of grass and grain. Did you realize that they were scooping up insects on the wing? Other birds do this. The chimney swift plies a similar trade higher in the air. Have you never seen the spectacular plunge of the nighthawk whose swoop of several hundred feet toward the earth is accompanied by a curious guttural sound? With these birds the premium is on the extent to which the mouth can be spread. Where the insect has to be extracted from the wood or bark, however, the bill has to be differently adapted and so we find the woodpecker provided with a long, chisel-pointed bill for drilling into trees, and a barbed and hard-pointed tongue so long that it lies coiled around the head close to the skull. It is thus enabled to make deep thrusts into the runways of insects buried in trees.

NECTAR EATERS. The humming bird poised over the vase of a honeysuckle is sipping nectar through a long bill perfectly fitted to procuring liquid food from such deep-cupped flowers.

LEGS AND TOES. An examination of the feet of the foregoing birds will show that all except the parrot and the woodpecker are alike in having three toes in front and one behind. Corroborate this with your canary, hen, or dove. In the two exceptions the toes are arranged two in front and two behind, and are utilized by these birds for climbing purposes. The tail is also a supporting aid in the case of certain birds like the woodpecker and chimney swift. The woodpecker slants the tail against the tree and the chimney swift against the inside of the chimney, so that stiff projecting ends of the shafts act as extra props for both birds.

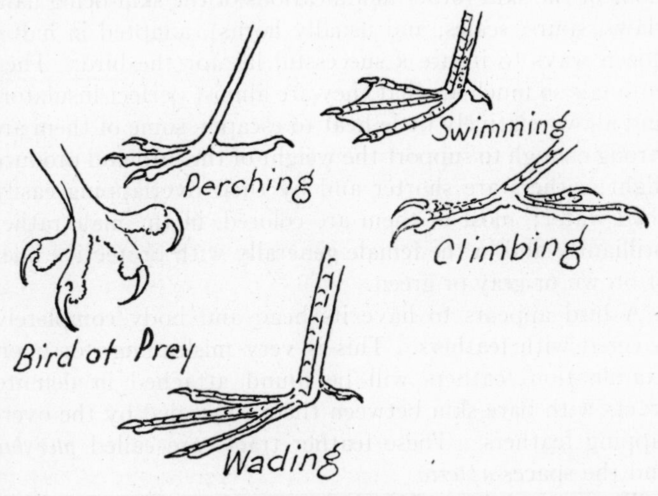

TYPES OF FEET

In the case of certain wading birds, like the heron and bittern, the legs and toes are unusually long, and the bill is a veritable spear point for offense, for securing a luckless fish, frog, or muskrat, or for defense against attack. The kingfisher also has a bill of abnormal length with which it easily gets fish by diving from a height.

The webbed feet of the duck, goose, grebe, and loon are peculiarly adapted for rapid swimming or diving. The loon is one of the most powerful swimmers in the world, comparing favorably with a fish or seal either on or underneath the surface of the water. In the case of the duck, the wide, shovel-shaped bill is peculiarly fitted for grubbing in the mud and it is provided with stiff strainers on each margin to retain food and yet allow the water to escape.

FEATHERS. The most prominent characteristic distinguishing birds from all other animals is the possession of feathers. These curious structures are really only modifications of the skin (other modifications of the skin being hair, claws, spurs, scales, and usually horns), adapted in half a dozen ways to insure a successful life for the bird. They entangle so much air that they are almost perfect insulators and allow relatively little heat to escape; some of them are strong enough to support the weight of the bird and produce flight; others are shorter and by their overlapping easily shed water; most of them are colored, in the male rather brilliantly and in the female generally with protective hues of brown or gray or green.

A bird appears to have its head and body completely covered with feathers. This is very misleading, for upon examination feathers will be found attached in definite tracts with bare skin between them concealed by the overlapping feathers. These feather tracts are called *pterylae* and the spaces *apteria*.

There are at least three types of feathers. Close to the skin are down feathers, fluffy structures especially valuable for retaining heat. The contour feathers are somewhat larger and make up most of the surface of the bird. They are protective in character. The quill feathers are the large feathers of the wings and tail. Upon these the bird depends for flight.

Watch one of the gulls soaring on wide-spread and motionless wings astern your steamer, or circling over the harbor. It rides the air as lightly as down. But shear the supporting wings and its heavy body would drop like a plummet.

A typical wing feather is a structure which must be light,

yet strong. Examine patiently such a feather and see if it does not reveal amazing adaptations to this end. Extending through the middle is a stiff, more or less hollow, shaft, the lower and larger part of which — the quill — contains at the extremity an opening by means of which blood vessels and nerves enter the structure during its early stages. On either side of the shaft is the vane, an extension of material flattened in one plane and easily separating into divisions when pulled apart, yet cohering when the edges are brought together and stroked. Under your hand lens or microscope, the vane is seen to be composed of separate, parallel units, each called a *barb*. On both sides of each barb are rows of oblique extensions called *barbules*, which being entangled and held by their tiny hooklets, practically unite all the barbs into a unit. Fluffy feathers lack these hooklets on the barbs.

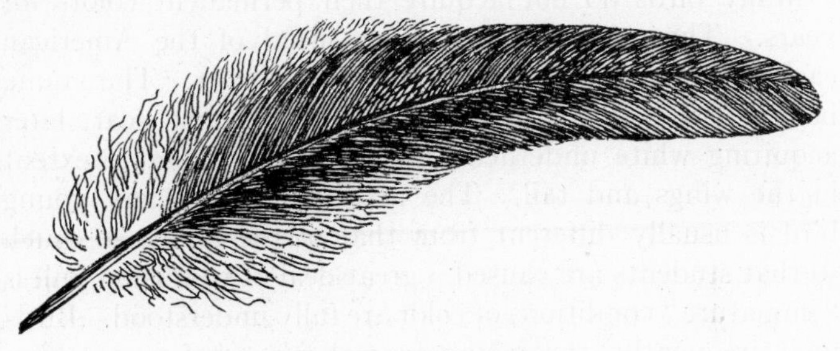

A Typical Feather

Colors. Among the birds the male is distinctly a beau brummel; upon him nature has generously lavished the most brilliant hues from her palette. Many male birds, while not so demonstrative and frank about their charms as is the male peacock, nevertheless at the mating season strut, bow, and otherwise display their gorgeousness. All scientists have seemed impressed with the special value of color in the matter of selecting mates in birdland, though we are not so sure about the explanation of the phenomena as we thought we were when Darwin first announced his theory of sexual selection.[1]

There is no question but that the nest of young is especially protected through the inconspicuous gray and brown of the mother bird who does most of the incubating. Brilliant colors here would only serve as an advertisement, attracting the attention of all sorts of enemies.

From an optical standpoint, we know that the gorgeous effects seen in the "eye" of a peacock's tail or the burnished throat of a humming bird, are due largely to iridescence or the breaking up of white light by the tiny parts of the feathers into color effects. In some birds, however, there are true color pigments in the feathers. Stripped of all its feathers, even the most beautiful bird becomes a wretched object. In a bird beauty is truly "skin deep."

Many birds do not acquire their permanent colors for years. Thus the feathers of the head of the American eagle become white only after the third year. The young herring gull is a streaked brown for the first year, later acquiring white underneath and to a considerable extent in the wings and tail. The first plumage of any young bird is usually different from that of the adult, so much so that students are caused a great deal of confusion unless "immature" conditions of color are fully understood. Birds molt frequently, the young several times before reaching maturity. Both the adults, after rearing the young, pass through what is known as the "post-nuptial" molt, in which the male sometimes loses his jaunty colors and becomes like the female. An example is the bobolink. Changes in color have always seemed difficult to explain, but the modern scientific interpretation is that they are

[1] Darwin's idea was that in general females, especially birds, were attracted by color and so were more likely to mate with particularly brilliant males, thus giving rise to a line of descendants markedly colored.

caused mostly by the wearing away of the outer parts of the feathers, thus exposing new areas. Do not be too hasty in correcting someone who is identifying a bird by colors noted in the field. Allowances must be made for the many variations of plumage due to age, sex, or season.

SONGS. Birds have call notes and songs, both produced primarily by a curious vocal organ called the *syrinx*. It is a sort of swelling in the windpipe, controlled by muscles. Usually the male birds alone do the singing. While the human voice box (larynx) is situated at the top of the windpipe, the syrinx of the bird is at the lower end of the trachea. The inimitable bubbling song of the wren, the warble of the vireo, the musical preachment of the brown thrasher, the fluted notes of the white-throated sparrow, the ecstasy of the ovenbird, and the ascending hymn of the hermit thrush, are expressive of the rhapsody of bird music, a freedom and joy unique among all creatures. Approach too closely and the reticent singers stop. If their nests are near, their changing emotion may produce staccato alarm notes and calls. It is quite possible through practice to whistle imitations of bird notes which approximate the original musicians, and when well done serve to attract the birds.

MIGRATION. The fact that birds fly means that they can be cosmopolitan creatures at will. They are the world's travelers, untroubled by the prospect of a sustained flight of hundreds or even thousands of miles. But not all of our birds fly away seasonally. Some live rather permanently in a given region throughout the year. Such birds are called *permanent residents*. Those which migrate in fall and return in spring are called *summer visitants*. Those which migrate in the winter from a region further north are known as *winter visitants*.

The migration of birds has always had a strange fascination for all who gave it any attention. There is no scientific explanation of how they find their way except the admission of a "sixth sense" of direction, which is not even a reasonably good, man-made label behind which to hide ignorance. Here man must acknowledge his limitations. A little feathered mite launches itself on the first trip to South America. Probably accompanied by others of its kind but without compass, baggage, or Baedeker, without the assistance of a signboard throughout the entire route other than the moonlight dancing on the water course of a great river system, or along the coast line (and on stormy nights without even that faint aid), flying now by day and now by night it comes into its own port. Each species has its own time-table which is followed rather closely, arriving in any locality at about the same date every year — sometimes a day earlier and sometimes a day later, but amazingly punctual, everything considered.

The longest non-stop flight probably is that of the golden plover which flies 2,500 miles from Nova Scotia to South America. The arctic tern travels the farthest, a round trip of 22,000 miles each year.

Just why the birds should desire to travel so far is difficult to see. It is certainly not because they cannot withstand the cold, though it is obvious that in the case of insectivorous birds their food supply is largely cut off in winter, and they are obliged to travel into a warmer climate. The glacial period in North America may have started this racial habit. The homing instinct may bring them back, once they have gone to the South.

Few birds have any permanent homes or abiding places. The great birds of prey — eagles, hawks, vultures, condors, and the like — which mate for life, are likely to retain their usually inaccessible and precarious nesting sites year after year, making many additions to the uncouth nest. The multitude of smaller birds, however, erect the nest not for a home but rather for a cradle, which is abandoned after their young are reared. When birds are "at home," then, we may expect to find them almost anywhere throughout the particular environment or region preferred by them, though many of our birds are known to return seasonally to exactly the same place.

NESTS. Once here, they mate and start nesting. The nests of birds vary with the species, from the grass structure of the field sparrows to the more intricate nest of the red-eyed vireo adorned with strips of birch bark. In size, the variation is tremendous, from the tiny, lichen-covered thimble of the humming bird to the coarse structure of the hawks, several feet in diameter. The nest of a certain fish hawk on Long Island was found to weigh 600 pounds. Certain species like the kingfisher and the bank swallow burrow into banks. Others, such as the woodpeckers, drill into trees.

Courtesy of Rex Green

NEST AND FLEDGLINGS

A black-throated green warbler's nest in a rhododendron bush.

All sorts of materials are used in making nests, selected mainly from the best available in the region. Since the nest of our smaller birds is freshly built each year it is in no sense despoiling the property of the birds to gather such nests after they have been abandoned. Much can be learned from such a collection if the nests are well cared for and labeled. Professor Arthur A. Allen of Cornell University states that 90 per cent of the nests commonly found in the northeastern states will be products of nine common birds: catbird, chipping sparrow, goldfinch, Baltimore oriole, redstart, robin, song sparrow, red-eyed vireo, and yellow warbler.

EGGS. In the completed nest, itself — mute witness of the skill of mind and bill — soon appears the first egg. The egg of the bird is the largest single cell known. The enveloping membrane is covered with a hard shell to prevent evaporation of the liquid contents. Eggs are large because food must be provided for considerable development prior to hatching. Eggs that are laid in dark places are usually white; other eggs frequently match their environment by being greenish or brown, and are usually covered with spots, lines, or different markings.

Courtesy of Oliver P. Medsger

NEST OF THE WHIPPOORWILL

The eggs are laid in a little hollow without any nest construction.

The entire number of eggs laid by a bird for incubation at one time is called the *clutch*. This number is usually constant for a given species. The passenger pigeon, now extinct, laid but one egg; the mourning dove lays two; the robin, three or four; and the kingfisher, six or eight. Birds like the grouse or bobwhite may lay from twelve to eighteen.

While formerly collections of birds' eggs were as common as stamp or tobacco tag collections among country boys, conservation laws and a new public opinion now effectively safeguard the eggs of wild birds.

When the clutch is completed, usually within three or

four days, incubation begins. The female bird — sometimes the male — sits on the eggs to keep them constantly warm. This supplies to the vital cell in the egg the heat which must be maintained continuously until the young hatches. Under the influence of this enveloping warmth, the living cell, always uppermost in the egg, grows into an embryo which in about two weeks breaks the shell and sprawls out a naked, ugly, helpless, little creature in most cases, which will have to be fed and cared for another half month or more. Such birds are called *altricial*. A few birds like the grouse, turkey, duck, chicken, killdeer, and nighthawk have a plumage of soft down when hatched, and are soon able to run around. Such birds are called *precocial*.

SUGGESTIONS FOR BIRD STUDY[1]

Bird study is fascinating because, just as in a game of chess, the unexpected is forever happening. It calls for alertness and quick thinking. Since birds in summer are most active during the two hours following daybreak, the early morning is a good time for birding. From April to July in the northern states, the trees and bushes are full of birds at all hours of the day, and one can usually get a fair record almost any time. The height of the migrating season is in May.

The group going on a bird trip should be limited to about ten, though double that number can be taken after they are more experienced. The smaller the group the more successful the trip. Conspicuously colored clothing should not be displayed as it is alarming to birds. Sudden movements and loud talking, calling, or shouting are distinctly taboo. Avoid narrow paths where the party must go single file, and never go facing the sun.

Sometimes excellent results are obtained by selecting a

[1] See "Bird Trip" in Chapter XXVI.

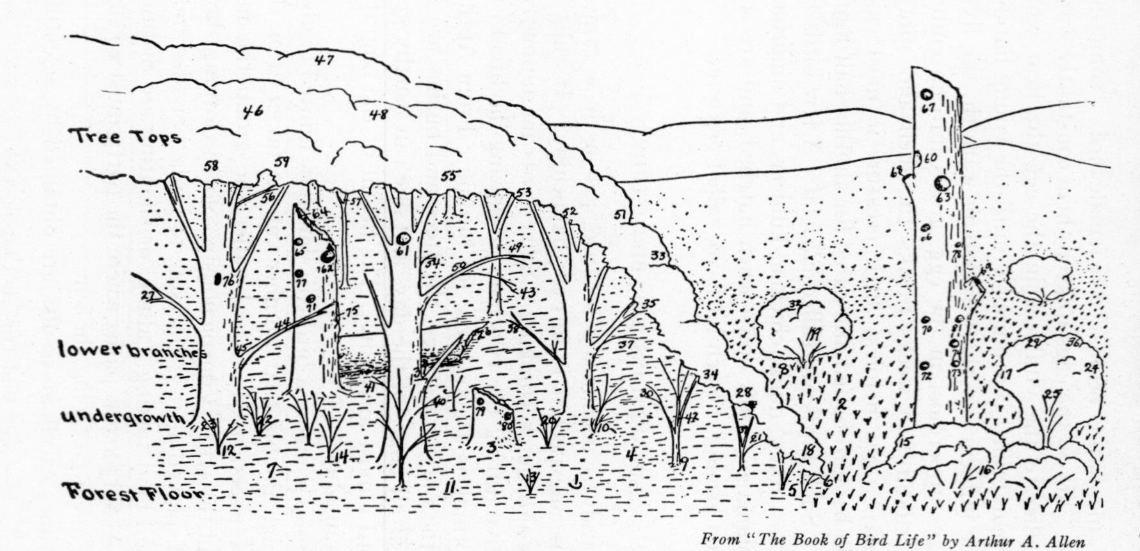

From "The Book of Bird Life" by Arthur A. Allen

NESTING SITES OF BIRDS OF THE WOODLANDS AND WOODLAND BORDERS

Ground-nesting Birds

1. Woodcock
2. Bobwhite
3. Ruffed Grouse
4. Whippoorwill
5. White-throated Sparrow
6. Junco
7. Pine-woods Sparrow
8. Towhee
9. Black and White Warbler
10. Nashville Warbler
11. Ovenbird
12. Canadian Warbler
13. Veery
14. Hermit Thrush

Birds of the Undergrowth and Low Bushes

15. Field Sparrow and Yellow-breasted Chat
16. Song Sparrow
17. Cardinal
18. Indigo bird
19. White-eyed Vireo
20. Black-throated Blue Warbler
21. Chestnut-sided Warbler
22. Mourning Warbler
23. Hooded Warbler
24. Mocking bird
25. Catbird and Brown Thrasher
26. Winter Wren

Birds of High Bushes and Lower Branches

27. Mourning Dove
28. Black and Yellow-billed Cuckoos
29. Kingbird
30. Acadian Flycatcher
31. Blue Jay
32. Chipping Sparrow
33. Goldfinch
34. Rose-breasted Grosbeak
35. Scarlet Tanager
36. Cedar Waxwing
37. Red-eyed Vireo
38. Blue-headed Vireo
39. Yellow Warbler
40. Magnolia Warbler
41. Myrtle Warbler
42. Redstart
43. Golden-crowned Kinglet
44. Wood Thrush
45. Robin

Birds of the Higher Branches and Tree-Tops

46. Herons, Great Blue and Black-crowned Night
47. Bald Eagle
48. Hawks, Red-shouldered, Red-tailed, Broad-winged, Goshawk, Cooper's and Sharp-shinned, Osprey
49. Olive-sided Flycatcher
50. Wood Pewee
51. Baltimore Oriole
52. Purple Finch
53. Pine Siskin
54. Yellow-throated Vireo
55. Warbling Vireo
56. Cerulean Warbler
57. Black-throated Green Warbler
58. Blackburnian Warbler
59. Pine Warbler

Birds that Nest in Holes

60. Wood Duck
61. Barn Owl
62. Barred Owl
63. Screech Owl
64. Great Horned Owl
65. Woodpeckers — all species
66. Crested Flycatcher
67. Sparrow Hawk
68. Starling
69. House Sparrow
70. Tree Swallow
71. Prothonotary Warbler
72. Carolina Wren
73. Bewick's Wren
74. House Wren
75. Brown Creeper
76. White-breasted Nuthatch
77. Red-breasted Nuthatch
78. Brown-headed Nuthatch
79. Tufted Titmouse
80. Chickadee
81. Bluebird

good place near bushes or trees and quietly watching the birds as they come and go. If you are well concealed or remain motionless close to some tree trunk, you can attract birds to your hiding place by "squeaking." This is usually done by drawing the breath in through closely pursed lips. A louder sound can be produced by holding the lips to the back of your moistened hand. The sound simulates a young bird in distress.

BIRD HOUSES

The openings should be small enough to prevent the entrance of the English sparrow. When the bottom is hinged, as in the house at the left, the house may be cleaned after occupancy.

Since most birds are small and very active, a pair of field glasses is desirable, though not absolutely essential. A small book should be carried for recording field observations and notes. Care should be taken not to make final decisions as to color when birds are seen against the sky, as they will invariably appear black or very dark in such light. A check list is important if you expect to make real progress in learning the birds seen on field trips. Small pamphlets or lists are procurable for this purpose and will be noted in the bibliography.

The establishment of a bird bath and a bird feeding station will be of great assistance in attracting common birds. A shallow pan, sunk flush with the surface of the ground and kept filled with water, will, in one season, return dividends far in excess of the slight expenditure. The important thing is to remember to add water daily.

If this bath is the only water near by, it will be very attractive to the birds. Care should be taken in locating the bird bath where there is no cover for cats to lie concealed within jumping distance.

In the winter time a piece of suet wired to a tree, window sill, or blind, or seeds scattered on a window tray, will bring a variety of birds. While photographs of wild birds can be quite easily made by attaching a string to a camera concealed and prefocused on the bird bath or feeding station, many of the best pictures of wild birds have been taken from blinds or tents. The chapter on bird photography in *The Book of Bird Life* by Arthur A. Allen covers important details of procedure.

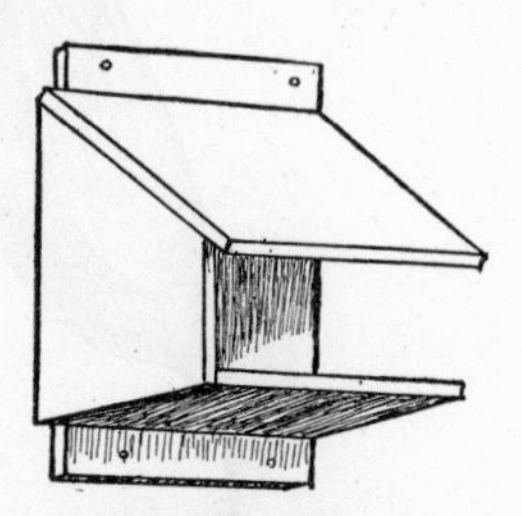

NESTING SHELF

The phoebe and robin will not nest in a box but will appreciate such a retreat for its protection in rainy weather.

Some naturalists belong to the Bird Banding Association. After a permit has been received from the United States Department of Agriculture at Washington, D.C. allowing you to band birds, you may add your quota to the hundreds who have aided in making possible fascinating discoveries of the traveling habits of birds. The procedure is simple. A small numbered band of aluminum is fastened loosely around the leg of a young bird just above the foot. The number is recorded and a report also sent to Washington. Whenever banded birds are captured, the number on the band and the locality in which the bird was found are reported.

After you have gained a fair degree of bird knowledge, become a leader and encourage others to join in bird study. The National Audubon Society will help with literature and in other ways. In your school or camp you might prepare exhibits of nests, feathers, maps showing migration

TYPICAL BIRDS DRAWN TO SCALE

It is difficult to estimate the size of a bird when seen even at a short distance. One usually underestimates the length, often guessing it to be not more than half what it really is. Few people would think the robin was 10 inches long, or a crow nearly 20. To make the judging of size easier, the representative birds shown above are commonly used as standards.

routes, models of bird houses, casts of tracks, conservation laws concerning birds, etc. It is quite possible that your enthusiasm may be the stimulus for developing public interest in the cause of birds and in stimulating the establishment of farms or other territory as bird sanctuaries.

It will not be feasible to present detailed descriptions here of the numerous groups of birds, as such notes, to be adequate, would require more space than can fairly be accorded to one chapter in this book. There are many books devoted to birds, and to these students are referred.

However, 75 of the commonest birds have been listed according to size, with the hope that such information may be of some help in learning to recognize birds.

A. SMALLER THAN AN ENGLISH SPARROW

LESS THAN 6.33 INCHES LONG

Bird	Inches	Bird	Inches
Ruby-throated Humming Bird	3.74	Brown Creeper	5.66
Golden-crowned Kinglet	4.07	Field Sparrow	5.68
House Wren	5.	Warbling Vireo	5.80
Goldfinch	5.10	Tree Swallow	5.90
Yellow Warbler	5.10	Tufted Titmouse	6.
Chickadee	5.27	Nuthatch	6.07
Black and White Warbler	5.30	Vesper Sparrow	6.12
Maryland Yellow Throat	5.33	Ovenbird	6.17
Chipping Sparrow	5.37	Red-eyed Vireo	6.23
Redstart	5.41	Junco	6.27
Chimney Swift	5.43	Louisiana Water Thrush	6.28
Indigo Bunting	5.59	Song Sparrow	6.30
		English Sparrow	6.33

B. A LITTLE LONGER THAN AN ENGLISH SPARROW

SLIGHTLY LONGER THAN 6.33 INCHES

Bird	Inches	Bird	Inches
White-throated Sparrow	6.74	Barn Swallow	6.95
Downy Woodpecker	6.83	Phoebe	6.99
Snow Bunting	6.88		

C. A Little Smaller Than a Robin

FROM 7 TO 9.75 INCHES LONG

Bluebird	7.01	Wood Thrush	8.29
Cedar Waxwing	7.19	Towhee	8.35
Scarlet Tanager	7.25	Starling	8.50
Bobolink	7.25	Kingbird	8.51
Yellow-breasted Chat	7.44	Yellow-bellied Sapsucker	8.56
Spotted Sandpiper	7.50	Catbird	8.94
Veery	7.52	Screech Owl	9.40
Baltimore Oriole	7.53	Red-winged Blackbird	9.51
Horned Lark	7.75	Whippoorwill	9.75
Rose-breasted Grosbeak	8.12		

D. The Size of a Robin or Slightly Larger

FROM 10 TO 12 INCHES LONG

Robin	10.	Brown Thrasher	11.42
Sparrow Hawk	10.	Blue Jay	11.74
Bobwhite	10.	Mourning Dove	11.85
Meadow Lark	10.75	Flicker	12.
American Woodcock	11.		

E. Between the Size of a Flicker and That of a Crow

FROM 12 TO 19.3 INCHES LONG

Yellow-billed Cuckoo	12.20	Laughing Gull	16.50
Purple Grackle	12.75	Ruffed Grouse	17.
Kingfisher	13.02	Crow	19.3
Wilson's Tern	15.		

F. Larger Than a Crow

LONGER THAN 19.3 INCHES

Red-tailed Hawk	20.	Turkey Vulture	30.
Great Horned Owl	22.	Common Loon	32.
Mallard Duck	23.	Bald Eagle	32.85
Herring Gull	24.	Canada Goose	35.-43
American Bittern	28.	Great Blue Heron	42.-50

BIBLIOGRAPHY

ALLEN, ARTHUR A., *A Key to Bird Nests.* Slingerland-Comstock Company, 1929.

A convenient, well-illustrated pamphlet with a workable key.

—— *The Book of Bird Life.* D. Van Nostrand Company, 1930.

Field observations with excellent hints for bird study.

—— *American Bird Biographies.* Comstock Publishing Company, 1934.

Graphic life histories of twenty common birds.

BAILEY, MRS. FLORENCE M., *Handbook of the Birds of the Western United States* (7th edition). Houghton Mifflin Company, 1921.

Rather technical keys and full descriptions of the birds of the Great Plains, the Pacific Slope, and the Lower Rio Grande Valley.

BURGESS, THORNTON, *Bird Book for Children.* Little, Brown and Company, 1919.

One of the best books for young children.

CARR, WILLIAM H., *Glimpses of Familiar Birds.* Samuel Gabriel Sons and Company, 1931.

Colored illustrations and descriptions of seventy-two birds.

CHAPMAN, FRANK M., *Handbook of Birds of Eastern North America.* D. Appleton and Company, 1932. Revised edition.

The standard manual of the birds of the East.

—— *What Bird Is That?* D. Appleton and Company, 1920.

A useful book for determining the birds seen, though the illustrations are much too small.

COLLINS, HENRY H., *Field Marks of the Birds of Northeastern North America.* H. H. Collins, Chester Hill, Pa., 1931.

A pocket-size booklet giving essentials for determining birds.

DICKEY, FLORENCE V. V., *Familiar Birds of the Pacific Southwest.* Stanford University Press, 1935.

A book for field use with colored photographs and simple descriptions of the more common birds. Size and color keys help in identifying birds seen.

EATON, E. H., *Birds of New York State.* New York State Museum, 1914.

Magnificent plates, full descriptions, tables of migrations, etc. The plates, which are valuable for many purposes, may be purchased separately.

HOFFMAN, RALPH, *Birds of the Pacific States.* Houghton Mifflin Company, 1927.

An excellent manual of all the birds of the region, with black and white illustrations and ten colored plates.

MATTHEWS, F. S., *Field Book of Wild Birds and Their Music.* G. P. Putnam's Sons, 1925.

A unique work on the subject, attractive and usable.

PEARSON, T. GILBERT, editor, *Birds of America.* Garden City Publishing Company, 1936.

A magnificent book, at a fraction of its original price.

PETERSON, ALVIN M., *A B C of Attracting Birds.* Bruce Publishing Company, 1936.

PETERSON, ROGER TORY, *Field Guide to the Birds.* Houghton Mifflin Company, 1934.

Field book emphasizing distinguishing characteristics of birds.

REED, CHESTER, *Land Birds East of the Rockies.* Doubleday, Doran and Company, Inc., 1925.

—— *Water and Game Birds.* Doubleday, Doran and Company, Inc., 1906.

—— *Western Bird Guide.* Doubleday, Doran and Company, Inc., 1913.

Probably the most used and popular bird guides. Pocket size.

ROBERTS, THOMAS SADLER, *Bird Portraits in Color.* University of Minnesota, 1934.

Ninety colored plates from the author's *Birds of Minnesota.* Shows most of the birds found east of the Rocky Mountains.

SUTTON, GEORGE MIKSCH, *Birds in the Wilderness.* The Macmillan Company, 1935.

Stories of the author's experiences with birds in many places.

WYMAN, LUTHER E. and BURNELL, ELIZABETH F., *Field Book of Birds of the Southwestern United States.* Houghton Mifflin Company, 1925.

All the birds of Arizona, part of Nevada and Southern California described briefly and illustrated.

Bird Calendar and Check List. Slingerland-Comstock Company, 1926.

A valuable aid in learning birds.

Bird Cards, National Association of Audubon Societies.

Sets of 50 winter birds, 50 summer birds. Postcard-size.

Bird Key. Slingerland-Comstock Company, 1923.

Excellent drawings by Fuertes, named or numbered (for tests).

Book of Birds, The, 3rd edition. National Geographic Society, 1927.

Colored plates by Fuertes, with notes and descriptions.

Educational Leaflets, National Association of Audubon Societies.

Each leaflet has a colored plate, an outline drawing to be colored, and a description. Too well known to need comment.

CHAPTER IV

LEGLESS REPTILES — THE SNAKES

A narrow fellow in the grass
Occasionally rides;
You may have met him, did you not?
His notice sudden is.

The grass divides as with a comb,
A spotted shaft is seen;
And then it closes at your feet
And opens further on.[1]

— Emily Dickinson

For unreckoned ages the snake has been cast in the rôle of villain. His sinuous and rapid locomotion is mysterious. Biblical and other stories have portrayed him as the personification of evil, and as cursed. Some snakes are poisonous and this fact has made it difficult for the average person not to believe that all snakes are harmful.

So the catching of a reptile may be both a psychological victory and a real adventure. Possibly there is a more or less unconscious idea of doing something brave, of running a risk, or of showing off. If children could be shown early in life how simple it is to handle the non-poisonous snakes, and how easily these animals may be kept and cared for, it would do much to counteract the fear and disgust with which most children in their earliest years are taught to regard reptiles. Of course they must be shown how to recognize the few poisonous snakes and how to handle the

[1] From *The Poems of Emily Dickinson,* Centenary edition. Copyright and reprinted by permission of Little, Brown and Company.

non-poisonous ones to prevent being bitten, and quite as much, to avoid injuring the snakes. Snakes may be found almost anywhere in fields or woods. Often they may be found under old logs or near stone fences or other hiding places. Nearly all snakes, even the poisonous ones, are beneficial because of their food habits, since they eat insects, worms, rats, and mice. The harm they do in nature is chiefly through eating frogs and toads and young birds.

Photograph by Paul B. Mann

WHO'S AFRAID?

The black snake, though not poisonous, would bite unless carefully held by the neck. It has powerful muscles and can travel at the speed of a running boy.

STRUCTURE. Snakes are generally regarded as reptiles which have degenerated in certain particulars. The legs are lacking or have been reduced to tiny vestigial leg bones as in the case of some of the larger snakes. It will be interesting when visiting the museum to see these actual leg bones. No eyelids are present. There is no breast bone. This allows the ribs to expand and thus accommodate large food masses when swallowed. Also, strange to say, there is only one functioning lung — the right; the shrunken left lung is so small that it is difficult to find.

The number of vertebrae and ribs is amazingly large,

running up to three hundred in certain snakes. The snake, through its ability to dislocate its jaws, can swallow an animal considerably larger than itself. The victim is held securely by the backward-slanting teeth. The halves of the lower jaw are loosely connected in front by a strip of ligaments so elastic that they can be separated considerably. By thrusting out each half separately, hooking the teeth up into the prey and then pulling back, alternately releasing the grip to get a fresh hold, the animal is slowly pulled into the mouth. Powerful muscles of the gullet then slowly force it into the stomach. With large victims the process of swallowing is laborious and may continue for hours.

All snakes, whether harmless or poisonous, possess a forked tongue which is being darted out of the mouth much of the time. This has been erroneously thought by some people to be a sort of "stinger," but it is harmless and is undoubtedly a sense organ, used as a feeler, to taste with, and possibly to catch vibrations in the air as our ears do, for the snake, like the fish, lacks any external evidence of ears. The tongue of the snake, unlike that of amphibians and lizards, is never of any assistance in getting food.

Molting. Snakes have a curious habit of "molting" or shedding the entire scaly covering. This does not occur at any set time but is likely to happen two or three times a year. A new skin forms beneath the old one which becomes loosened. Even the skin covering the eyes is loosened and looks milky, making the snake temporarily blind. During this period snakes do not eat.

When the skin is sufficiently loosened, the snake rubs his head around in the ground until he has broken the connections of the skin around the jaws. Then by crawling through a crevice among stones or through grass or brush, the skin is peeled off wrong side out like a glove. Such molted snake skins are frequently found in the fields. At least one bird, the crested flycatcher, makes a specialty of including a piece of snake skin in her nest.

LOCOMOTION. Snakes glide in a sinuous, double curve, using the broad plates or scales (*scutes*) on the ventral surface with which to grip the ground, holding on for a moment by their scales and the associated ribs and muscles to any projecting objects, such as sticks, stones, and plants as they pass over them.

American Museum of Natural History

THE PUFFING ADDER

This snake is molting its skin, a process which begins at the head. The outer skin is eventually shed from the entire body. Note the curiously flattened front end of the head.

Some snakes are very swift. You will have to run to keep up with a black snake, frequently called the "blue racer" because of its speed.

REPRODUCTION. Like birds, all snakes develop from eggs, though with the snake the eggs are usually placed in the ground. This method of reproduction is called *oviparous* (*ovum* means "egg"; *paro* means "to bear") and the term is also applied to animals practicing it. While in general the female snake deposits her eggs, in some cases — such as DeKay, garter, and water snakes — the eggs are retained within her body until the baby snakes are ready to hatch. When the young emerge, apparently they are being "born," but properly that term applies only to mammals. The term *ovoviviparous* is given to such

American Museum of Natural History

Milk Snake Eggs and Partly-grown Milk Snake

Eggs of snakes are laid under dead leaves or logs or otherwise hidden.

snakes and a few other animals such as tropical fishes like guppies and swordtails, where the eggs hatch within the body of the female, to distinguish them from viviparous animals (*vivum* means "alive"; *paro* means "to bear"). The eggs of snakes are not so pointed as those of birds, and the covering is leathery, more like that of a soft-shelled egg of a hen. Oviparous snakes lay from 5 to 25 eggs, reproduction usually taking place in the middle of the summer. There is no metamorphosis in the case of the snake; the young closely resemble their parents except in size.

SNAKES IN CAPTIVITY. The small snakes, brown, red-bellied, ring-necked, green, milk, and puffing adder can be picked up with little likelihood of being bitten. Black snakes and water snakes are apt to strike viciously when caught and the bite is unpleasant, though no more dangerous than any small cut or scratch. A stick for holding non-poisonous snakes may be made of any forked branch. The stick should be about three feet long, the fork not over an inch and one-half deep. If the fork is deeper than this it will be possible for snakes to wriggle out from under. With a snake stick, a snake can be pinned down, with the stick as near the head as possible. Once held, shift the stick quickly just back of the head or have two sticks and get the head hold with the second. Then take hold of the snake just behind the head with one hand, holding the body, if the snake is large, with the other to prevent its twisting around the arm and pulling its head free. Poisonous snakes are too dangerous to be handled by anyone but an expert and then only with extreme care.

A stout cloth bag about two feet long should be provided in which to carry the snake. The snake can safely be left in such a bag for hours. In school or camp the easiest and most frequently made snake cage is a wooden box with wire netting tacked over the top. A box of this kind is unsatisfactory in every way. It is difficult to observe the snake inside the box, the netting must be loosened to add food or water, and if a corner is left unfastened, the snake is almost sure to work its way out. Any cracks in the box, too, give opportunity for escape as snakes can go through holes that seem altogether too small for them.

Cages with glass fronts and solid or netting backs are far more satisfactory. Boxes a foot high, a foot deep, and two or three feet long are convenient. If a board long enough for the top, bottom, and ends is secured at a lumber yard, have a groove cut with a buzz saw about $\frac{1}{4}$ inch deep and $\frac{1}{2}$ inch from one edge. Cut the top and bottom pieces just 2 feet long, the end pieces $11\frac{5}{8}$ inches. One end piece should be trimmed off even with the saw cut, making it a little more than $\frac{1}{2}$ inch narrower than the rest of the pieces. Nail or screw the pieces together, making sure the grooves in the top and bottom exactly meet that in the end. A piece of glass 2×1 feet will slide in the groove as a front, projecting slightly at the end making it easy to remove. If it is not convenient to have the grooves cut in the board, two thin strips of wood may be fastened close to the edges of the end, top and bottom, just far enough apart for the glass to slide between them. If preferred the groove may be on the two ends and the bottom, the top hinged as a cover and the glass slid down from the top. The wood of the cages may be painted or varnished, though this is not necessary. The back may be another piece of wood, or of netting, securely tacked on.

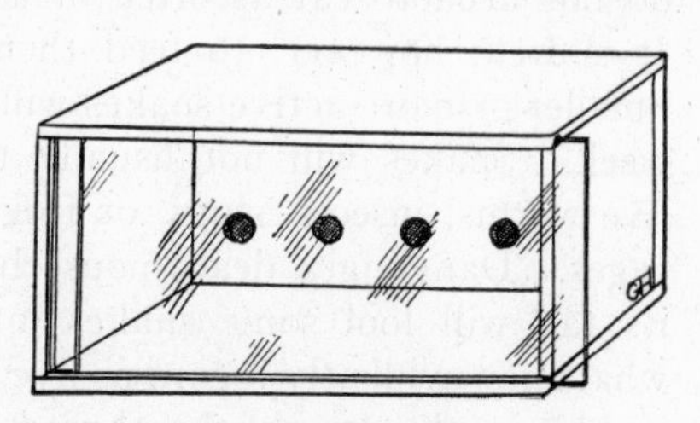

A SNAKE CAGE

A few stones and dry leaves and a small pan of water in the cage make it ready for an occupant. Too many stones or leaves will enable the snake to hide so that it cannot be seen. A label telling the kind of snake and something of its habits can be fastened on the upper edge. The cage should be set on a table or shelf so as to be nearly at the eye level of the observer. In such cases the idea of protective coloration, the adaptations for movement, the method of getting food and other habits, perhaps including the molting process, can be observed.

If snakes or any other living things are kept they should be well cared for. It is far better to have no living animals about than to have them neglected. Snakes and other cold-blooded animals do not need food to keep up the body temperature as do warm-blooded animals and consequently do not need to eat as often or as regularly as the latter. It is well, however, to feed them at least once a week. Smaller or more active snakes will eat two or three times a week. Snakes will not usually touch anything dead, so live worms, insects, slugs, or frogs should be put into the cages. Dangling a dead mouse by a black thread tied to its tail will fool some snakes into capturing and eating what they evidently regard as live prey. After the swallowing has really begun the thread can be cut. Sometimes small pieces of raw meat will be eaten if they can be fastened lightly to wires or straw and moved about to suggest that they are alive. Every few days the cages should be cleaned and fresh water put in the pans.

SUPERSTITIONS ABOUT SNAKES. From time immemorial scaly monsters and cold-blooded dragons with fiery breath have persisted in myths. Even today a dragon is seen in every parade in China. Perhaps there may be a subtle relationship between such superstitions and the attitude of most people toward reptiles, especially snakes.

Besides the common idea that all snakes are poisonous there are dozens of other erroneous ideas about snakes that may be corrected. They are not slimy; touching one will prove that. They do not chase people, but on the contrary will do their best to get away and only show fight or threaten when cornered. (Black snakes will occasionally follow a person who runs from them, but will not attack.) None of our native snakes can spit or throw out poison — though the spitting cobra of India can do this — nor can a coiled snake leap like a released spring. When a snake is killed its tail does not keep on moving till sundown, though as in some other cold-blooded animals, reflex movements may continue for some hours. Neither do snakes swallow their young. They do not charm or hypnotize birds and small mammals, though possibly at times such animals, confronted by a snake, may be too frightened to move for a few minutes. The milk snake does not suck milk from cows. There is no such creature as a hoop snake, so called, reputed to put its tail in its mouth and go rolling down hill. Nor are snake skins, snake oil, rattles, or other parts of snakes of value in the cure of diseases.

Some Common Snakes. There are only five families of snakes in the United States with about one hundred and seventy species. Many of these are rare or confined to small areas. Moreover, in a number of cases the different species within a genus are very similar. For these reasons only a few notes will be given on the common forms.

Poisonous Snakes. The poisonous snakes of the United States come under four popular heads. The copperhead and water moccasin, though belonging to the same genus, are generally thought of as quite distinct from each other. The coral snakes, of which there are two species, comprise the third group. The last consists of the rattlesnakes, which are the most widely distributed of the poisonous forms. The rattlesnakes are divided into two genera, pigmy rattlesnakes and true rattlesnakes. There are three species of the first and thirteen of the latter in the United States.

In the northeastern states are found only the copperhead and the pigmy and timber rattlesnakes. South of Virginia we also encounter the water moccasin and the coral snake. In the extreme western states the only poisonous forms are the rattlesnakes and it is here that the majority of the species are found.

Three of the four so-called "kinds" of poisonous snakes are again grouped, the copperhead, water moccasin, and rattlesnakes being called pit vipers because they have a depression or pit on either side of the head between the eye and nostril. As yet no one knows positively what this pit is for. They also have rather flat, triangular heads and stout bodies with distinct necks. The pupil of the eye in these forms is a vertical slit. Contrary to popular belief, however, neither this nor the triangular shape of the head is a definite characteristic of poisonous snakes. The coral snake has a round head and no distinct neck.

Courtesy of Oliver P. Medsger

THE COPPERHEAD

A poisonous reptile which is especially dangerous in the woods because its brown markings blend with dead leaves and conceal it.

The poison apparatus of such snakes consists of two hollow (sometimes grooved) fangs, one on either side of the upper jaw attached to a modified maxillary bone which is usually movable. These fangs connect, through ducts or tubes, with the poison sacs situated back of and below the eyes. In the pit vipers reserve fangs may always be found under the skin just back of the active fang. These quickly replace the fangs as they are shed or become broken.

The copperhead, rarely over three feet in length, is

brown or reddish with a coppery luster. The head is of a particularly rich color, dark on top and lighter on the sides, but lacking distinct markings. The body is light, with long saddle marks like dumb-bells which flare out very wide on the lower part of the snake's sides. The edges of these blotches are always darker than the centers.

American Museum of Natural History

THE GARTER SNAKE

Unfriendly, yet harmless, this is probably the commonest snake in the United States. Like most snakes it is beneficial because it feeds on insects injurious to man.

The rattlesnake has a series of rattles on the end of the tail that distinguish it from all other snakes. The number of rattles, unless some have been lost (which is often the case), shows not how old the snake is but how many times it has shed its skin. A snake with eight rattles may not be more than three years old.

Timber rattlesnakes may be yellowish or nearly black, with darker blotches down the back. The other species are usually either gray or brown, with darker blotches on the back and sides. In some these marks are diamond-shaped.

The typical diamond-back rattler is found in Florida. Another, the western diamond-back, is lighter and grayer in color. One species is a beautiful rusty red color. The timber rattler may reach six feet in length but in the north it is seldom over four. The diamond-back, the largest, occasionally grows to a length of over eight feet.

American Museum of Natural History

THE RIBBON SNAKE

This name has been applied to a variety of the garter snake which has ribbon-like bands extending the length of the body.

The water moccasin, or cottonmouth, is found from southern Virginia to Florida and Texas, always in wet places or where it can easily get into the water. It is greenish-brown with obscure darker markings on the sides. The lips of the water moccasin are cream-colored. The name "cottonmouth" is derived from the snake's habit of facing an enemy with its mouth wide open showing the cottony-white interior.

Non-poisonous Snakes. The most widely distributed of the ten or twelve common kinds of non-poisonous snakes are the garter snakes. They are easily recognized by their stripes of brown and yellow with brownish spots on the sides. There are several species, all much alike. They are likely to be vicious and bite upon slight provocation, though they are not in any sense poisonous. They give off a strong odor when handled.

American Museum of Natural History

The Green Snake

Perhaps the most beautiful of our native snakes is this harmless little creature found in grass and thickets.

The ribbon or ribboned garter snake has no spots on the sides; it is slender, with narrow, light yellow stripes contrasting with the chocolate brown above and on the sides.

There are two gentle little snakes of a grass-green color. One has smooth scales and is the common grass or green snake of the northern states. It seldom reaches twenty inches in length. The other is larger, more slender, and has rough or keeled scales. It is found further south, not occurring above southern New Jersey. It is arboreal, being found in low bushes where its color renders it very inconspicuous. Both these species are insectivorous.

The ring-necked snake is slender, and bluish-black with a yellow ring around the throat. It grows to be a foot and a half long, but most specimens found are under a foot in length.

There are two small chocolate-brown snakes often found under stones or pieces of wood. One is the red-bellied snake or Storer's, the other is light brown below and is known as the DeKay's snake. Both snakes are easily tamed and will readily eat in captivity, if provided with earthworms.

The black or blue racer is of a bluish-black color with white on the under side of the head and throat. The scales on the back are all smooth and the snake usually has a satiny appearance. It prefers small mammals, mice, and young rats for food, but also takes other snakes, frogs, toads, birds, and insects. Though this snake fights fiercely when cornered, it will not attack of its own accord. It does not charm animals, birds, or people; is not a constrictor, and does not go out of its way to attack rattlesnakes. It is interesting to know that the young black snake looks much like a small milk snake, having dark brown blotches on a grayish body. They are over two years old before they acquire the uniform black color. A large black snake measures about six feet in length.

The pilot, or mountain black snake, superficially resembles the common black snake. On close examination it may be seen that the scales along the back are slightly keeled, that is, have a ridge down the center of each scale. It also is usually more glossy than the other snake. On close examination white spots may be seen between the scales when the skin is distended. In reality the two snakes belong to different genera. Both species of black snakes sometimes climb trees in search of birds and their eggs, but they also eat great numbers of destructive rodents and other small animals.

The water snake is rather stout, dark brown, with a row of irregular darker blotches on the back and a row of smaller ones on the side. The under side is white or yellowish with reddish blotches.

The puffing adder or hognose snake is often supposed to be poisonous, but it is one of the most harmless and easily handled of snakes. It is rather stout with a short tail, brown or reddish-brown with darker spots on the back and sides, or in one form is uniformly black. The up-turned nose or snout is a characteristic by which it has earned one of its names. When disturbed it flattens its neck, swells up, and hisses in a manner that terrifies those who do not know what a bluffer it is. If much disturbed it may "play possum."

American Museum of Natural History

THE WATER SNAKE

This snake lives near streams and does not hesitate to enter the water where it seeks fish and frogs.

The pine or bull snake is a conspicuous snake reaching six feet in length, whose general whitish color includes chestnut brown blotches margined with black. There are three series of lateral blotches.

The milk snake is one of the handsomest, being milky white or gray with large reddish-brown spots on the back. It sometimes reaches a length of three and a half feet.

The king snake, with its brown and yellow markings, is a familiar and protected form in southern states. It frequents the neighborhood of houses and may often be seen just as it is disappearing down a hole or under the barn, searching for rats and mice. This snake is actually immune to the poison of the rattlesnake which it kills and eats.

BIBLIOGRAPHY

BARBOUR, THOMAS, *Reptiles and Amphibians, Their Habits and Adaptations* (revised edition). Houghton Mifflin Company, 1934.

A well-written, semi-popular account of the representatives of these two groups.

DITMARS, R. L., *Reptiles of North America.* Doubleday, Doran and Company, 1936.

A new and revised edition of *The Reptile Book.* An invaluable book for those who wish to know about the snakes, lizards, and turtles of America. With many illustrations, some in color.

—— *The Snakes of the World.* The Macmillan Company, 1931.

Will probably prove to be the standard reference book on the subject. Not too technical.

HASSLER, WILLIAM, *Reptile Study.* Boy Scouts of America, 1927.

A paper-covered book containing the material needed to pass the Scout merit-badge test for reptile study.

HOOPES, ISABEL, *Reptiles in the Home Zoo.* Boston Society of Natural History, 1936.

An inexpensive guide for the care of reptiles kept as pets.

CHAPTER V

OTHER REPTILES

"When we were little," the Mock Turtle went on, "we went to school in the sea. The master was an old Turtle — we used to call him Tortoise." [1]

— LEWIS CARROLL

TURTLES. At first sight a turtle does not betray much relationship to a snake, though they are both reptiles. It is toothless, has eyelids, legs with toes and claws, and seems built on a completely different plan of architecture.

Courtesy of Abraham Mandelstam

STUDYING A SNAPPING TURTLE

But the additional fact that it possesses scales, yet is not a fish, places it at once in the class Reptilia. It is actually more reptilian than is the snake, which shows many signs of modifications of structure due to probable degeneration.

[1] From *Alice in Wonderland* by Lewis Carroll.

STRUCTURE. Turtles are strange animals, adapted by many peculiarities of structure for their mode of life. All the softer tissues of the body are inclosed between bony "shells" which in most turtles are themselves covered with a coat of horny plates or scales. The legs, head, and tail can to a degree be pulled under the shelf of the shell.

In the case of the box turtle there is complete withdrawal and closure by means of a hinge in the *plastron* or lower shell. Perhaps the slow movements of this turtle betray its consciousness of this omnipresent protection. The upper "shell" is the *carapace*, formed from the eight pairs of ribs and from flattened parts of the dorsal vertebrae. Unlike other reptiles, the dorsal vertebrae are thus rendered immovable. The lower "shell" or plastron is formed by bony parts of the sternum or breast bone. Both the carapace and the plastron are made up of plates which differ enough in different species to be used in identification.

The turtle's mouth is toothless but the horny edges of the jaws are formidable shears. A snapping turtle has been known to cut out a triangular piece from the front of a shoe, shearing at one bite both top and sole.

The epidermal scales or plates on the shells have lines or ornamentations peculiar to the family concerned. Some authorities think that in the case of turtles which hibernate, each of the tiny lines found in a scale represents a year's growth.

Turtles have large lung capacity and can remain under water for an hour or more without coming up to breathe. They have keen eyesight and acute hearing, as you can testify after trying to approach a turtle sunning itself on a log or stone in a pond.

Turtles that live on land are sometimes called tortoises. Such turtles and some of the aquatic species are herbivorous. The common box turtle, for instance, eats berries, mushrooms, and ripe, soft fruits. It may also eat worms. Some turtles are carnivorous like the snapping turtle, which eats fish, earthworms, freshwater clams, young birds, etc. Some, like the pond turtles, are omnivorous, though preferring animal food.

EGGS. All turtles lay their leathery eggs in the ground. The aquatic forms come out on the land, dig a hole with the hind legs in a sandy region, and deposit there from three to thirty eggs, according to the species. After replacing the sand the mother turtle abandons the eggs. Musk turtles lay their eggs in a rotten log.

Turtles are long-lived, "marked" turtles having been observed in the same fields for many years. Authentic records reveal cases where they have existed fifty to seventy-five years. The huge Galápagos tortoises are thought to live 200 to 300 years.

Because of their abundance and the obvious timidity of most forms turtles are often captured. Their curious structure and method of defense make them interesting subjects for observation.

TURTLE PENS. Snake cages with or without tops are excellent for small turtles. With soil or sod in the bottom, level with the edge of the water pan, a few stones, and a small plant, it is ready for use. Small aquatic turtles may also be kept in aquaria, but should have some kind of a float on which they can climb. For larger turtles, pens can be made with wire netting — ordinary chicken wire may be used — fastened on stakes driven into the ground. The bottom of the wire should be set in a shallow trench, about six inches deep, and stones or soil filled in to prevent the turtles from digging out. A pan should be set in the ground and kept filled with water. Land turtles, which are legally protected in some states, will climb the netting, so the top edge should be turned in about three inches, or narrow boards may be fastened over the tops of the stakes with the netting fastened to the outer edges. Turtle pens should be placed where some part at least will be in the shade all day long. They may be of any convenient size, but preferably not smaller than three by six feet. Land turtles will eat many fruits and vegetables, and it is interesting to make a list of just what they will eat. Water turtles may be fed dead fish or scraps of meat. Care should be taken to keep the pen clean, and to remove uneaten food each day.

COMMON TURTLES

SOME COMMON TURTLES. There are five families of turtles common to the eastern United States, with thirty-one species.

Two turtles are distinctly terrestrial, being called land turtles: the box turtle, which has a hinged lower shell so that it can draw in its head and feet and close the shell, and the wood or red-legged turtle. The latter is flatter across the top than the box turtle, has no hinge in the lower shell, and the scales of the back are marked with concentric lines as if engraved.

The common water turtles are the spotted turtle with small yellow spots on the black shell, and the painted turtle with yellow and red on the black shell and on the skin of the neck.

The musk turtle is small, with a rough upper shell, rather small under shell (plastron) and has a habit of snapping at things. It gives off a musky odor, hence its name. The lower shell is large enough to allow the head and legs to be withdrawn. The snapping turtle is the largest of our turtles and also the most vicious. The lower shell is so small that the legs and head cannot be drawn in.

FENCE LIZARD

These agile creatures are common in the warmer parts of the United States.

LIZARDS. These animals are seldom found within the United States north of latitude 40°, i.e., the line connecting Philadelphia, Indianapolis, Kansas City, and Denver. They prefer a hot climate.

In the arid regions of the Southwest are found certain lizards especially adapted to their environment, notably the horned toad and the Gila monster. In other parts of this region, iguanas may sometimes be seen. Elsewhere in the southern states occur the common skink and the anolia, or American "chameleon." A legless lizard called the glass snake is found in the same places and in the central states as far north as Wisconsin. The blue-tailed skink has been found as far north as Massachusetts; the fence swift as far north as New Jersey and sometimes Long Island.

Like all reptiles the skin of the lizards is decidedly scaly, and their toes are provided with definite claws. These two characteristics distinguish the lizards from the salamanders, and make it easy to avoid confusing these animals, as is frequently done by a novice in the field.

IGUANA

Another strange characteristic of many of the smaller lizards is their ability to part company with their tails when captured and held by that part of their anatomy. Certain lizards can break off the tail at will and scamper to safety, leaving the enemy occupied with the dismembered appendage, which wriggles about for some time in the liveliest manner. In these cases, a new tail grows out, but without vertebrae. Lizards, unlike the amphibians, never possess gills at any stage of their development and, unlike their closer relatives—the snakes—have movable eyelids. They hatch from tough-shelled eggs laid generally in the ground and slowly incubated by the heat of the sun. They closely resemble the form of their parents and do not pass through a metamorphosis of developing stages as do the young amphibia.

Because they feed mostly upon insects our smaller lizards are generally regarded as beneficial. With the exception of the Gila monster, the lizards native to the United States are entirely harmless. In the case of the Gila monster the poison seeps into the wound from grooved teeth in the lower jaw and this unusual arrangement compels the animal to turn on its back, as the shark does, to bite effectively.

REPTILES OF THE DESERT
Horned toad at the left; Gila monster at the right.

Many tropical lizards are brightly colored, and some, like the chameleons, can change their color by rearrangement of the pigment cells in the skin. Lizards living under desert conditions are protectively colored. In the case of the horned toad, a little flattened creature which, in spite of its name, should never be classed with the true toads, there are protective spines all over the upper surface of the body. This little animal will easily survive a trip across the country in a box, without food or water, and will probably thrive for a considerable time if kept in a warm place with a sandy bottom and fed now and then with meal worms. The American "chameleon" can also be kept in captivity.

The ability of the horned toad to live for a while without food has undoubtedly given rise to the strange tale which crops up from time to time about a horned toad having been taken out of a recess in solid rock or from a corner stone of a building where it must have been alive for perhaps a century more or less! Nothing could be more impossible. Certain beetles deprived of food were known to have remained alive for about five years, and the Regal Python, when first brought to the New York Zoölogical Park, refused to eat for almost two years. These represent probably the maximum period that animals can exist without food.

The iguana is killed for food by natives who consider it a great delicacy. Of late years the skin of lizards, when tanned, has been used to a great extent for bags and shoes and other similar articles.

ALLIGATORS. These animals are found only in Florida and parts of Mississippi and Louisiana, and need only be referred to here as the largest reptiles in the United States.

BIBLIOGRAPHY

BARBOUR, THOMAS, *Reptiles and Amphibians, Their Habits and Adaptations* (revised edition). Houghton Mifflin Company, 1934.

A well-written, semi-popular account of the representatives of these two groups.

DITMARS, R. L., *Reptiles of North America.* Doubleday, Doran and Company, 1936.

Describes lizards and turtles as well as snakes. *The* book of its class.

CHAPTER VI

FROGS AND THEIR RELATIVES

Have you heard the blinking toad
Sing his solo by the river,
When April nights are soft and warm,
And spring is all a-quiver? [1]

— JOHN BURROUGHS

The name *amphibia* comes from two Greek words, *amphi* meaning "both sides" and *bios* meaning "life," and refers to a group of animals most of which can live both on land and in water. The amphibians are smooth-skinned, cold-blooded vertebrates. They differ from the fish and reptiles in the absence of scales, but show probable relationship to the fish by starting life as aquatic fish-like forms with external gills. Some of them retain these external gills throughout life, others develop internal gills. Some have lungs in the adult stage. The heart in all of them has three chambers, two auricles and one ventricle.

EGGS. Compared with those of fish, their eggs are larger and fewer in number, but are like them in that they are without shells. They are frequently protected by gelatinous coverings, sometimes resembling masses of beads in jelly. Like fish eggs they are deposited in water (a few exceptions occur where they are placed under bark or stones in damp places). When the eggs are laid in water, hatching consists in the emergence of tiny fish-like forms called tadpoles. This usually occurs in early spring. The eggs of frogs or other amphibians brought into the classroom or museum

[1] From "Song of the Toad" in *Bird and Bough* by John Burroughs. Copyright by Houghton Mifflin Company.

furnish some of the most interesting chapters of any observable life history.

LIFE HISTORY. It is well to note that the length of the life cycle varies with different species; the tadpoles of toads, tree frogs, and wood frogs transform in one season, while the larger tadpoles of the green frog and bullfrog require

American Museum of Natural History

THE BULLFROG

This is the largest of American frogs and has a voice which can be heard over water for more than a mile.

two or three years for the transformation to adults. Bullfrog tadpoles in various stages of development are therefore common in the shallow water of ponds and sluggish streams. From laboratory experiments it is now known that shallow water and warmth hasten the larval transformation, while deeper water and cold retard it. The fact that the body temperature of amphibia, as that of other cold-blooded animals, varies with their surroundings, provides an easy method of meeting the rigors of winter in cold latitudes by hibernating. All bodily functions can be slowed down almost to lifelessness, without injury. In the process of hibernation the animal appears dead. Most of the amphibians hibernate in the mud at the bottom of the pond or stream, or under a rock or in some hole in the ground. The skin of the animal is the sole organ of respiration in the case of lung-bearing amphibia during hibernation, and to a large extent at other times. It is extremely important, therefore, that frogs and most other terrestrial amphibia, if kept in vivaria, be provided with plenty of water or be given a damp retreat to avoid death through the drying of their skins.

The males of frogs, and some other amphibia, can make distinctive sounds by means of what are called croaking sacs, located under the skin on the sides of the throat or neck. The females are not voiceless but in no sense rival the males. In croaking, the frog never opens its mouth; instead the air is forced from the lungs through the glottis into the mouth and croaking sacs and back again by the pressure exerted by the elastic walls of the swollen air sacs. The sound produced varies from the high treble notes of the tree frog to the deep bass of the bullfrog, whose bellowing "jug-o'-rum" has been heard a distance of two miles over the water.

The best known representatives of the amphibia are the frogs, toads, and tree frogs. They are the tailless amphibia. In general they are similar in appearance, having a short and usually broad body, no teeth as in the toad, or teeth in the upper jaw only as in the frogs and tree frogs, and with strong hind legs adapted for leaping. The long tongue is fastened at the front of the mouth and is cleft at the extremity. This sticky organ is of great assistance in catching insects, slugs, and worms.

One especially interesting thing to look for in a live frog is the so-called lymph heart on the dorsal side at the rear of the body. There are two of these organs whose regular beat can be easily observed. Their purpose is to aid in the movement of the lymph through the body.

An especially important adaptation of the frog is its webbed feet. The breast stroke taught by your swimming instructor is almost a copy of the strokes of a swimming frog. While the frog does not use its "arms" which are folded against the body, its stroke is particularly effective because of the large webbed area of the hind feet.

Another distinct adaptation is the elevation of the eyes so that all of the rest of the body can be submerged and the vision still remain unimpaired. The relatively enormous mouth, the sticky tongue, and the agility of the muscular hind legs are also of peculiar significance in the procuring of food.

American Museum of Natural History

THE PICKEREL FROG

This is the common frog of the mountainous regions of eastern United States.

Only when you begin to look for frogs in their native habitat do you appreciate how closely they resemble their environment. Their colors are like the neighboring plants with which they blend. In many cases they are camouflaged by their blotches which resemble the shadow spots around them where leaves and stems interrupt the sunlight.

Besides secreting a slimy substance which protects the skin and makes them difficult to hold, both frogs and salamanders are capable of secreting a poison through the skin. Some species do this more than others. This poison is rarely injurious to one's hands, but is an irritant when taken into the mouth and thus protects the amphibians from many animals which would otherwise eat them. The common western toad has been known to kill dogs that mouthed them. Certain South American frogs are used for their poison which is put on arrow points.

SOME COMMON FROGS. The typical frogs belong to the family *Ranidae* of which there are twenty species common to the United States. The largest is the bullfrog (4 to 8 inches long), with a pale green head, toes widely webbed, and very large eardrums or tympana. The green frog (3 to 5 inches long) resembles the bullfrog but is a lighter green and not so blotched and has a ridge or "lateral fold" extending on each side of the body from just back of the eye. In the bullfrog the fold extends only from the eye to the tympanum.

Courtesy of Oliver P. Medsger

THE WOOD FROG

One of the terrestrial frogs which is common in damp woods.

Two other frogs which are often confused are the leopard and pickerel frogs (each 2 to 3 inches long). The leopard frog is green or olive with irregular black or dark brown blotches which are bordered with white. It is generally distributed throughout the United States. The pickerel frog is light brown with darker blotches on the back. The upper jaw is white with black spots. There is a dark line from the nostril to the eye and the under surface of the legs is yellow or orange. The pickerel frog is fairly common in the eastern states. The wood frog (2 inches long) is more truly terrestrial than most of the others. It is common in damp woods throughout the East. It is a pale reddish-brown color varying to almost black, with a dark spot or "mask" over each eye, closely resembling the dry leaves of the forest floor.

The tree frogs (or tree toads) belong to the *Hylidae* family, and are distinguished by having fingers and toes dilated into sticky disks. They also possess large vocal sacs which swell out their throats like miniature balloons when they make their call notes. Many of the tree frogs consistently "call" through the season. After a little practice, the beginner will be able to avoid the natural confusion of the voice of tree frogs with bird or insect calls, some of which they closely resemble. In fact, tree frogs will always be more frequently heard than seen, since their colors so completely match the immediate surroundings that they usually escape discovery, except when actually moving. Perhaps the chief characteristic of the call of the tree frog is its monotonous repetition.

American Museum of Natural History

THE SPRING PEEPER

The dark x on the back between the arms makes it easy to distinguish this common tree frog.

The *Hylidae* embraces three genera. One of these contains but one species, the little brownish cricket frog one inch long. Though grouped with the tree frogs it is really confined to the ground since the disks on its fingers are too small to enable it to cling. It lives along the edges of ponds, and the strong webbing between the toes makes it a powerful swimmer. The skin is warty and between the eyes is a dark triangular blotch with others on the sides. The call is a distinct clicking which may be imitated by rubbing one coin over the slightly separated edges of three others. This frog occurs throughout the eastern states.

The swamp tree frogs also have small disks but belong to another genus. They too stay near the ground, but because their toes are poorly webbed they are not such good swimmers as the cricket frog. They are striped longitudinally and lack the triangle of the other group. Several species are found east of the Rocky Mountains. They are all small, an inch or less in length.

The genus *Hyla* includes fourteen species in the United States, one or more of them being found in every state of the Union. Strangely enough the call of one of these is familiar to nearly all of us, but the frog itself is seldom seen. This is the spring peeper. It is usually straw or light tan in color, about an inch long, and is easily distinguished by a dark x on the back. Its call is a continuous series of high-pitched peeps, one of the most characteristic sounds of early spring near ponds or hidden bayous from meandering brooks in the woods.

The tree frog — rain toad or tree toad — (2 inches long) common throughout the eastern part of the country varies in color from gray to green or brown with darker blotches and yellow underparts. Its skin is slightly warty. Its call is a clear trill given more frequently in the evenings and in damp weather. Like some other amphibians, this frog can change its color to match its environment by expanding or contracting black pigment cells in the skin. When these are expanded the skin appears darker. It also has yellow pigment in spherical cells. When the black pigment cells are contracted, a general greenish or yellowish color appears, due to the reflection of light from the yellow pigment cells. Even more prone to change color is the

Pacific tree frog which is smaller than our common tree frog and also more active. It lives near the ground. In the southern states is a slender delicate tree frog about two inches long, of brilliant green color, found frequently in marshes where it lives among the green leaves and reeds. It has long legs and a white stripe along each side of the body.

All the North American tree frogs breed in the water in early spring, but they soon leave the water and during the rest of the season they stay on trees and coarse vegetation, climbing frequently to inaccessible places by their viscid disks.

American Museum of Natural History

THE TOAD

This shy and beneficial animal is familiar to all. Its warts are not "catching."

Tree frogs easily adapt themselves to captivity in a vivarium or terrarium in which there are a few growing plants in whose leaves they may find concealment. Insects must be provided, which they will stalk and capture as in the woods. Their acrobatic ability, color changes, their ability to jump and capture insects, and their vocal efforts will attract attention.

TOADS. The family *Bufonidae* includes the common American toad and the Fowler's toad, the latter being smaller and more active and frequently without spots on the white underparts. Toads are warty creatures, but it is an error to think the warts are "catching." Generally regarded as being ugly in appearance, they have eyes as beautiful as any animal in the world, a statement you can easily confirm the next time you have a toad in your hands.

Other species of toads, of which there are sixteen in the United States, are very similar in appearance to the two already mentioned. In the Southwest is found the largest of the genus, a toad with smoother skin than most, and reaching five inches or more in length. On the other hand the oak toad of the southeastern states is the smallest — a little fat mite with short legs and a body only a trifle over an inch in length.

Although the toad is a land animal, it begins its existence in the water and returns there to spawn. When the shallow water of ponds and stagnant pools is warmed by April sunshine the toads enter it and for days there is much commotion. Each female deposits in ropes of jelly about 10,000 eggs, which soon hatch into tiny black tadpoles. It is not easy at first to distinguish between the tadpoles of frogs and toads, but the toad tadpole, even late in summer, is generally smaller and blacker.

Toads remain in the same general locality as long as they live. Instances are on record where toads have traveled long distances in returning to their native haunts, after having been carried away.

The toad is a prodigious eater, consuming as much as four stomachfuls of insects in 24 hours. While frequently seen during the daytime, it is really a nocturnal animal and seems most appreciative of man's invention, the electric light, which attracts insects. It is a common thing to find a fat toad regularly visiting such a lighted zone night after night. Toads are of enormous value to agriculture through their destruction of injurious insects.

SALAMANDERS. The other order of Amphibia comprises the salamanders, a group known as the *Urodela*, all of which in the adult form have tails. The salamanders also have teeth in both jaws and breathe either by gills or by lungs when adult. They are frequently mistaken for lizards, but have a smooth, naked skin instead of scales as do the lizards. They also lack the claws with which the toes of lizards terminate. Lizards in general require a warmer habitat, and therefore are rarely found where it is cold in winter. They also demand a drier habitat than the salamanders, which must keep the skin moist as in the case of frogs.

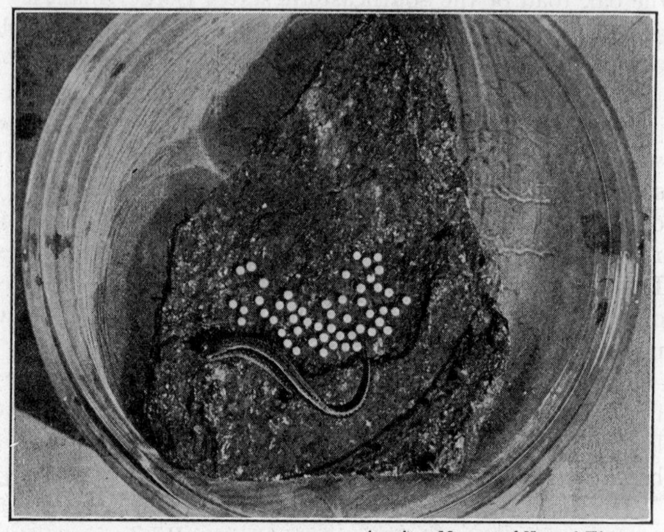

American Museum of Natural History

TWO-LINED SALAMANDER AND EGGS LAID IN CAPTIVITY

The eggs are normally deposited in the waters of stagnant brooks.

The salamanders vary in size from the two-lined salamander, only 3 inches long, to the relatively huge hellbender, 24 inches in length. None of them is harmful in any way, and some of the smaller salamanders are so exceedingly active that the would-be capturer has to be extraordinarily quick to thwart their escape. Practically all of them lay their eggs in water, in which medium they begin their life cycle. Many of them later leave the water and hide under stones, old logs, and débris in the woods around springs, brooks, or other damp places. In general, these forms can be found by overturning the objects under which they are likely to be concealed. Under good conditions they may be induced to breed in captivity.

American Museum of Natural History

SALAMANDERS

Above is the common newt; below is the red-backed salamander, a very active form commonly found under logs. (See page 96.)

Terrestrial salamanders will thrive under artificial conditions in a vivarium if provided with bark or moss under which they can find sufficient concealment and dampness. A few meal worms, or other insects, or an occasional small earthworm will be appreciated as food.

SOME COMMON SALAMANDERS. One of the most abundant and widespread salamanders is the newt ($3\frac{1}{2}$ inches long). It is found in most ponds and streams and may be recognized by its olive-green or reddish appearance. Its sides have small scarlet dots bordered by black, which among those found in the South become lines. It is bright yellow beneath. The northern form usually undergoes a terrestrial period in its life when it becomes brick red in color and is to be found among the dry leaves in woodlands. The skin at this time is rough and dry and the animal is often miscalled a lizard. This red stage lasts for a year or two following the larval stage and preceding the true adult form, when it again takes to the water to live and breed.

American Museum of Natural History

THE TIGER SALAMANDER

This is strikingly colored, with yellow blotches on a brown background.

The tiger salamander (8 inches long) is dark brown or black with irregular yellow blotches and bands. The immature salamander may, under certain conditions, breed while still retaining the larval external gills. In this form it is called the *axolotl*. The animal is widely distributed from Mexico through the central and eastern states.

The spotted salamander (6 inches long) is black with yellow spots on the sides. Its skin may exude a milky fluid. The eggs of this common form resemble frogs' eggs but may be distinguished by the fact that the eggs are clustered together inside a large mass of jelly which forms a thick layer entirely surrounding them instead of each egg having its own jelly coating.

There is a large group of lungless salamanders in the United States comprising some fourteen genera and forty-eight species, the representatives of which are distributed widely in damp woods. Those most likely to be seen are the following:

The dusky salamander and its relatives are very common in wet places, such as under stones in and along the sides of streams. They are brown with darker mottlings and stripes and range in size from 3 to 6 or 7 inches.

American Museum of Natural History

THE RED SALAMANDER

This form is vermilion red, with many black spots.

The two-lined salamander is a common eastern form. It is yellowish in color with a narrow dark line extending down each side of the back. One member of the same genus is found in limestone caves.

The red salamander is purely aquatic and may be recognized by its large cylindrical body, colored red and covered with small black spots.

The purple salamander resembles the red, but is brown in color. It also lives in streams and is common in some sections of the East.

The red-backed salamander is small ($3\frac{1}{2}$ inches long), grayish-brown in color, and may or may not have a reddish-brown stripe down its back. The eggs are laid in little grape-like clusters in hollows in rotten logs or under rocks and in other damp places. They are usually five to nine in number and are guarded by the female.

American Museum of Natural History

THE SLIMY SALAMANDER

The slimy salamander is about 6 inches long and is slate black with minute white spots on the sides and sometimes on the whole body, and lighter gray underneath. The slime given off by it when trying to escape is very difficult to remove from your fingers. Its body is very slippery.

There are several other species in the West and in our southern mountains, most of which are blackish in color, though one has bright red cheeks and another red legs.

The salamanders of another genus are arboreal, being found under bark and loose wood in trees. Two other varieties live only in deep wells or caves. These are pinkish-white and compared with their relatives are considered colorless. They have no vision, as constant living in utter darkness has caused them to lose both pigment and eyes.

The largest of our salamanders is the ugly hellbender (24 inches long), found in swamps and large streams of the eastern and southern states. It is harmless, but most unprepossessing. The eggs laid in water look like long strings of translucent beads. The male guards these eggs, really with the purpose of safeguarding his own food supply. Fortunately for his family he rarely consumes all of the eggs before they hatch.

The mud puppy, or *Necturus*, (12 inches long) is dark, with bushy red external gills on each side of the head. It is found in the eastern states. The northern species lays its eggs on the under surfaces of flat stones in streams. The eggs remain fixed to the stones and the female curls underneath them to guard them.

Amphiuma, the Congo eel (36 to 40 inches long), has a long black body with very small legs and has a spiracle on each side of the neck. It is found in streams and ditches of the southern states. The *Siren*, or mud eel (24 to 30 inches long), resembles the Congo eel, but has no hind legs and its jaws are provided with horny coverings instead of teeth. It has external gills.

BIBLIOGRAPHY

Barbour, Thomas, *Reptiles and Amphibians, Their Habits and Adaptations* (revised edition). Houghton Mifflin Company, 1934.

A well-written, semi-popular account of these two groups.

Dickerson, Mary C., *The Frog Book.* Doubleday, Doran and Company, Inc., 1906.

A popular, illustrated book on the frogs of the United States.

Noble, G. Kingsley, *Biology of the Amphibia.* McGraw-Hill Book Company, 1931.

A comprehensive work, both descriptive and experimental.

Wright, Anna A. and Albert H., *Frogs and Toads.* Comstock Publishing Company, 1933.

Descriptions, photographs, and keys of the more than eighty varieties of frogs and toads of the United States and Canada.

CHAPTER VII

FINS AND SCALES

Slowly, silently, now the moon
Walks the night in her silver shoon;

. . . .

A harvest mouse goes scampering by,
With silver claws and silver eye;
And moveless fish in the water gleam,
By silver reeds in a silver stream.[1]

— Walter de la Mare

Who wouldn't throw his cap in the air at the prospect of "goin' fishin'"? The excitement of matching wits against the fish, the possibility of catching the biggest fish, the getting away from office, home, school, or camp routine, spending hours out in the woods or on the lake, hearing new sounds, experiencing new thrills is a composite delight which makes a tremendous appeal.

Where the water in stream or lake is shallow enough to allow observations, some notes on the habits of fish may be possible. By procuring a permit from the proper authorities allowing netting or seining for educational purposes, living specimens can be obtained including practically all local fish. It is best to select the smaller fish, putting them promptly in a can or pail of water and transferring them as soon as practicable to the camp or school aquarium.

Structure. Fish are peculiarly adapted in structure to their aquatic existence. Their streamline body more or less covered with mucus, overlapping scales, laterally placed

[1] From "Silver" in the *Collected Poems* of Walter de la Mare. Copyright by Henry Holt and Company.

eyes, powerful muscles, membranous fins, large mouth provided with numerous teeth, and delicate gills protected by gill covers, are some of the more obvious adaptations.

There are no external ears, sound waves being transmitted by the water directly to the inner ear, which is probably more an organ of balance than of true hearing. A so-called lateral line on each side also seems to be of some assistance as a sense organ. Scattered on the surface of the body are nerve endings which correspond to the taste buds in the mouth of animals higher than fish. It is not a misstatement, then, to say that to a degree a fish can taste with its skin. For smelling, there are two tiny nostril openings in front of the eyes, though they are unlike our nostrils because they are blind sacs and are never used for breathing. Some fish, like the catfish and cod, have filaments around the mouth known as *barbels*, which doubtless aid in feeling. Fish have no eyelids since the eyes are kept continuously moist from the water.

Fish are the only aquatic animals which possess a special apparatus for rising and sinking in the water. This is the swim bladder which, in some forms like the garpike, bowfin, sturgeon, catfish, and lungfish, is connected by a tube with the gullet. The lungfish actually use the swim bladder or air bladder for respiration. This seems to indicate that the true lungs of air-breathing vertebrates have developed from such an organ as the swim bladder.

Most fish are protectively colored, being darker above and lighter beneath. This is important in the case of smaller fish, which are preyed upon from above by birds such as kingfishers, herons, gulls, and terns, and from beneath by larger fish such as bass, pike, pickerel, etc. The dark color of the back thus blends with the dark-colored stream if seen from above, and likewise the pale-colored underparts if seen from beneath merge with the light coming down through the water from the surface. If the back of fish were light-colored and the belly dark, it is easy to see how much more conspicuous they would be to their enemies. Tropical fish in some cases gain immunity from danger by being colored like the marine landscape where they live. Others can afford to be conspicuous because they can dart into a niche in the rocks or under friendly plants if alarmed. By rearrangement of their color pigments, certain fish are also able to change their color patterns to match their environment more closely. In temperate waters the flounder probably shows the best example of this function, though its ability is more than matched by tropical species. The colors of fish are primarily due to pigments in the skin and do not come off with the transparent scales.

The fins consist of two structures, each valueless without the other. The membrane obviously is necessary to push against the resisting water and thus secure locomotion. But the supporting rays, either soft or spiny, are as necessary to the functioning of the fins as are the ribs of an umbrella when one desires to open it. Many people remembering that the chemical formula for water is H_2O, seem to have the idea that fish in breathing take out of the water this oxygen which has combined with the hydrogen. Of course it is impossible for these two gases to be separated except by an electric current. It is quite possible to drown a fish, simply by placing it in water which has been cooled after having had all the air driven out of it by boiling. The oxygen, which in breathing is commonly extracted from the water by the capillaries in the fish's gills, is simply a part of the atmosphere which has previously been absorbed by the surface of the water, or else comes from aquatic green plants as a waste product of their starch-making.

FOOD. The food of fish varies greatly. Practically all smaller forms of plant and animal organisms are devoured.

The carp, for instance, is vegetarian; the bass, trout, and bluefish are examples of carnivorous fish; while minnows and suckers represent a group which will eat either kind of food.

Sunfish Guarding Its Nest

The male fish is a pugnacious fighter at the breeding season.

Reproduction. The breeding habits of certain fish are interesting. Marine species and some fresh-water forms abandon their eggs after fertilization. This may account for the tremendous numbers laid by certain fish, which run up to 10,000,000 in the case of a single female cod. Some fish migrate to spawn. The salmon, shad, sturgeon, and trout all go upstream, the eels on the contrary pass them as they go downstream en route to the ocean. Among the fish which do not migrate are several which show parental care, either in the preparation of a sort of nest or the actual care of the eggs and young.

The spawning season of most fish is the spring of the year, but there are many exceptions. For instance, members of the salmon family spawn during the fall or winter and the sunfish spawn during early summer.

The spawning habits of fish are not so well known as they should be. Two, in particular, are very interesting: the sunfish and the stickleback. The male sunfish excavates by means of his tail a shallow, circular nest near the shore, frequently under an overhanging waterplant. These nests are easily observed in clear water. After the female has deposited her eggs, she leaves them in charge of the pugnacious little male who faithfully watches over them till they hatch. During the mating season, the male will fight any approaching fish. The stickleback is a small fresh-water fish which builds a true nest out of *spirogyra*, the green water algae which is sometimes called pond-scum. The male secretes a sort of waterproof glue from the opening of the kidney, near the anal fin. With this glue he pastes together the threads of his filmy house, leaving a round entrance like the opening of a muff. Then he seeks a mate who enters and deposits her eggs. After she has left, he induces other female sticklebacks to come in and lay their eggs. He seems to like family cares for he fertilizes all the eggs that can be got into his green bower. Then like the male sunfish he watches over them until all the eggs are hatched and the little sticklebacks have scurried away in the water.

Other fish have interesting spawning habits. The parent

bullheads take care of their young, which look like small black tadpoles, conducting them in a large "school" for a long time after hatching.

Fish eggs lack the shell found in the eggs of birds, because in the water there is no danger of the contents being dried up as there would be if exposed to the air like birds' eggs or the eggs of reptiles.

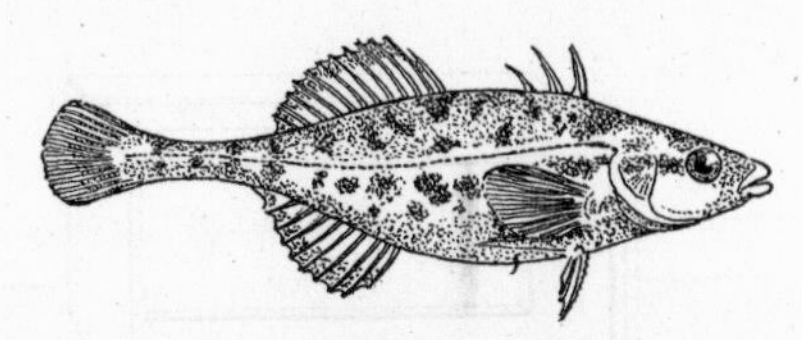

FOUR-SPINED STICKLEBACK

Fish are so valuable for food and other purposes that both the United States Fish Commission and the different states have coöperated in developing numerous fish hatcheries. If there is a state hatchery near enough to visit, the details of propagation of fish will be better understood.

AQUARIA. One of the best and most interesting ways of studying fish is to keep them alive in aquaria. These may be purchased at any of the supply houses at prices ranging from two dollars up and there should be several for different kinds of fish. Those made of thick glass with metal frames and slate bottoms are the best — and most expensive. Nearly as satisfactory and cheaper are those with metal frames and bottom and thinner glass sides. Either of these is better than the rectangular one made entirely of glass. The round fish bowls are quite unsatisfactory, distorting the fish as seen from the sides, and exposing comparatively small surfaces of water to the air. Aquaria 10 by 6 by 6 inches holding about six quarts of water, or those 12 by 8 by 8, holding twelve quarts are very good for small fish.

Home-made aquaria are satisfactory if carefully constructed. To make an aquarium 14 by 8 inches, secure two pieces of glass of that size for the sides and a board

1 inch thick, 9 inches wide, and 32 inches long. Have a groove cut with a buzz saw half an inch from each edge of the board and about a quarter of an inch deep. Then cut the board into three pieces; one, 15½ inches long, and two, 8¼ inches long. Set the short pieces on the long one and hold the glass in the grooves to mark the position where the end pieces are to be fastened. Then fasten the ends with screws to the bottom, making sure that the grooves of the ends and bottom exactly meet. Give the boards two coats of a good outside paint. When dry fill the grooves half full of white lead, slide the glass in place, and fasten strips of wood an inch wide by half an inch thick across the top over the glass sides. The small aquaria described for aquatic insects in Chapter IX can be used for minnows.

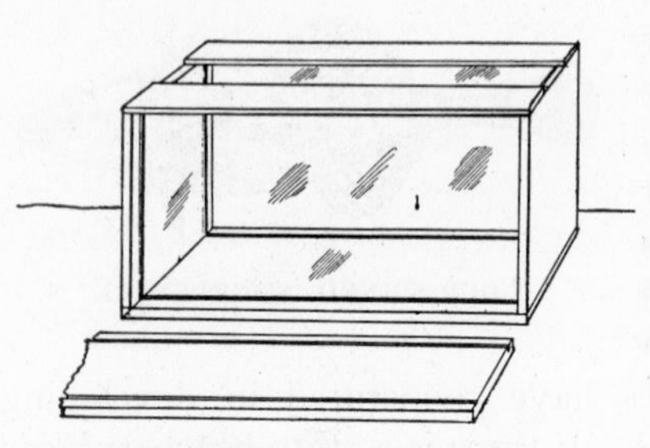

A HOME-MADE AQUARIUM

In stocking the aquarium, first put about half an inch of washed sand or gravel in the bottom — that taken from the shore of the lake or stream is best — fill two-thirds full of water taken from the lake or stream and put in water plants secured if possible from the place where the fish are to be caught. The plants can be weighted down by lead wire wound around the lower ends, or may be tied with string to small stones and the bottoms buried in the sand. There are several species of aquatic plants, the most valuable of which for an aquarium are the wide and long-leaved species, *Vallisneria* and *Sagittaria*, or the abundant-leaved *Elodea* and *Myriophyllum*, all good producers of oxygen. Put the aquarium in a place where it is light without, however, being in the direct sunlight, for if the water becomes too warm most of the fish will die, and in bright light algae grow rapidly on the walls.

After the water plants have been in the aquarium for a few days, the fish may be added. A dip net or dredge should be successful if used in the nearest body of water, or a fine-meshed seine may be used if permission has been secured from the State Game or Conservation Commission. Collect a variety of small fish, together with any newts, tadpoles, snails, or water insects that may be caught. Put these in pails of water at once to be carried back. Small sunfish, perch, bullheads, or minnows will usually do well in aquaria. Trout or bass are not likely to live unless the water can be constantly aërated, as by a stream of water falling from some height. Game fish protected by law should not be kept unless a permit has been secured. Do not put too many fish in an aquarium; half a dozen small ones with a few snails, a newt or two, and some tadpoles are enough. After the aquaria have been stocked they should be watched daily to see how the occupants are getting on. Very likely some fish will make a meal of others. Such predacious ones thereafter should have no smaller fish put in with them. The plants will furnish food for most fish while small worms, insects, or tiny bits of meat will be relished by others. Fish in an aquarium should be fed very sparingly. They thrive better and there is less chance of contaminating the water.

When the water plants in an aquarium give off enough oxygen to supply the respiratory needs of the aquatic animals therein, and through their own starch-making utilize the excess carbon dioxide given off by the animals, the aquarium is said to be balanced. Such an aquarium should continue for weeks with no required changes except adding water from time to time.

There is another kind of balance which one should strive

to gain and maintain in an aquarium, namely a balance among the microörganisms in the water. The reason why the water for the aquarium should be taken from the lake or stream from which the specimens are obtained is that such water is already balanced, i.e., the microörganisms have acted and reacted against each other until each, to a degree, is checked by the other forms. If unbalanced water is used, one special organism may start to run wild, then die for lack of food or other reasons, causing serious trouble to all the other organisms in the aquarium.

Just as the water plants balance the aquatic animals and the microörganisms balance each other, so do the scavengers, snails and tadpoles, balance the algae, excess food, and dirt.

In addition to aquaria, outdoor ponds may be made by lining a shallow excavation with cement. If placed where partly shaded, and a small stream from a brook can be deflected to run through it, such a pool may be made so like a natural one that any kind of fish can be kept in it. Another method is to enclose part of a brook with galvanized netting of quarter-inch or finer mesh, and stock the enclosure with fish.

A further project with fish is to make a plaster cast. This will be fairly simple if one side is done at a time, according to the general directions given in Chapter II.

The preparation of a fish skeleton is rather difficult, but should prove instructive and interesting. Ants and beetles will be of assistance in the later stages of the preparation.

Some Common Fish. There are too many species of our common fish to attempt to present a complete key. However, some of the more common forms are here briefly described.

Every brook and pond contains some of the minnow family which includes the carp, dace, and minnows. There are over one thousand species in this one fresh-water family,

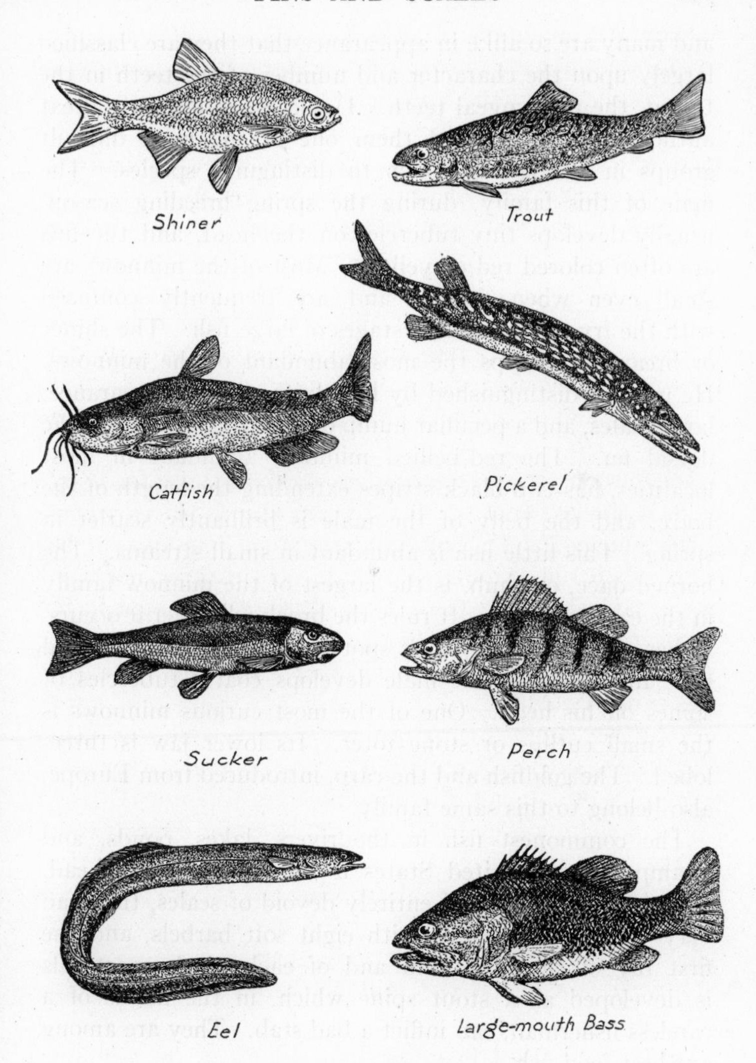

COMMON FRESH-WATER FISH

and many are so alike in appearance that they are classified largely upon the character and number of the teeth in the throat, the pharyngeal teeth. David Starr Jordan, a great authority on fish, called them one of the most difficult groups in zoölogy in which to distinguish species. The male of this family, during the spring breeding season, usually develops tiny tubercles on the head, and the fins are often colored red or yellow. Most of the minnows are small even when adults, and are frequently confused with the fry and fingerling stages of large fish. The shiner or bream is perhaps the most abundant of the minnows. He may be distinguished by his bluish-silvery appearance, large scales, and a peculiar hump on the back in front of the dorsal fin. The red-bellied minnow, abundant in most localities, has two black stripes extending the length of the body, and the belly of the male is brilliantly scarlet in spring. This little fish is abundant in small streams. The horned dace, or chub, is the largest of the minnow family in the eastern states. It rules the brook wherever it occurs. It has a conspicuous black spot at the base of the dorsal fin. In the spring the male develops coarse tubercles of spines on his head. One of the most curious minnows is the small cutlips or stone toter. Its lower jaw is three-lobed. The goldfish and the carp, introduced from Europe, also belong to this same family.

The commonest fish in the rivers, lakes, ponds, and swamps of the United States is the catfish or bullhead. The skin is smooth and entirely devoid of scales, the head very wide and provided with eight soft barbels, and the first ray of the dorsal fin and of each of the pectorals is developed as a stout spine which, in the hands of a careless fisherman, can inflict a bad stab. They are among our best food fish.

Another family, comprising 60 species, is the sucker family. These fish are toothless, with fleshy, protractile lips. Some grow to a large size but the flesh is tasteless and filled with small bones.

True eels represent another family. These strange, snake-like fish are exceedingly voracious, even burrowing in the mud in search of food. When mature, eels travel downstream to the Atlantic Ocean, where they spawn in the open sea beyond the Bermuda Islands.

Salmon and trout as a rule prefer very cold water. During the breeding season the males have a tendency to develop a hook on the lower jaw.

Pike and pickerel are examples of carnivorous fish, built for speed and voracious in the extreme, as the projecting lower jaw with its many sharp teeth would indicate. Although bony fish, their flesh is good to eat.

KILLIFISH

Killifish are generally confused with the minnows. The marine species are the small fish always seen about rocks and piers. The fresh-water forms are similar and frequently live at the bottom of streams.

Bass and sunfish are keenly voracious. The two kinds of black bass, large-mouth and small-mouth, are perhaps the gamest fresh-water fish of our deep streams and lakes.

Darters are probably the most interesting and peculiar of our small fish. They are found only east of the Mississippi River. They are peculiar-looking little fish, with eyes somewhat bulging like a toad's and located nearly on the top of the head. Some are very plain in appearance, but the males of some species are colored like the rainbow. They have no air bladder and depend upon their large pectoral fins with which they fairly fly through the water, and with which they also crawl up water plants.

The yellow perch is valued for food. It is numerous in all fresh waters and is easily recognized by its golden yellow color, banded with dark rings. The wall-eyed pike or pike perch is a large fish of the same family, as is the white perch. Both are excellent for food.

BIBLIOGRAPHY

BREEDER, CHARLES M., *Field Book of Marine Fishes of the Atlantic Coast.* G. P. Putnam's Sons, 1930.

A popular account of the structure and distinguishing characters of the fish that may be seen along the Atlantic coast.

FULLER, RAYMOND T., *Along the Brook.* John Day Company, Inc., 1931.

A popular account of the life of small streams.

GOODE, GEORGE B., *American Fishes.* L. C. Page and Company, 1926.

A large book, well illustrated, on game and food fishes, with especial reference to their habits and the methods of capture.

JORDAN, DAVID STARR, and EVERMANN, B. W., *American Food and Game Fishes.* Doubleday, Doran and Company, Inc., 1923.

A standard and complete work on the subject. Nothing better for reference.

LEDERER, NORBERT, *Tropical Fish and Their Care.* Alfred A. Knopf, 1934.

A valuable treatise on the breeding and care of tropical fish.

MANN, MRS. LUCILLE QUARRY, *Tropical Fish.* Leisure League of America, 1934.

A popular and inexpensive pamphlet on the subject.

MELLEN, J. M., *Young Folks' Book of Fishes.* Dodd, Mead and Company, Inc., 1927.

Stories and descriptions, written in simple language, of many fish of both fresh and salt water.

MORGAN, ALFRED, *An Aquarium Book for Boys and Girls.* Charles Scribner's Sons, 1936.

Tells how to make an aquarium and how to keep fish, frogs and toads in it.

The Book of Fishes, National Geographic Society, 1924.

The colored plates alone make the book worth while, but with these are excellent descriptions and accounts of the life histories.

CHAPTER VIII

AT THE SEASHORE

The quivering terns dart wild and dive,
As the tide comes tumbling in.
The calm rock pools grow all alive,
With the tide tumbling in.
The crab who under the brown weed creeps,
And the snail who lives in his house and sleeps,
Awake and stir, as the plunging sweeps
Of the tide come tumbling in.[1]

— CALE YOUNG RICE

The conjunction of the seashore with the salt water, encroaching or retreating under the influence of waves, storm, or tide, produces a region of unending and kaleidoscopic interest to the naturalist.

Many of the plants and animals are steadfast residents of their various haunts throughout the year. Others migrate or hibernate to avoid the rigors of a winter which makes adamant and impenetrable the once oozing mud and the shifting sands. The sea wrack, flung on the beach as the aftermath of a storm, will be sure to contain some exotic treasures like the Portuguese Man-of-War, jellyfishes and shells, or even a huge blackfish — foreign perhaps to that immediate shore, but related because part and parcel of the abounding ocean.

Animals like sponges, oysters, and mussels, which cannot migrate because they are anchored with self-imposed links, together with slow-crawling forms like sea urchins, are

[1] From "As the Tide Comes In" by Cale Young Rice. Copyright by The Century Company.

sometimes called *benthos* (depth of the sea). To the active and free-swimming organisms, the term *nekton* (swimming) is applied. A third term, *plankton* (wandering) describes animals and plants, often minute, which float close to the surface. The animal organisms of the sea can all be classified under one or the other of these terms. Just as the wide distribution of bird life is dependent, somewhat, on environmental factors, so the organisms of the seashore are sensitive both to the temperature and depth of the water,

Photograph by Paul B. Mann

A STRANDED BLACKFISH

This small whale pursued its prey into shallow water and was left on the beach when the tide went out.

as well as to food supply. The animals of the shallow water near the shore are often called *littoral* (of the shore), in contrast to the *pelagic* (the open sea) forms living in the ocean far from land. Deep-sea forms are called *abyssal* (the depth). Sometimes abyssal forms, which normally seem to prefer the cold depths of the tropical oceans, may be found in the shallower waters of northern seas, if they find there a temperature to their liking. Such an animal is the English whelk found in the cool waters of the New England coast, north of its accustomed latitudes. Probably to an extent far greater than we are yet aware, temperature and food supply are determining factors for much of the life of the seashore.

American Museum of Natural History

A MUDDY BEACH

Here are hidden great numbers of marine worms and other small organisms. Note the periwinkles scattered in the foreground.

The character of the shore itself is of great significance. Sandy shores with lagoons, rocky ledges with tide pools, mud flats, and coral strands are four types of shores, each characterized more or less by distinctive organisms. Mud flats may not be so enjoyable to explore, but they are worth investigating. Eel grass is usually abundant there and the mud beneath it harbors a multitude of creatures such as marine worms, and other small organisms like the pipefish. Such shores are treacherous to the naturalist because of deep pockets of soft mud here and there on the bottom, and because of the danger of cutting one's feet on shells.

From Cape Cod southward sandy shores are perhaps the

most common. The exposed beaches of pure sand are relatively barren, though characteristic species may be found near and below the low tide limit. The most productive regions are the sandy mud flats where the sand is somewhat darkened by combination with fine particles of mud. Here great numbers of forms find homes or temporary concealment beneath the soft contours of the sandy mud, the fine texture of which is so pleasing to the touch and so easily retains impressions to be considered by the sleuthing naturalist.

Sandy shores where there is a rather precipitous slope to the bottom are not the best for our purpose. A shore of gradual descent is preferable; still better, a region where the ebb tide makes a profound difference in the amount of new territory exposed.

Photograph by Gladys Parker

WHEN THE TIDE GOES OUT

Fascinating new stretches of territory, rich hunting ground for the naturalist, may be explored at ebb tide.

The strange inflood and retreat of waters constituting the tide may amount to a difference of as much as ten feet in vertical measurement between tidal levels produced in a constricted area such as Cape Cod Bay. Twice a day this phenomenon takes place. There is no escape; animals must adapt their living or perish. Some mollusks simply close their shells, or if a univalve, withdraw into the shell and close the entrance with a protecting operculum. Many more organisms, however, will burrow into the moist sea bottom and thus avoid the dangerous exigency of being exposed to the air. Some animals wait in the tide pools around rocks; others hazard the wet strands of eel grass now lying flattened — inert compasses pointing to the direction of the ebbing tide.

Photograph by Paul B. Mann

A SANDY BEACH

The pebbly stretch and the sand beyond are submerged at high tide. A broken horseshoe-crab shell lies by the windrow of dead eel grass.

In studying the life of sandy seashores, it is important to observe every mark or disturbed condition, because each trace is a telltale to keen eyes. Footprints of birds, furrows of clams, grooves of undulating worms, indentations of crawling crabs, blowholes of buried mollusks, and round holes drilled in abandoned snail shells, all have a story to tell to those who will take the trouble to investigate. Let us take our notebooks and go down to the shore. If we expect to collect and study any of these forms, we should also have a pail, shovel or old iron spoon, long-handled knife, sieve, strong net, hand lens, and several small bottles. A pair of good field glasses is necessary in order to study shore birds.

American Museum of Natural History

DRILLED CLAM SHELLS

The small holes in the upper shells were drilled by a sponge. Those in the lower shells were made by sea snails.

Wild grape, wild rose, beach plum, beach pea, milkweed, false cranberry, and reindeer moss grow down as close to the high tide level as they can. Where they hesitate, the beach grass, here solitary and there in clumps, wrests a precarious living closer to the water. Some of these plants have marked the sand with a tiny indented circle where the tip of the leaf has bowed to the winds and swung back and forth in a fixed arc. Near by are masses of Russian thistle; over there is a kind of spurge, and close by is a rampant pigweed — all strange visitors. It seems a miracle that any plant could live in these hot sands. Yet several allied forms may be found if one searches. And where it is not so sandy and is distinctly wetter, one may find sea lavender and even cranberries mingling with reeds, rushes, cattails, sedges, and grasses. As we walk along, mottled grasshoppers become apparent as they launch themselves into the air, but seemingly disappear when they alight, for when they are quiet the eye cannot distinguish them from the sandy environment.

Brown Bros.

A Sand Dune

The beach grass and other plants prevent further drifting on the landward side.

The sticks and timbers projecting from the sands are smoothed by nature's sand blast as though some old man of the sea had used them for his own throughout the ages. The frosted windowpanes of life-saving stations bear similar testimony to the effectiveness of the wind-blown sand. The contour and physical character of the beach itself may be changed from season to season by the fickle winds, especially when aided by a nor'-easter. Dunes may come, and dunes may go, unless held intact by beach grass or other vegetation; but the life of the shore is adaptable to such minor fluctuations in environment, and will be fairly constant.

The shore is likely to be covered by windrows of "seaweed," so-called, really the brown or bleached leaves of

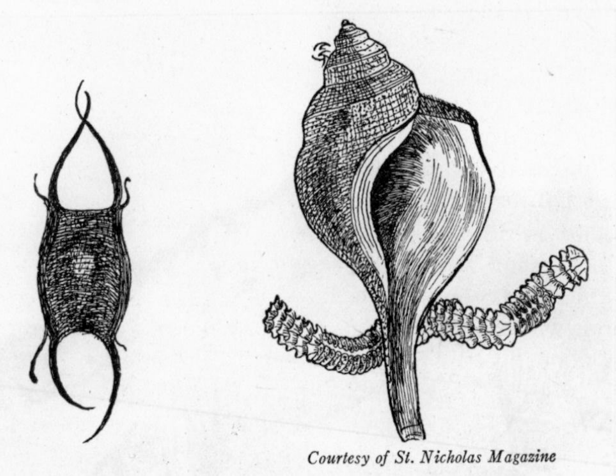

Courtesy of St. Nicholas Magazine

MERMAID'S PURSE AND WHELK WITH EGG CAPSULES

dead eel grass cast on shore by waves and tide. Turn over a clump with your foot or stick. Out of the moist layers leap innumerable sand hoppers or beach fleas. Perhaps a green crab will scuttle back under a protecting mass.

A further examination of the shore may reveal some Mermaid's purses — those strange egg cases of the skate; swollen, black, rectangular objects with a tendril-like extension at each corner. The split across one end shows how the young occupant got out. In certain localities, and especially after a storm, the string of seed-like capsules of the channeled whelk, or the compact egg cases called sea-corn may be found. Sand dollars may be picked up, brown with tiny specks if only recently exposed, or white and smooth if old, revealing the symmetrical rows of perforations through which projected the tiny ambulacral feet.

Here and there will probably be found clear or brown or purplish masses, the remains of jellyfish left on the shore by the waves. If we look for them when we return, we may find nothing more than a moist spot on the sands, since they are about 99 per cent water and dry down to an impalpable film.

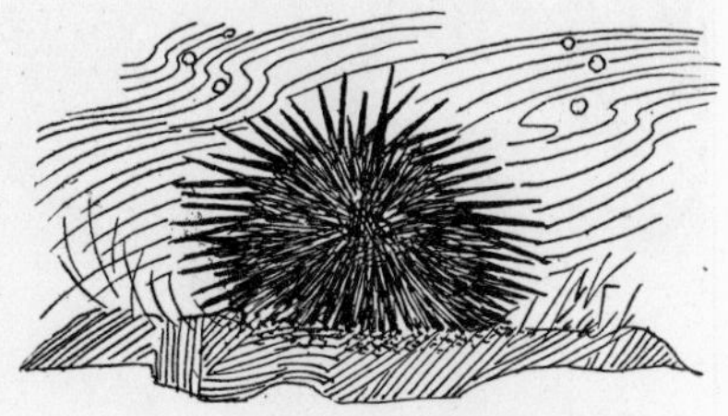

Courtesy of St. Nicholas Magazine

SEA URCHIN

If tomorrow you chance on tide pools of a rocky shore, you will see many of the same forms with some additions. Sea urchins may be seen moving about like living pincushions in the midst of hydroids resembling animated plants. Starfishes, caught out of water by the hot sun and killed by exposure, are slowly drying. Whether the shore is rocky or sandy, periwinkle shells of many species will be in evidence as we approach the water, which harbors many millions more of these small univalves. Fiddler crabs, the burrowing crab *Hippa*, sand crabs, and other crabs will be encountered. In some localities many beautiful shells may be picked up, as well as bleached sponges and occasional corals.

Courtesy of St. Nicholas Magazine

STARFISH

If we use our spade or iron spoon, we begin to realize that

the shores which appear so empty are teeming with hidden life. In the mud flats the *Nereis* or clam worm, the richly colored opal worm, the slender "red thread," the fierce "four-jawed worm," the ribbon worm, the tiny "blood spot," and other tubeless worms may be easily caught by washing the mud through a sieve. The four-jawed worm

American Museum of Natural History

MARINE WORMS AT HOME

Tube worms may be seen in the foreground, whelks in the background.

and clam worm are carnivorous and their bite should be avoided. There are other worms which construct a tube within which they live. One of the commonest is the tufted worm, which builds a leathery U-shaped tube. Another, the shell worm, secretes the little white tubes which are frequently found zigzagging over the outer surface of marine shells. *Spirorbis* is a tiny worm which makes little coiled tubes slightly larger than a pinhead. They are usually found attached to *Fucus* or to eel grass.

On rock-bound shores an abundance of life clings to the surface of rocks normally submerged but exposed when the

American Museum of Natural History

SEA ANEMONE

The tentacles encircling the mouth are armed with stinging cells to aid in capturing prey.

tide ebbs. Oysters may be found in profusion, attached toward the base of the rock or on the shell bottoms. Wherever the black-ribbed mussels can get a foothold they, too, hang on as for dear life by skeins of thread called *byssus*.

Above them, and also growing on both mussels and oyster shells, are hosts of white-shelled barnacles. The upper flanks of such rocks will undoubtedly be covered with mats of *Fucus* or rockweed, one of the brown seaweeds. Great streamers of kelp are found along some coasts. Formerly most of the world's supply of iodine came from these plants. Various-hued sea anemones should also be common here below the low water-mark. Leave them undisturbed until each expands its tentacles like an unfolding bud of innumerable stamens. The strong knife will play its part in loosening such specimens as may be desired.

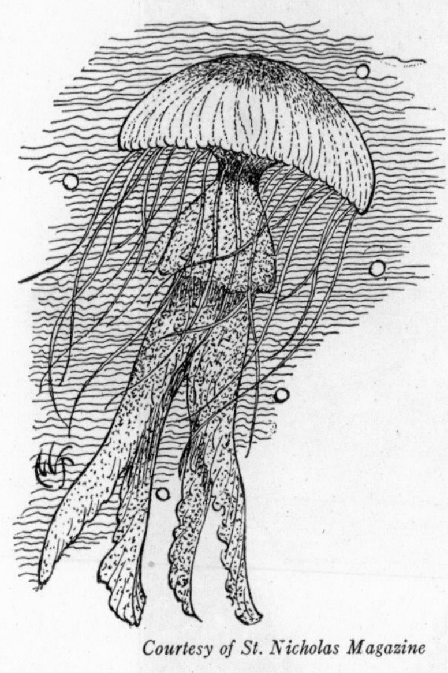

Courtesy of St. Nicholas Magazine

JELLYFISH

The old wharf yonder looks as though it might repay a visit. Some of the boards may be gone from the top, but the piling seems solid enough. What masses of colored creatures cling to its flanks, when we peer through the water surface below the lowest limit of the receding tide! Barnacles with their white cockades, mussels in black and purple profusion, sea squirts or tunicates with two protruding openings, tiny red and yellow sponges, mats and floral designs constructed of living anemones and delicate hydroids, encrust the entire outer surface. And within the old piles, we suspect, are plenty of shipworms, prisoners in their strange tunnels, whose devastating tubes, pushed deeper and deeper though never intersecting, can disintegrate and ruin wood exposed to sea water faster than the millions of bacteria of decay accomplishing the same end. If we watch long enough we may be rewarded by seeing a jellyfish or two, idling slowly through the water with frequent pulses of its tenuous cup of jelly. If it has long tentacles do not touch them, for those streaming filaments are armed with hundreds of sting cells.

The bird life of the seashore is characteristic. The sandpipers are probably as sociable as any of these birds, and they are most interesting as they feed, incessantly agitated, taking to wing on alarm in a group that banks and turns as one bird. Herring gulls, the most abundant of the larger gulls, are conspicuous in the winter everywhere along the Atlantic coast, straggling south during the summer and autumn. In the spring they go north to their nesting grounds. Their continuous cackling squawks, especially over food exposed on flats by the low tide, is a characteristic sound of many seashores. The black-headed laughing gull is much more common during the summer. There are other gulls and there are terns, frequently mistaken for gulls, but distinguished from them by a more slender body, a downward-pointing bill, and a definitely forked tail. Skimmers, shearwaters, plovers, and curlews

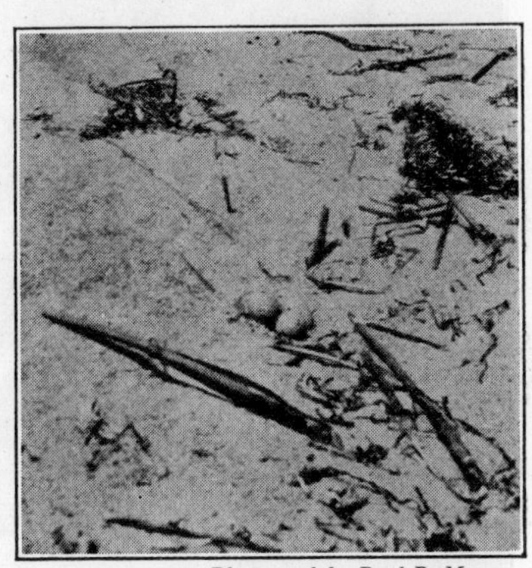

Photograph by Paul B. Mann

EGGS OF A PIPING PLOVER

The piping plover frequently lays its eggs in a hollow of a sandy beach.

sooner or later will be observed, though probably not all on the same day. In many regions, herons — especially the little night heron — and crows make regular trips to the shore for food. Blackbirds and certain sparrows sometimes visit the shore for the same reason. Birds of inland, fresh-water localities, such as the loon and various ducks and geese, may be seen frequently during their migrations in spring and fall.

American Museum of Natural History

THE LARGEST OF OUR CRUSTACEANS

The lobster digs with its claws holes into which it backs.

On some of your wanderings along the shore you may have the good fortune to discover the nesting place of one of the shore birds like the piping plover. The bird utilizes a slight depression in the sand and there the spotted eggs are laid without any attempt at concealment more than their excellent protective resemblance to the surroundings.

Sometimes sand bars are exposed offshore at low tide,

and are worth investigating, especially if one has to wade out to reach them. Don a bathing suit and put sneakers on your feet to avoid possible cuts from shells. How strange and how difficult it is to walk through water! Wherever you traverse deeper pools, frightened killifish, the minnows of the sea, dart for the protection of the surrounding eel grass. With good luck you may surprise a flounder and capture it, too, if you are alert with your net. Here on the sea bottom may be picked up some of the frail sand collars or Tom Cod houses, the strange egg-cases of the *Lunatia* (*Polynices*) snails, resembling lamp shades. They are somewhat tenacious while wet, but after they have dried in the sun and air they crumble at a touch. Crawling everywhere, and fighting continuously with one another, are hermit crabs of varied sizes. A purple lady crab or a green crab edges away. In some pools timid squids may be seen, suffused with changing colors. Catch one in the net and holding it by the body now out of the water and now in, get it to shoot out ink forward through its siphon. Under good conditions, a squid may be induced to throw a stream of inky water ten or fifteen feet. Normally the squid relies on the reaction from such expulsions of water to dart backward. The ink is added when it wants to produce a concealing cloud in the water. Avoid a bite from the parrot-like, horny jaws. The female squid hangs her eggs from eel grass or other seaweed in long fingers of jelly from which the little embryos escape after hatching.

Courtesy of St. Nicholas Magazine

GREEN CRAB

The omnipresent eel grass is one of the few flowering plants growing in salt water, and its long, floating leaves afford a relatively safe home to myriads of creatures. Tiny shrimps and prawns cling to the swaying leaves, and scallops make their brief spurts as we approach. A bubbling hole may betray a soft-shelled crab, a quahog, or a razor-shell clam. Possibly you can get the razor-shell to show how he goes underground, pushing his muscular foot down below, then anchoring it by swelling it full of blood, and suddenly yanking the rest of the body down an inch or two.

American Museum of Natural History

KILLIFISH IN EEL GRASS

A scallop may be seen at the left above the middle of the picture.

With a series of such jerks he rapidly disappears. Gently pick up one of the larger sea snails abundant everywhere, and tap its broad foot. You will be amazed at the sudden reaction. Quantities of water will be shot out, and an extraordinary amount of living tissue pulled quickly within the shell, and the opening sealed with the horny operculum.

You continue to wonder how such a large animal could completely withdraw into such a small shell.

Pick up any old stick that has lain in the water a long time, and you may find it harboring forms like planarian worms, ascidians (seasquirts), delicate plant-like hydroids, polyzoa, sponges, and possibly sea urchins, besides showing evidence of the internal borings of the shipworm.

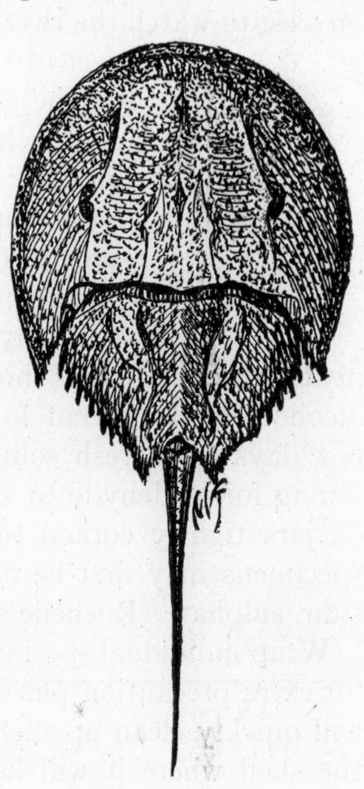

Courtesy of St. Nicholas Magazine

HORSESHOE CRAB

Perhaps you may find a horseshoe crab moving slowly away from the zone of danger, or burying itself in the oozing sand. He is a venerable descendant of ancient types, a kinship obvious when the related fossils are seen. Before you let him go, loosen with the knife one of the flat shells with which he is fairly covered. You have in your hand a decker or shelf-shell (*Crepidula*) and its living inhabitant. Find the "shelf" at one end.

Such specimens as you want to exhibit alive may be temporarily kept in your pail. A marine aquarium is rather difficult to maintain unless you have running sea water, or an aquarium directly connected with the sea, or plenty of oxygen-producing plants like sea lettuce. Otherwise, small animals are likely to die, and the water then becomes quickly polluted, especially in hot summer weather. By frequent observation and prompt removal of any dead animals, and by changing the water twice a day, a temporary salt-water aquarium without any oxygen-producing plants can be conducted long enough to display many of the living marine forms described in this chapter. It would be a sad mistake however to attempt to crowd many animals at one time into such an exhibit. After it is set up and the water has cleared, it will be of particular interest to watch the rhythmic, muscular movements of the feet of the snail as it crawls up the inside of the glass; to note how the starfish or sea urchins use their tubular feet in locomotion; to see the row of steel-cut, beaded eyes just inside the mantle of the scallop, and to observe the activities of shrimps, prawns, and other marine forms.

Courtesy of St. Nicholas Magazine

SCALLOP SHELL

If any specimens are desired for permanent collections they should be immersed in a solution of alcohol, or 5 per cent formaldehyde, and changed after a few days to a fresh solution made by adding 5 parts of strong formaldehyde to 100 parts of water. Keep bottles or jars tightly corked to prevent evaporation. Delicate specimens may first be narcotized in a solution of magnesium sulphate (Rochelle salts) and sea water.

Wrap individual specimens in cheesecloth or muslin, and for extra precaution place them in large cloth bags. Ants will quickly clean up shells, though a quicker way is to tie the shell where it will lie in sea water and let the small crustaceans known as amphipods clean it up. This will be accomplished in a few hours. Dry specimens may be wrapped in portions of newspapers. If a collection of shells is being made, a good plan is to number each shell temporarily with a lead pencil and to make notes as to date, locality, and other details. Never write with ink on specimens or on paper to be placed in the preservative liquid. Later the shell may be permanently numbered or labeled with India ink, then brushed over with a layer of shellac.

In certain seashore localities many kinds of true seaweeds

will be found floating in the water. If you want to add them to your collection, gently lift such specimens into a pail or basin of sea water, making sure that no sand adheres. When you reach the workshop, take out each specimen in turn and float it in a smaller dish of water, so that you may trim it as desired. Now pass beneath it a sheet of paper, preferably of the consistency of Bristol board or regular herbarium paper, and lift the specimen from the water, rearranging parts if necessary. Lay the specimens thus mounted on blotting paper or newspaper, cover with a cloth and more blotting paper. If there are many specimens repeat this procedure. Finally place the layers between flat boards with moderate weights. One authority suggests changing blotters and cloth frequently for the first few days, then discarding the cloth entirely. The important thing is to get the specimens dried as quickly as possible, and blotters should be changed often enough to accomplish this result. A little glue may be advisable to secure parts of specimens that have not adhered of themselves. Finally, label each specimen as you would in making an herbarium.

Whatever marine lore we have gained from sojourning at the sea, whatever fascination we have felt for wisps of living colors and for twisted shells, whatever respect has been engendered by stinging filaments and piercing spines, we can hardly leave such a marine laboratory without a special appreciation of the amazing variety of adaptations peculiar to sea life. We should realize that most marine animals have gills which are thin structures kept moist by the water and provided with blood by means of which breathing (the exchange of carbon dioxide and oxygen) can take place. They swim either with fins or tails or other flattened parts, with collapsible umbrella-like structures, or with cilia or flagella. Sometimes they spurt through the water by rapidly opening and closing their shells. They may walk or crawl with a muscular foot, or with hundreds of tube feet, or with slender jointed legs. They procure their food by creating currents which suck it in, or by using stinging cells, or suckers on long arms, or by swimming and seizing their prey. Since their eyes — if they possess any — are continually moistened by the sea water, they are lidless, and since ears would be an incumbrance, they have none, but are sensitive to vibrations through specialized areas. Furthermore, the creatures not protected by sting or claw or shearing teeth, or by impervious shells into which soft tissues can be withdrawn, have special structures for digging their way into sand or boring into wood.

BIBLIOGRAPHY

ARNOLD, A. F., *Sea Beach at Ebb Tide.* The Century Company, 1901.

A finely illustrated book on the animal and plant life of the shore and the water along the shore.

BURGESS, THORNTON, *Seashore Book for Children.* Little, Brown and Company, 1929.

A well-illustrated book with accurate descriptions suited to young readers.

BUTLER, MRS. EVA L., *Along the Shore.* John Day Company, Inc., 1930.

A book for children describing the creatures to be found along the seashore. Drawings by the author.

CROWDER, WILLIAM, *A Naturalist at the Seashore.* The Century Company, 1928.

Fascinating accounts of explorations along familiar shores and of experiments conducted with sea animals.

—— *Between the Tides.* Dodd, Mead and Company, 1931.

A large and well-illustrated book describing the life to be found at the seashore.

—— *Dwellers of the Sea and Shore.* The Macmillan Company, 1923.

A popular account of the forms of life along the shore with one chapter on the life of the open sea.

GUBERLET, MURIEL L., *Animals of the Seashore.* Metropolitan Press, 1936.

HENDERSON, D. M., *Children of the Tide.* D. Appleton and Co., 1926.

Short stories about seals, fish, and lower marine animals.

KEEP, JOSIAH, *West Coast Shells.* Revised by Joshua L. Bailey. Stanford University Press, 1935.

Excellent descriptions of the marine and fresh-water shells of the Pacific Coast. The illustrations largely make up for the lack of keys.

MAYER, A. G., *Seashore Life.* New York Zoölogical Society, 1911.

An excellent book, well illustrated, giving brief descriptions of typical forms.

REED, WILLIAM MAXWELL, and BRONSON, WILFRED SWANCOURT, *The Sea for Sam.* Harcourt, Brace and Company, 1935.

Fascinating chapters on all sorts of things found in the sea. Graphic illustrations.

ROGERS, JULIA E., *The Shell Book.* Doubleday, Doran and Company, Inc., 1914.

Covers all the shells of the world. Has fine colored plates. So many shells are described that the book is difficult to use in determining species.

RUSSELL, F. S., and YOUNG, C. M., *The Seas.* Frederick Warne and Company, Inc., 1928.

An attractive book describing some of the animal life from the shore to the deep sea. Many illustrations; about half in color.

SHANNON, HOWARD JOHNSON, *Book of the Seashore.* Doubleday, Doran and Company, 1935.

An excellently written book narrating the observations of the author covering plant and animal life of the shores of the Atlantic Ocean.

WELLS, HARRINGTON, *Seashore Life.* Harr Wagner Publishing Company, 1936.

CHAPTER IX

SIX-LEGGED ANIMALS

THE TAX GATHERER

"And pray, who are you?"
Said the violet blue
To the Bee in surprise
At his wonderful size,
In her eyeglass of dew.

"I, madam," quoth he,
"Am the publican Bee,
Collecting the tax
Of honey and wax.
Have you nothing for me?" [1]

— JOHN B. TABB

Of all creatures in the world insects are not only the most numerous — comprising perhaps four-fifths of all animal species — but they are the most successful and therefore the most dominant. Merely to exist, man must wage a constant and increasingly costly warfare with his tiny competitors when they are his enemies. With little or no natural immunity from their attacks, all organisms of the earth, plant and animal, pay direct or indirect toll to insects.

Many insects play a deadly rôle in the carrying of disease germs. Fleas may carry bubonic plague germs; flies, the germs of tuberculosis and typhoid; mosquitoes, the organisms that cause malaria and yellow fever; lice are associated with typhus and trench fever, and tsetse flies with African sleeping sickness.

[1] From "The Tax Gatherer" by John B. Tabb. Published by Dodd, Mead and Company.

Probably the greatest nuisances in the world are certain less deadly insects — mosquitoes, black flies, "punkies," and others which are the bane of campers and hikers, while wasps and yellow jackets resent a too intimate acquaintance in a way that will leave unpleasant memories for years.

HARMFUL INSECTS. Insects unfriendly to man increase the cost of living. To the farmer "bugs" mean an army of would-be destroyers of his crops. Even with all the aid of science in controlling them, it is estimated that insects continue to eat up annually about one-tenth of all the produce of the United States, of a total value of over one thousand million dollars each year! We all help to pay the cost in increased prices for grains, fruits, vegetables, and fibers.

Courtesy of Oliver P. Medsger

SPHINX MOTH CATERPILLAR

The back is covered with the cocoons of a small ichneumon fly.

Many of the obnoxious forms of insect life have been imported from foreign lands; in fact, over 70 species of undesirables reached our shores in grains, fruits, lumber, exotic plants, and even in fabrics before our present strict quarantine. Such insects usually arrive unattended by their natural parasites and enemies and in their new freedom are likely to flourish like the proverbial green bay tree. One of the first steps, therefore, in the control of such insect pests is to introduce their parasites from their original homeland. The bronze-green Calosoma beetle, now common in the northeastern part of the United States, was originally introduced into New England to fight the gypsy moth. Several kinds of small insects have been introduced to fight the Japanese beetle. Ladybird beetles were brought from Australia to save the orange trees of California from the San José scale insects, which threatened the total loss of the crop and trees.

Among native insects the ichneumon flies parasitize the caterpillars of many harmful forms; ground beetles capture and eat other insects; dragon flies feed on mosquitoes and flies; the praying mantis is always on the watch for insects which it may devour; the aphis lion helps suck the body juices from plant lice; and many others help in keeping the hordes of harmful forms in check. Our insectivorous birds are invaluable allies of predacious insects in controlling obnoxious forms. The statement has been made that if all the birds were exterminated, harmful insects would develop so fast that in five years' time there would not be a green leaf!

Courtesy of Oliver P. Medsger

CLAY JUGS OF THE POTTER WASP

The jugs are stored with small caterpillars or grubs, with the one egg of the wasp in each.

BENEFICIAL INSECTS. Of the 400,000 species of insects that have been named, only a few hundred are in the "rogues' gallery" while many kinds are of direct value to man. Aside from the silk of the silkworm, the honey and wax from the bee, and the shellac from the lac insect, we should pay homage to the bees, butterflies, flies, and others which cross-pollinate our flowers. Many crops would not mature without their aid and, with no seed produced, the plants themselves would disappear from the earth.

Courtesy of Oliver P. Medsger

YELLOW-NECKED APPLE WORM

When disturbed the worms assume a threatening attitude with head and "tail" raised.

STRUCTURE OF INSECTS. Typical adult insects have the body divided into three regions, head, thorax, and abdomen, with three pairs of legs and often two pairs of wings attached to the thorax. Structural exceptions occur in certain degenerate forms such as scale insects. All insects breathe by means of openings on the sides of the body, the *spiracles*, which lead into tubes called *trachae*. The mouth parts of insects vary in character, but four types may be recognized: biting, by means of mandibles and maxillae, as in beetles and grasshoppers; piercing and sucking by means of lancing and sucking tubes, as in the stable fly and mosquito; lapping by means of a proboscis, as in the house fly; and sucking and biting, as in the case of the bee.

Most insects have a complex life history, or complete metamorphosis (indirect development), being hatched from eggs in the form of a larva variously called caterpillar, maggot, or grub — always very unlike the mature insect — and resting for some time in the form of a pupa or chrysalis before changing into the adult. Often the larva lives under

Courtesy of Oliver P. Medsger

GREAT-SPANGLED FRITILLARY ON FLOWERS OF DITTANY

Visiting flowers for nectar, the butterfly unwittingly helps in pollination.

entirely different conditions and usually on different foods from those of the adult. Sometimes the larva lives under water, as in the case of the mosquito, May fly, caddice fly, and others; under the bark or inside of tree trunks, like boring beetles; in buds, like the cotton bollworm; in pods, like the pea weevil; or under the ground, like the cicada and the May beetle. Other insects, like the grasshopper and cricket, hatch from the egg into forms not essentially different from the adult. Such insects are said to have incomplete metamorphosis (direct development).

Observing Insects. In observing insects the most important thing to learn is something of their habits and life histories. Watch a bee or butterfly to see how many flowers and what kinds it visits in succession. Find what kinds of plants are eaten by caterpillars and how they eat. Or spend an hour by some blossoming plant, such as a lilac, sumach, thistle, or privet, and see how many kinds of insects visit it. Observations may be continued indoors if living insects are kept. The small glass boxes described in Chapter XXII, or fruit jars covered with mosquito netting, do well for insects. Feed them with the leaves on which they were found, or which you wish to test as food. A small potted plant may have a lantern globe set over it, the top covered with netting, and caterpillars kept till the cocoons or chrysalids are formed. A jar of pond water with mosquito larvae is of great interest and the development from wriggler (larvae) to adult can easily be watched. In this case a piece of netting should be placed over the jar, for mosquitoes are by no means domesticated simply because they were hatched in a schoolroom or camp museum. Various water insects, dragon-fly nymphs with curious lower lips that mask their faces till some other insect or small fish comes within reach, water beetles, the back swimmers, and others will live well in an aquarium which may be no more than a quart jar.

The small aquaria described by Dr. Frank E. Lutz, of the American Museum of Natural History in New York City, are excellent for water insects. To make one of these, get two pieces of glass of selected size. Cut a block from a smooth two-inch plank so that it is one inch shorter than the glass and one and a half inches narrower. If the glass is five by seven inches the block should be three and one half by six inches. Coat the block (A) with vaseline. Stand it on end and put the pieces of glass (B, C) one on each side; put narrow strips of glass (D, E) at the ends and tie together with cord. Wedges of wood between the cord and the glass sides will hold them firmly against the block. Place the

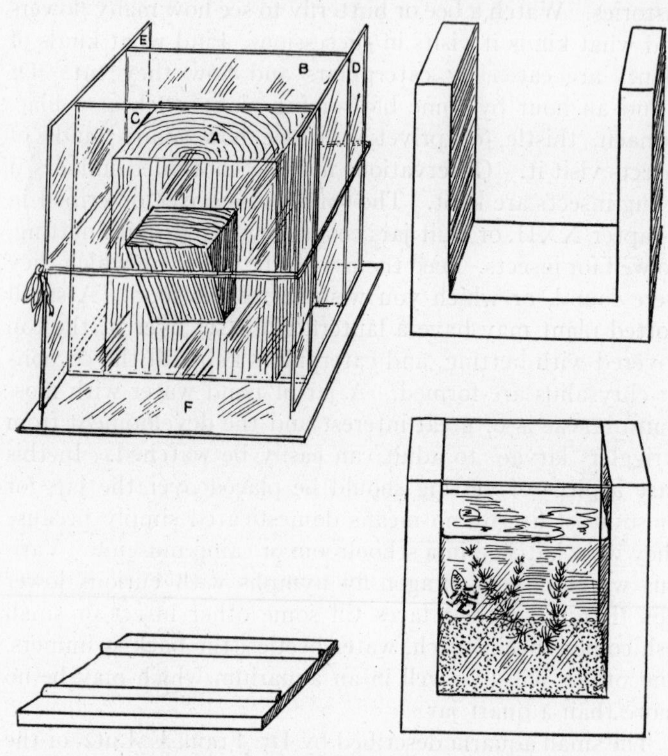

MAKING AN AQUARIUM FOR INSECTS

Above at the left the wooden block has the glass fastened around it, ready to pour the plaster. At the right, the plaster form has been removed from the mold. Below is the finished aquarium, and a base to hold it.

structure on a piece of glass (F) and put plasteline about the base on the outside along the lines where the side glasses join the ends. Now prepare sufficient plaster of Paris mixture [1] to fill the space around the block and pour it in, covering the block to the top of the glass. When the plaster is thoroughly hardened, dismantle the glasses and remove the block. (If the long edges are beveled slightly it will come out more easily.) After drying for a day, place this U-shaped piece of plaster in melted beeswax and

Courtesy of George Rex Green

COLLECTING AND STUDYING INSECTS AT PENNSYLVANIA STATE COLLEGE NATURE CAMP

let it stand about fifteen minutes. Then take it out and when the wax has hardened, brush more wax on what is to be the front and back sides of the aquarium. Now, after heating the side glasses in an oven till they are hot enough to be uncomfortable to handle, place one glass on a board that has a few nails driven in so as to hold it in place. Put the plaster form on this glass and the other glass on top. The hot glasses will melt the wax which, when it hardens, will hold the glasses firmly. To finish the aquarium, adhesive plaster one and one-half inches wide may be placed over the sides and bottom of the aquarium and

[1] See Chapter II for details of preparing and using plaster of Paris mixture.

painted if desired. A stand like that illustrated may be used to keep it from tipping over. Place a little sand or a few pebbles in the bottom with a small water plant, fill the aquarium with pond water and it is ready for the insects.

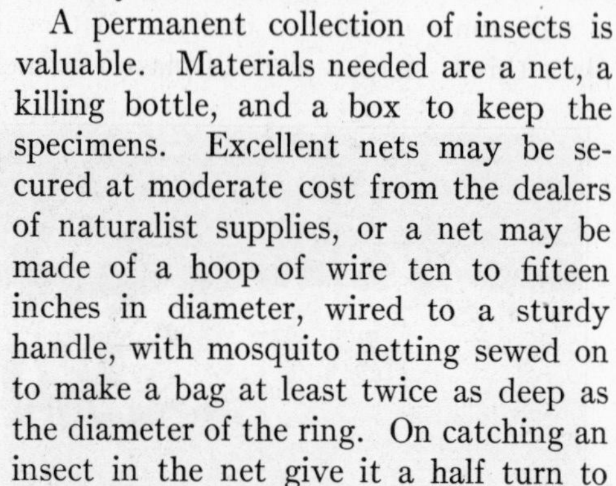

A Home-made Insect Net

A permanent collection of insects is valuable. Materials needed are a net, a killing bottle, and a box to keep the specimens. Excellent nets may be secured at moderate cost from the dealers of naturalist supplies, or a net may be made of a hoop of wire ten to fifteen inches in diameter, wired to a sturdy handle, with mosquito netting sewed on to make a bag at least twice as deep as the diameter of the ring. On catching an insect in the net give it a half turn to fold the lower part over the ring and prevent the escape of the insect. If bees and wasps are caught, the part of the net they are in can be put in a killing bottle for a minute till the insect is safe to handle. Butterflies should be allowed to stand on the side of the net as it hangs over the ring, then caught by the thorax and pinched firmly between the thumb and forefinger to paralyze them and prevent beating and breaking of their wings when put into a killing bottle. Cyanide of potassium makes an effective killing bottle, but it is a deadly poison. A safer killing bottle is made in the following way. Take a large-mouthed bottle and place a little cotton on the bottom. A small amount of carbon tetrachloride or Carbona is then poured into the bottle and more added every few days as it evaporates.

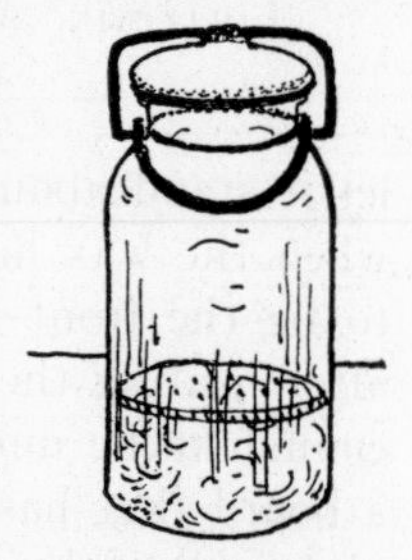

Killing Bottle with Carbona on Cotton

A piece of paper over the cotton will keep insects from becoming entangled in it. Insects should be left in the bottle for some time after they are apparently dead as they will revive if taken out too soon.

Dragon flies, butterflies, and moths should have the wings spread before mounting. A mounting board can be made of two strips of soft wood fastened side by side on a board and separated by a space wide enough to allow the body of the insect to lie between. The wings are spread by placing a pin point back of one of the large veins and gently moving the wings to the desired position where they are held by a piece of glass laid on top or by strips of paper pinned across them. A day or two on the mounting board is usually enough to harden the wings in position. Insects when ready to be mounted may be fastened on pins in boxes, or put on cotton in glass-covered boxes. For the former, if regular insect cases are not available, cigar boxes do very well. Corrugated paper in the bottom of the box does nearly as well as the sheets of cork or balsa wood sold to line the bottoms of insect boxes. Regular insect pins are an inch and a half long and should be put through the insect so that one quarter of the pin stands above the back. A small gauge of wood or cardboard will make it easier to secure uniformity of height and make the collections much more attractive. Beetles should be pinned through the right wing cover; other insects through the middle of the thorax. The use of Riker mounts is more attractive and easier, but more expensive. They may be purchased in various sizes.

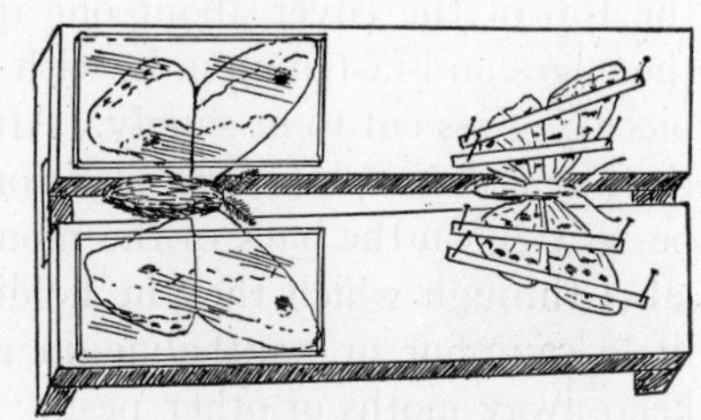

SPREADING BOARD

Butterflies may be held in position in either of these two ways.

In using the Riker mount the insect is placed in position on the cotton, then the cover is put on and fastened with pins. If the box is large enough several insects can be put in one box. The scientific value of such work could be enhanced by preparing complete life histories showing each stage of development, food plant or prey, nest, or any other pertinent items. Boxes similar to the Riker mounts can be made by taking a shallow pasteboard box, cutting out the top of the cover about one quarter of an inch inside the edges and fastening in it, with passe partout binding, a piece of glass cut to fit snugly. After the insect is mounted, the name, date, place, and plant on which it was found can be written on the back of the mount or written on a small label through which the pin holding the insect is run. A little camphor or napthaline in a corner of the box will keep away moths or other pests.

Galls. Everyone is familiar with the round ball with the spongy interior found on oak leaves, the oak apple or oak gall. There are hundreds of other kinds of galls. Almost every plant has one or more special types. The hard ones on the stems of golden-rod, or the round bunches of small leaves on the tops of the plants, are very common. Many witch-hazel leaves bear little conical galls and on the ends of branches of willows may often be found the inch-long "Pine cone" galls. Most galls are made by insects — flies, aphids, or wasp-like gall flies. Each kind of gall-making insect seems attracted to certain kinds of plants. There the female lays her egg in leaf or stem and the plant makes the characteristic growth around it.

Just what causes the variations in growth is not known. Possibly the insect injects some peculiar poison when the egg is laid, or perhaps it is a mechanical stimulation from the egg or the developing larva. Each kind of insect causes its own particular kind of gall. A species of aphid causes the strange coxcomb gall on the elm; another causes the spiny balls on the witch-hazel twigs. In every case the gall provides a home and food supply for a young insect. Within the gall the fly or wasp passes through its larval and pupal stages, to emerge when developed. Sometimes the aphids may develop a whole colony inside the gall, the young of which come from unfertilized eggs. If when gathered galls are put in jars the tops of which are then covered with netting or cheese cloth, the adults may be caught as they emerge. If no insects appear, it may be because the insects are not far enough developed, but it may also be due to the fact that the gall was caused by a certain fungus growing inside the plant, not by an insect at all. Generally fungus galls are irregular in shape and have no cavity within.

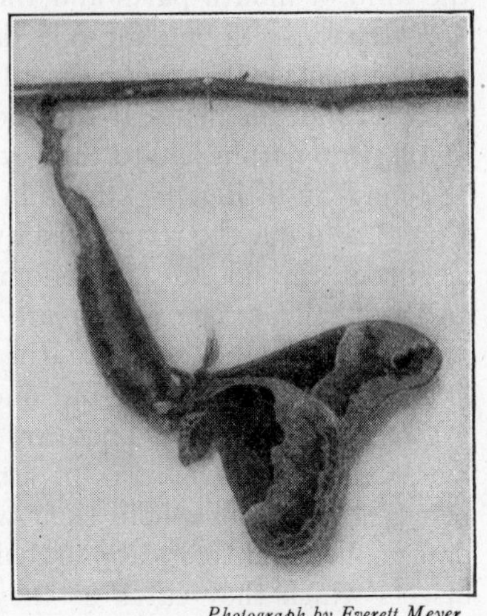

Photograph by Everett Meyer

PROMETHEA MOTH

If cocoons are brought indoors the moths may be seen in the process of emerging.

SOME COMMON ORDERS OF INSECTS. According to structure, insects are classified in orders, from a dozen to forty; the number depending partly on the judgment of the entomologist who classifies them. Of these about a dozen orders include most of the insects commonly seen. It is comparatively easy to learn the characteristics of these orders and begin to classify the insects seen. Wing structure is one of the features considered in determining orders; the names of the orders ending in most cases with the suffix –*ptera* from the Greek *pteron* meaning "wing," while the prefix suggests the principal characteristic of the wings. Two other characteristics used in distinguishing orders are the kind of mouth parts and the kind of development.

Ephemerida (living for one day only). May flies are small insects with two pairs of filmy wings and two or three slender filaments at the end of the body. The larvae live in water from one to three years. They are usually to be found by lifting the stones in a brook or at the edge of a pond, and may be recognized by the tufts of fine filaments or gills on the sides of the abdomen and the three filaments at the "tail." The adults are sometimes found in vast numbers near the water in the evening. Some of them live in the adult form for but one night.

Odonata (toothed). These are the dragon flies and damsel flies. All have two pairs of straight, slender wings. At rest the dragon flies hold their wings out horizontally, the damsel flies fold theirs above their backs. All live on other insects which they catch as they fly; none, however, can harm human beings, though superstitious people think they can sew up lips or ears. The eggs are laid in water and the young (called nymphs) feed on insect larvae, small fish, and other water life.

Plecoptera (pleated wings). The stone flies have two tail filaments and two pairs of gray or greenish wings. When at rest, the hind ones are folded lengthwise and covered by the narrow front wings. The larvae may be found under stones in streams or ponds. Their flattish bodies, the two tail filaments, and the gills at the base of the legs, never on the abdomen, distinguish them from other aquatic insects.

Megaloptera (great wings). The fish flies and dobson flies, while not numerous, are so peculiar as to be often noticed. They are large insects with rather soft wings, the hind ones folded fanwise. The fish flies are from one to two inches long, gray or brown with white spots on the wings, and with feathery antennae. The dobson flies or hellgrammites are about three inches long with slender antennae. The

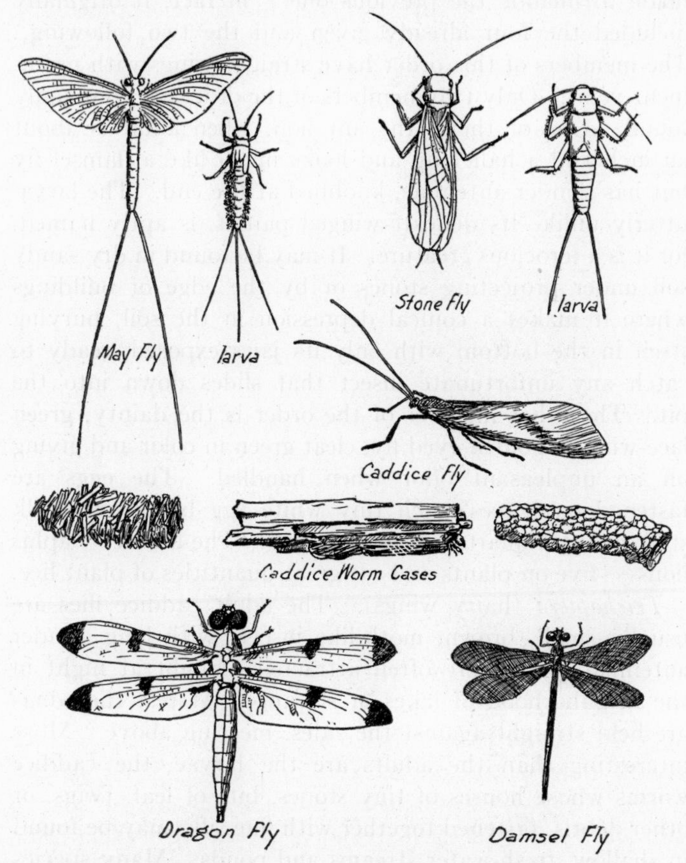

REPRESENTATIVE INSECTS OF THE ORDERS EPHEMERIDA, PLECOPTERA, TRICHOPTERA, AND ODONATA

male has very large curving jaws which appear to be formidable but which cannot be used in biting. The larvae live in streams or ponds, and are frequently used as bait by fishermen.

Neuroptera (netted wings). (This order is sometimes made to include the previous one — in fact, it originally included the four already given and the two following.) The members of this order have straight wings with prominent veins. Only two members of the order are commonly found. One of them, the ant lion, when adult is about an inch and a half long and looks much like a damsel fly but has slender antennae, knobbed at the end. The larva, utterly unlike its delicate-winged parent, is aptly named, for it is a ferocious creature. It may be found in dry sandy soil under projecting stones or by the edge of buildings where it makes a conical depression in the soil, burying itself in the bottom with only its jaws exposed, ready to catch any unfortunate insect that slides down into the pit. The other member of the order is the dainty, green lace-wing or golden-eyed fly, clear green in color and giving off an unpleasant odor when handled. The eggs are fastened on leaves, each tiny white egg being on a silk stalk about a quarter of an inch long. The larvae — aphis lions — live on plants and eat great quantities of plant lice.

Trichoptera (hairy wings). The adult caddice flies are usually small, brown, moth-like insects with long slender antennae. They are often attracted to light at night in the neighborhood of lakes or streams. At rest the wings are held straight against the sides, meeting above. More interesting than the adults are the larvae, the caddice worms whose houses of tiny stones, bits of leaf, twigs, or other débris, fastened together with fine silk, may be found in shallow, fresh-water streams and ponds. Many species build houses that can be dragged around as the owner puts its head and feet out the front door, but others fasten their houses firmly and crawl out to get their food from small nets they spread between stones in the streams.

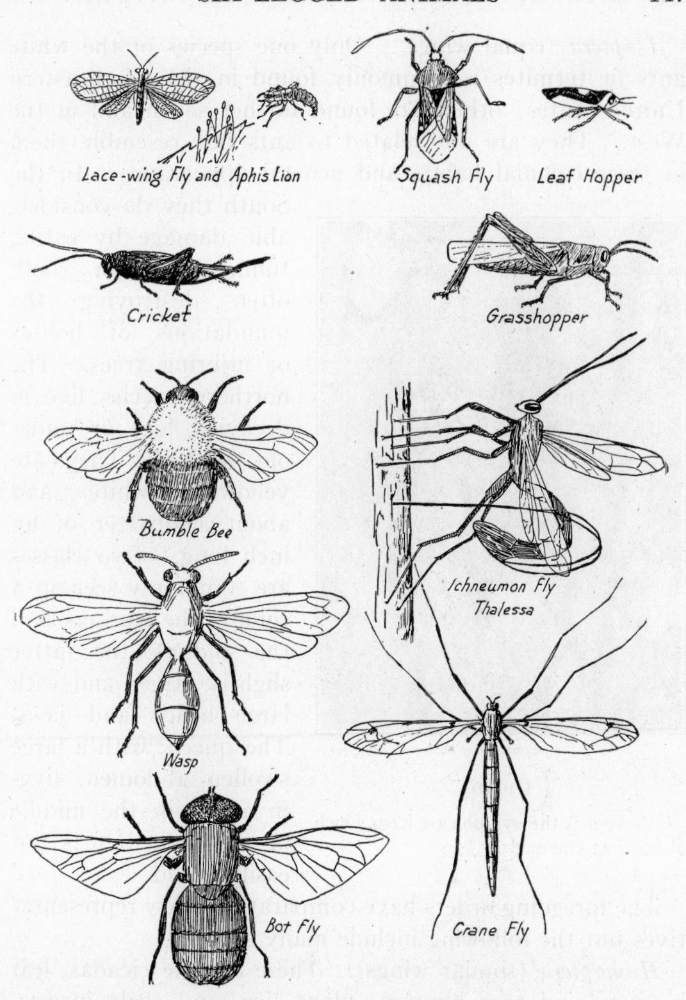

REPRESENTATIVE INSECTS OF THE ORDERS NEUROPTERA, HOMOPTERA, HETEROPTERA, HYMENOPTERA, AND DIPTERA

Isoptera (equal wings). Only one species of the white ants or termites is commonly found in the northeastern United States; others are found farther south and in the West. They are not related to ants but resemble them in their colonial habits and general appearance. In the South they do considerable damage by eating tunnels through wood, often destroying the foundations of houses or injuring trees. The northern species live in decaying logs or under old boards. They are yellowish white and about a quarter of an inch long. Two classes are commonly seen in a colony, the workers and the soldiers, the latter slightly larger and with large heads and jaws. The queen, with a large swollen abdomen, lives in a cell in the middle of the nest but is not easily found.

Courtesy of Oliver P. Medsger

CICADA

Above it is the nymph case from which it has just emerged.

The foregoing orders have comparatively few representatives but the following include many species.

Homoptera (similar wings). These are the cicadas, leaf hoppers and tree hoppers, plant lice, and scale insects. They are all alike in having sucking mouth parts arising from the under side of the head close to the thorax. They live on juices of plants. Many of them are serious pests on cultivated plants.

Heteroptera (different wings). (This order was formerly included with the *Homoptera* in an order known as the *Hemiptera* or true bugs). Here belong the water striders, squash bugs, stink bugs, and hundreds of others. The front wings are thicker near the body, with a thin membranous part near the tip. The wings lie flat on the back when at rest, with the membranous tips overlapping. The sucking mouth parts arise from the front part of the under side of the head.

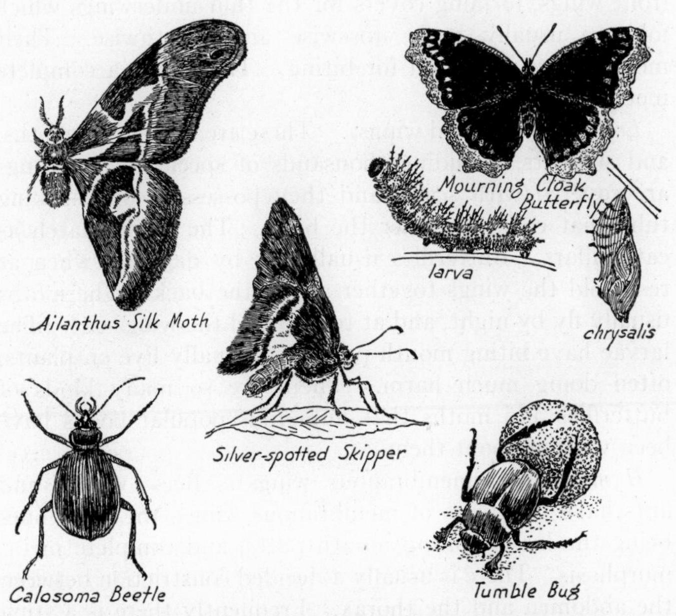

REPRESENTATIVES OF THE THREE GROUPS OF THE ORDER LEPIDOPTERA AND TWO MEMBERS OF THE ORDER COLEOPTERA

Orthoptera (straight wings). These are grasshoppers and locusts, the crickets, katydids, walking sticks, cockroaches, and mantids. If wings are present the front pair are membranous and cover the hind ones, which fold underneath like fans when at rest. They have biting mouth parts. The young when hatched resemble the adult but have no wings. (The walking sticks in the North are wingless in the adult stage.)

Coleoptera (sheath wings). Beetles — of which there are probably more thousands of species than there are in any other order — are represented by May beetles, potato bugs, ladybugs, tiger beetles, and water beetles. All have hard front wings, forming covers for the thin underwings which fold up usually both crosswise and lengthwise. Their mouth parts are fitted for biting. They have a complete metamorphosis.

Lepidoptera (scaled wings). These are butterflies, moths, and skippers, including thousands of species. The wings are covered with scales and they possess a long sucking tube that coils up under the head. The young hatch as caterpillars. Butterflies usually fly by day and when at rest hold the wings together above the back. The moths usually fly by night, and at rest spread the wings out. The larvae have biting mouth parts and usually live on plants, often doing much harm. There are so many kinds of butterflies and moths that numerous popular books have been written about them.

Hymenoptera (membranous wings). Bees, wasps, and ants have two pairs of membranous wings, the front ones being the larger, biting mouth parts, and complete metamorphosis. There is usually a decided constriction between the abdomen and the thorax. Frequently there is a sting at the end of the abdomen of the female. Bees, wasps, and ants are sometimes called social insects, as many of them live in communities with a high degree of division of labor. However, some are solitary.

Diptera (two wings). These are the flies, gnats, and mosquitoes. The members of this large group have but one pair of wings, the hind wings being represented by a tiny pair of knobbed threads. They have complete metamorphosis. To this order belong a large number of pests — the house fly, horse and deer flies, mosquitoes, black flies, punkies, and the Hessian fly which does serious damage to grains. Some are harmless, as the long-legged crane flies, which are sometimes mistaken for gigantic mosquitoes; while a few, such as the robber flies, are distinctly beneficial.

BIBLIOGRAPHY

COMSTOCK, JOHN H. and ANNA B., and HERRICK, GLENN W., *Manual for the Study of Insects*, 21st edition. Comstock Publishing Company, 1936.

One of the most comprehensive American texts on the subject.

COMSTOCK, JOHN H. and ANNA B., *How to Know the Butterflies*. (New edition.) Comstock Publishing Company, 1936.

A popular book, well illustrated, partly in color.

FABRE, J. H. C., *The Mason Bees*. Garden City Publishing Company, Inc., 1925.

Excellent translations of the fascinating insect stories and studies by the great French naturalist. This author has written several other equally interesting books on insects.

FELT, E. P., *Popular Guide to the Study of Insects*. University of the State of New York, Albany, N. Y., 1928.

A small, paper-bound volume, adapted for beginners.

HOLLAND, W. J., *Pocket Butterfly Guide*. Doubleday, Doran and Company, Inc., 1923.

One of the best of the pocket guides, both in the colored plates and in the descriptions.

—— *The Butterfly Book*. Doubleday, Doran and Company, Inc., 1914.

A valuable aid to a knowledge of butterflies.

HOWARD, L. O., *Insect Book*. Doubleday, Doran and Company, Inc., 1923.

A large and valuable book by the "dean" of American entomologists.

—— *The Insect Menace*. The Century Company, 1931.

A thoroughly readable and graphic portrayal of past, present, and probable future relationships between insects and man.

KELLOGG, V. L., *American Insects.* Henry Holt and Company, Inc., 1908.

Another large volume, describing all the orders of insects and the commoner species in each.

—— *Insect Stories.* D. Appleton and Company, 1923.

A series of stories on insect behavior.

LUTZ, FRANK E., *Field Book of Insects* (3rd edition). G. P. Putnam's Sons, 1935.

A most convenient book for learning what insect one has found. With interesting descriptions and characteristic comments by the author.

MORGAN, ANN, *Key to Aquatic Insects.* Slingerland-Comstock Company, 1929.

At least the orders, and in many cases the genera, of water insects can be determined with the aid of this little leaflet.

WEED, C. M., *Butterflies.* Doubleday, Doran and Company, Inc., 1926.

A valuable book for determining specimens of the ever-popular butterflies.

Key to Galls, Slingerland-Comstock Company, 1927.

A convenient leaflet describing common galls, arranged according to the plants on which they are found.

Our Insect Friends and Foes and Spiders. National Geographic Society, 1935.

Fascinating accounts of typical insects and spiders. Lavishly illustrated in natural colors.

CHAPTER X

THE SPINNERS

In wheel and fan along a wall embossed,
The spider's handiwork shows fine
With jewels girdling every airy line;
Though the small mason in the cold be lost.[1]

— LOUISE IMOGEN GUINEY

Probably none of the common invertebrates of the field furnish more unusual facts than the spiders. Although they are often called insects, the briefest inspection will reveal eight legs instead of the six of true insects.

Most people, old and young, shun spiders, having an almost superstitious belief that they have a poisonous bite. While a spider may bite, the effect at most is hardly worse than a mosquito bite. The venom which a spider injects may be sufficient to kill an insect, but people living in regions outside the tropics need not be afraid of spiders, except possibly the tarantulas and the Black Widow. The latter is usually considered quite poisonous, especially in the South and West where it is fairly common. The female is about three-quarters of an inch long, and black with a red mark underneath that is shaped like an hourglass. Any of the small spiders in the North, and almost everywhere else in the United States, may be picked up with no risk whatever.

One of the characteristics which differentiate spiders is their silk spinning, so that it is frequently easier to classify the web than it is the spider. Spider silk cannot approach

[1] From "Cobwebs" in *Happy Ending, Collected Lyrics* of Louise Imogen Guiney. Copyright by Houghton Mifflin Company.

the enduring quality of that of the caterpillars of moths, the silk-makers par excellence. Unlike the silken product of the insect larvae, which is spun from the head, spider silk is spun from spinnerets at the tip of the abdomen.

Photograph by Paul B. Mann

WEBS ON A MISTY MORNING

It is easier to distinguish webs than their makers, who are frequently concealed. In the foreground are the flat webs of *Agelena naevia* (grass spider) with a few domed webs of *Linyphia*.

STRUCTURE. The adaptations of spiders to their interesting activities and habits is a fascinating study. The body of a spider is divided into two parts. Unlike the insect, but like its relatives the lobster and the crab, the head and thorax are combined in what is called a *cephalothorax*. The other region of the body is the abdomen.

Crowning the front part of the head segment are the eyes, from two to eight pairs. They are simple, and vary in size and position in the different species. But with all their eyes they can see clearly for only a few inches. Certain spiders living in the dark have pearly-white "nocturnal" eyes.

The cephalothorax bears six pairs of appendages: the first two are used for grasping and crushing insects, the other four are legs functioning in locomotion. The first pair of appendages are the "jaws," properly called *chelicerae* (pincers). Each consists of a large basal segment supporting a terminal, hooked, clawlike segment. Near the tip of this claw is a tiny opening through which the venom passes out of the poison gland. The chelicerae differ considerably among spiders. Some possess files, others have a brush of hairs, or are sawlike on one edge. Certain burrowing spiders have teeth on the chelicerae by which they excavate their holes.

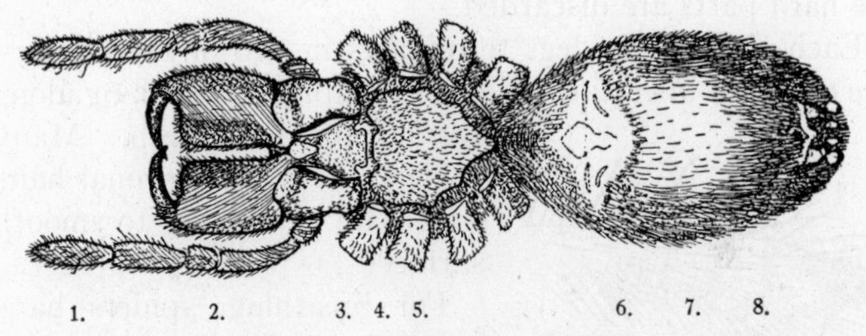

VENTRAL VIEW OF A SPIDER

1. Palpus or pedipalp. 2. Chelicera. 3. Labium. 4. Basal segment of the leg. 5. Cephalothorax. 6. Lung-book. 7. Abdomen. 8. Spinnerets.

Immediately behind the chelicerae is a pair of leg-like appendages called *palpi* or *pedipalps* (foot feelers). These have a huge basal segment used in crushing and squeezing the insect prey. On the inner surface of this segment is a toothed structure which lacerates the body of the insect to release the desired juices. In adult male spiders the terminal part of each palpus becomes greatly modified into a swollen, hollow organ for the transfer of the seminal fluid to the female during mating. Most naturalists make use of the various types of palpi in classifying the species of spiders. These organs are undoubtedly the most complicated structure in the animal. John H. Comstock, in *The Spider Book*, enumerates forty-four separate parts of a single palpus.

Between the palpi is a sort of upper lip called the *rostrum* (beak), the lower part of which contains grooves leading to a central slit. These grooves aid in conveying the juices of the insect victim to the slit where they flow through a tube to the so-called mouth. A *labium*, or lower lip, helps to prevent the loss of the juices. Spiders never eat the insects they capture, but poison them, then hold their bodies tightly till they have sucked them dry, after which the hard parts are discarded.

Each of the eight legs terminates in two or three claws, one of which in certain spiders is adapted for walking along the strands of the web. Many spiders also have terminal hairs which aid in clinging to smooth surfaces.

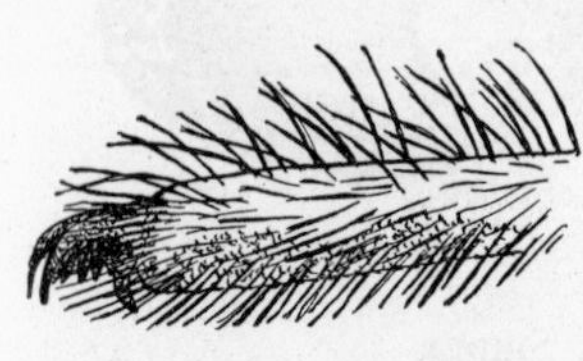

After Comstock

TIP OF LEG

The terminal claws allow the spider to walk over the web without breaking it.

For breathing, spiders have internal air tubes like the insects, the opening to these tracheae being found on the ventral, or lower side of the abdomen. In addition, a spider has what is called a lung-book, a series of gill-like structures within the body, opening by one or two pairs of slits on the ventral side.

EGGS. The female spider lays from five hundred to twenty thousand eggs in a mass inside a silken cocoon. The nursery-web weavers and the wolf spider, as well as some others, carry the egg case with them till the young are hatched. More often the cocoon is attached to the underside of a piece of loose bark or of a stone, concealed among the leaves of weeds or bushes, or otherwise hidden. Usually the mother dies after laying her eggs. The eggs hatch in a few weeks or, if laid in the fall, may remain throughout the winter and hatch in the spring. In either case the little spiders still imprisoned in the egg case turn on each other, the stronger devouring the weaker. Eventually the survivors work their way out of the case and start life for themselves.

Photograph by Lynwood M. Chace. Courtesy of "New York Herald Tribune"

COCOON OF THE GARDEN SPIDER

The female, shown above, constructs her egg case late in the season among bushes or weeds and fastens it securely by cables of silk to withstand winter storms.

The male spider is usually smaller than the female. He has to be very cautious when he comes near his mate for he is likely to be pounced upon and eaten by her.

SILK SPINNING. The spinning apparatus of the spider is on the ventral side of the abdomen at the rear. A magnifying glass will reveal the spinnerets, usually six. Each spinneret has about one hundred spinning tubes through which the silk passes from the body in a viscid fluid which immediately solidifies. It seems incredible that a composite of five hundred or six hundred such strands, joining as they issue, could be so delicate as to be scarcely visible even in a strong light.

The character of spider silk differs greatly according to the species spinning it and the purpose for which it is to be used. It may be dry or viscid, elastic or inelastic, heavy or light. A single, orb-weaving spider may spin five different kinds of silk. It uses both dry and viscid threads in making its symmetrical web, but when it entangles an insect, it spreads the spinnerets apart and throws out a broad band of silk to wrap around the struggling victim. The soft, fluffy mass on the inside of the cocoon which it hangs up in late summer, and the tough outer layer of the cocoon, are quite different from the silk spun for the web or the shroud of its prey.

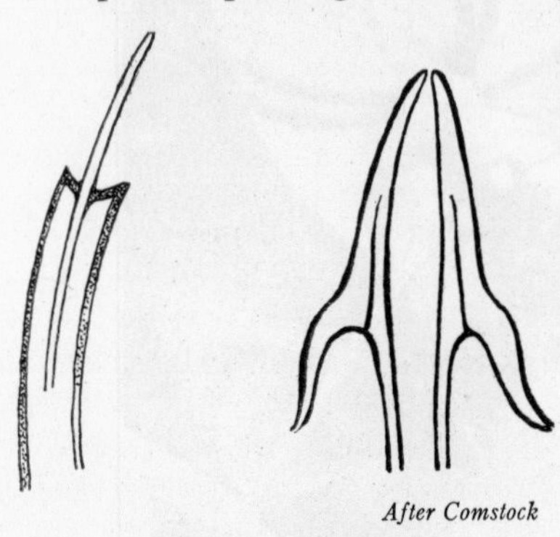

After Comstock

SPINNING TUBES

At the left is a long cylindrical type with a tip; at the right is a spigot.

Most spiders spin out what is known as a *drag line* wherever they go, suspending themselves by it when they drop from a height. It is thought to be spun from two enlarged silk tubules called *spigots*. When moving about on plants and trees the drag line is ordinarily attached at frequent intervals by patches of silk called *attachment disks*. The drag line is a "life line" to a spider. One strange use of this drag line is that shown by the young of various species of spiders, who on warm days fling out into the air a single gossamer strand, spinning it out until the upward-moving breeze catches both it and the spider and whirls them away, like little balloons, to other regions. Irregular webs are largely composed of drag lines, which also make the foundation threads of orb webs. The drag line is dry silk but the orb weavers also spin an elastic and very sticky line called the *viscid thread* for use in trapping insects. This sticky silk is passed out on the surface of a thread more elastic than the usual type and immediately seems to break up into minute droplets.

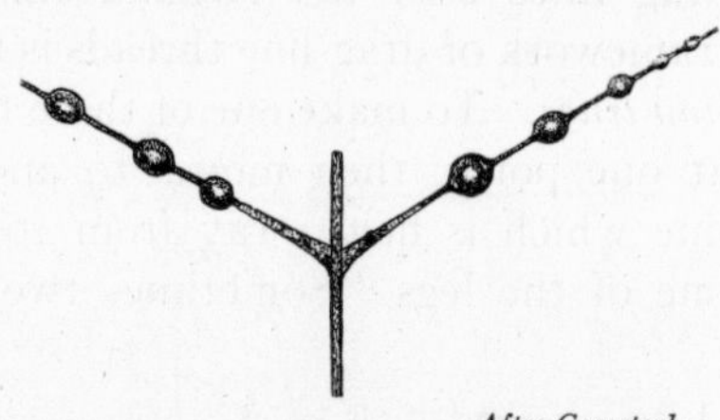

After Comstock

PHOTOMICROGRAPH OF A RADIUS AND TWO VISCID LINES

WEBS. Many types of webs are made to catch insects and to serve as homes for the makers. Some spiders make only a meager nest of their silk. The trapdoor spider, for example, makes a burrow in the ground, lining it with silk and even constructing a hinged lid of silk covered with soil particles. The wolf spider uses silk sparingly to fasten together a small turret of tiny sticks which becomes a little barrier around the top of her tunnel. Orbs, domes, triangles, mazes, sheets, and funnels are all found among the webs of spiders. Since spiders are usually concealed, and since the web itself is difficult to see except in misty or foggy weather, or in the early morning when the dew has strung the slender filaments with sparkling jewels, patience and alertness are essential in acquiring a field knowledge of spiders.

The construction of a spider's web calls for engineering and architectural skill not at all comprehended by most people. It is fascinating to watch the web-building of such a spider as one of the orb weavers. The first strand spun is the *bridge*. This is a delicate thread spun out and blown off by the wind — it takes very little movement of the air to carry such a light thing — until it catches on to some near-by object; then it is pulled tight and fastened. Next the spider strengthens this bridge by depositing several drag lines over it. Around this heavy thread an outer framework of drag-line threads is formed, called the *foundation lines*. To make one of these the spider fastens a thread at one point, then moves to another place, spinning the line which is held away from contact with the bridge by one of the legs. Sometimes two bridges are constructed.

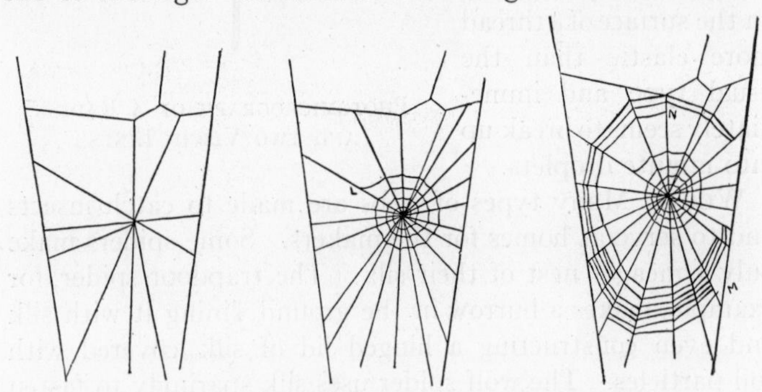

STAGES IN THE CONSTRUCTION OF THE WEB OF AN ORB WEAVER

Left: Foundation lines and first radii. One of the middle lines was the bridge. *Center:* More radii have been spun and the hub has been formed. The temporary spiral guy line has been laid down, starting at the hub and ending at L. *Right:* Viscid spiral threads have been formed in the area M–N.

When enough foundation lines have been constructed the *radii* are made. The spider goes to the point of the bridge where the center of the web is to be, fastens a thread there, and holding the radius clear of other threads walks along the bridge to the desired point on the outer framework. This thread is now pulled tight and fastened to one of the foundation lines. By a similar process all the radii are placed, one by one, the spider returning to the center each time. Sometimes to reach the center the spider walks along a radius thread to which it adds a drag line, thus thickening it.

Courtesy of Oliver P. Medsger

GARDEN SPIDER AND A CAPTURED FRITILLARY BUTTERFLY

The spider is resting over the hub of the web, made stronger by the stabilimentum which extends upward as a zigzag band of silk. Note the radii and spiral lines.

After the radii are completed, the spider makes a mat of more or less closely woven lines at the very center of the web. This mat is the *hub* of the web. The central area of the web is further strengthened by the placing of several spiral turns crossing the radii just beyond the hub. This spiral zone is called by Comstock the *notched area.* The spider then spins a *temporary spiral guy line* from this notched area to the outer foundation lines, crossing the radii at right angles. Now comes the most important part of the web, the *viscid spiral*. Following the spiral guy lines, but starting at the outer margin, the spider spins an elastic and viscid thread, attaching it to each radius as it crosses it. The temporary spiral guy lines are cut away as the spider works inward, laying down the viscid spiral almost to the notched zone. The area between the viscid spiral and the notched zone is called the *free zone*. Frequently an irregular mat or band of silk is placed at or near the center. This is the *stabilimentum* because it strengthens the web.

Photograph by Paul B. Mann

WEB OF LINYPHIA COMMUNIS

The central part of the web resembles a bowl suspended over a horizontal mat, and has caused its maker to be called "the bowl and doily spider."

The spider normally stays at the hub. Certain spiders, however, wait on one side of the web, holding a thread called the *trap line* which connects their retreat with the hub. This line serves to betray to the waiting spider any disturbances in the web.

SOME COMMON TYPES OF WEBS. There are several recognized types of webs with a great number of variations. The grass spider, *Agelena naevia*, spins a flat web, sometimes with a second irregular net above it, among support-

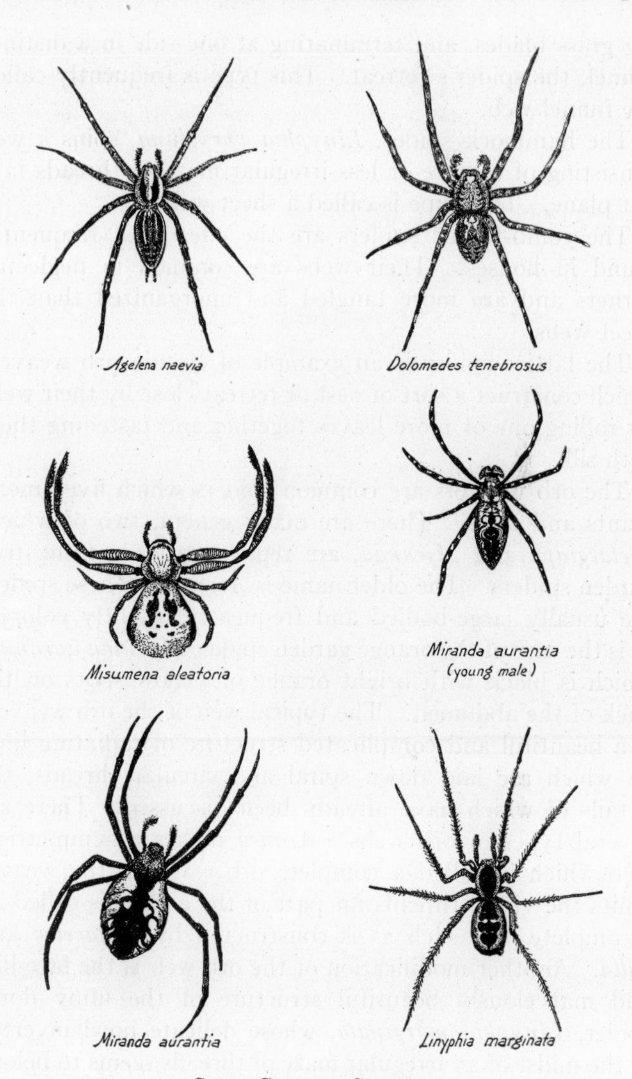

SOME COMMON SPIDERS

ing grass blades, and terminating at one side in a distinct funnel, the spider's retreat. This type is frequently called the funnel web.

The hammock spider, *Linyphia phrygiana*, spins a web consisting of a more or less irregular maze of threads in a flat plane. This type is called a sheet web.

The comb-footed spiders are the ones most frequently found in houses. Their webs are common in neglected corners and are more tangled and unorganized than the sheet webs.

The lattice spider is an example of certain orb weavers which construct a sort of nest or retreat close by their webs by rolling one or more leaves together and fastening them with silk.

The orb weavers are common spiders which live among plants and trees. There are many genera, two of which, *Metargiopa* and *Miranda*, are representatives of the true garden spiders. The older name is *Argiope*. These spiders are usually large-bodied and frequently brightly colored, as is the case of the orange garden spider, *Miranda aurantia*, which is black with bright orange or yellow spots on the back of the abdomen. The typical web of the orb weavers is a beautiful and complicated structure of radiating lines on which are laid down spiral and circular threads, the details of which have already been discussed. There are several types of orb webs. *Aranea* makes a symmetrical web which is called a complete orb. Where the weaver omits the viscid threads for part of the area it is called an incomplete orb, such as is constructed by *Metaerira* and *Zilla*. Another modification of the orb web is the lace-like and marvelously beautiful structure of the filmy dome spider, *Linyphia marginata*, whose delicate bowl inverted in the midst of an irregular maze of threads seems to belong to fairyland.

The triangle spider, *Hyptiotes cavatus*, is a tiny form which spins a little web of four radiating lines converging in a point and crossed by transverse lines, looking very much like rope ladders leading up the mast of a sailing vessel. This simple but beautiful web is usually found at the tips of dead branches of evergreen trees.

Photograph by Paul B. Mann

WEB OF LINYPHIA MARGINATA

This delicate, inverted dome is one of the most beautiful of all spider webs.

One of the strangest webs is the tubular structure of the rare purse-web spider, which extends a foot or more above the base of the tree along the side of which it is fastened.

WEBLESS SPIDERS. There are several spiders which rarely or never make webs. The *Attidae*, or jumping spiders, are common on tree trunks, plants, posts, and buildings. Some of them are brightly colored. They may be recognized by their short legs, prominent eyes, and quick movements. They can jump sideways or backward as well as forward. One authority says that he has seen them jump away from the side of a building, catch insects, and then recover their first position by means of a drag line.

The crab spiders, *Thomisidae*, are often found in the same localities as the jumping spiders. The first two pairs of legs are longer than the others and they move sideways more often than forward. They are usually gray or brown and thus are protectively colored when on wood or bark. Certain crab spiders live in flowers and they are either white or bright-colored like the flower in which they are ambushed. The most common crab spider of flowers is *Misumena vatica*, which is white in early summer when it lives in white flowers but becomes yellow in late summer when it is found on golden-rods. This color change takes about ten days to be completed. If in a field of daisies one looks for flowers in which two or three rays are bent down together over the center, he is almost sure to find one of these spiders hiding in the little tent thus made.

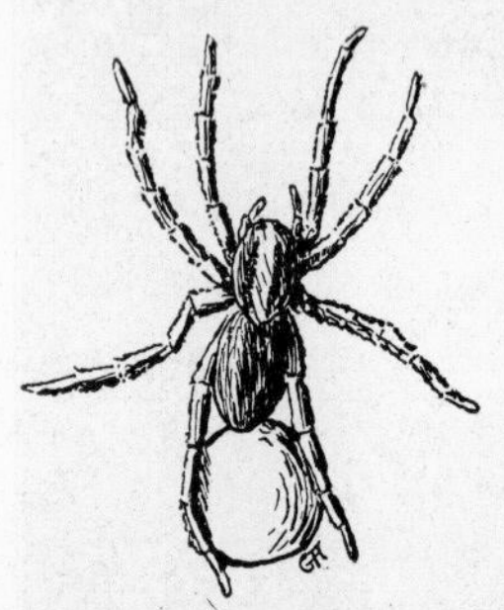

LYCOSA (WOLF SPIDER) WITH EGG CASE

The most interesting of the webless spiders, other than the trapdoor spider, are the representatives of the genus *Lycosa*, the wolf spiders. They dig a vertical burrow, varying in width and depth with the size of the spider; some are an inch across and almost a foot deep. The female drags her egg case with her until the young hatch out, after which they crawl to her back and for weeks thereafter are carried around.

There is another group of spiders widely distributed and attaining large size, so frequently seen around water, even running over it or diving into it, that they have been popularly called water spiders. These species belong to the genus *Dolomedes*. These should not be confused with the water striders, true insects found commonly on ponds and slowly running streams, floating quietly on the surface or darting off quickly on the four long legs, the shorter front pair held above the surface.

One of the commonest spiders of the fields, found under stones, is *Castianeira descripta*. On the sides of such stones may be found their egg sacs, which look somewhat like paper caps used in toy pistols by children, only they are grayish white with a metallic luster.

The largest spiders found in the United States are the tarantulas. They are found only in the South and West and are considered poisonous. Their bodies are covered with hair. They are chiefly nocturnal.

The giant crab spiders are about as large as the tarantulas. They are found in the United States only in the South. They have very long legs but are not hairy like the tarantulas.

Suggestions for Spider Study

Most people do not seem to like spiders, but when they learn how to handle these harmless creatures, and begin to observe their ways, an absorbing interest captivates them before they are aware of it.

One of the best ways to begin the study of spiders is to hold a spider with the under side uppermost and then to touch the spinnerets with the point of a pencil or the end of a twig. When the silk adheres, have someone walk slowly away carrying the pencil or twig. If the air is quiet a drag line of unbroken silk, fifty to one hundred feet long, may be obtained. Under a magnifying glass the silk can be seen streaming out of the spigots on the spinnerets.

The silk is very delicate, yet is quite elastic and has enough tenacity to move the dial of a small postal scales before it breaks. Other devices can be contrived to measure its strength. Silk is the one commodity a spider uses under almost all circumstances. Place a living spider in a large bottle or glass jar and watch it closely with the aid of a lens as it begins to spin its web. This may not take place immediately, and if it does not readily spin introduce a twig or stick. Note how it first fastens the drag lines with attachment disks to the sides of the glass. Left to itself, a single night usually suffices for the completion of an entire web.

The processes employed by a spider in making and repairing the web must be observed closely to appreciate fully the skill of the tiny architect. Likewise, the dexterity and speed with which a spider swathes and captures a partially entangled insect is a mere statement until seen for one's self.

Photograph by Paul B. Mann

COBWEBS AMONG THE PINES ON CAPE COD

Fogs bedew the webs and reveal loveliness unseen before. With such a setting one instinctively looks for a Puck to enter the fairyland.

There are several ways of making permanent records of spider webs: photography, mounting, and drawing. To photograph the web, stop the diaphragm of the camera to a minute opening and make a time exposure, with the camera resting on a solid support such as a tripod or a chair. Careful focusing is also necessary to show the delicate details of the web. A foggy morning is about the only time spiders' webs are clearly visible and the precious early hours of such a morning should be promptly utilized. If there is no fog, somewhat the same effect may be secured by spraying the web with water from an atomizer, taking care not to break the web by too much water. A black cloth behind the web will make it more distinct.

Webs, such as those of the orb weavers, can be permanently mounted by taking two pieces of clear glass of the same size, around the edges of one of which has been placed a narrow strip of adhesive tape. Carefully press one of the glasses against the web, which will adhere to it. Wipe away the excess threads from the edges without disturbing the web. Now bring the second glass into position over the first, and bind the two together with passe partout or lantern-slide binding.

An excellent sort of laboratory work, necessitating close observation, is the making of a drawing, to scale, of a spider's web. The orb weaver is again probably the best for this purpose. All parts should be labeled.

Another worth-while study is the investigation of a spider's cocoon. Having observed the exterior, open it carefully and look through a lens at the eggs or spiderlings, which represent such an important phase in the life history.

The homes of burrowing spiders may be visited. If the hole of a wolf spider, for instance, can be found, the spider herself may be revealed by reflecting down the shaft a beam of sunlight from a mirror. Frequently she may be tempted to come to the top by introducing a long straw and dangling it as though it were alive. The burrow can then be dug out by starting about six inches away and slowly undercutting until the spider is seen. Having destroyed her home, it seems only fair to leave the spider finally at the entrance to an abandoned burrow.

If spiders are to be collected they must be preserved in alcohol or formaldehyde solution. It is useless to attempt to keep them as one does insects, as their bodies are so full of fluids that they shrivel and the legs curl as they dry.

For studying and collecting spiders one should have a bottle of alcohol, an empty bottle for living specimens, a lens, and a square of black velvet as a background for photographs.

BIBLIOGRAPHY

COMSTOCK, JOHN H., *The Spider Book.* Doubleday, Doran and Company.

A very complete account of the spiders of the United States.

DUNCAN, F. M. and L. T., *Spiders and Scorpions*, Vol. 6: *Wonders of Insect Life.* Oxford University Press, 1913.

A book for young people, describing some English spiders.

FABRE, J. H. C., *Life of the Spiders.* Dodd, Mead and Company, Inc., 1927.

An intensely interesting account of the lives of spiders. It should inspire anyone to a study of these animals.

Our Insect Friends and Foes and Spiders. National Geographic Society, 1935.

Fascinating accounts of typical insects and spiders. Lavishly illustrated in natural colors.

CHAPTER XI

SOME LOWLY ANIMALS — MOSTLY AQUATIC

Ye little snails,
With slippery tails,
Who noiselessly travel
Along this gravel.

— ANONYMOUS

If you were asked to name an animal, the chances are one thousand to one that your answer would refer to a vertebrate. Except for the insects, practically all the animals one commonly sees are back-boned forms. Yet familiar as are the fishes, toads and frogs, reptiles, birds, and mammals, they are but a trifling minority of all animals. In fact, all the vertebrates of the world total but seven per cent of the 500,000 named species. The invertebrates or spineless animals comprise most of the known species and are represented by millions and millions of individuals, inhabiting land, air, and water, and infesting almost every plant and animal. We are not so well acquainted with the members of this horde, because most of them are small, many are microscopic, and the majority are aquatic. Yet they are of great significance. They are of direct economic value as the most important food supply for higher animals. The accumulated shells of certain forms have built great deposits, some of which have been raised from the ocean and form beds of chalk. Some of the microscopic forms are of tremendous importance in affecting the health of man and beast. Others influence the welfare of plants and animals in other ways. Widespread in their distribution, they are members of every environment, and their strange ways are of unending and absorbing interest.

Let us begin our investigations of invertebrates (other than insects and spiders) by procuring some bottles of water taken at random from stagnant pools. It is a good plan to collect some decaying parts of water plants along with the samples of water and to add some scrapings from submerged branches or other objects in the pool.

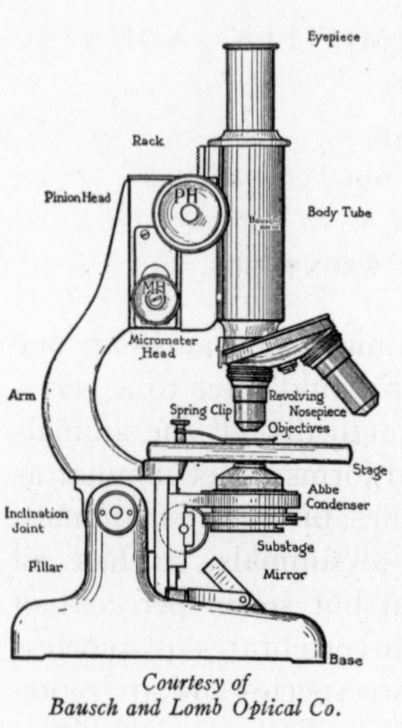

Courtesy of Bausch and Lomb Optical Co.

A LABORATORY MICROSCOPE

When you are ready to proceed, take a pipette (medicine dropper) and fill its stem from one of the bottles. Hold it to the light. Nothing in particular can be seen. Even with your pocket magnifier (see page 405) it is doubtful whether you could catch much more than an impression of some apparently free-swimming spots, most of which are probably inert and lifeless particles swirled about by the currents in the water. We shall require the lenses of a compound microscope to enhance our limited eyesight.

Transfer a drop from the pipette to a glass slide, place a cover glass over it and put it in position in the middle of the aperture on the stage of the microscope. An instrument of such delicacy and precision calls for a working knowledge of its parts, and so it is assumed that someone experienced in its use will aid the beginner in acquiring a knowledge of what is called microscopic technique, otherwise costly lenses and slides may be ruined. One or two hints may be given here. First place the microscope where you can catch a beam of clear light (never direct sunlight) in the mirror and, by turning the mirror, reflect this light through the aperture in the stage up to your eye as you look into the instrument. Always begin with the low-power objective (lens at lower end of the microscope), turning the coarse adjustment wheels until the objective, moving downward, almost touches the slide. Lower the objective while looking *at the microscope from the side, not looking down through it.* Otherwise you may get the objective too close and break the slide or injure the lens. Now, looking through the ocular (upper lens of the microscope) slowly turn the coarse adjustment in the *opposite* direction until the structure or object on the slide is seen clearly. If nothing appears, try some other spot and repeat the maneuver. If conditions warrant it, greater magnification can be gained, though the "field" will be correspondingly reduced, by turning the high-power objective into place and focusing with the fine adjustment. The use of the low-power objective in the average compound microscope gives a magnification of about 50 to 100 diameters; while the high-power objective may give from 150 to 500 diameters.

If these directions are followed and the material is good, the neophyte is likely to have one of the surprises of his life, as he gazes into a circular "field" — actually less than $\frac{1}{100}$ of the original drop of water — and finds this sample of the transparent globule transformed into a teeming world, alive with myriads of forms! Though ordinarily invisible, these creatures are as truly living organisms as are birds, fishes, and trees, with structures and functions and habits and life histories. Most of them are free-swimming wanderers in the pool, but many forms congregate along the surfaces of leaves and decaying vegetation in the water.

Move the slide slightly. You will soon get accustomed to the fact that it apparently moves in a direction exactly opposite to the one in which it is pushed, and you will govern your probings of the slide accordingly. You will find that you can gaze longer at the strange and amusing antics of these minute creatures and study them without eye-strain if you *learn always to keep both eyes open when looking through the microscope.*

Since most of the microscopic forms are one-celled animals, classified by the biologist under the phylum *Protozoa* (first animal; see Table of Classification, page 421) it may be best first to discuss this group, the more common members of which you are likely to find.

PROTOZOA. These one-celled creatures may be found anywhere in the world where there is moisture, unless it is too hot. Not only do they live in oceans, lakes, ponds, streams, and springs, but they are frequently inhabitants of temporary pools in ditches and fields, into which they were blown by the wind which picked them up as dust when dried or encysted. In an hour or two they are again active and remain so until the pool dries up, when they probably will become encysted again. Protozoa are able to endure excessive cold, but not high temperatures. Some species live as parasites in the living structures of plants, of other Protozoa, or in the blood or tissues of so-called "higher" animals (i.e., higher in the scale of biological development). Most of them are solitary, but some are colonial (many individuals structurally united and thus living together). There are over 8,500 species of Protozoa, divided into four classes. Only a few common representatives of these groups can be referred to here.

Amoeba. The amoeba, of which there are many species, is the typical representative of one class. In appearance it resembles a tiny globule of jelly. It can usually be found in the slimy coating of a submerged and decaying leaf or in the scrapings from a piece of wood long under water. It changes its shape continuously, though slowly, by thrusting out finger-like extensions of the body called pseudopods ("false feet"), into which the granular protoplasm may be seen to flow. It is generally regarded as the simplest animal

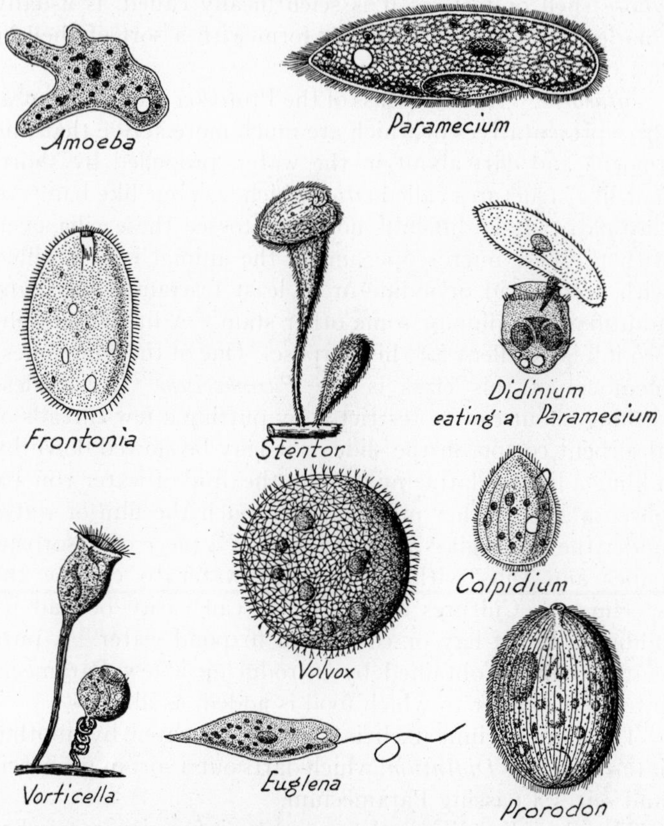

SOME COMMON PROTOZOANS

in the world. Certain representatives of the same class bear shells through which the pseudopods project. There are many marine species of shelled Protozoa, some of which are amazingly beautiful structures as seen under the microscope. Accumulations of these microscopic shells are used commercially for polishing purposes. Some of the fresh-water Protozoa also produce shells, notably the *Arcella* whose shell or test, as it is scientifically called, is usually colorless. *Difflugia* is another form with a sort of shell or test covered with mud, sand, etc.

Infusoria. Another class of the Protozoa is the Infusoria, the representatives of which are much more active than the amoeba and dart about in the water, propelled by short, hair-like structures called *cilia*, which lash out like banks of tiny oars. It is difficult, however, to see these cilia even with the best microscope, unless the animal is first killed with acetic acid or iodine or at least restrained by slight additions of iodine or some other stain. A little fountain-pen ink is excellent for this purpose. One of the commonest members of this class is the *Paramecium.* Its aimless rushing about can be restricted by putting a few threads of absorbent cotton on the slide or it may be slowed down by adding a little gelatine mixture to the drop of water you are observing. Another method is to touch the film of water under the cover glass with the edge of a piece of absorbent paper and thus withdraw enough water to confine the specimens. Cultures of Paramecia can easily be had by adding a bit of hay or corn meal to pond water. A pure culture can be obtained by introducing a few Paramecia into sterile water to which food is added, as above.

The Paramecium itself is hunted and eaten by another infusorian, the *Didinium*, which darts out a sort of proboscis and seizes a passing Paramecium.

The *Colpidium* is another common infusorian somewhat more abundant than the Paramecium, but smaller and rounder.

Another infusorian likely to be seen is the *Prorodon*, a fairly large protozoan, symmetrically rounded, which may frequently be observed devouring the one-celled plants called *Desmids*. *Frontonia* also somewhat resembles a Paramecium but it is plumper and rather sharply pointed at one end.

Stentor is another infusorian which looks like a miniature cornucopia with rows of sweeping cilia adorning the wide rim at the top. It adheres with a sort of tail to plants or to the bottom of the pool.

One of the most interesting of the Infusoria is the *Vorticella*. This animal seems more like a microscopic plant, since the upper part is cup-shaped and is supported on a coiled stem. When it is disturbed the stem suddenly contracts like a released spring. Then the stem slowly lengthens, only to have the action repeated. The rim of the upper part is fringed with cilia which are continually lashing a current inward, thus bringing particles of food into the interior. Vorticella may be looked for on the stems and leaves of water plants. They usually occur in clumps of so many individuals that they seem to be colonial.

A third class is of forms characterized by the possession of a long whiplike extension called a *flagellum*. A good example is the *Euglena*, a strange little creature which often possesses the same green stuff as plants. By the aid of this chlorophyll, these animals can make their own starchy food as do the green plants.

One of the strangest of all organisms, the *Volvox*, is also classified by many zoölogists as a member of this class. Some scientists, however, consider it to be a plant. This is a spherical form which whirls through the water like a spinning ball. It is really a colonial type consisting of hundreds of individuals. The Volvox produces two kinds of reproductive cells — the rounded eggs and the elongated sperm cells. These will generally be observable in the interior of the spherical mass. Besides these, Volvox may produce numerous daughter colonies which are set free by the breaking of the original ball.

Sometimes the surface of ponds and lakes is covered with a scum for a few days or weeks during the summer when the lake is said to be "working." This scum is sometimes made of blue-green algae of various kinds, but often among them, or making up all of the scum, are countless numbers of Volvox, Euglena, or other protozoans.

Common Inhabitants of the Shore Line of Fresh-water Ponds and Streams

Rotifers. Another interesting animal which is sure to be seen sooner or later under the microscope is one of the many rotifers (wheel-bearing). They are larger than the Protozoa and are usually colorless and somewhat elongated, generally marked off into six folds or segments. The body ends posteriorly in what seems to be a sort of tail by means of which it attaches itself. At the front end on either side of the mouth are two lobed disks provided with one or two bands of cilia which sweep food into the mouth in the manner of the infusorians, Vorticella and Stentor. The name "rotifer" refers to these disks which are used for locomotion as well as for collecting food. Like other aquatic organisms they are enormously productive. Thompson states that he found 5,000,000 rotifers in a square yard of lake water!

Fresh-water Sponges. Did you ever pull up a "snag" caught in fishing and forget your annoyance long enough to examine the gray or green lump attached to it? Probably you did not realize that you held in your hand a fresh-water sponge. It is rather rough and looks like a sort of coarse, wrinkled growth, with several holes. Yet it is a true animal and closely related to the marine sponges. These fresh-water sponges differ from the marine forms in producing winter buds, or statoblasts, rounded structures about as big as a pinhead, which survive the cold of winter and continue the species (the adult sponge dies and disintegrates at the end of summer). The development of new individuals in the spring is dependent on the statoblasts. All sponges, marine and fresh-water, have a sort of skeleton made either of tiny rods, fibers, or spicules. These can be seen if you tear apart one of the fresh-water forms and look at it through the microscope.

Hydra. Some day you may find a strange little gray or green creature about an eighth of an inch long attached to the leaf or stem of a water plant — a *Hydra*. It is almost too large to put under the compound microscope, in fact, the hand lens of about 10x power is more suitable for observing it. It responds quickly to stimuli. A slight rap on the table on which the jar containing it stands causes it to shrink to a bulging mass. Then it cautiously extends itself to its previous length. The Hydra attaches itself temporarily at the base while at the other end are from six to ten slender arms called *tentacles* surrounding a mouth opening. These aid in getting food; not only do they grasp it somewhat as an elephant's trunk does, but by means of special stinging cells, they paralyze such creatures as Cyclops or Daphnia upon which they feed. Then the victim is seized by the tentacles and pushed into the mouth. Sometimes the Hydra releases its hold on the plant and by the aid of the tentacles turns a somersault, thus moving to a new spot. Unlike the sponges, there is no supporting skeleton of any kind.

Bryozoa. Colonial forms, called *Bryozoa* — or moss animals — are very common. They may be found attached to submerged stones, boards, or leaves and stems of water plants. The individual animals of the colony, each called a zoid, are too minute to see without at least a hand lens.

Plumatella is the commonest fresh-water bryozoan. It is much branched and can usually be found in great quantities around the sluiceways of reservoirs.

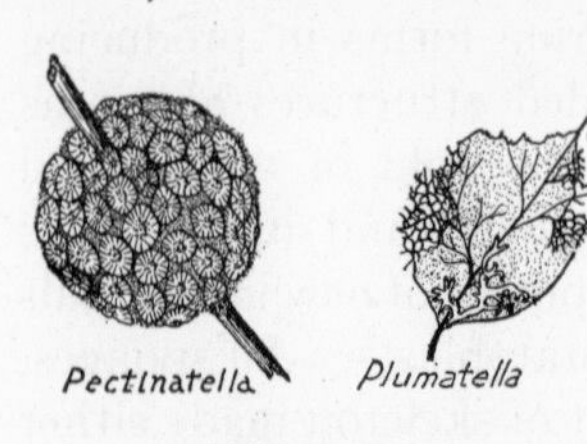

BRYOZOA

It is difficult to realize that these clusters are composed of fresh-water animals gathered together in colonies.

Pectinatella grows in a gelatinous mass resembling a cantaloupe in size, shape, and markings. It may be found attached to sticks or stems in shallow water. If a mass of Bryozoa is taken into the museum or laboratory and placed in water, when everything is quiet each little zooid slowly protrudes a feathery crown of tentacles.

FLATWORMS. In turning over logs or stones in a pond or brook, a curious flattened creature may be found clinging to some support or swimming away with wavelike, muscular contractions. This is one of the flatworms, probably *Planaria*. It is quite harmless, though often confused with the leech, which is segmented and has a sucker at each end of the body. The power of regeneration in this little creature is remarkable. If cut into pieces each part may grow a complete animal. Planaria can easily be kept in an aquarium.

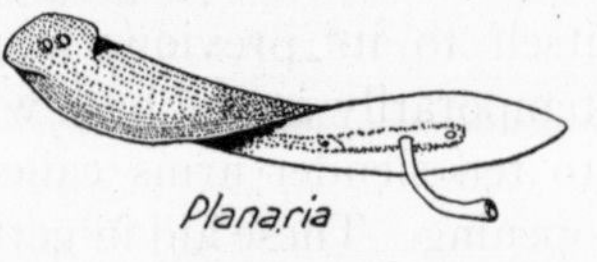

PLANARIA

Note the two eyespots on the head, and the mouth at the end of the hanging tube some distance away.

SEGMENTED WORMS. The common angleworm or earthworm, of which there are several species all much alike, is distributed practically throughout the world. Without sight or specialized sense organs, with no weapons for offense or defense, a tasty morsel of food for most birds and many other animals, it still survives all vicissitudes. In general, a nocturnal animal like the earthworm is possibly better protected than animals with definite defensive adaptations. Certainly during the time that it hides in the earth it is safe except, perhaps, from moles. It may be driven out of its burrows when they fill up with water from rains. Unless the refugee worm is successful in finding or making another burrow, it is likely to have its skin dried by exposure to sun and air. Like all animals which breathe through the skin, it must be continuously moist or it dies.

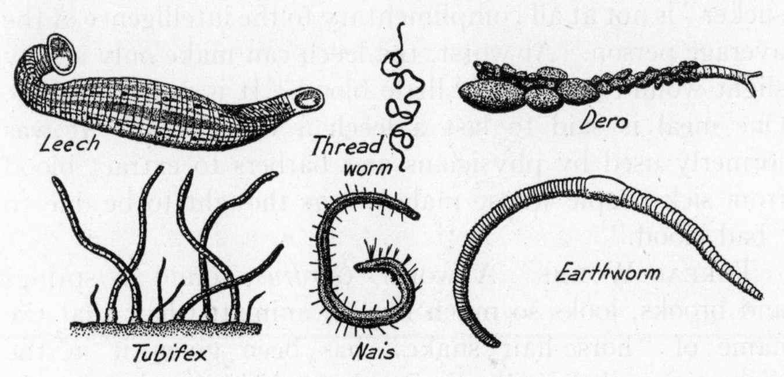

VARIOUS KINDS OF WORMS

If you steal out on a grass plot at night and search with a flashlight, you may find large earthworms entirely out of their burrows except for the last few segments. Some may be found apparently joined along their sides. These are mating. Each earthworm, strangely enough, produces both sperms and eggs, though in mating it transfers its sperms to another individual from which it at the same time receives sperms.

The earthworm literally eats its way into the earth in making its burrows. Most of this earthy material is passed off in little turrets of mud pellets at the mouth of its burrow. With care it is possible to make a plaster of Paris cast of such a turret. The scientist Darwin estimated that one acre of land may contain 50,000 earthworms and that during one year more than eighteen tons of these pellets would be brought up by the worms. Land is thus made more porous and fertile.

Leeches are aquatic relatives of the earthworm, the several species differing in size, form, and color. Most of them are greenish or black above and reddish below, and swim actively in undulating fashion. The leech is only a few inches long, yet the consternation and even panic which usually occurs in a group of bathers at the cry of "blood-sucker" is not at all complimentary to the intelligence of the average person. At worst, the leech can make only a very slight wound and suck a little blood. It is not poisonous. One meal is said to last a leech a whole year. It was formerly used by physicians and barbers to extract blood from sick people whose malady was thought to be due to "bad blood."

THREAD WORMS. A worm, *Gordius*, found in springs and brooks, looks so much like an animated hair that the name of "horse-hair snake" has been given it in the superstitious belief that it is a horse hair that has lain in water till it became alive. Actually it was first an internal parasite in the body of some aquatic insect, then later in the body of another animal, such as the minnow, from which it escapes to the water when full grown. In its last stage it may live in the body of a cricket or a grasshopper. Another thread worm is the little "vinegar eel" found in mother-of-vinegar, the mass often found floating in vinegar. This worm must be looked at with a microscope in order to see it clearly. Then there are the dangerous parasite worms — trichina or pork worm, and the hookworm.

Several other worms are found in stagnant water: *Dero*

constructs a tube for itself and is commonly found near the surface. *Nais* is a segmented worm bearing frequent bristles of varying lengths. *Tubifex* lives on the bottom where it builds a tiny burrow projecting slightly above the mud. From this case the reddish worm extends its inquisitive form, retreating instantly if danger threatens. Many of these worms live close together.

THE CRUSTACEANS. The members of the Crustacea, in addition to an armored covering, the exoskeleton, have jointed legs and usually gills for breathing. They vary in size from microscopic forms to the huge horseshoe crab.

Entomostraca. The tiny crustaceans are often grouped in a sub-class, the *Entomostraca*. Though apparently negligible, they have been termed "the most important animals in all fresh waters." Feeding on minute plants, they in turn constitute the food supply of small fish. They include the fairy shrimp, water fleas, and copepods.

Fairy Shrimp. The fairy shrimp is the largest of this sub-class, a beautiful little creature about an inch and a half long, transparent, yet resplendent with all the colors of the spectrum. It swims on its back. Hatching in the spring in temporary rain-water pools, it lives for a few days or weeks, then lays eggs and dies. The mussel shrimp of the western states is a related form which is enclosed in a shell.

Water Fleas. Water fleas are very common. All of the body except the head is covered with a thin bivalve shell. The shell is delicately marked and so transparent that under a microscope one may see the elongated, pulsating heart, the blood streaming through the body, the tiny muscles, and the feathery gills attached to the feet. The posterior part of the body is fashioned somewhat like a knife blade with a curved tip for which the two valves of the shell act as a sort of sheath. There are two black eye spots on the head, and branched antennae by means of

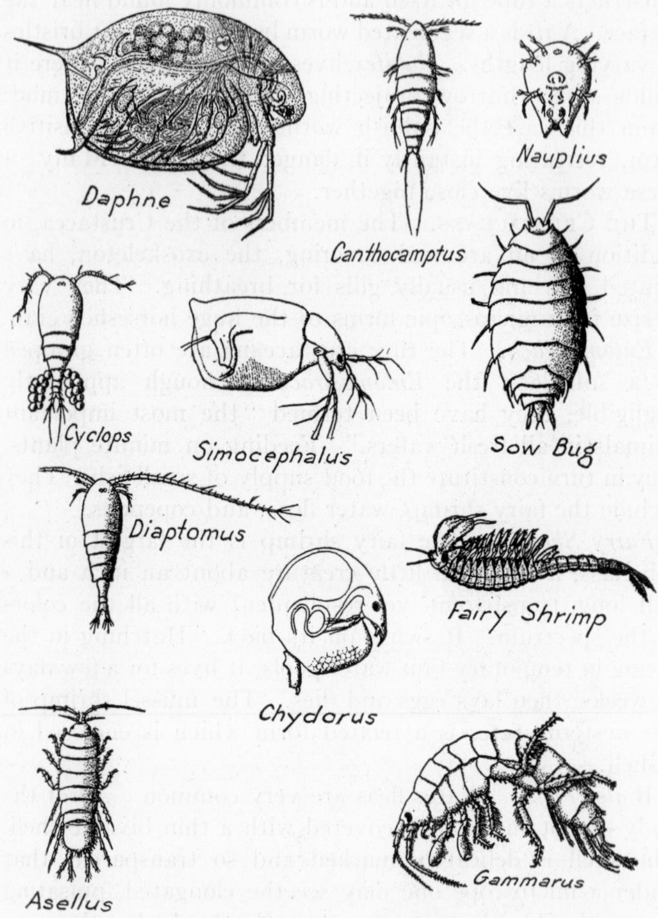

Adapted from "Guide to the Study of Fresh-water Biology" by Needham and Needham

SOME OF THE SMALLER CRUSTACEANS

Many of the fresh-water crustaceans are microscopic.

which the water flea swims in a jerky fashion. The water fleas eat diatoms and other algae. Through the warm weather they are found near the surface of all quiet ponds where plants abound.

Courtesy of General Biological Supply House

USING A PLANKTON NET

Many kinds of minute organisms can be caught in such a net.

The commonest water flea is *Daphne* or *Daphnia*, but there are numerous other forms such as *Chydorus* and *Simocephalus*. To collect specimens of any of these small crustaceans, drag a tapering net made of bolting cloth (a plankton net) along the surface of the water on a still day toward the evening when these animals come nearer the top of the pond. From time to time turn the net inside out and wash off the tip in a jar of the pond water.

Copepods: Copepods are found in ponds both summer and winter. These creatures have an elongated body divided into segments. The body tapers to the rear where it is forked, unlike the single posterior point of the water fleas. There is a single relatively large eye on the top of the head between the bases of the single pair of antennae. There are four pairs of swimming legs beneath the body, but they are of little value in locomotion, since the copepods depend on the sweeping movements of the antennae to propel themselves through the water in a characteristically jerky fashion. The best known member of the group is *Cyclops*, named because of its solitary eye. Other copepods are *Diaptomus*, usually red in color, with very long antennae, and *Canthocamptus*, with larger tails and shorter antennae. The female of Cyclops or of other copepods may be seen carrying her eggs in a pair of rounded pouches attached to the rear of the body. All copepods pass through a stage of development called *Nauplius*, in which they differ markedly from the adult form.

Amphipods: Gammarus and *Asellus*. The scuds or amphipods are small, pale, greenish crustaceans usually found among water plants from which they dart away to some other shelter when disturbed. One of the commonest of the scuds is *Gammarus*, a very active creature, about 25 mm. long. *Asellus* is another crustacean, about half the size of Gammarus, which lives in the muddy bottoms of stagnant pools.

Sow Bugs. One common crustacean lives on land, the so-called "sow bug" or "pill bug." Found under logs or in decaying vegetation, it promptly rolls up into a tight ball when caught. It is interesting to hold one of these compact balls in the cup of your hand and watch it relax, unroll, and scurry off.

Crayfish. The crayfish or crawfish is the largest of the fresh-water crustaceans. They are widely distributed in fresh-water streams where they may be seen crawling over the bottom or may be found by turning over submerged stones. To all intents they are what they are commonly called "fresh-water lobsters." Heavily armored by the exoskeleton and the powerful pincers, they are ready to battle any enemy. In picking them up hold them firmly by their sides to avoid a bad nip. They eat almost anything, and in a very real sense are valuable scavengers. They can easily be caught in the hand or in a small net or may be fished for, as are crabs, with a piece of meat tied to a string. When they have caught hold of the meat, lift them gently to the surface, then with a quick jerk take them out of the water. They make satisfactory inhabitants of an aquarium if the water is not too deep and if they are given a piece of meat or fish from time to time. In the aquarium it may be possible to see the process of molting. The exoskeleton prevents the constant growth seen in most other animals so it must be shed at times. Molting is a curious proceeding and is so strenuous that sometimes the crayfish dies in the struggle. The exoskeleton splits a little way down the back, starting at the head, and through this aperture the animal somehow manages to withdraw all the soft tissue, even the contents of the long legs, antennae, and eyes. The molted shell looks exactly like a very pale crayfish.

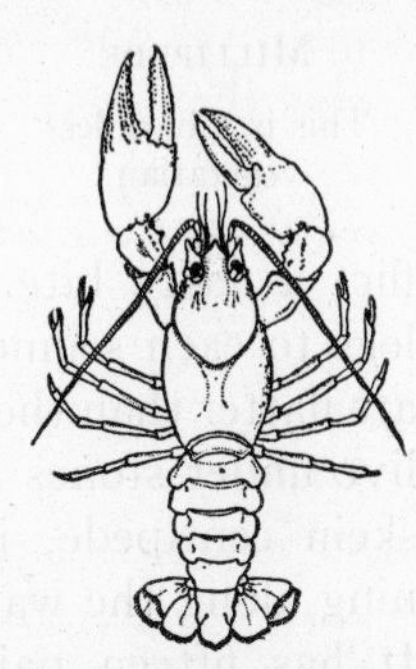
THE CRAYFISH

Lobsters, crabs, and certain shrimps or prawns are marine cousins of the crayfish and are referred to in Chapter VIII.

MYRIAPODS. "Thousand-leggers" or *Myriapoda*, as the scientist knows them, are of two distinct kinds, the millipedes or thousand-legged worms, and the centipedes or hundred-legged worms. The millipedes are harmless little creatures that curl up when disturbed. They have two pairs of legs on each segment. The commonest are dark in color and are to be found under old boards or logs. The largest one in the north is called *Spirobolus*. It is dark reddish-brown with greenish edges to the segments. When handled it gives off a peculiar odor like bitter almonds. All the millipedes are vegetarians. The centipedes are carnivorous and some of the tropical forms can inflict a nasty bite. They have one pair of legs to each segment of the body and they are flatter than the millipedes. They usually live under stones and logs. One form, the skein centipede, is occasionally seen running along the walls or floors of buildings. It has fifteen pairs of long legs. As it feeds on various kinds of household insects it is of real benefit, though most people will not tolerate its presence.

MILLIPEDE

This is a harmless vegetarian.

CENTIPEDE

All centipedes found in northern latitudes are harmless.

CLAMS. Along the shores of ponds and streams will often be found piles of empty shells of fresh-water clams, mute evidence of a muskrat's banquet. The inside of these shells is usually a pinkish color with a pearly luster; on the outside they are greenish or brownish with many lines of growth. There are numerous species of fresh-water clams, differing in size, shape, thickness, and color, but to separate them into their species is work for a specialist. Their tracks may often be seen in muddy or sandy bottoms where they have plowed along, pulled by the muscular "foot." They are edible but those who have tried them say that shoe leather is no tougher.

FRESH-WATER CLAM

These clams produce valuable pearls. The shells are used for buttons.

SNAILS. Snails are related to the clams. Some, like the

slugs, have no shells, others carry univalve shells into which they can retreat in time of danger. The pond snails are excellent scavengers in the aquarium, slowly gliding from place to place along the glass sides and feeding by the rasping tongue on the algae which coat the glass. They may breed in the aquarium, and the tiny eggs in the mass of gelatinous material are worth repeated observations with a hand lens. As the embryos develop they may be seen slowly revolving inside the surrounding jelly; then after a few days the tiny young snails may be found crawling about in the aquarium. The living snails and slugs are well worth close observation. There is one breathing opening which suddenly appears, much like an iris diaphragm, then a moment later shuts tightly. The eyes are dark spots on the ends of stalks, which, when touched, quickly telescope and are withdrawn close to the head. A little later they cautiously reverse the motion and, when fully extended, the eye stalks begin again to wave slowly about. Two tentacles similar to the eye stalks also project from the head.

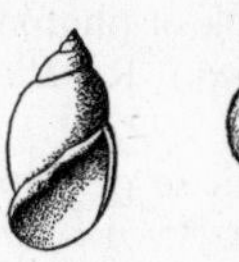
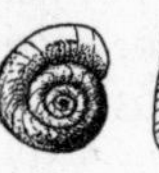

FRESH-WATER SNAILS

Snails are interesting and helpful in an aquarium.

There are three common genera of fresh-water snails: *Planorbis*, having a shell with a flat coil like a watch spring; *Limnaea*, with a sharp pointed shell having a clock-wise or right-hand spiral; and *Physa*, similar, but with a left-hand spiral. There are several genera of land snails with spirally coiled shells, the spiral being very low. The largest are a little over an inch across, and a half to three-quarters of an inch high. Most of the species are brown or tan, but some are marked with reddish spiral bands. The land snails may be kept in jars or the glass boxes described in Chapter XXII. A bit of lettuce leaf or a piece of fruit will furnish all the food they need.

BIBLIOGRAPHY

CALKINS, GARRY N., *The Protozoa.* Lea, Lea, and Febiger Company, 1926.

A standard book for study or reference.

DISRAELI, ROBERT, *Seeing the Unseen.* John Day Company, 1933.

A book of photomicrographs of all sorts of things.

KUDO, RICHARD R., *Handbook of Protozoölogy.* Charles C. Thomas, 1931.

A concise description of the protozoa, valuable for reference.

MINCHIN, E. A., *An Introduction to the Study of the Protozoa.* Longmans, Green and Company, 1922.

A large book, quite technical, with special reference to parasitic forms.

NEEDHAM, JAMES G., and LLOYD, JOHN T., *Life of Inland Waters.* Charles C. Thomas, 1931.

An excellent account of the life of ponds and streams, from the one-celled forms to the fish and flowering plants.

NEEDHAM, JAMES G. and PAUL R., *Guide to the Study of Fresh Water Biology* (3rd edition). Comstock Publishing Company, 1935.

A pamphlet of plates and keys to the genera of water insects, mollusks, crustaceans, algae, etc. Very useful for its purpose.

STOKES, A. C., *Aquatic Microscopy for Beginners.* John Wiley and Sons, Inc., 1918.

An excellent book for young microscopists.

WARD, H. B., and WHIPPLE, G. C., *Fresh Water Biology.* John Wiley and Sons, Inc., 1918.

This might well be considered *the* standard book on the subject.

YATES, R. F., *Exploring with the Microscope.* D. Appleton-Century Company, 1934.

This book develops microscopy as a possible avocation for young people; it also includes microscopic technique.

GETTING ACQUAINTED WITH PLANT LIFE

D. Warren Boyer

"THEN THINK I OF DEEP SHADOWS ON THE GRASS
OF MEADOWS WHERE IN SUN THE CATTLE GRAZE."

CHAPTER XII

TREES AND SHRUBS

The deep seclusion of this forest path,
O'er which the green boughs weave a canopy;
Along which bluet and anemone
Spread a dim carpet; where the twilight hath
Her cool abode; and, sweet as aftermath,
Wood-fragrance roams.[1]

— MADISON CAWEIN

Trees are among the easiest of living things to know. They are large and stay put. Their leaves are so numerous that they may be gathered without fear of injury to plants. In any one locality the number of kinds is so limited — fifty species within a radius of two or three miles being an unusual number — that it is easy to learn all of them. For a boy or girl to realize that all the trees can be known by name, when a few weeks before most of them were merely objects in the landscape, gives a sense of satisfaction and mastery that will add to the interest with which other phases of nature are taken up.

LEAVES. In beginning tree study, gather a few leaves from some of the trees, at the same time noting the general characteristics of each tree, such as height, shape, method of branching, bark, and flowers or fruit if in season. Leaves are classified first as to whether they are needle- or scale-like, or broad or thin. The first group, often called evergreens or conifers, comprises the pine, hemlock, fir, spruce, larch, red cedar, and white cedar. Of the broad leaves only a few kinds — maple, ash, horse chestnut and dogwood — grow opposite each other in pairs on the branches;

[1] From "Enchantment" in *Weeds by the Wall* by Madison Cawein. Copyright by John P. Morton and Company.

all the others grow alternately, that is, only one at a given point on the branch. The broad-leaved trees are usually called *deciduous* because in cold climates they shed their leaves in winter. Leaves are either simple or compound; the edges either entire, toothed, lobed, or notched; and the surfaces smooth, rough, waxy, or hairy.

Courtesy of Oliver P. Medsger

A TREE-SHADED ROAD

Much of the beauty of country roads is due to the bordering trees.

Leaves are important to the tree as the factories where food is manufactured, while the nature lover admires their beauty and basks in their shade and the student finds in them an easy way of distinguishing the various species. But to know the trees we must not only know the special details of the leaves, but those of the bark, twigs, and buds and the general characteristics of the tree as a whole.

Courtesy of Oliver P. Medsger

RIVER BIRCH

The curved, thin sheets of bark are quite unlike the bark of other birches.

BARK. A few trees have such characteristic bark that it serves as an immediate identification, such as that of the shagbark hickory with its long plates loosened at each end, the patched brown and white of the sycamore, the smooth gray of the beech, the chalky white of the white birch or the silvery curls of the yellow birch. The smooth brown bark of the black birch and the young black cherry look much alike, but close comparison shows that the cherry is more lustrous, often with bronze or purplish sheen and has broader horizontal streaks marking the surface where the tiny breathing pores of the young twigs have stretched and grown as the trunk has developed. With close observation, individual characteristics — ridged, checkered, or scaly bark, with shallow or deep markings — can be found for each species of tree, so that one who knows them well can recognize them even when blindfolded, if allowed to feel the trunks.

TWIGS AND BUDS. With twigs and buds there is always color to be noticed — browns and grays usually — but the green of sassafras twigs, the yellow of some willows, and the red of red and silver maples are conspicuous even at a distance. Buds are most noticeable in winter, when they are as useful in determining the kinds of trees as are the leaves in summer. To the trees, buds — within which are leaves or flowers more or less developed — are important as the growing points of branches. Some winter buds have in them all the leaves that are to develop the next summer, very tiny and folded snugly to pack into such close quarters.

It is extremely interesting to open a bud and separate carefully the little leaves in order to compare their number with the leaf scars that show the position and number of the leaves of past seasons. Buds are usually covered with overlapping scales that are waxy, varnished, or hairy to prevent the loss of water from the delicate parts within. Sometimes, as in willows and sycamores, only one scale can be seen; more often there are many. Occasionally, as in the black walnut and butternut, there are no bud scales; undeveloped leaves crowded together make up the buds. In a very few cases there are no buds visible on the twigs, as in the black locust where the tiny buds are hidden in cavities underneath the calluses of the leaf scars. Below each bud, except in the case just mentioned, is found a scar where a leaf had been attached. (Two or three flower buds may grow above one leaf scar in the maples, and in walnuts and hickories several buds may grow one above another.) Sometimes the leaf scar encircles the bud, more often it is

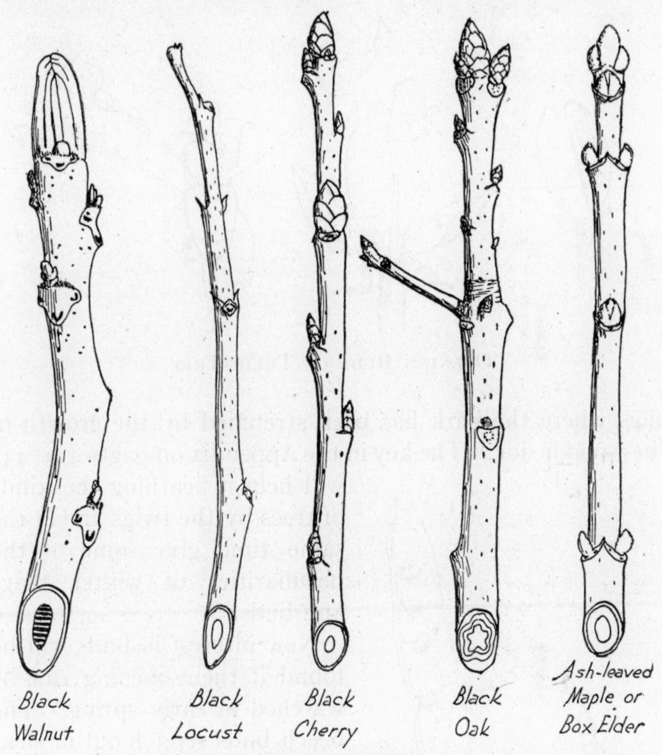

TWIGS AND BUDS

The walnut has chambered pith; the bundle scars give the leaf scars the appearance of animal faces. The locust has thorns at the side of the leaf scars and no terminal bud. The oak has star-shaped pith. In the box elder the leaf scars and buds are opposite.

crescent-shaped or elliptical. In the scar are tiny dots, the scars of the fibro-vascular bundles that connected the wood of the twig with the veins of the leaf. The arrangement of these bundle scars is characteristic for each kind of tree. On the twigs are found little dots — lenticels or breathing pores — very tiny on young twigs, larger on older

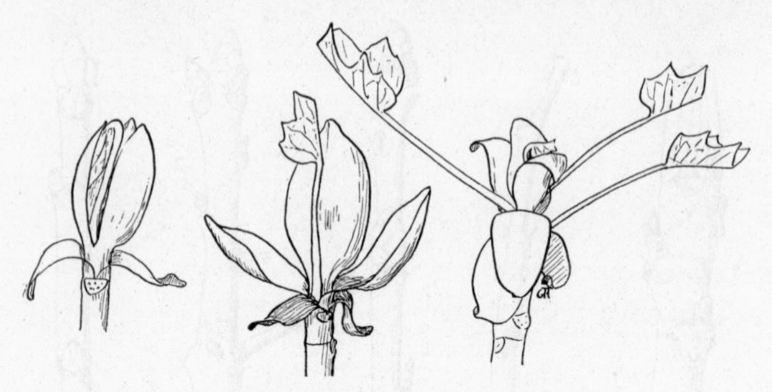

OPENING BUDS OF TULIP TREE

ones where the bark has been stretched by the growth of the wood inside. The key in the Appendix on pages 431–434 will help in learning the kinds of trees by the twigs and at the same time give some of the peculiarities of winter twigs and buds.

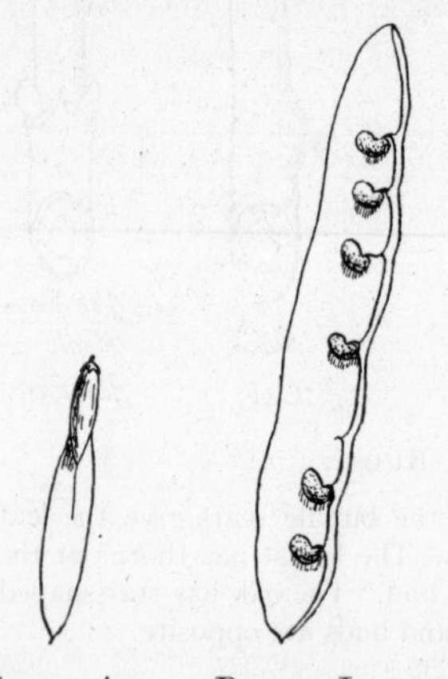

WHITE ASH BLACK LOCUST

New interest in buds will be found if their opening can be watched in early spring. The beech buds stretch out in slender, silky, green and brown fringes. The horse chestnut leaves are densely covered with brown wool as they push up from between the sticky scales. The bud scales of the oaks stretch out as if trying to enclose the developing leaves, and often take on a reddish color. Finest of all are the

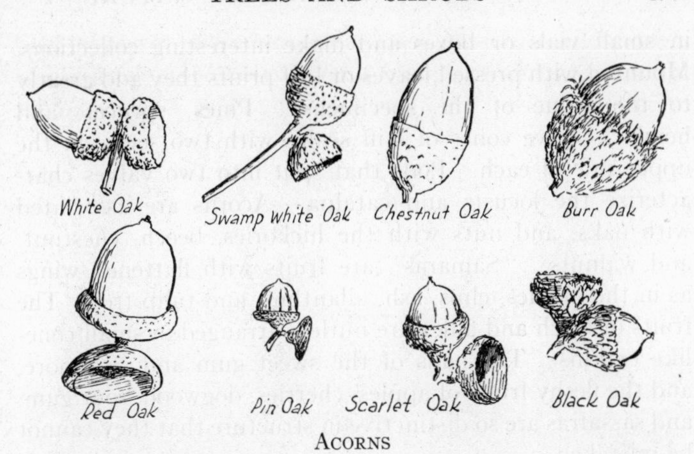

ACORNS

Those in the top row are from oaks of the white oak group. The lower ones belong to the black oak group.

flaming hickory buds, sometimes mistaken for flowers down the woodland vistas.

FLOWERS. All trees have flowers, but except for a few such as those of the fruit trees, magnolia, tulip tree, horse chestnut, and catalpa, the flowers are adapted for wind pollination and are small and inconspicuous. Most of them blossom in early spring before the leaves are fully expanded. Following the flowers come fruits, many of which ripen during the summer. Fruits may be used with as much ease as leaves in determining the kinds of trees, and often with more accuracy. Dry fruits and seeds may be kept

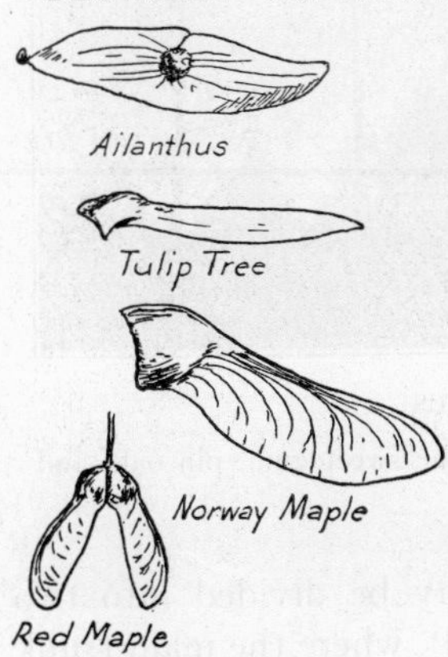

WINGED SEEDS

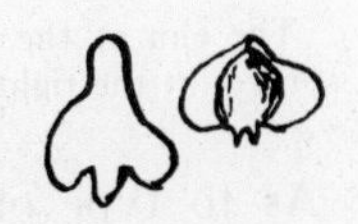

SCALE AND SEED OF YELLOW BIRCH

in small vials or boxes and make interesting collections. Mounted with pressed leaves or leaf prints they add greatly to the value of the specimens. Pines, spruces, and hemlocks have cones of stiff scales with two seeds on the upper side of each. Pods that split into two valves characterize the locusts and catalpa. Acorns are associated with oaks, and nuts with the hickories, beech, chestnut, and walnuts. "Samaras" are fruits with flattened wings as in the maples, elms, ash, ailanthus, and tulip tree. The fruits of birch and alder are nutlets arranged in small cone-like catkins. The balls of the sweet gum and sycamore, and the fleshy fruits of apples, cherries, dogwood, sour gum, and sassafras are so distinctive in structure that they cannot be mistaken.

TYPES OF TREES

The elm at the left is deliquescent. The sweet gum, pin oak, and spruces at the right are excurrent.

As to type of growth, trees may be divided into two groups: *excurrent* (running through), where the main trunk continues through the crown to the top; and *deliquescent* (dissolving), where the trunk repeatedly divides so that it cannot be traced to the upper part of the crown. To the first group belong the pine, spruce, hemlock, and other conifers, the tulip tree, lombardy poplar, pin oak, white ash, and many others. To the second group belong the widespreading trees such as the willow, elm, white oak, dogwood, sycamore, etc. Often young trees are of the excurrent type, while older ones of the same species are deliquescent. Some individual specimens are intermediate in type, so that this criterion is of little value in separating species.

Photograph by G. T. Hastings

Shrubs by the Stream

The stream bank is the natural habitat of many shrubs.

In habitat some trees prefer moist ground, others dry; some level land, others hillsides; still others show little preference. Willows, pin oaks, sycamores, some red maples, and black ash thrive in damp ground near streams or swamps; white oak, hickories, sugar maple, and white ash are found on higher, drier ground. Chestnut oak is characteristic of hillsides, while the little scrub oak is at home on the tops of rocky hills or in barren soil.

Photograph by G. T. Hastings

SHRUBS ABOUT THE HOME

A planting of shrubs adds greatly to the attractiveness of a house.

SHRUBS. Shrubs are naturally associated with trees; in fact it is frequently hard to tell whether a particular form should be called a shrub or a tree. In general, shrubs are woody plants without a definite trunk, with more than one stem, and usually low in height compared to trees. In size they vary from forms only a few inches high — the aromatic wintergreen is often called a shrub — to the tree-like forms of the sumachs and alders, which often grow as trees. Woody vines are usually classed with shrubs. The all too common poison ivy usually grows as a vine, clinging to tree trunks and walls, but not infrequently it is bushy in form. Shrubs may be studied just as trees are — by the leaves, fruits, or general characteristics. No key will be given here, though such keys may be found in some of the tree and shrub books. Suggestions, however, are given in the Appendix on page 427 of how a key may be worked out. It would be an interesting project to make a key for the shrubs of some particular region, illustrating it with outline drawings of leaves and fruits.

Leaf Prints. While the trees are being learned, it will add to the interest if leaves are pressed and mounted or leaf prints made. Pressing can easily be done between thicknesses of newspaper or in magazines placed under a weight. A weight of 15 or 20 pounds will prevent leaves from wrinkling as they dry. When dried the leaves should be mounted with glue or gummed strips on stiff paper, as described for flowers. Several kinds of leaf prints are described here and others may be devised.

In making photographic prints, probably the best results are obtained by the use of papers such as solio or velox. The leaf should be placed on the glass of a printing frame, the paper put over it, and then exposed to the sunlight. Velox requires a minute or less; solio may take several minutes. The length of the exposure will depend on the brightness of the light and the thickness of the leaf. The papers are toned or developed with the prepared chemicals according to the directions received with the papers. Both kinds must be fixed by soaking in a hypo solution for ten or fifteen minutes, then washed in running water or with several changes of water for at least half an hour, and then dried. The placing of the paper in the frames and the toning or developing must be done in dim light; in fact, a photographic dark room gives the best results. If the exposure is long enough every veinlet should show in the print. The necessary supplies are a printing frame, (5 by 7 inches is a convenient size), sensitive paper, toning solution for the solio, developer for the velox, and hypo. They can be secured from any dealer in photographic materials. After making a good print it may be rubbed with oil to make it translucent and then used as a negative to make prints with the veins dark and the background white. Prints may be colored with green crayon. Similar to the photographic paper is blue print paper. With this the printing is much slower, from two to five minutes being required in direct sunlight, and even then it is probable that the veins will not show well unless the leaves are young or very thin. The prints can be made in a printing frame as described for the other papers, but if no frames are available a board and piece of glass can be used. Place the paper, sensitive side up, on the board, on this the leaf, or spray of leaves, and on top of all the glass. Put the frame or board in the sunlight and wait till the paper exposed around the leaf is of a bronze or gray color. Then wash in running water, or with several changes of water, for about half an hour, and dry. Sprays of flowers can be used instead of leaves and very attractive results secured if care is taken in the arrangement.

Ink-pad prints. The simplest kind of leaf prints is made with a large ink pad, such as can be obtained at any stationer's. Put the leaf, lower side down, on the pad, cover with a piece of paper and press firmly down. Then put the leaf, ink side down, on a sheet of clean white (or pastel-tinted) paper to receive the impression. Again cover with a paper such as newspaper and holding firmly with the fingers of one hand, rub with the fingers of the other.

Smoke prints. These are very delicate and show the veining perfectly when well made. A piece of newspaper or any absorbent paper is first treated by rubbing into it a small quantity of vaseline, then the prepared surface is passed back and forth slowly through the flame of a candle till well blackened. A little practice will show how much vaseline to use and how much smoking is necessary. There should not be enough vaseline to show oily spots when smoked and the black should be evenly spread. The leaf is placed, lower side down, on the smoked paper, covered and rubbed firmly, then placed on the white paper on which the print is desired, covered with clean paper, and rubbed as before. Care must be taken not to let the paper or leaf slip during the rubbing or the veins will show double. A

Photographic Print of a Tulip Tree Leaf

print made in this way will not blur and is permanent. In smoking the paper there is always the possibility of its catching fire; it will surely do so if held still in the flame. In case this happens drop the paper quickly to the floor and extinguish the flame by stepping on it. Once prepared the paper can be used for a number of prints.

Paint prints. These are made with oil paints. Place a little of the tint desired, presumably green, on a piece of tin or glass. With the finger tip or a pad of cloth touch the paint, then lightly pat it all over the lower surface of the leaf. (If the paint is rubbed on, it will invariably show as parallel lines.) Place the leaf on the paper and rub as described before. In making ink, smoke, or paint prints, better results are secured if the paper to receive the impression is placed on a pad of newspapers or botany driers.

Printer's-ink prints. A little printer's ink is placed on a pane of glass and spread uniformly with an ink roller (brayer, the printers call it). The leaf is placed on the inked glass and the roller run over it firmly *once.* Now the leaf is placed inside a folded sheet of white paper and rolled once with a photographic mounting roller. Or, the lower side of the leaf is placed on the white paper and a piece of newspaper is placed over it before rolling, thus getting only the impression of the lower surface. In rolling to get the impression press down firmly.

Splatter prints. Lay the leaf on the paper, weighting the edges with bits of metal or pebbles, if it does not lie flat; then, with an old tooth brush dipped in ink, splatter ink around the leaf. The splattering is done either by rubbing a nail or twig across the brush, or better, by drawing the brush over a small square of wire mosquito netting. The movement should be all in one direction and if care is taken will give very clear outlines. A small air brush will give excellent results, with colored inks or solutions of aniline dyes. An atomizer will answer as an air brush.

LEAF PRINTS

Left: Pressed leaf; Printer's-ink print; Splatter print. *Right:* Ink-pad print; Smoke print; Combination print.

Combination prints of various kinds can be made. For instance, after making a blue print the leaf can be placed in a book or magazine till the print is dry, then be used to make a smoke print on the blue print. Or, after making a smoke print, the leaf can be left in position and a splatter print made with colored ink.

Courtesy of Boy Scouts of America

Studying the History of a Tree in the Stump

Interesting collections of leaf prints can easily be acquired. In every case enough information should accompany the print to identify it and give facts as to the tree from which it came and the locality where it grew. Leaf prints may also be used for ornamental effect on note paper, the covers of notebooks, borders of posters, etc.

Woods: Another division of tree study is that of woods. Wood is useful to man for such a great variety of purposes that something of its structure should be learned, but any detailed study is out of place in a nature program. A stump of a tree will furnish a fascinating project. By counting the rings of growth the age of the tree can be determined. Note the difference in the width of rings in different years: broad rings mean favorable growing seasons, warmth, and abundant rainfall. Note the age of the tree when it was growing most rapidly. Naturally the study of what causes annual rings will follow. In oaks and chestnuts the large pores of the early spring wood are easily seen with the naked eye and obviously account for the rings. With most kinds of woods it is not so easy to see the elements of structure unless a hand lens is available. With a 10x lens, or stronger, it is easy to see the larger cells formed in early spring and to note the contrast with the small ones formed at the end of the previous summer's growth.

With a lens, too, it is easy to determine in which of the three large groups any wood should be placed. If a small surface is cut across the end of a piece of wood, the uniform structure of the non-porous woods, the scattered pores of the diffuse-porous woods, and the arcs of large pores of the ring-porous woods can be made out. The non-porous woods are the conifers. In these the wood is made of long slender cells, square or rectangular in cross section, called *tracheids*. In the spring wood they are comparatively large, with thin walls; in the summer wood they are smaller, with thicker walls, resulting usually in a darker color. The line where the small cells of summer meet the large ones of the succeeding spring marks the year's growth. In the pines and spruces scattered resin canals can be seen, chiefly in the summer wood, but these are quite different from the pores found in the wood of the broad-leaved trees. The diffuse-porous woods, such as the willows, maples, and cherries, have small pores scattered through the whole season's growth and the rings are not very distinctly marked. The third group is the ring-porous, to which the oaks, ashes, and elms belong. In these woods there are large pores in the early spring wood and small ones, or none at

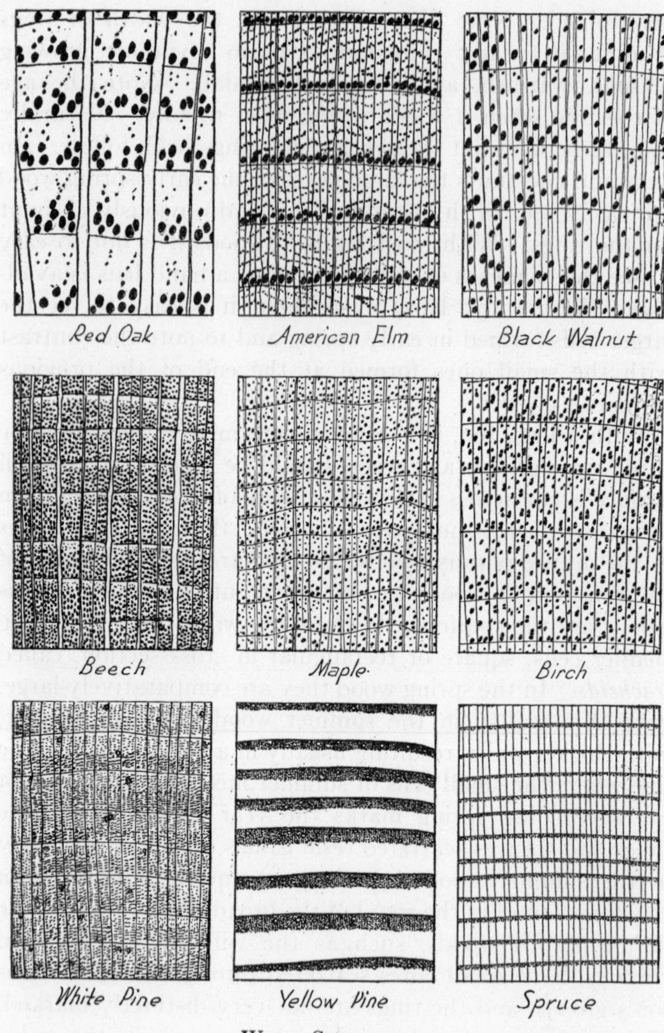

WOOD STRUCTURE

The upper sections are ring-porous; the middle ones, diffuse-porous; and the lower ones, non-porous. All are cross sections about twice natural size.

all, in the summer wood. Medullary rays run across the rings of growth from the pith to the bark. These are large enough to be seen easily in the oaks, may be seen with a lens in the maples, and are difficult to see even with a lens in the poplars. By these characteristics and such obvious ones as color and odor the kinds of wood may be recognized. The key in the Appendix on pages 434–436 will help if a further study of wood is desired.

WHITE OAK

Cut to show the grain.

A collection of wood specimens should be undertaken with care. Growing trees should be thought of as friends and be given corresponding consideration. Sometimes the camp wood pile, or piles of brush where clearings have been made, will furnish good specimens. Small twigs are of little value as the character of the wood does not show clearly. Branches or poles to furnish wood specimens should be at least two inches in diameter. If these are sawed to a uniform length of about eight inches, and cut half way down through the middle, as shown in the illustration, these specimens will show much of the character of the wood.

In winter most of our broad-leaved trees and the tamarack or larch and the bald cypress of the needle-leaved group lose their leaves. The ruggedness of the oak, the grace of the beech, the symmetry of the maple are better realized when we see them without leaves. And surely the tracery of branches seen against a snow-covered hill or silhouetted against the sky is as beautiful as the waving foliage of summer. It is as easy to learn the trees in winter by the bud and leaf scars as in summer by the leaves. The key in the Appendix on pages 431–434 will call attention to many of the details shown by the twigs.

We are often reminded of those who fail to see the forest because of the trees. In like manner we shall miss much if in studying details of leaves or buds we fail to see the tree as an individual and as a member of the society of the woods or forest. One way of learning to know the forest is to walk for a half mile or more and list all the trees within ten feet on each side of one's path. This makes an excellent project for a group of campers. Several may work at one time on a single path, and other groups may take different paths. By taking the total of all the trees counted and then finding the percentage of each species of tree, the composition of the forest is fairly well determined. At the same time notes may be made of the sizes and probable ages of the trees.

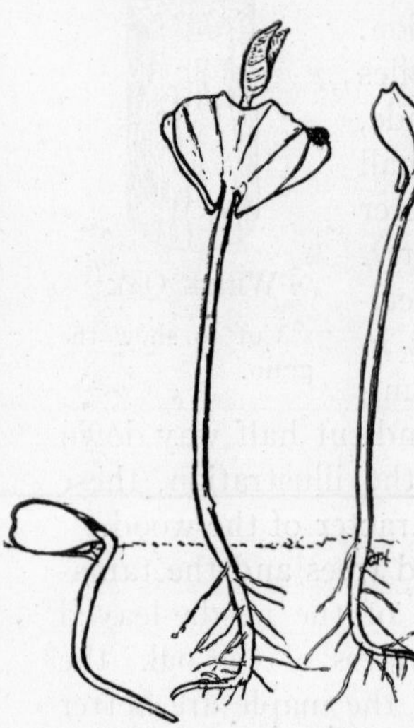

SEEDLINGS OF BEECH 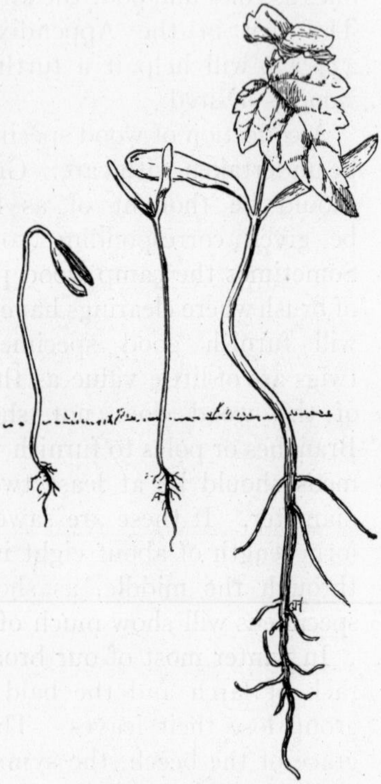 YOUNG RED MAPLE TREES

On a walk of this kind, or on another trip, look in the carpet of fallen leaves at your feet for the young trees which have sprouted from seeds. Many of them, such as young maples, oaks, and birches, resemble the mature trees in the shape of their tender leaves. Others, like the basswood, beech, and ash, have first leaves so unlike the leaves which come later that the novice will fail to recognize them unless a series of such tree seedlings of various ages can be found.

Courtesy of the Camp Fire Girls

PLANTING A PINE TREE

Some day it may shade the camp grounds.

TREE PLANTING. A practical thing to do at camp or school is to set out young trees. Nuts and acorns can also be planted where trees are wanted. Young seedlings can be found and transplanted. Take plenty of soil with them, and be sure the ground has been moistened thoroughly before taking the seedlings up and after replanting them.

For extensive planting, young trees can be purchased at a nominal sum from state forest nurseries. Young plants three or four years old that have been transplanted once or twice are more likely to grow than those taken up from a place where they have grown naturally.

Because of their beauty and suggestion of strength, their dominance in the landscape, and their age, trees appeal strongly to the emotions, and have long inspired poets. Some of the nature poems should be familiar to all. With hundreds to choose from we might mention Joyce Kilmer's "Trees"; Bryant's "A Forest Hymn"; Henry van Dyke's "Salute to the Trees"; Henry Abbey's "What Do We Plant?"; and the following poem by Bliss Carman:

TREES [1]

In the Garden of Eden, planted by God,
There were goodly trees in the springing sod,

Trees of beauty and height and grace,
To stand in splendor before His face.

Apple and hickory, ash and pear,
Oak and beech and the tulip rare,

The trembling aspen, the noble pine,
The sweeping elm by the river line;

Trees for the birds to build and sing,
And the lilac tree for a joy in spring;

Trees to turn at the frosty call
And carpet the earth for the Lord's footfall;

Trees for fruitage and fire and shade,
Trees for the cunning builder's trade;

Wood for the bow, the spear, and the flail,
The keel and the mast of the daring sail;

[1] From *Later Poems* by Bliss Carman. Copyright by Dodd, Mead and Company, Inc.

He made them of every grain and girth,
For the uses of man in the Garden of Earth.
Then lest the soul should not lift her eyes
From the gift to the Giver of Paradise,

On the crown of a hill, for all to see,
God planted a scarlet maple tree.

BIBLIOGRAPHY

BERRY, J. W., *Western Forest Trees*. World Book Company, 1924.
Accurate and concise descriptions, with outline drawings.

BLAKESLEE and JARVIS, *Trees in Winter*. The Macmillan Company, 1926.
Excellent descriptions of all the trees of the East, with full-page plates and complete keys.

BROWN, H. P., *Trees of New York*. New York State College of Forestry, 1922.
Illustrates and describes every native tree of the state, with both summer and winter keys.

CHENEY, E. G., *What Tree Is That?* D. Appleton and Company, 1930.
A small book with outline drawings of leaves for determining eastern trees.

COKER, WILLIAM C., and TOTTEN, HENRY R., *Trees of the Southeastern States*. University of North Carolina Press, 1934.
Descriptions with illustrations of the trees found from Virginia to northern Florida. Complete keys.

COLLINS, J. F., and PRESTON, H. W., *Key to Trees*. Henry Holt and Company, 1912.
A most convenient book for finding the names of native or commonly cultivated trees of the East, with illustrations throughout the book.

HARKIN, L. L., *Wild Flowers of the Pacific Coast*. Metropolitan Press, 1934.
A valuable handbook for Western flowers and shrubs.

HOUGH, ROMEYNE B., *Handbook of the Trees of the Eastern United States*. R. B. Hough, Lowville, N. Y., 1907.
A beautiful and comprehensive book. In addition to the descriptions of the trees, the structure of the wood of each is given with photographs of microscopic sections.

ILLICK, JOSEPH H., *Tree Habits, How to Know the Hardwoods.* American Nature Association, 1924.

Interesting descriptions of native and cultivated trees, with tabular comparisons of the trees in each genus.

—— *Trees of Pennsylvania.* Times Tribune Company, Altoona, Pa., 1925.

A small handbook of the trees of the state.

KEELER, HARRIET L., *Our Native Trees and How to Identify Them.* Charles Scribner's Sons, 1900.

An attractive book with descriptions and illustrations of most of the Eastern trees. Written in a popular style.

—— *Our Northern Shrubs and How to Identify Them.* Charles Scribner's Sons, 1903.

A companion book to *Our Native Trees.*

LONGYEAR, BURTON O., *Trees and Shrubs of the Rocky Mountain Region.* G. P. Putnam's Sons, 1927.

It is enough to say that this is one of the Putnam nature series. Of great value to the naturalists of the region.

MCFARLAND, J. HORACE, *Getting Acquainted with the Trees.* The Macmillan Company, 1924.

A series of informal but informative talks on different groups of trees with methods of distinguishing the species but without full descriptions and with no keys.

MCMINN, H. E., and MAINO, E., *Illustrated Manual of Pacific Coast Trees.* University of California Press, 1936.

An excellent manual, giving both native and commonly cultivated trees, with complete keys.

MATTHEWS, F. SCHUYLER, *Field Book of American Trees and Shrubs.* G. P. Putnam's Sons, 1915.

A convenient and attractive book. The inclusion of the shrubs makes it especially valuable.

SAUNDERS, CHARLES FRANCIS, *Trees and Shrubs of California Gardens.* Robert M. McBride Company, 1926.

Descriptions and stories of the trees and shrubs to be found in gardens and along the streets of California.

SCHAFFNER, JOHN H., *Field Manual of Trees* (4th edition). R. G. Adams and Company, 1936.

A pocket-size book with keys for winter and summer use. Describes all the native and commonly cultivated trees of the northeastern states.

CHAPTER XIII

FLOWERING PLANTS

With pillow of grass,
On Musashino Prairie,
Lying still, I see
Only a little wild pink,
But . . . it overtops Fuji.[1]

— Translated from the Japanese
by SEYMOUR G. LINK

From the trumpets of the morning-glory and honeysuckle to the tiny florets of the bluets and forget-me-not, beauty in form and color is so bounteously expressed in flowers that our interest in them is spontaneous.

You take in your hand a simple flower of good size, such as the wild rose, flowering raspberry, or buttercup. Each part seen is a physical tool for subtle uses, your knowledge of which will open the door to a deeper appreciation of the wonders of plant life.

Flowers are far from being standardized, and modifications in number, arrangement, and relations of floral parts should be expected. The special means of bud protection, of attracting special insects, of keeping out undesirables such as ants, of securing cross-pollination and preventing self-pollination are among the things to be noted. Even if one does not know all of the flowers found on a trip — and that is to be expected — these adaptations can be studied and the growing plants watched for insect visitors.

[1] Reprinted by permission of the author and *The Golden Book Magazine.*

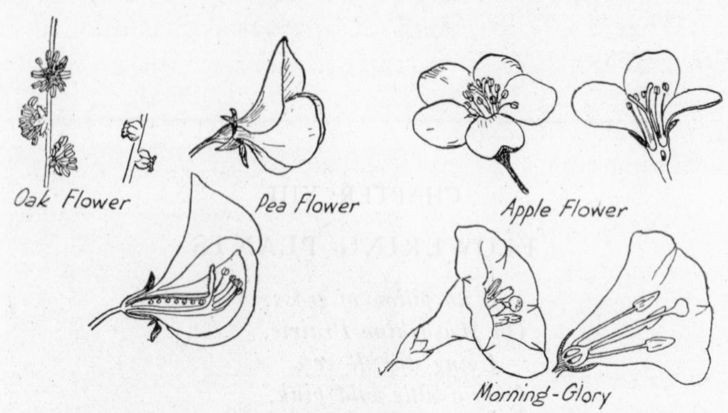

TYPES OF FLOWERS

The oak flowers have no petals, and stamens and pistils are in different flowers. The pea blossom is perfect and irregular, the apple perfect and regular, and the morning-glory perfect with the petals united.

Courtesy of Oliver P. Medsger

RHODODENDRON

The yellowish-green blotch on the upper lobe serves as a nectar guide for the bees. All parts of the flower show clearly.

"What is it?" is the first question asked regarding anything seen. Often the giving of a name satisfies the inquirer who feels that now he knows it. Generally it is best to withhold the name until some things about the plant are discovered. "He that names it shall never find it, he that finds it needs no name," said Sir Mortimer in van Dyke's *The Blue Flower*. The arrangement of the flowers on the plant, the order of opening of the individual blossoms, the maturity of stamens and pistils, are all things of more than passing interest. Even the commonest flower when observed closely reveals uncommon beauty.

Courtesy of Oliver P. Medsger

BUTTER AND EGGS

Stamens and pistils are hidden till a bee opens the flower to hunt for nectar.

For instance, let us examine one of the milkweeds. The milky sap which oozes when the stem is broken contains rubber of a fair quality, though of no commercial value at present. As with most flowers, the sepals cover the petals in the bud, but you will have to search carefully to find the sepals when the flower is opened, as they are concealed by the petals. Inside the reflexed petals note the erect ring of curious organs with the curving horn in each. Note the arrangement of the stamens close against the pistil. Slip a pin point between the stamens and pull out the tiny dark gland with the two pollen masses hanging from it. Watch to see if a bee, when she visits milkweed, will pull out these pollen masses. When she goes to another milkweed flower does she leave pollen masses on the stigma? Can you find any flower where a small bee has caught a claw in the gland of the pollen masses and been held prisoner? Find the plants with the pods beginning to develop. Compare the position of the young pods with older ones. Can you imagine the reason for the change in position? Possibly the problem must remain unsolved until you can find the ripened pods in the fall. Plan to get some of these ripened fruits. Besides the interest in the aërial scattering, the silky-haired seeds make beautiful backgrounds for insects in Riker mounts, or mounted in picture frames, and can be used for decorative effects in many other ways. Examine the plants for the black and green caterpillars or the beautiful jeweled pupa of the monarch butterfly.

Photograph by C. W. Johnson

MILKWEED IN BLOSSOM

Almost any plant will repay the same sort of careful observation and there is the possibility of making real discoveries regarding even the commonest of flowers. Jewelweed, from the time the first tiny bud with the curved spur shows until the fruit waits for some jar to snap it open throwing the seeds in all directions, presents many puzzles to be solved. The coöperation among the florets in the daisy, aster, or other composites; the different lengths of

Courtesy of Oliver P. Medsger

BLUETS OR QUAKER-LADIES

Dainty pale blue flowers. Some have long stamens and short pistils, others have short stamens and long pistils.

stamens and pistils in flowers of purple loosestrife or the pickerel weed; the dots on the petals and the arrangement of the stamens in the St.-John's-wort; and hundreds of other details of flower structure give opportunity for close observation and for the discovery of reasons for these variations. Notes and drawings will be valuable in making a record of these observations.

While nearly all the flowering plants of the fields and woods are green, there are exceptions, such as Indian pipe, pine sap, beech drops, coral root, and so on. "Are they kinds of fungi?" is often asked. No, they are flowering plants that get food by absorbing it from dead plants or by stealing it from living plants, since they have lost their

Photograph by G. T. Hastings

INDIAN PIPE

Waxy, white plants with scale-like leaves, sometimes called corpse plant. At the side is the rattlesnake fern.

green color and the power of making their own food. In a way they are degenerates, but of special interest not only because of their peculiar appearance but because of their adaptations to their mode of life.

Then there are the unusual plants that have adopted an

insect diet. In the neighborhood of sphagnum or cranberry bogs, pitcher plants and sundew can usually be found, and in slow streams or lakes the bladderworts. These are peculiar because so unlike other plants. The discovery of any of these may be made the occasion of reviewing or emphasizing the usual methods of food-making in plants and the importance of the process to man.

Courtesy of Oliver P. Medsger

FLOWER HEADS OF TIMOTHY

Grasses form a large family, widespread and very important to man.

To come back to the question of names, it *is* important to know by name as many of the flowers as possible, even though it is not the most important thing to know. Pictorial keys or any of the recent, well illustrated books that classify flowers according to color and season, make it possible for one with no botanical training to find the names of the more conspicuous flowers. But for careful determination nothing can take the place of a standard manual and a knowledge of a score or two of technical terms. It will facilitate identification and increase interest if the families to which plants belong can be recognized. Flowers are grouped according to structure, all those in one family being not only generally alike but closely related by descent from common ancestors. There are so many families of plants that a key to them such as is to be found in manuals is out of place here, but in the Appendix on pages 424–426 will be found a list of a dozen of the larger families which include two-thirds of all the flowering plants of most regions.

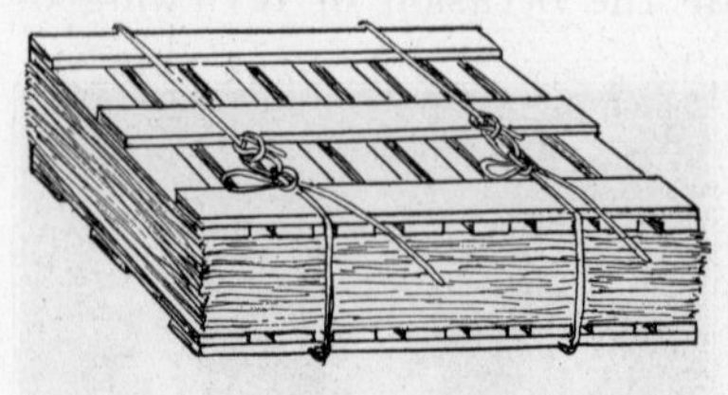

A Convenient Plant Press

Making a Collection. Flowers may be collected, pressed, and mounted. Here again the idea of conservation must be kept in mind. We must not love these beautiful things "to death," like the small child with a baby chicken. Roots should not be taken, except of weeds. The rarer or more unusual plants should not be gathered at all. A list of flowers that should not be gathered and a list of those that may be are given at the end of the chapter.

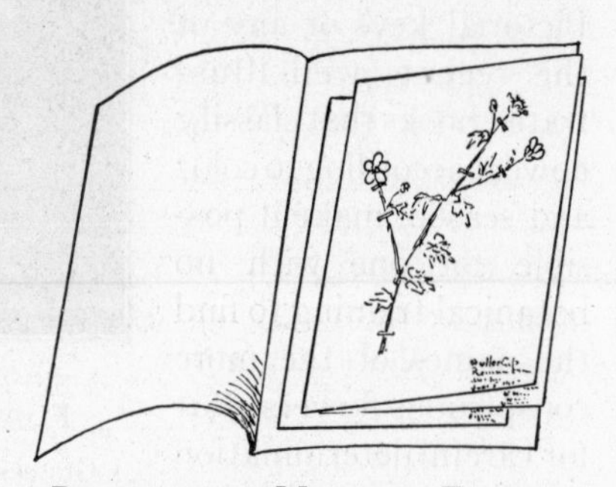

Pressed and Mounted Flower

In collecting, plants should either be put into a metal box such as a botanical collecting can or vasculum, or put directly into a press. A simple press for use in the field can be made of thin boards, heavy cardboard, or, better, of thin slat frames about 10 by 12 inches. Strips an inch wide cut from the sides of egg or orange crates do very well. Four to eight thicknesses of newspaper, folded to fit the press, make a drier. Single folds of paper will hold the plants between the driers, and the whole can be fastened with heavy cord or straps. Flowers for specimens should be carefully placed in the folders as soon after collecting as possible. Back at camp the press may be placed under a heavy weight. Fresh driers should be placed between the folders every day till the plants are dry, but the plants themselves should not be disturbed.

HEPATICA

One of the first flowers of spring. Easily transplanted to the garden.

When dry, the plants should be mounted on Bristol board or stiff white mounting paper secured from a biological supply company, a wholesale paper company, or a local printer. Cover or index paper is the kind to ask for. The best method of mounting is to glue the specimen directly to the paper. First spread a thin layer of liquid glue on a sheet of glass, diluting the glue with a little vinegar or water. Then lay the plant on the glass, lift it, and place it on the mounting paper in the position that gives the best effect. Lightly press it in place with a piece of newspaper. If glue oozes out from below the leaves it shows that too much was used on the glass. The excess in this case should be carefully wiped off the paper with a damp cloth. Each sheet should then be covered with a few thicknesses of newspaper, and the sheets piled one on top of another, and left under a weight for a day till the glue has dried.

Specimens may also be mounted with narrow strips of gummed paper for which labels cut into strips will do well.

After mounting, the name, locality where found, the date, and any other item that seems of interest should be written in the lower right-hand corner of each sheet.

PINK LADY'S-SLIPPER

Enjoy their beauty in the woods but leave them there.

Instead of collecting the flowers, drawings and notes may be made in the field, or outline drawings such as those of the Slingerland-Comstock series may be colored with crayon. A notebook of flower drawings, or the colored outlines with full notes, will be of more value to most boys and girls than the pressed flowers.

GARDENS. The camp or a school may increase interest in flowers by making a wild-flower garden. A place should be chosen generally similar to that from which the plants are to be taken. Plants growing in the woods usually will not grow well if put in unshaded places. The worst time to transplant is during the flowering time, but it can often be done satisfactorily if the ground is moist when the plant is taken up so that soil will adhere to the roots and protect the delicate root hairs from drying. Disturb the soil about the roots as little as possible and be sure the ground in which they are replanted is also moist. Following a rain is a good time to transplant, but if that is not convenient the ground around the plant may be soaked before digging. After plants are set out, labels should be placed beside them so that the name can be easily seen.

The camp museum may have on the wall pictures of flowers that are in blossom at the time, changing them as new flowers open and old ones fade. The separate plates from the *Wild Flowers of New York State* (see Bibliography) are among the best for this purpose.

Photograph by Martin Brown

MOUNTAIN LAUREL

The projections on the buds form pockets which hold the anthers. Pick this in moderation, if at all.

Following are lists of plants which should not be picked and of some which may be. These lists are adapted from those published by the Garden Club of America. In general no flowers should be picked where the entire plant above ground is taken with the flower, as in the trilliums and jack-in-the pulpit. Plants common in one region may be rare in another, and when rare, flowers should never be picked. Plants close to roads or paths should be left for others to enjoy, and of course plants legally protected should not be gathered. In this connection a committee might well ascertain wild flowers protected by state laws and post the list.

WILD FLOWERS OR PLANTS WHICH SHOULD NOT BE PICKED

Adder's-mouth
Arbutus [1]
Arethusa
Azalea
Bloodroot
Bluebells
Bunchberry
Calopogon
Cardinal flower
Columbine
Dogwood [1]
Fringed gentian [1]
Fringed orchis
Ground pine
Indian pipe
Jack-in-the-pulpit
Lady's-slipper [1]
Magnolia
May apple
Meadow lily
Partridge berry
Pipsissewa
Pitcher plant
Rattlesnake plantain
Sea lavender
Shinleaf
Spotted wintergreen
Trillium
Turk's-cap lily
Winterberry (Black alder)
Wood lily

WILD FLOWERS OR PLANTS WHICH MAY BE PICKED IN MODERATION

Anemone
Arrowhead
Bittersweet
Black haw
Blue flag (Iris)
Bluets
Bottle gentian
Butterfly weed
Buttonbush
Crane's-bill (Wild geranium)
Dog-toothed violet (Trout lily)
Dutchman's-breeches
False Solomon's seal
Flax

[1] Protected by New York State.

Foxglove
Fringed polygala
Galax
Hair bells
Hepatica
Loosestrife
Marsh marigold
Milkwort
Mountain laurel [1]
New Jersey tea
Rhododendron
Rose mallow
Saxifrage
Shadbush
Skullcap
Solomon's seal
Spring beauty
Star of Bethlehem
Swamp milkweed
Tansy
Trumpet creeper
Turtlehead
Water lilies
White azalea
White snakeroot
Wild bean
Wild calla

WILD FLOWERS OR PLANTS WHICH MAY BE PICKED MORE OR LESS FREELY

Agrimony
Asters
Bedstraws
Bee balm
Black-eyed Susan
Blazing star
Blueberries
Blue-eyed grass
Boneset (Thoroughwort)
Bouncing Bet
Bush clover
Bush honeysuckle
Butter and eggs
Buttercups
Cat-tails
Celandine
Chicory
Cinquefoil
Clovers
Coneflower
Daisy
Daisy fleabane
Devil's-bit
Dogbane
Elecampane
Evening primrose
Everlasting
Fireweed
Goldenrod
Hawkweeds
Heal-all
Henbit
Joe-Pye weed
Knotweed
Lousewort
Meadow beauty
Meadow rue
Meadowsweet

[1] Protected by New York State.

Milkweeds
Mints
Morning-glory
Mullein
Mustard
Partridge pea
Pickerel weed
Pokeweed
Purple gerardia
Queen Anne's lace
Robin's plantain
Sheep laurel
Silver-rod
Skullcap
Sneezeweed
Spikenard
Spurge
Star grass
Steeplebush
Stitchwort
St.-John's-wort
Stonecrop
Sunflower
Thistles
Trefoil
Vervain
Vetch
Viper's bugloss
Wild caraway
Wild cherries
Wild lettuce
Wild lily of the valley
Wild parsnip
Wild roses
Yarrow
Yellow rocket
Yellow wood oxalis

BIBLIOGRAPHY

Armstrong, Margaret, and Thornber, J. J., *Field Book of Western Wild Flowers.* G. P. Putnam's Sons, 1915.

A popular field book, well illustrated, with keys to genera. Describes a large number of the common and more showy plants.

Britton, N. L., and Brown, Addison, *Illustrated Flora of the Northern United States and Canada.* Charles Scribner's Sons, 1913.

A three-volume work with drawings and descriptions of 4,666 species of flowering plants and ferns. A standard reference text for serious-minded botany students.

Clements, Edith G., *Flowers of Coast and Sierra.* H. W. Wilson Company, 1928.

Beautiful plates which appeared first in the National Geographic Magazine, together with written descriptions.

Clements, Frederic E. and Edith G., *Rocky Mountain Flowers.* H. W. Wilson Company, 1928.

Illustrated guide to the flowers of this region.

GRAY, ASA, *Manual of Botany*, 7th edition. American Book Company, 1908.
A standard manual with illustrations of species in some of the more troublesome genera.

HARKIN, L. L., *Wild Flowers of the Pacific Coast.* Metropolitan Press, 1934.
A valuable handbook for Western flowers and shrubs.

HOUSE, H. D., *Wild Flowers of New York State.* New York State Museum, 1918. Two volumes.
Two large volumes with beautiful color plates. Sets of the plates may be purchased unbound.

JEPSON, WILLIS L., *Manual of the Flowering Plants of California.* University of California, 1925.
A standard work on the plants of California.

KEELER, HARRIET L., *Wayside Flowers of Summer.* Charles Scribner's Sons, 1917.
A pocket-sized book describing a few of the more common flowers. These are arranged systematically, but they are without keys.

LOUNSBERRY, ALICE, *Southern Wild Flowers.* Frederick A. Stokes Company, 1901.
An attractive, popular manual with keys to the orders but none to genera or species. Grasses, sedges, and some of the less noticeable plants are omitted. Beautifully illustrated.

MATTHEWS, F. SCHUYLER, *Field Book of American Wild Flowers.* G. P. Putnam's Sons, 1912.
A convenient volume describing most of the common wild flowers of the East. Well illustrated.

MUNZ, PHILIP A., *Manual of Southern California Botany.* J. W. Stacey, Inc., 1935.
For students of botany who wish to know the plants of the southern part of California, this book is more convenient than one covering the whole state.

PARSONS, MRS. F. T. D., (Mrs. Wm. Starr Dana), *How to Know the Wild Flowers.* Charles Scribner's Sons, 1900.
One of the first "how-to-know" books, still as useful as ever.

PARSONS, M. E., *Wild Flowers of California.* Cunningham, Curtis, and Welsh, 1897.
A popular book with a key to the more common or showy plants. The key unfortunately contains no page references. Flowers arranged by colors.

Reed, Chester, *Flower Guide; Wild Flowers East of The Rockies.* Doubleday, Doran and Company, Inc., 1922.

The book will enable the beginner to recognize many common wild flowers by their pictures but the illustrations are in many cases poorly colored.

—— *Flower Guide; Wild Flowers West of the Rockies.* Doubleday, Doran and Company, Inc.

A Western counterpart of the preceding.

Rydberg, P. A., *Flora of the Prairies and Plains.* New York Botanical Garden, 1932.

Covers the region from North Dakota and Minnesota south through Kansas and northern Missouri.

Saunders, C. F., *Western Wild Flowers and Their Stories.* Doubleday, Doran and Company, Inc., 1933.

A thorough treatise of the flowers of the Pacific States.

—— *The Western Flower Guide.* Doubleday, Doran and Company, Inc., 1917.

An ideal handbook of Western flowers, with colored plates.

Small, John K., *Manual of the Southeastern Flora.* The Science Press, 1933.

A standard work for the plants of the region.

Key to the Wild Flowers. Slingerland-Comstock Company, 1927.

Small outline drawings of some 200 common flowers, with a list giving the season, height, and color of each plant illustrated.

CHAPTER XIV

PLANTS WITHOUT SEEDS

FERN SONG

Dance to the beat of the rain, little fern,
And spread out your palms again,
And say, "Though the sun
Hath my venture spun
He hath labored, alas, in vain,
But for the shade
That the cloud hath made,
And the gift of the Dew and the Rain."
Then laugh and upturn
All your fronds, little fern,
And rejoice in the beat of the rain.[1]

— JOHN B. TABB

Many plants never have flowers and consequently produce no seeds. These plants are the ferns, mosses, fungi, algae, and bacteria. Of these the ferns are the largest and most easily studied.

FERNS. In size ferns range from less than an inch in height to the tree ferns of the tropics. In temperate regions they are of moderate size, rarely as much as six feet tall. They are commonly found in moist shaded places, though a few grow on rock ledges that may be dry in summer; some grow in swamps, and a few in water. Because we usually think of a fern as a plant with finely divided leaves, sometimes called fronds, several other plants having similar leaves are commonly mistaken for ferns, especially the

[1] From "Fern Song" by John B. Tabb. Published by Dodd, Mead and Company.

yarrow, wood betony, and asparagus "fern." The shrubby "sweet fern," common in sterile soil throughout the eastern states, is a relative of the bayberry, but not even distantly related to the ferns. On the other hand, some true ferns have simple undivided leaves, as the walking fern which takes root at the tip and the rare heart's tongue.

Photograph by G. T. Hastings

COMMON WOOD FERN

This shield fern has the lacy appearance usually connected with ferns. Great numbers are used by florists.

SPORES. The chief characteristic of ferns is the possession of fruit dots made up of peculiar spore cases (*sporangia*). In the grape ferns the spore cases are on stems separate from the leaf or growing from it; in the cinnamon, sensitive, and ostrich ferns special leaves are changed to produce sporangia; in the royal and interrupted ferns certain regions of the ordinary leaves are modified to masses of sporangia. In other ferns the fruit dots are on the underside of the green leaves. It is by the shape and position of these fruit dots and the presence or absence of a cover or indusium that the ferns are classified.

Photograph by G. T. Hastings

FIDDLE HEADS

Uncoiling leaves of the cinnamon fern are found in early spring in swamps.

The life history of ferns shows clearly the alternation of two generations. The spores from the fern leaf grow not into fern plants but into tiny heart-shaped, flat *prothallia*, rarely over a quarter of an inch across. On the lower side of these are produced the sperm and egg cases. The egg when fertilized by a sperm grows to form the fern plant.

In few places can more than thirty species of ferns be found, more often not over twenty, so that it is possible in one season to become familiar with all the ferns in the region and to make a complete collection.

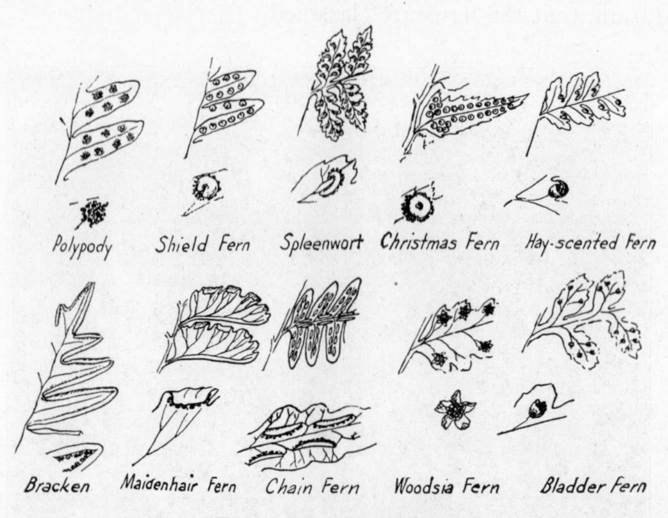

Fruit Dots of Ferns

For each species the upper figure is approximately natural size and the lower enlarged as it would appear under a pocket lens.

Collecting Ferns. In collecting ferns the fronds — or leaves — with fruit dots are desirable. But if the fern has fertile and sterile leaves, both should be collected. Fruit dots are not usually mature till midsummer, so ferns are best collected after July. The three *Osmundas* — the royal, interrupted, and cinnamon — and the grape ferns or *Botrychiums* produce their spores earlier in the season. In fact, the Osmundas have shed all their spores before camping seasons open and perfect specimens cannot be secured in the summer. The Botrychiums, because they have but a single leaf, should not be collected at all. Most ferns produce a number of leaves from the underground stems every season (all of our ferns are perennials), so that a few leaves taken in midsummer will not injure the plants so long as the roots and root stalk are not injured. With the adder's-tongue and grape ferns, however, there is but one stem sent up, which divides into fertile and sterile parts. Collecting these is likely to destroy the plant, so they should not be gathered unless a number of specimens are found close together. Any fern which is rare in a region should be carefully protected. For example, in the Bear Mountain section of the Palisades Inter-State Park, New York State, the walking fern has been found on only one boulder, with no other ferns of the kind within many miles. This one little colony is being carefully guarded. Of the smaller ferns photographic prints and blue prints give beautiful results, but with the larger forms it is impracticable to use more than a portion of the leaf. Other kinds of prints are difficult to make because of the delicacy of most ferns. Fern leaves are easily pressed, dry quickly, and make attractive mounts.

Photograph by G. T. Hastings

COMMON HORSETAIL

These yellow or brownish stalks with their spore-bearing cones will soon be replaced by green plants like tiny pine trees.

FERN ALLIES. With the ferns are grouped several kinds of plants that are very different in appearance but are like ferns in producing spores and in having bundles of conducting tubes in the stems. The most commonly seen of these fern allies are the horsetails, plants with ribbed green stems, leaves reduced to circles of tiny points at the joints, and the spore cases on small hexagonal scales that form cones at the ends of some stems. Another group of the fern allies are the club mosses — ground pine and trailing Christmas greens — with small green leaves thickly covering the stems. The spore cases are on the upper side of some of the leaves, which may be either ordinary ones on the sides of the stem, or special ones forming a cone at the ends. Most unfern-like of all are quillworts, looking like grass tufts in water or marshy places; the base of each leaf is hollowed out to contain the spore cases.

Photograph by G. T. Hastings

CLUB MOSSES

The tree-like club moss is at the left, the shining club moss at the right.

MOSSES. The next group of spore-bearing plants comprises the mosses and liverworts. Mosses are usually small and the distinguishing characteristics require a lens. It is worth while to know the thirty-five common species in the simple key of the Slingerland-Comstock Company. A few types are easy to recognize: the cushion mosses growing in rather firm, rounded, cushion-like masses, and the delicate branching fern mosses on moist soil, stones, or rotting logs. Somewhat similar but less finely branching are the *Hypnums*

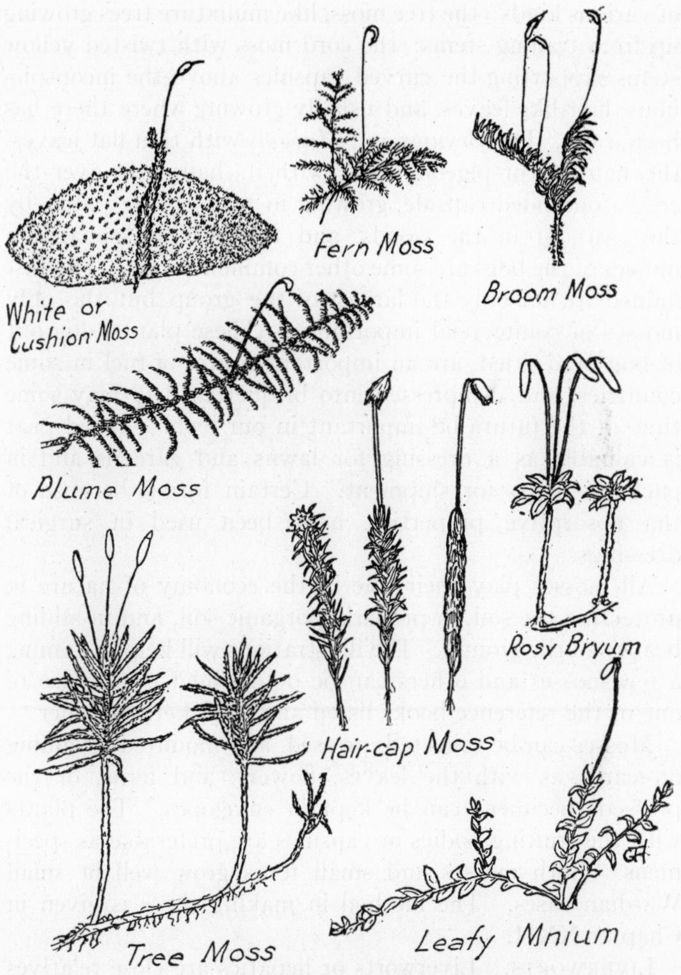

Drawn from "Mosses With a Hand Lens" by A. J. Grout

TYPES OF MOSSES

The white moss forms compact masses several inches in diameter. The individual plants are slender with the capsule stalks at the top. In the other mosses shown the individual plants are not so closely massed together.

of various kinds: the tree moss, like miniature trees growing up from trailing stems; the cord moss with twisted yellow stems supporting the curved capsules above the inconspicuous, hair-like leaves, and usually growing where there has been a fire. The *Bryums* and *Mniums* with thin flat leaves, the hair-cap or pigeon wheat with its hairy cap over the erect, four-sided capsule, growing in fields, along paths, by the road, or in the woods, and the peat or sphagnum mosses of the bogs are some other common forms. The last named are not only the largest of the group but the only mosses of commercial importance. These plants, dug out of bogs and dried, are an important source of fuel in some countries, and compressed into briquettes they may some time in the future be important in our own. Dried peat is valuable as a dressing for lawns and gardens and in packing plants for shipment. Certain forms, because of the absorptive properties, have been used in surgical dressings.

All mosses play their rôle in the economy of nature in protecting the soil, in preparing organic soil, and in adding beauty to the ground. The illustrations will help in naming a few mosses and others can be determined by the use of one of the reference books listed and a pocket magnifier.

Mosses can be collected, pressed, and mounted by gluing on cards as with the leaves, flowers, and ferns, or the pressed specimens can be kept in envelopes. The plants with the fruiting bodies or capsules are preferable as specimens. Both mosses and small ferns grow well in small Wardian cases. The method in making these is given in Chapter XXII.

LIVERWORTS. Liverworts or hepatics are close relatives of the mosses, but are simpler in structure. Those most commonly seen are not divided into stem and leaves but are flattened green bodies from one-eighth to one-half an inch wide and usually over an inch long, forking and notched at the tip. The leafy liverworts are flattened, with the leaves on opposite sides of the stem. Liverworts often look like lichens, but are greener. One of the commonest of the liverworts is *Marchantia*, with its reproductive bodies on stalks resembling tiny parasols.

Photograph by G. T. Hastings

MARCHANTIA

Often found where there has been a fire in the woods, sometimes on damp rocks.

FUNGI. The fungi that we see in the woods are the bracket forms growing on tree trunks or stumps, and the great variety of mushrooms (popularly called toadstools). "Is it poisonous?" is usually the first question asked about a mushroom. None is poisonous to the touch and only a few are poisonous internally. Yet some, especially the *Amanitas*, are deadly poison. As to the use of fungi for food, the only safe rule is to use only those one knows with certainty. *Do not consider this chapter sufficiently detailed to be your guide!* For general interest it is desirable to be able to recognize a few of the more common forms and to know at least a little about them.

The fungi all produce spores. These are usually on the sides of thin gills that radiate from the stem on the under side, or are found lining small tubes on the under side, but in the puffballs and cup fungi of various kinds they are formed on the inside or over the inner surface. To aid in knowing the fungi the characteristics of about twenty of the most common are given, but there are hundreds of others.

On Trees and Logs (Woody). Some woody fungi found growing on trees and logs are the following:

Shelf Fungus. This is common on either living or dead trees, increasing in size each year, and becoming very large. It is dark brown above, lighter near the edges, and white below. Pictures are often drawn on the lower surface of this fungus with a sharp-pointed instrument; the fungus dries and hardens and the pictures become permanent.

Labyrinth Fungus. This grows chiefly on oak logs and stumps. It is often as thick as it is wide, light gray or brown above, and white below, with an irregular labyrinth of narrow pores.

Versicolored Fungus. The group of thin shelves found commonly on dead wood is the versicolored fungus. The upper surface is velvety with bands of different shades of brown and gray; the lower surface is covered with minute pores.

Stereum Fungus. Much like the preceding is the stereum fungus, but the lower surface is without pores.

Varnished Hemlock Fungus. This is a shining reddish fungus. It is found on hemlock logs and stumps and has a distinct stalk from one side. It is leathery rather than woody.

On Trees and Logs (Fleshy). Some other fungi found on trees and logs are fleshy. Among these are the following:

Beefsteak Mushroom. This is found on dead hardwoods. It consists of stalked red shelves with pores below which are yellowish or reddish. It is edible but has a sour taste.

Sulphur Mushroom. This often grows in large masses of fluted or folded shelves. It is orange above and sulphur yellow below with fine pores. This mushroom is edible.

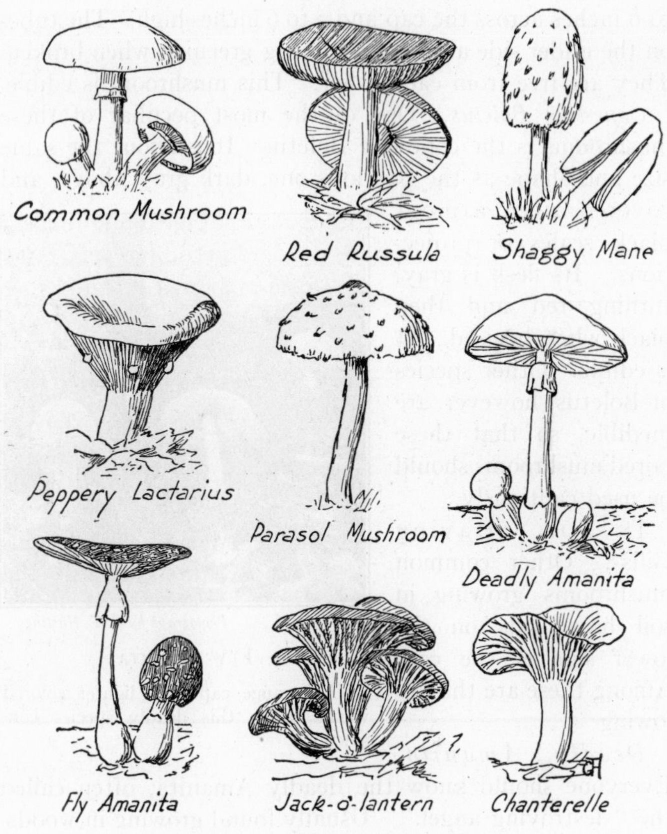

COMMON GILLED MUSHROOMS

Oyster Mushroom. Rather smaller than the sulphur mushroom is the oyster mushroom. Its white shelves have gills on the lower side. It, too, is edible.

IN SOIL (Having Pores). More abundant than the forms that grow on wood are those that grow in soil. Some are mushroom-shaped with pores on the lower side of the cap.

Edible Boletus. This is gray, reddish, or brownish gray, 4 to 6 inches across the cap and 2 to 6 inches high. The tubes on the under side are white, turning greenish when broken. They are free from each other. This mushroom is edible.

Cone-like Boletus. One of the most peculiar of these mushrooms is the cone-like Boletus. It is about the same size and shape as the previous one, dark gray above, and covered with almost black scales or projections. Its flesh is gray, turning red and then black when bruised. It is edible. Other species of Boletus, however, are inedible, so that these pored mushrooms should be used cautiously.

Photograph by G. T. Hastings

FLY AMANITA

The orange cap with lighter colored warts makes this deadly species conspicuous.

IN SOIL (Having Gills). Other common mushrooms growing in soil have gills on the lower side of the cap. Among these are the following:

Deadly Amanita. Everyone should know the deadly Amanita, often called the "destroying angel." Usually found growing in woods, it has a cup (death cup) at the base of the stem and a ring below the cap. It is 2 to 6 inches high, the cap 2 to 5 inches broad, and white or sometimes yellow, gray, or brown in color. It is deadly poisonous.

Amanitopsis. Quite similar to the Amanita is the Amanitopsis. It has a cup but no ring. It is from 3 to 5 inches high and 2 to 4 inches broad, white or fawn-colored or brownish and furrowed at the margin. The gills and cap are fragile. It is not poisonous.

Parasol Mushroom. This is found growing in fields or open woods. It is from 5 to 10 inches high, the cap is from 3 to 5 inches across, brownish in color or with brown scales. There is a knob in the center of the cap. The stem is bulbous at the base with a ring. It is edible.

Honey-colored Armillaria. This grows in large clusters on stumps or tree roots in open woods or clearings. The stems are from 1 to 6 inches high and the caps from 1 to 6 inches broad, pale to dark yellow in color with tiny sharp, blackish, erect scales near the center. The gills are white. This is another edible species.

Photograph by G. T. Hastings

JACK-O'-LANTERN

It makes a brilliant contrast to the dead leaves of the forest floor.

Jack-o'-lantern. Also growing in large masses is the jack-o'-lantern. Yellow or orange in color, it gets its name from the fact that it glows, or is phosphorescent, in the dark. The caps are from 3 to 6 inches across; when young they are convex with a knob in the center. The gills are forked, rather thin, and extend down the stem. It is slightly poisonous.

Lactarius. Several species of mushroom exude drops of milky juice when the firm, brittle flesh is broken. These are all called *Milky Mushrooms* and belong to a genus called *Lactarius.* They are usually funnel-shaped, at least when old, with the gills extending down the stems. The juice is usually acrid or peppery. They are edible when cooked, but are said to be indigestible.

Emetic Russula. Another peppery-tasting mushroom is

the common red one in the woods, the *Emetic Russula.* It grows singly or a few together, the stem is white and from 2 to 3 inches high. The red skin easily peels off from the white flesh of the caps. The gills are white and are rounded near the stem. It is usually considered somewhat poisonous but is edible when cooked.

Chanterelle. Found on the ground in the woods, the chanterelle has the stem yellow and solid, 1 or 2 inches high. The chrome yellow cap is convex when young but becomes depressed at the center (funnel-shaped) when old. The gills are blunt at the ends, fork freely, are far apart, and extend down the stem. It is edible.

Shaggy Mane. This grows in groups in pastures and waste ground. The stem is from 3 to 5 inches high. The cap is cylindrical or bell-shaped, white, and covered with many grayish or slightly yellowish scales. The gills are at first white, then turn pink, then black, and finally dissolve into a black liquid. It is edible when young.

Somewhat similar is another species of *Coprinus*, the *Ink Cap.* It is smaller, the cap is grayish without scales and ovate rather than cylindrical in shape. It, too, is edible.

Agaricus. One species is the meadow mushroom, commonly cultivated but also often found growing wild in pastures or lawns, singly or in groups. The stem is from 2 to 3 inches high, white, and with a ring. The cap is white and flattish. The gills are pink when young, brown when older.

In Soil (Neither Pores nor Gills). Some fungi found growing in soil have neither pores nor gills and are not shaped like toadstools.

Coral Fungi. These resemble little branching corals and are often found in woods. The common kinds are white or yellowish. All of them are edible, or at least are not poisonous.

Puffball. The common puffball grows in open woods and meadows. It is from 1 to 4 inches in diameter, white or grayish with tiny erect spines on the upper side when young. It is edible when white inside, before the mass of black spores have formed.

Giant Puffball. This puffball always excites interest. It is sometimes as much as 18 inches in diameter. When sliced, it can be fried or broiled.

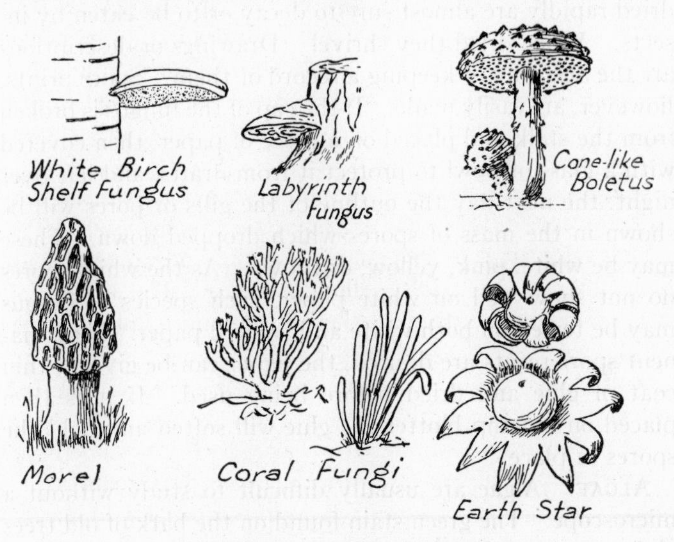

SOME FUNGI WITHOUT GILLS

Closely related to the puffballs is the *Earth Star* or *Geaster*. The hard outer skin splits into points which spread out when dry, like a star with from six to twelve points, with the small puffball in the center.

Scleroderma. Certain puffballs are hard and have an unpleasant taste so that they are not recommended as food. These are called *Scleroderma*. They are found in woods or pastures and are white or light gray with many dark gray or brown spots or a dark network. Inside they are mottled greenish or yellowish.

Morel. The morel is a slender cone on a short stalk with the surface coarsely honey-combed. It grows to be from 3 to 6 inches high and is from 1½ to 3 inches across at the base. It is highly prized for its delicate flavor.

MAKING COLLECTIONS. Collections of fungi, except the woody ones, are not satisfactory. The fleshy ones unless dried rapidly are almost sure to decay or to be eaten by insects. When dried they shrivel. Drawings or descriptions are the best way of keeping a record of them. Spore prints, however, are easily made. If the cap of the fungus is broken from the stalk and placed on a piece of paper, then covered with a glass or bowl to protect it from drafts, and left over night, the next day the outline of the gills or pores will be shown in the mass of spores which dropped down. These may be white, pink, yellow, or brown. As the white spores do not show well on white paper, each species of fungus may be tested on both white and colored paper. If permanent spore prints are desired, the paper can be given a thin coat of glue and dried before being used. If it is then placed on a damp blotter the glue will soften and hold the spores in place.

ALGAE. Algae are usually difficult to study without a microscope. The green stain found on the bark of old trees and posts, usually — though not always — on the north side, when examined under the microscope is seen to consist of myriads of individual plants of the one-celled *Pleurococcus*. Nearly all other algae live in the water. The ones commonly noticed in fresh water are bright green, such as the floating masses of tangled threads of *Spirogyra*, *Zygnema*, and other filamentous forms, or the green felt — *Vaucheria* — attached to the bottom of streams or on the edges of small cascades. Sometimes species of blue-green algae are found as dark masses on the bottom of quiet ponds, or floating as blackish or brownish-green masses or as yellowish dots. These blue-green algae may be so abundant in midsummer as to render the water murky and give it a disagreeable fishy odor. At such times the water is often said to be "working."

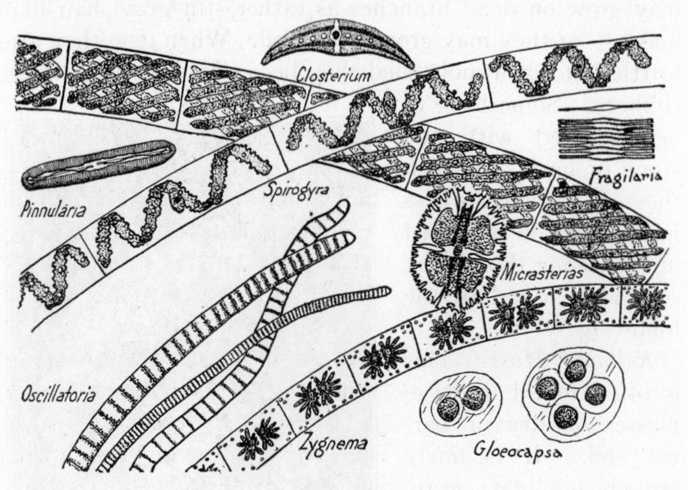

COMMON FRESH-WATER ALGAE

Fragilaria and Pinnularia are diatoms, brown in color. Gloeocapsa and Oscillatoria are blue-green algae, the others are green.

In salt water are found kelps and rockweed of the brown algae, sea lettuce and other forms of green algae, and scores of delicate fern-like and moss-like red algae. These various forms may be found on rocks or old piles exposed at low tide, floating in tide pools or washed up on the beaches. The red algae make especially attractive mounts. (See Chapter VIII for method.)

LICHENS. An intermediate group of flowerless plants is the lichens. A lichen represents a partnership between a fungus and an alga, each helping the other. The alga makes food for both, and the parasitic fungus, incapable of self-support, in turn forms reproductive bodies. Lichens may be found as black, gray, or yellow blotches on stone or wood, too firmly attached to be removed except by scraping off in bits. They may make rosettes of various colors (except a bright green) of somewhat leaf-like lobes; they may grow on dead branches as rather stiff gray, hair-like masses; or they may grow in the soil. When dry, they are brittle but when moistened they become soft or somewhat rubbery. Some have to be collected with the stone or bark on which they are growing, others may be cut off or pulled up. Among those most commonly found are the following:

Courtesy of Oliver P. Medsger

PARMELIA

One of the most abundant of lichens.

Reindeer Moss. This is often found in large masses on dry or barren soil. It is finely branched, light gray, and grows to be as much as four inches tall.

Scarlet-crested Cladonia. This sends up little gray stalks, sometimes branched at the top, with bright red knobs.

Pyxie Cup. Another species of Cladonia is the Pyxie Cup with grayish-green cups on the tops of short stalks. The cups are usually less than a quarter of an inch across and often have tiny brown dots or knobs on the margins.

Old Man's Beard. This consists of slender branching gray stems hanging from tree branches, especially in bogs. It resembles somewhat the hanging Florida moss, which is a flowering plant.

Parmelia. Several species of Parmelia grow as blue-gray or greenish-gray rosettes on the bark of trees and on stones.

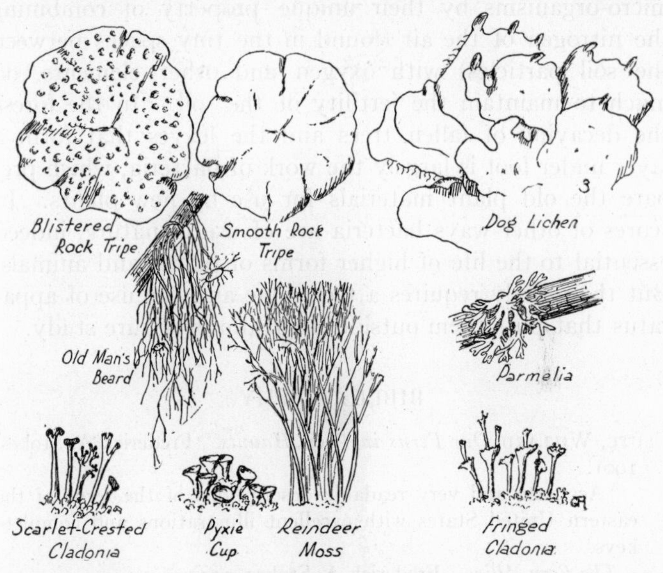

SOME COMMON LICHENS

Rock Tripe. Blackish disks fastened by their centers to rocks are Rock Tripe. This lichen is usually found at a considerable elevation. When moist it is greenish and rubbery. The Indians ground it with acorns for food. It is sometimes called a starvation food — of some value but only to be used in case of extremity.

BACTERIA. The last and simplest group of plants is the bacteria. These are all single-celled, though often grouped together in colonies. Most people think of them as the causes of disease, but besides these "bad" bacteria, against which we must be on our guard, there are great numbers of "good" bacteria. Pull up a clover plant in the field or a hog peanut in the woods and note the little nodules, the size of a pinhead or larger, on the roots. These are caused by millions of nitrogen-fixing bacteria in the roots. These micro-organisms by their unique property of combining the nitrogen of the air (found in the tiny spaces between the soil particles) with oxygen and other elements, do much to maintain the fertility of the soil. In the forest the decaying of fallen trees and the leaves that form a layer under foot is largely the work of bacteria, which prepare the old plant materials for use by new plants. In scores of other ways bacteria are of use in nature, indeed essential to the life of higher forms of plants and animals. But their study requires a technique and the use of apparatus that puts them outside the realm of nature study.

BIBLIOGRAPHY

CLUTE, WILLARD, *Our Ferns in Their Haunts.* Frederick A. Stokes, 1901.

Accurate and very readable descriptions of the ferns of the eastern United States with excellent illustrations and complete keys.

—— *The Fern Allies.* Frederick A. Stokes, 1905.

A companion to *Our Ferns,* describing the species of horsetails, club mosses, etc.

COLLINS, F. S., *The Green Algae of North America.* Tufts College, 1909.

An authoritative but technical work.

—— *Working Key to the Genera of North American Algae.* Tufts College, 1918.

A useful key to one who, with a microscope, would know the algae.

DANA, MRS. WM. T., (Mrs. F. T. D. Parsons), *How to Know the Ferns.* Charles Scribner's Sons, 1899.

A popularly written account of ferns, describing the eastern species.

DUNHAM, E. M., *How to Know the Mosses.* Houghton Mifflin Company, 1916.

A small book with keys and illustrations, helpful in learning the commoner mosses.

DURAND, H., *Field Book of Common Ferns.* G. P. Putnam's Sons, 1928.

Splendid habitat photographs, outline drawings, and concise descriptions. No key, and the rarer ferns omitted.

FINK, BRUCE, *Lichen Flora of the United States.* University of Michigan, 1935.

Describes nearly all the lichens of the United States. A valuable, rather technical book.

GROUT, A. J., *Mosses with a Hand Lens.* A. J. Grout, New Brighton, N. Y., 1924.

One of the best books to use in beginning the study of mosses. Full keys.

KRIEGER, LOUIS C. C., *The Mushroom Handbook.* The Macmillan Company, 1936.

Describes practically all the higher fungi of the northeastern states. Keys and also black and white and colored illustrations make the book a very desirable one for those wishing to know mushrooms.

MARSHALL, N. L., *Mosses and Lichens.* Doubleday, Doran and Company, Inc., 1914.

One of the large volumes of the Doubleday nature series. Well illustrated but no keys. One of the few books describing the more common lichens.

—— *The Mushroom Book.* Doubleday, Doran and Company, Inc., 1923.

One of the same series as the previous book, thoroughly illustrated.

McKENNEY, M., *Common Mushrooms of Field and Wood.* John Day Company, Inc., 1929.

A useful little book with clear descriptions of the more common mushrooms.

PRAY, LEON L., *Common Mushrooms.* Field Museum of Natural History, 1935.

An inexpensive booklet describing the commoner species of mushrooms. Illustrated from photographs.

ROBERTS, EDITH A., and LAWRENCE, JULIA RUTH, *American Ferns, How to Know, Grow, and Use Them.* The Macmillan Company, 1935.

A novel book on fern culture.

SMALL, JOHN K., *Ferns of the Vicinity of New York.* Science Press, 1935.

Full descriptions with drawings of the ferns found within 100 miles of New York City, including the fern allies.

THOMAS, E., *Field Book of Common Gilled Mushrooms.* G. P. Putnam's Sons, 1928.

A worthy member of the Field Book series. Describes and illustrates all of the common species.

TILDEN, JOSEPHINE E., *The Algae and Their Life Relations.* University of Minnesota Press, 1935.

A description of the genera and many of the species of American algae. Also gives a good deal on their structure, life histories, and uses.

TILTON, G. H., *The Fern Lover's Companion.* Little, Brown and Company, 1923.

The key is illustrated in such a way as to make it very easy to use. One of the best books for determining the species of ferns.

WILEY, FARIDA A., *Ferns.* American Museum of Natural History, 1923.

A pamphlet describing most of the common ferns, with outline drawings of each.

—— *Ferns of the Northeastern United States.* Published by the author, 1936. Address in care of American Museum of Natural History, New York City.

A book that fits the pocket easily, with concise descriptions and drawings of all the ferns found in the region covered. A convenient and useful book for those who wish to know the ferns.

WRIGHT, M., *Flowers and Ferns in Their Haunts.* The Macmillan Company, 1928.

A well-written narrative with accounts of the plants to be found in various habitats in the different seasons.

Key to Ferns. Slingerland-Comstock Company, 1927.

It should be possible to tell at least the genus of any of our ferns with this little leaflet.

CHAPTER XV

PLANTS NOBODY LOVES

You argue in your manner of a weed,
You did not make yourself grow from a seed,
You fancy you've a claim to standing room,
You dream yourself a right to breathe and bloom,

The sun loves you, you think, just as the rose,
He never scorned you for a weed, he knows!
The green-gold flies rest on you and are glad,
It's only cross old gardeners find you bad.[1]

— GERTRUDE HALL

Weeds are often neglected by nature leaders, but they deserve attention and study as much as other plants.

Weeds are sometimes defined as plants growing where they are not wanted. According to this, wheat or corn growing in a flower garden, or flowers in the meadow are weeds. Weeds are also defined as useless, unsightly plants. Yet sometimes plants generally considered as weeds are used as medicines, as salad plants, as ornaments, or for other purposes. By any definition, however, there are certain plants which are considered weeds by everyone. They are usually plants of the roadside, cultivated land, or recently tilled fields and gardens.

Most of our common weeds were introduced accidentally from abroad and have made themselves very much at home. Few of our native plants have become weeds here, though

[1] From "To a Weed" in *The Age of Fairy Gold* by Gertrude Hall. Copyright by Little, Brown and Company.

some have been taken abroad and have become serious pests in their new home, such as the cactus in Australia and the blackberry in New Zealand. The explanation for this is that in their native land a balance has been reached with insect or fungus enemies and the competition of other plants so that each kind is held in check. When introduced into new lands they are free from their natural enemies and from former competing plants and so may easily become troublesome. Most weeds have some adaptations that enable them to persist under unfavorable conditions, or to succeed better than other plants. Among these adaptations are abundant seed production — wild carrot, burdock, and sow thistle may produce over 20,000 seeds on a single plant; early ripening of seeds — dandelion, chickweed, and galinsoga begin ripening seeds before most plants begin to flower; ability to germinate under unfavorable conditions; rapid growth; strong, deep root systems — dandelion and dock send their roots down far below those of lawn grasses or cultivated crops; ability to stand drought or cold; and in some cases reproduction by runners or rhizomes.

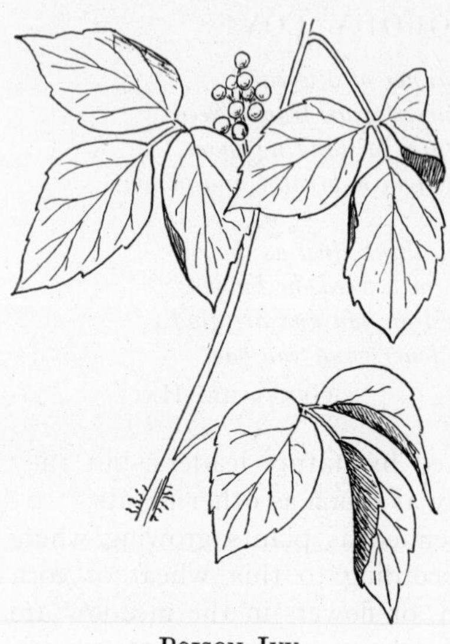

Poison Ivy

A plant everyone going into the out of doors should know. The leaf of three leaflets — the middle one with a stalk — white berries, and roots on the stem are characteristics.

Weeds belong to no definite group of plants, though

mosses and ferns furnish no weeds and, except for some grasses and the wild onion or garlic, few weeds are found among the monocotyledons. Among the families of dicotyledons many have no weeds, while in others weeds are as numerous as other forms. Among families where they are especially common are the buckwheat, goosefoot, amaranth (or pigweed), mustard, legume, parsnip, mint, and composite. Plants whose names contain the word "weed" are not always to be classed as weeds. Such are the pond-weeds, pickerel weed, jewelweed, and joe-pye weed. To the gardener, the only reason for studying weeds is in order to know how best to destroy them; the naturalist finds them interesting because of the adaptations that make them weeds; but the boy or girl who has spent hours that seemed meant for sport in weeding a garden will not easily find anything attractive in them.

In attempting to list and characterize a few of the more common weeds we shall omit some of the common roadside plants that are often found in old fields or pastures but which are not troublesome when the land is cultivated, such as bouncing bet, butter and eggs, evening primrose, or wild asters. In grouping them according to the areas where they are commonly found it will be evident that many are found in all the places mentioned, though most are characteristic of only one. Cultivated land has its special weeds. If the land is left uncultivated a few new types will soon appear and within three or four years these will be replaced with an entirely different set. Gradually these will be crowded out by vines and bushes — blackberry, raspberry, wild rose, and thorn apple among them. A few years later trees may spring up and the weeds will have entirely disappeared.

In Lawns and about Houses. The dandelion with its golden flower heads and feathery ball of seeds is one of the most common weeds.

The plantains of several species are equally common. The common plantain with broadly oval leaves and the slender spike of flowers and seeds is quite distinct from the ribgrass or buckhorn with narrow leaves and the long stem with a short spike of flowers at the top.

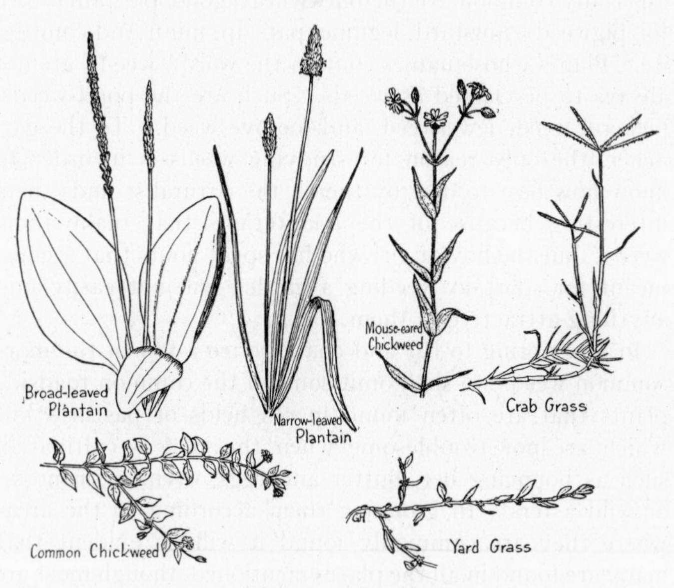

WEEDS OF LAWNS

Yard grass is not a grass but a species of knotweed. Mouse-eared chickweed is found in gardens as well as in lawns.

The flat, spreading chickweed, one of the most universally distributed of all weeds, opens its tiny white flowers with melting snow for a background and continues to flower and set seed all season.

Bermuda grass or wire grass in the South, and crab grass nearly everywhere are weeds that crowd out the better grasses.

In Gardens and Cultivated Ground. There are a great number of interlopers that keep the gardener busy. Among them are two vines.

Bindweed has arrowhead-shaped leaves and small morning-glory-like flowers and twines around and often over other plants. The black bindweed has leaves somewhat similar but the flowers are small and green and arranged in clusters like slender pyramids. The shining black seed enclosed in the keeled calyx lobes is triangular, showing that it belongs to the buckwheat family.

Dodder, a yellow vine with no sign of leaves, is sometimes found twining around garden plants. It is a parasitic plant that sends tiny roots into other plants to steal their sap.

Quack grass or quick grass sends long branching runners in all directions an inch or two below the surface of the soil, from which numerous branches grow up which are bright greenish-yellow on the lower parts. It is extremely difficult to eradicate this pest as any small part of the rootstock left in the ground will develop a new plant.

Wild oats is another grass that we could do well without. Resembling cultivated oats, the flowers and fruits are smaller with bent and twisted awns or bristles.

Several of the mustard family are among the common weeds. Black mustard and common mustard both have yellow flowers and slender pods. The first has pods from one-half to three-quarters of an inch long, and a short beak beyond the part containing the seeds; the second has pods over an inch long and a beak making up at least one-third of the pod in length.

Winter cress or yellow rocket is similar to the mustards, but the pod has no beak and the seeds are flattened instead of globular.

Peppergrass has very tiny white flowers and flat, round pods.

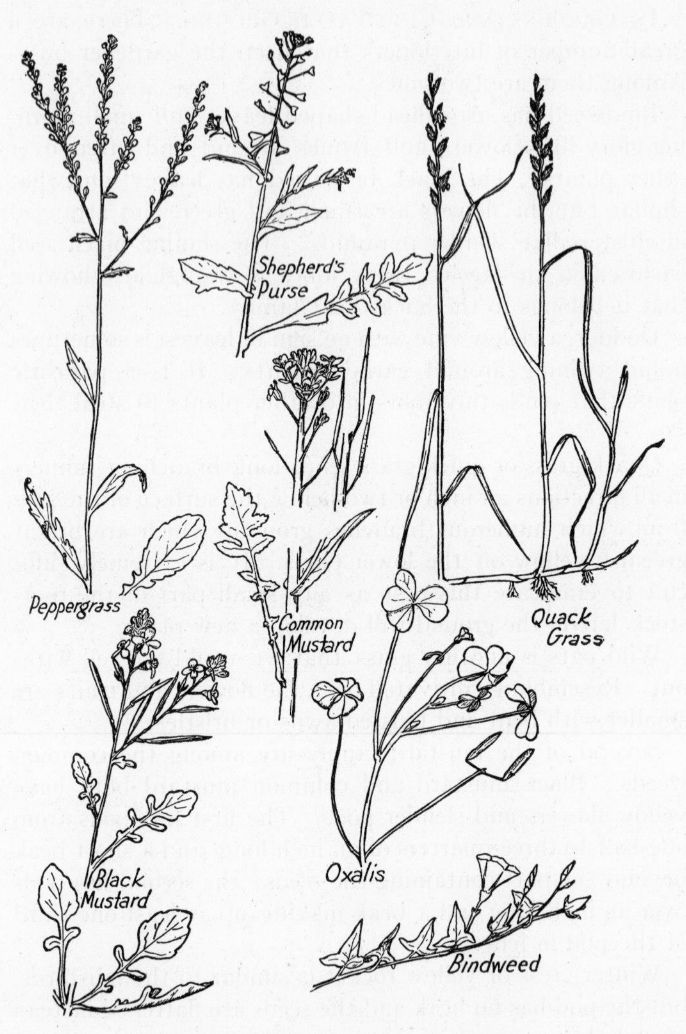

Common Weeds of the Garden

Shepherd's purse has white flowers but the pods are nearly triangular and slightly notched at the end.

Docks, curly, pale, and bitter, are tall plants with strong tap roots. The small seeds are three-angled and enclosed by three large sepals. The small greenish flowers and the fruits are crowded in large clusters at the tops of the stems.

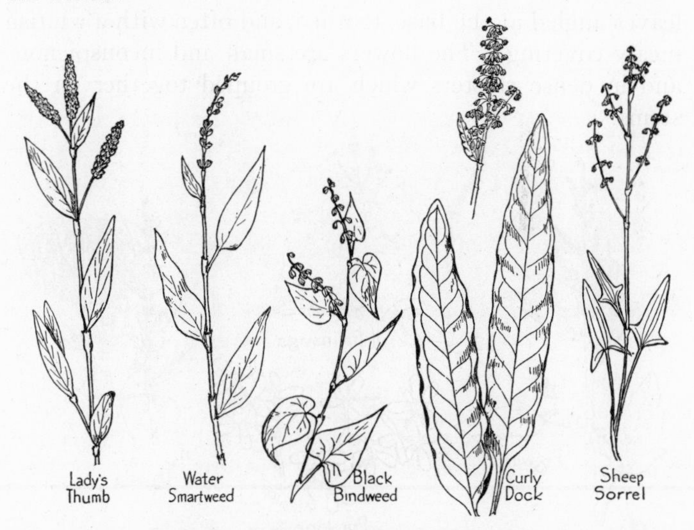

Common Weeds of Waste Ground

Sheep sorrel, a low plant with halberd-shaped leaves and small reddish flowers, is really one of the docks. Everyone is familiar with the pleasantly acid taste of the leaves. Another sorrel is the wood or lady sorrel, a species of oxalis, with yellow flowers and three-parted leaves somewhat like clover.

Knotweed forms small mats close to the ground and can be recognized by the sheath that surrounds the stem where each leaf is attached. The flowers are very small but numerous, and are produced all through the summer.

Smartweed and lady's thumb are close relatives of the knotweed, with similar sheaths about the stems where the leaves join, but the stems are erect and the flowers red or pink in slender clusters at the ends of the stems. Anyone curious as to the name "smartweed" may satisfy himself by eating a few of the triangular seeds.

Pigweed, or goosefoot, of several species, usually has the leaves angled at the base, toothed, and often with a whitish mealy covering. The flowers are small and inconspicuous and in dense clusters which are grouped together on the stems.

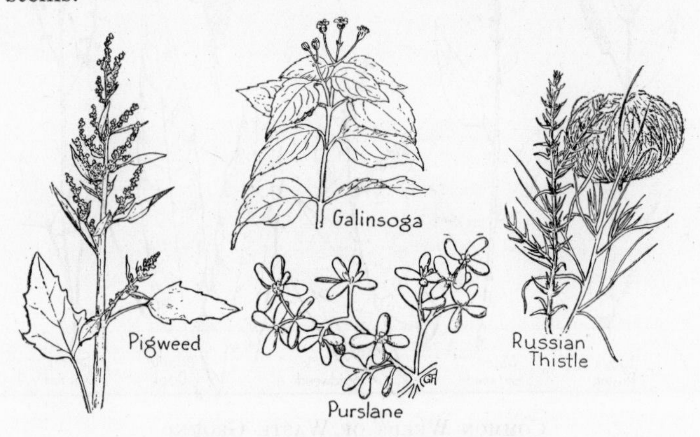

WEEDS OF GARDENS AND FIELDS

The Russian thistle is not related to other thistles. It is especially troublesome in the central and western states.

Russian thistle, related to the pigweeds, is a bushy plant, a foot or a foot and a half high, with very slender, bristle-pointed leaves.

Purslane grows flat, with fleshy stems and small, thick leaves. It is sometimes used as a salad plant.

Ragweeds are erect composites, bearing greenish flower heads; the staminate flowers hang inverted in slender racemes at the top of the stems, and the pistillate flowers are at the base of the racemes. The common ragweed has the leaves finely dissected, the giant ragweed has them deeply three-lobed. Both species produce abundant pollen in the fall and are among the worst of hay-fever plants.

Galinsoga is a small composite with flower heads less than a quarter of an inch across, with four or five white rays surrounding the few yellow disk flowers. An annual with weak roots, it is successful as a weed because of the abundant seed produced from early spring till late fall. Examine the fruit under the lens. The lobed pappus scales make the "seeds" very attractive.

In Pastures and Meadows. Here are found many of the garden weeds, but other weeds are more characteristic of these places.

Common buttercup and daisy are familiar to everyone. The small, daisy-like flower heads of the fleabane, with very slender rays, are almost as well known.

Hawkweed and devil's paintbrush are also common, the first with yellow, the second with orange-colored flowers resembling small dandelions, though with several flower heads on each stem, which may be six to twelve inches high.

Thistles with their prickly leaves, stems, and involucres and the feathery fruits (or "seeds") are among the best known of weeds. The Canada thistle has flower heads an inch or less across, the bull thistle two to three inches in diameter. Both kinds are favorites with many butterflies and other insects. The goldfinch is sometimes called the thistle bird because of its fondness for the seeds, and because it uses their downy tufts as lining material for its nest.

Wild carrot or Queen Anne's lace with its flat, circular cluster of small white flowers is a dainty plant worthy of a place with those cultivated for their beauty. Examine a number of flower clusters to compare the flowers near the center with those near the edge in shape and size. And

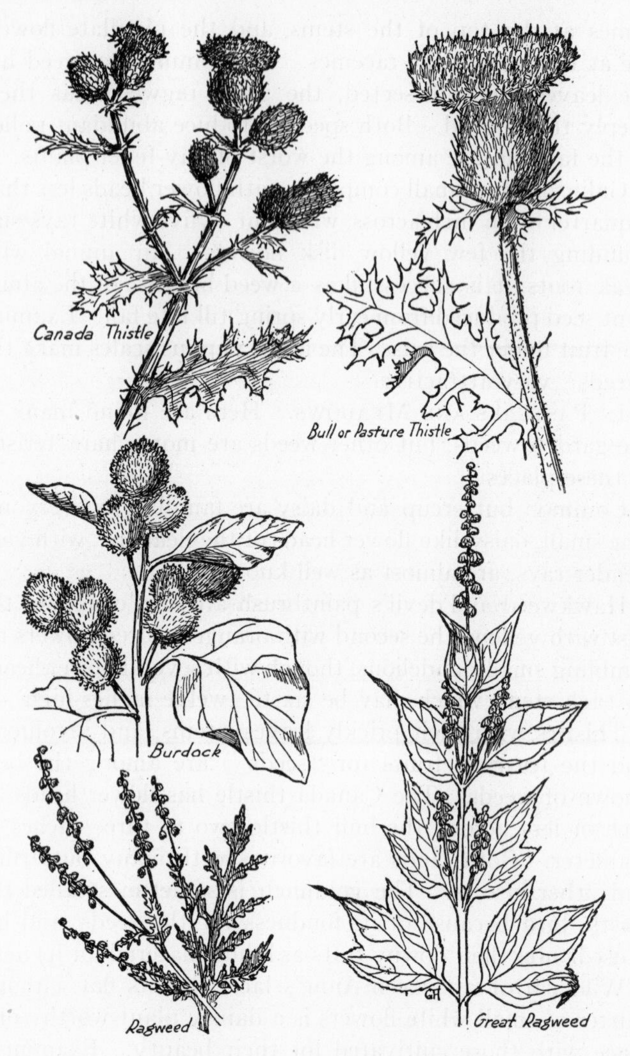

PASTURE OR MEADOW WEEDS

can you find a dark purple flower in the very center of the cluster?

Yarrow is sometimes confused with Queen Anne's lace, but what at first seem like separate flowers making up the flat-topped cluster are really flower heads of from ten to twenty florets each. The leaves are more feathery than those of the carrot and the odor of the crushed leaves is pleasantly aromatic.

Common mullein is found more often in dry pastures than in good soil. Put one of the woolly leaves under a lens to see what makes them so soft. The first year the mullein forms a rosette of large leaves close to the ground. Next year a stem grows up from the center to a height of from three to seven feet, with yellow flowers scattered along the sides near the top. After the seeds are formed the plant dies, and the dead stalks often stand for years in old fields.

Burdock, a large, bushy plant, also flowers in its second year, then dies. The dry flower heads covered with hooked bracts, constitute the burs. Their sharp hooks easily catch in the fur of passing animals or the clothing of people, and so are carried away to drop the seeds as the burs are rubbed or pulled off.

Bidens, or devil's pitchforks, is another plant that is a troublesome sticktight. The fruits, following the yellow flowers, have two or four backwardly barbed prongs that are all too familiar. It is sometimes found in pasture land, though more often it grows along roadsides or in waste places.

Wild onion and garlic are small weeds that are chiefly troublesome because of their odor, as it may be transmitted to milk if cattle eat them. There are several species with slender leaves growing from the bulbs. Often the flowers in the clusters terminating the erect stems are replaced by small bulbs.

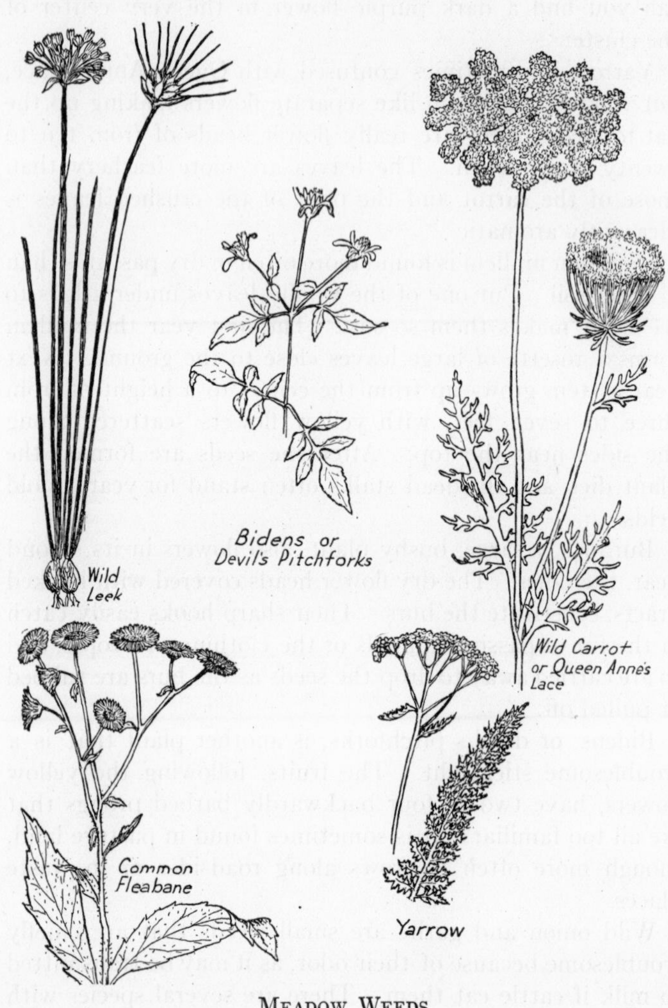

MEADOW WEEDS

Troublesome as weeds are to us, their seeds are the most important item in the bill of fare of many of the birds, especially in the winter when the dead stalks rise above the snow.

BIBLIOGRAPHY

GEORGIA, ADA, *Manual of Weeds.* The Macmillan Company, 1914.
Descriptions, with illustrations, of practically all weeds found in this country.

MUENSCHER, W. C. L., *Weeds.* The Macmillan Company, 1935.
Descriptions and illustrations of all common weeds and some that are not often thought of as weeds. The most complete book on weeds.

PAMMEL, L. H., *Weeds of Farm and Garden.* Orange Judd Company, 1911.
Descriptions of common weeds of North America with suggestions for their control.

GETTING ACQUAINTED WITH EARTH AND SKY

CHAPTER

D. Warren Boyer

THE RUSHING STREAM, THE MISTS ON THE MOUNTAIN SIDE, THE CLOUD ABOVE ARE ALL OF ONE BIRTH

CHAPTER XVI

THE SURFACE OF THE LAND

Near Pulpit Rock I sat, looking away
Over a valley sheerly cut through land
As gracious as land ever ought to be.
On the far side I saw the quiet hills
By the great distance touched so tenderly
That they seemed lovelier than nearer things.[1]

— MARGUERITE WILKINSON

Look through the nearest window or doorway and your vision will probably include many inequalities of land surface. Take a long walk and you will traverse land forms more striking, including hills, valleys, level plains, areas which have been deposited by water, and others which show evidence of erosion by stream action, and possibly cliffs, beaches, and other features of topography.

If we begin to speculate on the cause of these formations or their degree of permanence we shall want to look at them again and with more thoughtful inspection. Suppose we begin first with the more evident land features right in the neighborhood. Hills and valleys always reveal something of their history. Hills are frequently the final resultant of the wearing away of land about them. Valleys that have steep sides are young, from a geological point of view; broad valleys are old, their sides having been eroded through the ages into gentle slopes. Sometimes in the bottom of an old valley the stream has begun rapid cutting, forming a new and narrow valley in the bottom of the broad one.

[1] From "Near Pulpit Rock" in *The Great Dream* by Marguerite Wilkinson. By permission of The Macmillan Company, publishers.

If there are small streams, follow them looking for places where the banks are being cut away, or where beaches or bars are being formed in shallows or below rapids. Try to find evidences of higher stream levels, such as terraces or deserted channels. If there are ravines, either in rock

Courtesy of Oliver P. Medsger

ALONG THE BROOK

Whenever the water is high, part of the bank is cut away.

or in unconsolidated materials, there are sure to be falls, rapids, or quiet pools where later exploring will be in order for water insects, snails, fish, and salamanders. In the sides of the stream there may be potholes, left years ago before the stream had cut so deeply. Overhanging ledges, beneath which the nests of phoebes may be found, give evidence of undercutting, probably partly due to some strata being of softer rocks than others. Joint planes may cut across the strata at right angles, or possibly fault lines may be seen.

By the lake shore, beaches of sand or mud, sometimes with ripple marks, can be noted and the action of the waves in cutting or depositing observed. In sandy areas, evidences of deposition by the wind will be apparent. In swamps or bays there may be filling in by vegetation. Where streams enter larger bodies of water, deltas may be found.

Photograph by G. T. Hastings

EROSION IN THE ROAD

It spoils a road to have such miniature canyons cut by the rains but the power of running water is splendidly shown.

Observations after a local rain will disclose, on a small scale, explanations for many topographic forms. Look for the action of streamlets by the roadside to find where miniature ravines have been cut, or deltas built at the side of the lakelet that filled the gutter. Look to see if the deposited sand and mud particles have been sorted out according to size by the water. Compare the cutting on steep and moderate slopes, on bare soil by the roadside, and on ground covered by grass or dead leaves. Such observations may be continued after several rains to see the varying effects of light and heavy precipitation.

Photograph by Paul B. Mann

A TERMINAL MORAINE

The small hills suggest uneven deposits.

If you are walking where the country was once covered by the great ice sheet, which some twenty thousand years ago retreated to the North after covering all the northern part of the United States and Canada for other thousands of years, there will be different things to look for. Stretching in a long irregular line from Long Island on the Atlantic coast, across northern Pennsylvania, southern Ohio, Indiana, Illinois, to the Rocky Mountains are found peculiar hills and ridges of boulder clay forming the terminal moraine along what was once the southern edge of the ice sheet. If these hills are elliptical with smooth slopes, rather gentle toward either end and steeper on the sides, they are drumlins; those which are irregular in shape and arrangement are usually known as kames; long ridges parallel to the direction the glacier moved are eskers. Between the hills

American Museum of Natural History

BOULDER CLAY

The cut end of a glacial hill. Note the rounded stones in the foreground.

may be found kettle holes — depressions with no outlets, possibly formed by great masses of ice that remained covered by sand and gravel for many years after the glacier retreated and in their melting let the soil sink down. These kettle holes are often occupied now by ponds or small lakes. Boulder clay — a mixture of clay, sand, and stones of various sizes and kinds with no evidence of sorting out by sizes — is an almost sure proof of glacial carrying and deposit. Other evidences of the work of the glaciers are revealed by polished stones, grooves, or scratches in the bed rock, parallel and running more or less in a north and south direction, and by strange "balanced rocks" in unusual places.

If possible get copies of the topographic maps published by the United States Geological Survey. They are not expensive and give many details of the country that will be valuable for field trips. By writing to the Geological Survey in Washington it is easy to find out what regions have been mapped. On the back of these maps is a series of symbols and explanations that will aid in understanding them. After examining a map of this kind, large-scale maps of the school neighborhood or the camp grounds or of some near-by places of interest can be made, showing the physiographic features. Sometimes different groups can work on different areas, making maps on the same scale that can be joined when completed. Instead of maps, relief models may be made of clay from the neighborhood, or of plasteline or damp sand. More permanent models can be made of plaster of Paris. If the plaster is poured into a frame the surface can be shaped into the general form wanted as it begins to thicken. After hardening, additional plaster can be added to build up the hills. Valleys and slopes can be carved out with a knife either while the plaster is only partly hardened or by moistening the dry model. Later the model can be colored with ordinary house paint, making streams and lakes blue, hills and valleys green, and roads brown. Other color combinations may appeal to the makers.

Shallow trays or boxes filled with sand can be used in making a great variety of models or in demonstrating how hills and valleys were formed. By tilting the tray and sprinkling water on the sand, streams can be formed and their action noted. If a valley is made down the center of the tray with hillsides about equal on the two sides, one sandy hill can be covered with sheets of moss; the other, left bare, will be rapidly eaten away by the water. The effect of such cover in preventing soil loss demonstrates the value of the forests in preventing erosion.

Maps and models of the kind suggested may later become part of the camp or school museum. Carefully labeled with the names of the makers, such records of the region will have permanent value.

BIBLIOGRAPHY

Bradley, J. H., *The Earth and Its History.* Ginn and Company, 1928.
A well written, fully illustrated elementary textbook of geology.

Fabre, J. H. C., *This Earth of Ours.* Century Company, 1923.
Popular accounts of the earth and its movements, the tides, rivers, mountains, volcanoes, earthquakes, etc., by a great naturalist.

Hobbs, W. H., *Earth Evolution and Its Facial Expression.* The Macmillan Company, 1921.
An explanation of the origin of the earth, the formation of mountains, volcanoes, and features of erosion.

—— *Earth Features and Their Meaning.* The Macmillan Company, 1912.
An excellent college textbook of physiography.

Reed, W. Maxwell, *The Earth for Sam.* Harcourt, Brace and Company, 1930.
The story of the earth told in the way a boy would like to hear it.

Reeds, Chester A., *The Earth—Our Ever-changing Planet.* The University Society, Inc., 1931.
A graphic and well illustrated popular account of the subject.

CHAPTER XVII

THE EARTH BENEATH

The rock strata, miles thick, may be being flexed now under our feet, and we know it not. — JOHN BURROUGHS[1]

Rocks and soil are to be found everywhere; they are the foundation of the earth itself; on or in them grow our plants; from them we build our roads and homes; the minerals they contain have made possible modern industrial civilization, and yet they are commonly neglected by nature students as by others.

The earth core is composed of solid rock covered in most places by a layer of unconsolidated soil which varies in thickness from a few inches to several hundred feet. The surface rock which we see has probably been changed — much of it several times — through the action of natural forces, so that it is quite different from the original material.

Rocks are made up of definite chemical compounds called minerals, which in turn are composed of elements. Sometimes one of the 92 elements is found uncombined, as in pure gold, copper, silver, diamonds, and graphite (the last two are forms of carbon), but more commonly two or more elements are united to form a mineral. These minerals may occur in large masses or in such small particles that they are invisible to the unaided eye. The more common minerals should be learned first, as the rocks are made of them. In studying minerals it is important to observe

[1] From *Time and Change* by John Burroughs. Copyright by Houghton Mifflin Company.

the hardness, color, luster, cleavage, and crystalline form which characterize them.

MINERALS. Minerals are classified as to hardness on a scale of ten, ranging from the softest, talc and graphite, to the hardest, the diamond. If a set of minerals to show hardness be obtained from a dealer — usually the first nine only because diamonds are too valuable to be handed about — any mineral can easily be tested, as it will scratch any softer than itself or be scratched by any harder. However, a simple way of testing is to know that the finger nail will scratch talc and gypsum, numbers 1 and 2 in the scale; copper (a one-cent piece, for example) will scratch calcite, number 3; a knife blade will scratch fluorite and apatite, numbers 4 and 5; glass will scratch feldspar, number 6; while quartz, one of the commonest minerals, is number 7 and about the same hardness as glass. The harder minerals, all of which will scratch glass, are topaz, number 8; corundum, number 9; and diamond, number 10.

Color is a less definite characteristic since one mineral may show several variations in color. For example, while pure quartz is colorless or glassy, slight impurities may cause it to be smoky brown, yellow, pink, or blue.

Luster refers to the way in which light is reflected, and is referred to as glassy, as in quartz; pearly, as in opal; or dull, as in talc.

In form, minerals may be either (1) crystalline; (2) noncrystalline, but splitting in smooth surfaces in one, two, or three planes (cleavage planes); or (3) with neither crystal form nor cleavage planes. Quartz sometimes is found in crystals that are hexagonal (six-sided) prisms. Garnets usually are in twelve- or twenty-four-sided crystals; hornblende is usually in slender crystals. Calcite has perfect cleavages in three planes so that it breaks into quite regular rhombohedrons (six-sided solids, whose sides are more or less diamond-shaped); feldspar has perfect cleavage in two planes at right angles to each other, or nearly so; mica has perfect cleavage in one plane. Flint, agate, soapstone, or talc have neither crystalline form nor cleavage.

ROCKS. Rocks are usually divided into three groups according to their origin: igneous (by fire), sedimentary (from deposits), and metamorphic (changed shape). The igneous rocks are those that have solidified from molten material; granite, basalt, and lava are examples. Sedimentary rocks are made of fragments of other rocks worn away by the action of water, ice, or wind and deposited in layers which later have become solidified into sandstone, shale, or limestone. Metamorphic rocks originally were either igneous or sedimentary but have been changed by heat, pressure, or chemical action to other forms, such as gneiss, marble, or quartzite. To determine any particular kind of rock, it is important to know both the kind and size of the mineral particles composing it.

Photograph by Paul B. Mann

JOINT PLANES

Fractures sometimes occur in sedimentary rocks at right angles to the face of the rock.

Horizontal layers of rock usually indicate a region that has not been disturbed by mountain-building forces. In many places the slow but titanic stress and strain of a changing earth has caused the tilting, folding, or crumpling of rock layers, much as one might develop twisted effects and other combinations in molasses candy.

Photograph by Paul B. Mann

HORIZONTAL LAYERS OF LIMESTONE

This is an example of typical sedimentary rocks.

SOILS. While the material of the earth's crust was at one time solid and massive, the effects of wind, of water freezing in crevices, of expansion and contraction with changing temperatures, and other forces have all combined to break up parts of the surface into small particles. The oxidation of certain minerals, especially mica and iron, also contributes to the same end. Gradually enough particles accumulated to make what we know as soil. If you step out of doors wherever you are and pick up a handful of soil, consider whether it was made where you found it. It may have been, but in many parts of the world the chances are that it has been transported from a distance either by rivers or glaciers, whose ancient courses sometimes lie revealed today as dry and carved valleys.

Courtesy of Oliver P. Medsger

GLACIAL BOULDERS

The melting ice dropped its load here thousands of years ago.

The fact that the glaciers covered all of the area of North America north of an irregular line along the southern border of New York, through Ohio, and westward through the states north of the Missouri River to the Rocky Mountains, may to a degree account for some of the rich farm lands of those regions, the surface soil having been brought from the North by the encroaching rivers of ice. Glaciers also brought down huge amounts of boulders, pebbles, sand, and clay which they deposited in unsorted mixtures. The pebbles and boulders when carried long distances became rounded and polished and are usually found characteristically distributed in a helter-skelter fashion, throughout deposits of rock flour called boulder clay. Sometimes the bed rock over which the glacier moved has had parallel grooves or scratches cut into it by the stones carried along in the bottom of the river of ice.

Courtesy of Oliver P. Medsger

GLACIAL GROOVES

Rocks frozen in the bottom of the glacier were the tools used in cutting these gigantic grooves.

Soils may be classified according to the size of particles composing them and according to their chemical composition. The common soils are composed of (1) mineral matter, made up of gravel, sand, and clay, and (2) humus, the result of decaying organic matter. Loam is a fine, rich soil made up of sand and clay with considerable humus mixed in. Soils may be acid, due to the chemical composition or to the lack of proper drainage, or they may be alkaline, as is common in regions where there is limestone. The character of the soil is also determined in part by the kind of organisms that live in it: bacteria, molds, protozoa, worms. In any region the kinds and abundance of plants depend largely on the soil, so that some knowledge of soil composition is important to a full understanding of plant life and should be a part of any nature work. The erosion of soil can be noted after every storm, and the types of soil transportation observed by collecting bottles of muddy water from rivulets formed by the rain and letting the soil particles settle.

MAKING A COLLECTION. Collections of rocks and minerals are valuable, because careful examination and comparisons are necessary for knowledge about them. Rocks may be collected almost anywhere, but the best places are where blasting has laid bare large masses of fresh surfaces. Outcrop ledges on hillsides or in stream gorges, quarries, and ledges cut along roadsides, are excellent places. In regions containing glacial deposits, gravel pits will furnish rocks of many kinds. Samples of all the common rocks and of the different types of the same kind should be collected.

Specimens of rock should be approximately the size of the palm of the hand, or about 3 by 4 inches and an inch or two thick. With minerals, especially the crystalline ones, the size may be smaller. Fresh surfaces should be shown by breaking off parts discolored by weathering. Before carrying, wrap each specimen in paper to prevent scratching or chipping.

Every specimen should have a label giving the name, place found, date, and other information of interest. The labels may be written on adhesive tape and attached to the specimen. This is probably the simplest method, but as is often the case, the easiest way is the poorest. If specimens are kept in paper or wooden trays (such as cigar boxes without covers) the labels may be written on cards, and fastened to the trays. In any case, each specimen should be numbered and a corresponding number put on the label. Numbers may be on paper glued to the specimens, but the best way is to put a small circle of white paint on the specimen and after this paint dries, make the number with waterproof India ink. For the camp or school museum, specimens mounted in plaster of Paris show well and are not easily lost, but for the personal collection it is probably better to keep them in trays so that all sides may be examined. A geologist's or stone mason's hammer is a desirable accessory for collecting specimens.

Some Common Minerals

Feldspar. This is the most abundant rock-forming mineral, making about sixty per cent of the earth's crust. The hardness is 6, and it has cleavage in three planes, one rather imperfect, at about right angles. Its color is white, gray, or pink, and its luster glassy. It makes up the larger part of granite, gneisses, and lavas, and while usually found in small particles it is sometimes in large masses.

Quartz. This mineral comprises about twelve per cent of the earth's crust. Its hardness is 7, and it is found in hexagonal crystals or in masses that break with irregular surfaces like glass. It is colorless or white, pink or smoky, and has a glassy luster. It is found in masses in granites and gneisses, also as sand or sandstone. Agate and flint are varieties of quartz.

Hornblende. Hornblende and closely related minerals make up about sixteen per cent of the earth's crust. The hardness is 5.5, and it occurs in slender, six-sided crystals or grains, usually black or dark green, and with a glassy luster. It is found in some granite and gneiss, and by itself in large masses with a granular appearance.

Calcite. Next in abundance to quartz is calcite. Its hardness is 3 and it is colorless or white or may be tinted pink, yellow, brown, or blue, with a glassy or dull luster.

American Museum of Natural History

ROCK SPECIMENS

From left to right, top row: diorite, dolomite, schist. Middle row: granite, diorite (the form sometimes called basalt), sandstone. Bottom row: serpentine, shaly limestone, conglomerate.

It has cleavage planes inclined at angles of 75 degrees. It is frequently found in crystal form and often in veins of rocks or making stalactites in caves. Calcite and limestone will dissolve in hydrochloric acid; a drop of acid placed on them causes effervescence (bubbling).

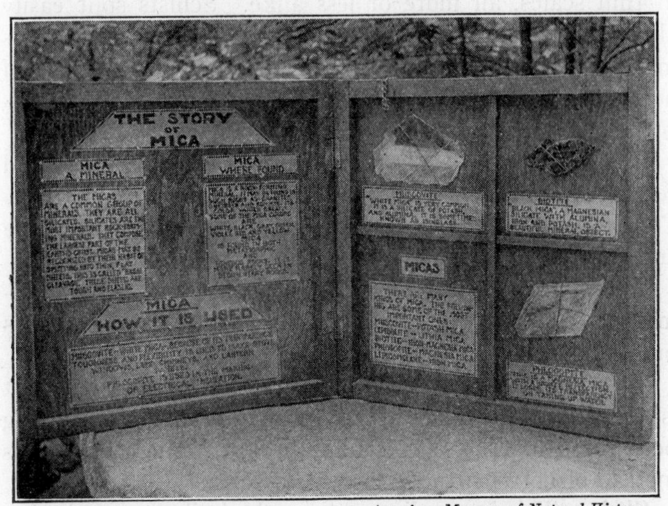

American Museum of Natural History

AN EXHIBIT OF MICA ON THE NATURE TRAIL AT BEAR MOUNTAIN

Micas. These are common minerals, easily recognized as they split into thin elastic sheets. The hardness is about 2.5 and the luster glassy. Muscovite is colorless or gray; biotite, dark brown or black. They occur in large masses or in small grains in granites, gneisses, and schists.

SOME COMMON ROCKS. *Granites.* These are very hard rocks composed of quartz, feldspar, mica, or hornblende, and often other minerals. The mineral particles are small but easily seen. Granites may be nearly white, pink, or red, or dark. They are igneous rocks.

Gneiss. Gneiss is metamorphosed granite. The quartz, hornblende, or mica and feldspar are arranged in bands, sometimes straight but often curved or contorted. The particles of minerals are large enough to be seen easily.

Schists. Schists are metamorphic rocks with the particles in thin scales, all more or less alike. Schists split easily along the plane in which the particles lie. Mica schist is made mostly of mica and quartz; hornblende schist of hornblende and quartz; chlorite schist of chlorite (a greenish mineral) and quartz.

Conglomerate. This is a rock made of pebbles and sand cemented together usually by silica, lime, or iron oxide. Conglomerates vary greatly in hardness, also in the size and color of the pebbles composing them.

Sandstones. Sandstones are composed of sand grains cemented together. They vary widely in color and hardness but the sand grains can always be distinguished.

Quartzite. Quartzite is a metamorphosed sandstone. It is very hard and glassy, the original sand grains having been fused together. A fracture breaks through the grains instead of between them as in sandstone.

Shale. This is a sedimentary rock similar to sandstone, but the particles are too small to distinguish without the aid of a lens. It is really solidified mud, as is evidenced by an earthy odor like clay which is given off when the surface is broken or the rock is breathed on. It splits into thin layers often resembling slate.

Slate. This is a metamorphic shale and splits along cleavage planes at an angle to the lines of bedding of the shale. The bedding lines usually show across the smooth surfaces of the slate.

Limestone. Limestone is formed by the deposit of calcium carbonate from solution or by the accumulation of shells or corals. It may be light or dark gray, bluish or brown, and it effervesces with hydrochloric acid. When metamorphosed, limestone becomes marble, showing crystalline structure and sometimes a great variety of colors.

BIBLIOGRAPHY

BAYLEY, W. S., *Minerals and Rocks.* D. Appleton and Company, 1915.

A good laboratory manual, with keys, for the determination of rocks and minerals.

ENGLISH, GEORGE L., *Getting Acquainted with Minerals.* McGraw-Hill Book Company, 1934.

A book for the beginner in the study and collecting of minerals.

GREATACAP, L. P., *Popular Guide to Mineral Collections.* D. Van Nostrand Company, 1912.

The fundamentals of mineralogy, with a descriptive survey of minerals as they will be found in large collections and museums.

LOOMIS, F. B., *Field Book of Rocks and Minerals.* G. P. Putnam's Sons, 1923.

A popular work on the subject, with general directions for study, simple keys, and excellent descriptions.

REED, THOMAS THORNTON, *Our Mineral Civilization.* Williams and Wilkins.

An interesting little book which supplies a great deal of information about the earth and its minerals and metals.

SPENCER, L. T., *The World's Minerals.* Frederick A. Stokes, 1916.

Well written, with beautiful colored plates.

WHITLOCK, H., *Story of the Minerals* (reprinted 1932). American Museum of Natural History.

An attempt to answer popular questions about the minerals exhibited in the Morgan Memorial Hall of the American Museum of Natural History.

—— *The Story of the Gems.* Lee Furman, Inc., 1936.

A lavishly illustrated and fascinatingly written account of gems and jewelry, including the art of the lapidary.

CHAPTER XVIII

FOSSILS — IMPRESSIONS OF THE PAST

I do not think she ever saw
Light through a leaf,
Or traced a dragon's rusty claw
Across a reef
Of ancient rock, or watched the sea
Lift to the moon.[1]

— PATIENCE EDEN

Eons upon eons ago strange creatures roamed the earth. They lived and died with no one to take note of them. Their existence would never have been guessed if they had not left in the rocks indelible records of themselves. These traces and remains of once-living forms tell a story as intact as the sedimentary rocks where they are found.

One of the most fascinating things in science is the way in which paleontologists (scientists who study fossils) piece together bits of fossil evidence and from these make skeletal restorations of these weird animals. Painters dare to clothe these bones and to depict probable scenes in prehistoric times when dinosaurs plowed through swamps and winged reptiles flapped across uncharted waters. In any museum one can now see horses the size of dogs, four-toed camels, great sharks with teeth like mowing-machine blades, armored fishes, and hosts of small fry — shell fish, and corals resembling a cow's horn. Some are found complete or nearly so; many of them are only portions of the original skeleton or structures from which the whole can be reconstructed.

[1] From "But, Does It Matter?" by Patience Eden. Copyright by *The New Yorker.*

There is a strange thrill that comes when one breaks off a piece of rocky ledge and for the first time in his life holds the imprint of an animal whose form and shape the rocks have kept intact for ages. An insignificant shell, perhaps, yet it is ten thousand times as old as any civilization.

Hunting for Fossils

Fossil-forming. Just what is this thing we call a fossil and how could it get into the rocks? The general agreement among paleontologists is that most fossils are the remains of animals or plants that once lived in the waters of the prehistoric ocean, land organisms whose remains were washed there by streams and floods, and the footprints of frequenters of the shore. Presumably drifting sand and mud then buried the remains, caught like raisins in a cake. Gradually the weight of additional layers of mud, together with heat coming from the interior of the earth, changed this sand and mud into rock, much as man today changes soft clay into bricks. Where bricks are made in a few days, fossil-making in nature seems to have taken hundreds and perhaps thousands of years. No fossil could be thrust into the rocks; it really had to out-date the rocks themselves. The term "fossil" may be applied to almost any structure of prehistoric origin, such as fossil ripple marks, fossil rain-drops, and fossil beaches, but most of these formations resulted from the deposit of organic structures in either salt or fresh water.

The question may arise, "If fossils are formed only under water, how is it that people now find fossils in high inland regions such as mountains?" The answer is quite simple. Throughout the geological (referring to rocks and their ages) history of the world, land levels have had tremendous changes. For example, the white cliffs at Dover, England, are the remains of enormous quantities of a little marine Protozoan called chalk. Originally deposited at the bottom of the ocean, they must have been pushed upward by tremendous upheavals of the land, several hundred feet above their early beds. One is safe in thinking that the presence of fossils in rocks always means that at some remote time that particular region was covered with water.

But not all remains have been elevated. Beds of coal represent swamps which sank below sea level, allowing the vegetation to become covered with mud. Coal itself is made of the carbon of the plants, and often — especially in the shales close to the layers of coal — the leaves and stems of the swampy vegetation consisting of tree ferns and their relatives are preserved so perfectly as to show all the veins on the leaves or the scales on the stems.

The petrified forests of the West were formed where trees and logs were carried by streams into lakes or inland seas. Becoming water-logged, the wood sank, and as it slowly decayed it was replaced, molecule by molecule, by quartz dissolved in the water, until at last a stone log showing the grain of the original wood was formed. Animal fossils are sometimes formed by this process of infiltration and replacement of the original structure by a silicate (a mineral like sand).

Sometimes the fossil is part of the actual plant or animal imbedded in the rock. Usually only the harder parts, such as shells and bones, are thus preserved.

Again fossils may be casts of the original organism. In this case, the original structure must have been slowly dissolved by water and decay. The cavity or mold thus left was later filled with a deposit of limestone, quartz, or some other mineral from the water, and an excellent cast of the original animal was thus left as a fossil in the rocks. Many fossils of mollusks were formed in this way. Such fossils as these may reveal either the outer or the inner surfaces of the shells, with the original structure and shape perfectly imitated.

Another class of fossils consists of the remains of trails made by animals or imprints left in sand or mud, just as the impression of a leaf or a footstep is often preserved in a cement walk. These might be the footprints of prehistoric reptiles and birds, tracks of a wandering mollusk or a burrowing worm, marks produced by raindrops, fruits, twigs, etc., falling in the mud, or ripple marks or lines caused by the wind on primordial beaches.

Fossils of vertebrates, excepting fish, are rare because these animals did not normally go into the water.

On dry land the soft tissues of dead bodies were sought as food by carnivorous animals or rodents, or were reduced quickly by bacteria and insects hatching from eggs laid therein. Even bones were ultimately reduced to powder through exposure to the disintegrating effects of the sun's rays and cold, coupled with the accompanying action of moisture and bacteria. In some cases, however, enveloping amber and tar have revealed specimens as perfect as the day they were caught or mired. Thus the remains of some insects of the tertiary period have been preserved in the gum of certain coniferous trees, with original colors and with structures intact. Southern California tar beds have yielded the bones of enormous numbers of prehistoric animals.

Most fossils are imperfect, as would naturally be expected, considering the stress and strain of the rocks through countless years, and incomplete because in most cases the soft parts were not preserved at all.

While fossils show that prehistoric life was different from the forms of today, there are enough striking resemblances to impress us with the probability that in most cases, when we examine a fossil, we are looking at the remains of a remote ancestor of certain living forms of today.

From the time of the Greeks curious and fantastic ideas have been held regarding fossils. They have been variously explained as sports of nature, as rejected models of the Creator, as discarded shells of crusaders (whose badge was a scallop), and as plant and animal remains stranded by the receding waters of Noah's flood. These superstitious ideas were quite generally believed up to the early part of the nineteenth century, when Cuvier and others founded the science of paleontology.

Fossil Ages. Next to what the fossil is, the most interesting question is, "How old is it?" This cannot be answered definitely in years, but the approximate age can be told if the geological formation in which it occurs is known. By examining state geological reports, or by writing to the Geological Survey at Washington, D.C., the periods to which the rocks of any region belong can be ascertained. The accompanying table shows the chief geological periods with the estimated ages in years and the kinds of animals and plants living in each. It must be remembered, too, that while trilobites or corals or other forms of life persist through many periods, possibly even to

TABLE OF GEOLOGICAL PERIODS AND THE LIFE DURING THEM

Age	*Period*	*Years ago*	*Animals*	*Plants*
Cenozoic	Quaternary	1,000,000	Man Primates	Modern Forms Palms
	Tertiary	20,000,000	Many mammals Modern reptiles	Angiosperms
Mesozoic	Cretaceous	45,000,000	Birds	Modern Conifers First angio-sperms
	Jurassic		First birds Crabs and lob-sters	Cycads
	Triassic	75,000,000	Cuttlefish Many reptiles (Dinosaurs)	
Paleozoic	Carboniferous	100,000,000	Reptiles Last of the trilo-bites Spiders Amphibians	Seed Ferns Conifers
	Devonian	140,000,000	Insects Many kinds of fish Last of cup corals	First ferns Lycopods Horsetails
	Silurian	155,000,000	Graptolites Star-fish Scorpions	First land algae
	Ordovician	190,000,000	First fish First insects Typical crinoids	
	Cambrian	225,000,000	Corals Sponges Brachiopods Mollusks Primitive cri-noids Trilobites	Seaweeds
Archaeozoic		500,000,000	Protozoa (Eozoon)	Bacteria Simple algae

the present, the particular kinds or species usually change from period to period.

Scientists use different methods in determining the age of rocks: the rate at which sand or other material is deposited in lakes or seas, the amount of salt in the ocean, the cutting of river valleys, and the change of radio-active minerals. These different methods give different results so that the figures given are only approximate. But modern investigation is lengthening rather than shortening these estimates. It is evident that geological time must be measured not only in millions but hundreds of millions of years, and that the fossils we find are correspondingly old.

FIELD STUDY. Fossil study in the field may or may not be possible. If the searcher finds himself in the midst of granite or other forms of volcanic rocks, it will be useless to hunt for fossils. The fiery origin of such rocks means that all such traces were destroyed ages ago. Fossil-bearing rocks are of the type called sedimentary — shale, sandstone, and limestone or clay, sand or marl — usually in layers, which are or were originally nearly horizontal. Sometimes fossil-bearing rocks are found loose where a glacier or stream left them, but more commonly fossils are found imbedded in rock strata in some quarry, ravine side, or cliff.

For collecting fossils in the field the equipment is the same as for the study of rocks and minerals, except that a few small cold chisels will be found useful. In collecting the fossil, the stone around it should be chipped away carefully to expose it as fully as possible and to remove the unnecessary stone at the sides. Great care must be taken to avoid cracking the fossil by chiseling too close to it. Wrap each specimen in newspaper for protection against rubbing, especially if several specimens are to be carried at one time.

SOME COMMON FOSSILS. *Brachiopods* (arm-footed). These were bivalve (two-shelled, like an oyster, or clam) animals resembling certain mollusks of today, but quite different in internal structure. A few are found living today, but they were vastly more numerous both in varieties and in number in early geological ages.

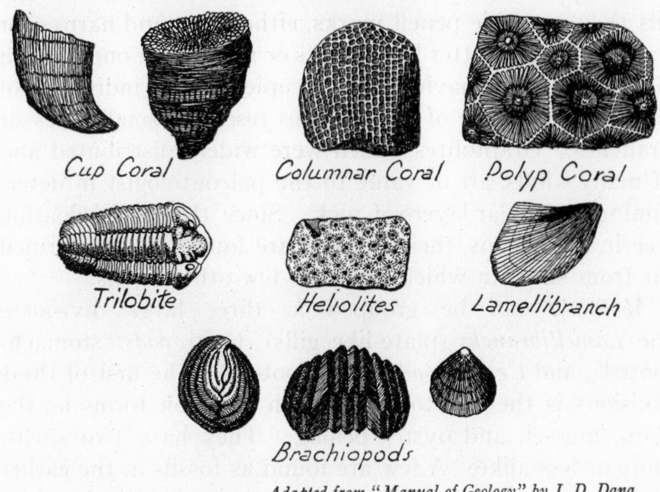

Adapted from "Manual of Geology" by J. D. Dana

SOME COMMON FOSSILS

Corals. Most of these were colonial animals, the tiny individuals building hard skeletons well adapted to form fossils. In the older rocks several types of coral are found. The cup corals, sometimes called staghorns, were abundant in early times, but disappeared before the Carboniferous Period. In these forms the individuals were relatively large.

Crinoids (lily-like). Sea lilies, also known as crinoids, are found in small numbers in warm ocean waters today, some floating, a few fastened by long stalks to the bottom. In ancient times, especially during the Silurian and Devonian Periods, they were very abundant. The long stalks, divided into rings or disks, usually separated when the animal died.

These disks are common in the rocks. However, the head or body, the lily-like part, is uncommon.

Graptolites (like writing). These were small colonial animals, abundant during the first part of the Paleozoic Age but disappearing by the end of the Silurian Period. As fossils they resemble pencil marks, either long and narrow, or branching; the latter bear marks or notches on one or both sides, each notch having been occupied by one individual of the colony. Some of the colonies resemble small trees or branches. Graptolites, which were widely distributed and of many kinds, are of value to the paleontologist in determining particular layers of rock. Since they lived floating free in the oceans, their remains are found in rock formed far from shore in which there are few other fossils.

Mollusks can be grouped in three large divisions: the *Lamellibranchs* (plate-like gills), *Gastropods* (stomach-footed), and *Cephalopods* (head-footed). The first of these divisions is the one to which such common forms as the clam, mussel, and oyster belong. They have two shells, more or less alike. A few are found as fossils in the earlier rocks, where they are much less important than the brachiopods. In succeeding periods they became more abundant while the brachiopods became less so, till they were the dominant form of shell fish.

To the gastropods belong the snails and hundreds of forms of one-shelled (univalve) mollusks. A few fossil gastropods are found in the earlier rocks of the Paleozoic Age and, as with the previous group, the number increases down through the following ages.

The highest group of mollusks living today, the cephalopods, have tentacles around the head, and they may have a single shell of peculiar form or none at all. In early rocks we find horn-like shells of cephalopods, long and slender, divided crosswise by partitions, each new division being longer as well as wider than the preceding one. Some are only an inch long and an eighth of an inch wide at the large end; some reach a length of ten feet and a diameter of one foot and there are a great variety intermediate between these two. In general, these straight forms are known as orthoceras (straight) or orthoceras-like forms. Evidently from this type developed those with spiral shells, of which the nautilus of today is a descendant. Orthoceras is found in the rocks of the Cambrian Period, becoming abundant during the succeeding periods and dying out during the Triassic. The coiled cephalopods later developed many forms; some of the Ammonites became very complex and beautiful in structure. Most of the prehistoric coiled cephalopods disappeared by the end of the Mesozoic Era.

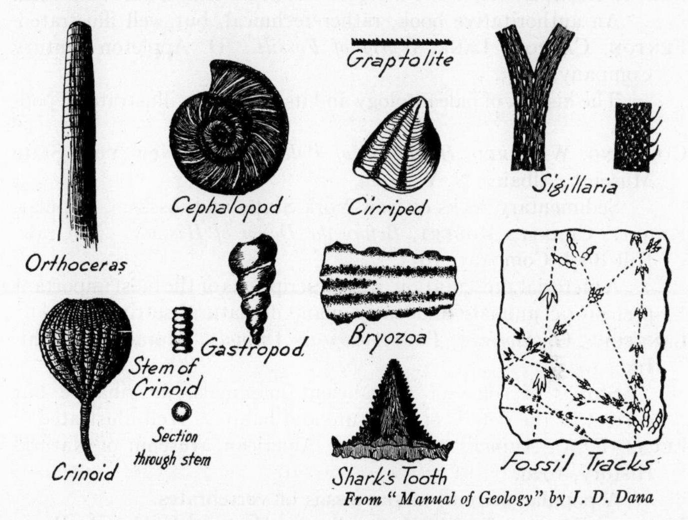

From "Manual of Geology" by J. D. Dana

PLANT AND ANIMAL FOSSILS

Trilobites (three-lobed) were the primitive ancestors of our crabs and lobsters. Many species are found in the rocks but all show the division of the body into three regions, head, center part, and tail, with the center and tail parts divided lengthwise into three rows of segments. Abundant during the early periods of the Paleozoic Period, they became extinct during or just before the Carboniferous Period.

While the first vertebrates were primitive fish, appearing first in the Silurian Period and becoming so abundant during the Devonian that it is called the "Age of Fishes," young people will not ordinarily find these fossils. Nor are they likely to find fossils of reptiles which appeared first in the Carboniferous Period and flourished in the Triassic, a period which might well be called the "Age of Dinosaurs."

BIBLIOGRAPHY

BERRY, EDWARD W., *Paleontology.* McGraw-Hill Book Co., 1929.
An authoritative book, rather technical, but well illustrated.

FENTON, CARROLL LANE, *World of Fossils.* D. Appleton-Century Company, 1933.
The history of paleontology and its methods; illustrated; popular.

GOLDRING, WINIFRED, *Handbook of Paleontology.* New York State Museum, Albany, N. Y., 1929.
Sedimentary rocks of New York State, and fossils. Popular.

KNIGHT, CHARLES ROBERT, *Before the Dawn of History.* McGraw-Hill Book Company, 1935.
A pictorial presentation, with descriptions of the most important prehistoric animals and early man, in natural settings.

LANGFORD, G., *Stories of First American Animals.* Horace Liveright, Inc., 1923.
Stories of some of the ancient mammals, imaginative but correct in the details of structure and habits. Well illustrated.

LUCAS, F. A., *Animals of the Past.* American Museum of Natural History, 1929.
A popular account of the fossils of vertebrates.

MATHER, KIRTLEY F., *Old Mother Earth.* Harvard University Press, 1929.
The story of the geological history of the earth and of the development of its plants and animals.

The Age of the Earth, Bulletin 80. National Research Council, 1931.
Scientific estimates of the age of the earth, based on radioactivity, ocean salinity, sedimentation, and astronomical data.

CHAPTER XIX

THE HEAVENS ABOVE

The heavens declare the glory of God;
And the firmament showeth his handiwork.
Day unto day uttereth speech,
And night unto night showeth knowledge.

— PSALM 19, 1–2

No form of nature work appeals more to young people than the study of stars. Nothing else does so much to give a feeling of wonder and reverence. In cities with their street lights the real beauty of stars is never realized. Away from artificial lights, their glory on clear nights gives a sense of the beauty and vastness of the universe afforded by nothing else.

For star study, utilize a cloudless night when the moon is between the last and first quarters. In early July the brighter stars may be seen about ten o'clock, in August by nine, and in midwinter before six. In each case, within a half hour, the fainter stars of the 4th and 5th magnitude will be visible. On bright moonlight nights stars are not easily studied, though those of the 1st and 2nd magnitudes may still be seen. The moon itself is our nearest heavenly neighbor and belongs especially to our earth. It will become more interesting to us if we are able to name some of its plains (oceans as they were first called), craters, and mountains instead of merely making out fanciful animal or human forms. Field glasses make its elevations and plains distinct. Records can be kept of the time of rising and setting of the moon and of its phases through a month.

THE MILKY WAY. One of the strangest of the heavenly phenomena is the Milky Way, the starry belt which forms the rim of the galaxy to which our solar system belongs. Galilei (his full name was Galileo Galilei) was the first to resolve this bright haze into millions of stars. One opinion of today is that our universe is shaped somewhat like a cookie in which the earth is located not far from one edge. When we look at the Milky Way, therefore, we are practically looking at our universe on edge, or through the thickest part, so that we get the effect of an enormous concentration of stars.

Photograph by Yerkes Observatory

THE MOON THROUGH A TELESCOPE

The small circles are craters, some over one hundred miles across. The dark areas are plains.

METEORS. The celestial fireworks known as "shooting stars" are not stars at all, nor parts of stars, but small fragments of matter which move around the sun in an elliptical orbit. When the earth passes through the orbit of these bodies many of them are drawn to the earth by gravitation and then heated white-hot by the friction developed in their fierce rush through the atmosphere. They should more truly be called *meteors* or *meteorites*.

The earth passes through the orbit of a large number of these about the tenth or twelfth of August, when a vivid display will usually reward the watchers. Even though we may see few of these meteors it is unquestionably true that they enter our atmosphere by thousands every day. The great majority are completely consumed as they pass through the air, but a few reach the earth. Most meteors are composed of stony material, but some are largely of iron and it is these latter that have most often been found. Almost every natural history museum has some of these heavenly visitors on display.

American Museum of Natural History

AN IRON METEOR

The cavities were burned out in its passage through our atmosphere. Found by Lieut. Peary in Greenland it is now in the American Museum of Natural History.

COMETS. These are luminous wanderers whose orbits bring them into sight at comparatively rare intervals. They are always sufficiently advertised by magazine and newspaper articles so that no one need ever fail to see a prominent comet.

NORTHERN LIGHTS. On some evenings observers will be sure to see great streamers or bands of light in the sky to the north. These are electrical phenomena known as "northern lights." Sometimes they are magnificent spectacles of impressive beauty.

American Museum of Natural History

CONSTELLATIONS ABOUT THE POLE STAR AS PICTURED BY THE ANCIENTS

No form of nature work is easier to begin and none needs less equipment than star study. A star chart for the month that may be found in a newspaper or magazine or purchased for a few cents is all that is necessary.

Additional charts can easily be made as observations are carried on. Be sure to record the hour and date on each chart. If arrangements are made for a group to study stars, it is best to have only five or six the first time so that the leader may be sure that all see the stars which are pointed out.

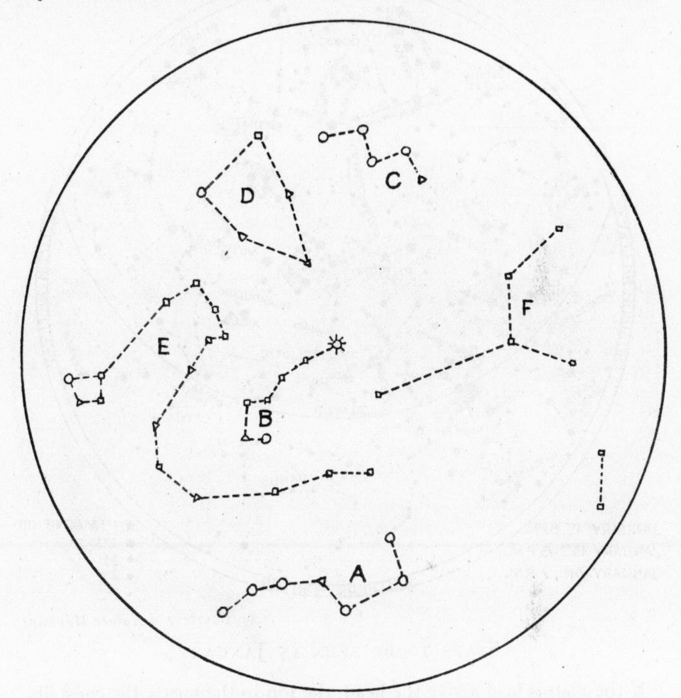

CONSTELLATIONS ABOUT THE POLE STAR AS SHOWN ON MODERN MAPS

A. Big Dipper. B. Little Dipper. C. Cassiopeia. D. Cepheus. E. Draco. F. Camelopardus.

A larger group may be successful after the students are more experienced. It might be well in the meantime to read in astronomies about planets and stars: their sizes, distances, and motions, and other absorbing facts.

Constellations are groups of stars that appear close together. They were named by the Greeks or the Arabs centuries ago for mythological characters and animals.

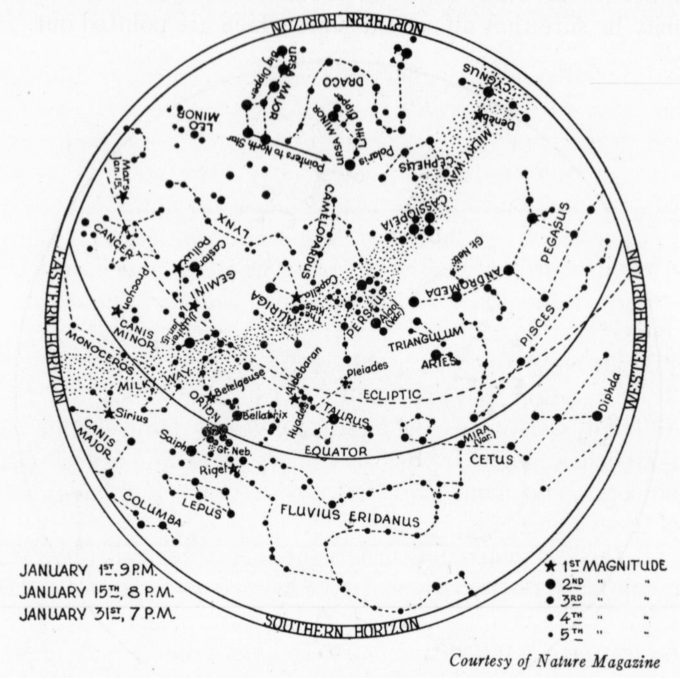

Courtesy of Nature Magazine

STARS TO BE SEEN IN JANUARY

If the map is held above the head, the top to the north, the constellations will appear as they are in the sky.

Actually the stars are very far apart and not connected in any way. The stories associated with the stars are interesting and some of them should be learned, but it is difficult in most cases even with a vivid imagination to outline in the sky the figures of the men or animals for which the constellations were named.

STAR MAPS. The making of star maps will help fix in mind the constellations and stars. Beginners may construct a simple chart from stiff paper or cardboard, preferably blue, but if that is not available the side of a large carton such as those in which boxes of cereal or bread are packed may be used, coloring it with blue-black ink or paint. Blue-print paper may also be used. Gummed silver or gold stars can be bought, or smaller stars may be cut from paper by a conductor's punch which may be secured from a dealer in stationery. The small stars so cut are preferable to the larger ones. In gluing the stars to the paper it is convenient to use two toothpicks. With one, put a drop of glue in the place desired; and move the stars with the other. Avoid crowding the stars and include only a few constellations on a single sheet. Older observers will not be satisfied with the simple charts just referred to. Their maps might well show variations in magnitude of the different stars. To be of greatest value, maps should be sketched at night from direct observation and completed indoors. Star maps made by copying charts and books are of less value.

If the star maps and flash lights are taken out on star-study trips, constellations can be located by examining the maps and comparing the stars of a known constellation with neighboring stars on the map. Too many lights may make it difficult to see the stars well, but each member of the party should have an individual map.

STAR STUDY. In beginning star study the group of constellations about the North Star is usually chosen. If a chart is made on a large disk of cardboard, showing the Big Dipper, Little Dipper, Cassiopeia, Cepheus, and the Dragon, it can be used to show apparent motion of the stars in the sky. Put a pin or small nail through the North Star, and hold the chart behind a table so that the lower edge is partly hidden and the Big Dipper just shows when it is on the lower side of the chart. Revolve the chart slowly and note that the stars below the North or Pole Star seem to move in an opposite direction from those above the pole. Of course stars further away from the pole than those shown would be below the horizon as represented by the table edge. The further north the location, the more constellations will be above the horizon continuously, with the North Star higher in the heavens.

American Museum of Natural History.

THE BIG AND LITTLE DIPPERS

The stars at the end of the bowl of the Big Dipper are known as the pointers.

After an explanation of the constellations the group should go into the open and locate them in the sky, beginning with the Big Dipper, part of a larger constellation, the Great Bear. Bears either had long tails in the olden days, or their tails stretched out when Jupiter seized them and threw them into the sky! The Big Dipper was called the "plow" by the ancients and in Europe is often called the "wagon." Can you see the outline of these objects in the group of stars?

Locate the pointers and from them the North Star. It is the "North Star" because the axis of the earth appears to point to it and it can be seen from all points in the northern hemisphere. Actually it is $1\frac{1}{4}$ degrees away from the true celestial pole. This star has been important in guiding men from the earliest times. It is fifty light years away from us. A light year is the distance traversed by a ray of light in a year, at a speed of 186,000 miles a second. This is about six trillion miles. The most distant stars are many thousand light years away.

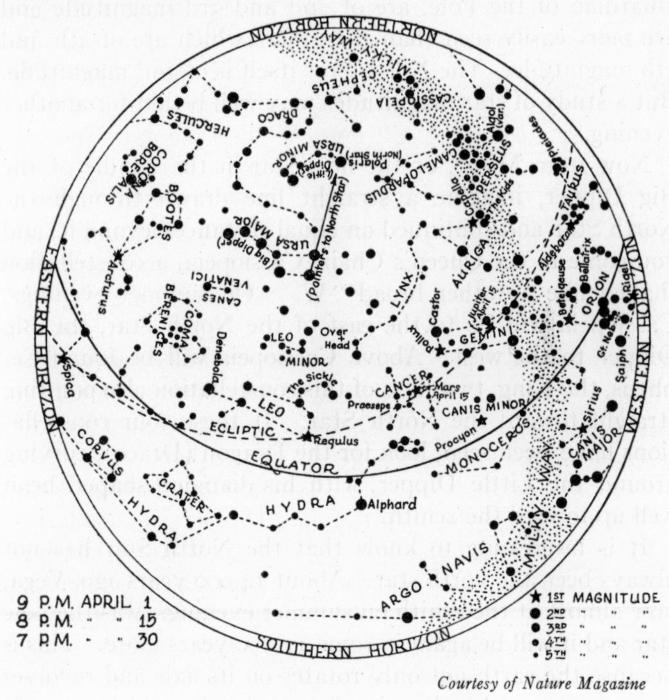

Courtesy of Nature Magazine

STARS TO BE SEEN IN APRIL

Find Mizar, the second star in the handle of the dipper, and see if you can make out the small star, at the side. The Indians called the two stars the "squaw and papoose"; the Arabs called them the "horse and rider." It is a test of good eyesight to be able to see this small star, and a good illustration of things we never see till they are pointed out to us. With field glasses it is plainly seen.

Now come back to the North Star and make out the

Little Dipper. In summer evenings, it stands upside down as if pouring its contents into the Big Dipper. The two stars at the end of the bowl of the Little Dipper, the Guardian of the Pole, are of 2nd and 3rd magnitude and are more easily seen than the others which are of 4th and 5th magnitude. The North Star itself is of 2nd magnitude. But a study of star magnitudes may well be left for another evening.

Now from Mizar, or the next star in the handle of the Big Dipper, imagine a straight line drawn through the North Star and continued an equal distance beyond it, and you come to the Queen's Chair, Cassiopeia, a constellation shaped like a rather broad "W." On summer evenings, Cassiopeia will be to the east of the North Star, the Big Dipper to the west. Above Cassiopeia will be found Cepheus, the King, two stars of this constellation also pointing straight toward the North Star. If these four constellations have been seen, look for the Dragon (Draco), curving around the Little Dipper, with his diamond-shaped head well up toward the zenith.

It is interesting to know that the North Star has not always been the north star. About 14,000 years ago, Vega, now almost at the zenith on summer evenings, was the pole star and it will be again in some 12,000 years more. This is because the earth not only rotates on its axis and revolves around the sun but has a third motion by which the axis swings in an apparent circle through the sky. This motion, called the Procession of the Equinoxes, takes about 26,000 years to complete. During this time the earth's north pole points at one time toward Thuban, the third star in the Dragon's tail, which was the north star 2,800 years ago, then swings toward its present position, passes through Cepheus, on to Lyra, and around to its present position again.

On the next trip the number and apparent size of stars might be considered. In spite of the fact that the stars seem innumerable on a clear night, there are only about 2,000 in sight at one time and only 5,000 to 7,000 visible to the eye in all the sky. With good field glasses the number that can be seen is about 100,000 and it is estimated that the largest telescopes reveal at least 100,000,000.

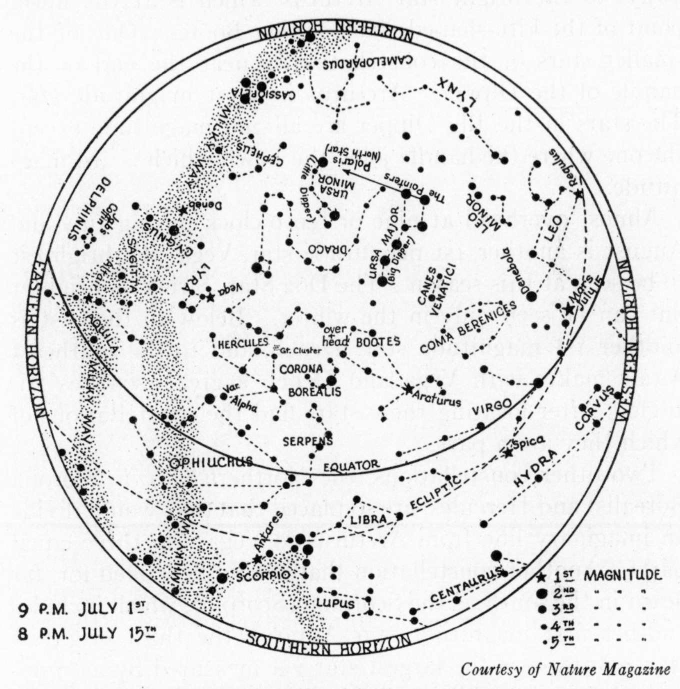

Courtesy of Nature Magazine

STARS TO BE SEEN IN JULY

Since remote times, the stars have been ranked according to brightness as of 1st, 2nd, 3rd, 4th, 5th, and 6th magnitudes, the last being the faintest the unaided eye can see. There are only twenty stars of 1st magnitude, and of these only six can be seen on a summer evening. The brightness of a star may be due to its distance or to its size; a comparatively small star near the earth (the nearest star is 4 light years or 25,000,000,000,000 miles away) may seem brighter than a large one farther away.

After reviewing the five constellations already learned, project the curve of the handle of the Dipper twice its length away, to the bright star Arcturus, which is at the lower point of the kite-shaped constellation Boötes. One of the smaller stars of the constellation is near the end of the handle of the Dipper. Arcturus is a 1st magnitude star. The stars in the Big Dipper are all 2nd magnitude except the one where the handle joins the bowl, which is 3rd magnitude.

Almost overhead at nine or ten o'clock during July and August is another 1st magnitude star, Vega, the brightest to be seen at this season. The Dog Star, Sirius, is brighter but can be seen only in the winter. Below to the east is another 1st magnitude star, Deneb, and to the southeast Altair makes with Vega and Deneb a great isosceles triangle. After locating these stars find the constellations of which they are a part.

Two other constellations, the Northern Crown (Corona Borealis) and Hercules, are so placed that they would divide an imaginary line from Arcturus to Vega into three equal parts. Another constellation that should be looked for, far down in the south, is the Scorpion (Scorpio), which includes another first magnitude star Antares, the third brightest star. Antares is the largest star yet measured by astronomers, being 400 million miles in diameter! If Antares were where our sun is, the earth would be only half-way between the center and the outer edge. But with its immense size, Antares is not dense — probably not as dense as our atmosphere. The variation in color of these stars is worth noting; Vega is bluish white, Arcturus yellow or orange, and Antares reddish.

After the middle of August other constellations may be

seen. The great square of Pegasus low in the east will suggest a baseball diamond. Below "second base" is the string of stars, Andromeda, curving over towards Perseus, who in mythology saved her from the dragon.

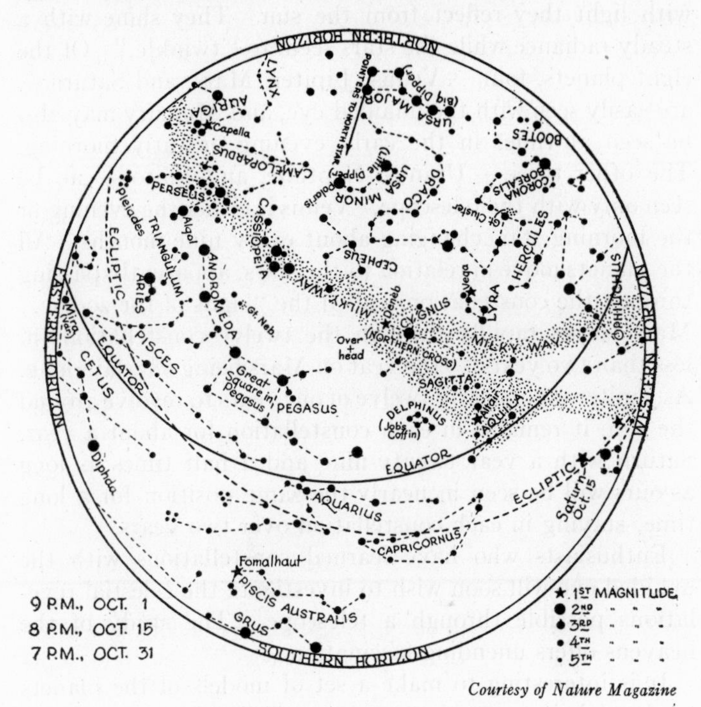

Courtesy of Nature Magazine

STARS TO BE SEEN IN OCTOBER

An early morning trip (four o'clock or earlier) devoted to star gazing might prove more than a novelty. Many constellations that usually are considered winter ones can be seen. Observe the Big Dipper under the North Star and to the east, instead of above and to the west as it was in the evening. Pegasus is overhead, the Northern Cross right side up in the west, and the Pleiades well up in the east.

PLANETS. The planets, usually mistaken for bright stars, belong to our own solar system and are very near compared with the stars. The stars are true suns giving out light, but the planets, like the earth and moon, shine only with light they reflect from the sun. They shine with a steady radiance while the stars seem to "twinkle." Of the eight planets, four — Venus, Jupiter, Mars, and Saturn — are easily seen with the unaided eye, and Mercury may also be seen at times in the early evening or early morning. The other three — Uranus, Neptune, and Pluto — can be seen only with the telescope. Venus is either the evening or the morning star, changing about every nine months. All the planets move in relation to the stars, apparently passing through the constellations called the "signs of the zodiac." Mars passes rapidly through the twelve constellations in less than two years — the year on Mars being 687 days long. As Jupiter takes nearly twelve of our years to revolve around the sun, it remains in each constellation for about a year. Saturn with a year twenty-nine and a half times as long as ours will be seen in nearly the same position for a long time, staying in each constellation over two years.

Enthusiasts who have learned constellations with the unaided eye will soon wish to investigate the celestial revelations possible through a telescope. The study of the heavens offers unending fascination.

It is interesting to make a set of models of the planets to show their proportionate sizes. Balls of clay or plasteline may be used, or such objects as mustard seed, peas, nuts, apples, and balls. If a disk of cardboard two feet in diameter is used to represent the sun, the following sizes and distances will be approximately correct for the planets. As the distances are too great to use conveniently they may be divided by one hundred, provided that everyone understands the scale.

Planet	Proportionate Size and Distance	
	in model	distance from sun model
Mercury	$\frac{1}{12}$ inch	84 feet
Venus	$\frac{1}{4}$ "	156 feet
Earth	$\frac{1}{4}$ "	220 feet
(Moon)	$\frac{1}{15}$ "	(7 inches from earth model)
Mars	$\frac{1}{9}$ "	330 feet
Jupiter	$2\frac{1}{2}$ "	1,100 feet or about $\frac{1}{4}$ of a mile
Saturn	2 "	2,000 feet
Uranus	$\frac{5}{6}$ "	4,200 feet or about $\frac{4}{5}$ of a mile
Neptune	$\frac{4}{5}$ "	6,500 feet or about $1\frac{1}{4}$ miles
Pluto	$\frac{1}{4}$ "	9,800 feet or about 2 miles

BIBLIOGRAPHY

BERNHARD, H. J., and others. *Handbook of the Heavens.* McGraw-Hill Book Company, 1935.

An excellent elementary book of the heavens with explanations and many illustrations.

BOHER, ROBERT H., *When the Stars Come Out.* Viking Press, 1934.

A valuable treatise in astronomy for older boys and girls.

CLARKE, E. C., *Astronomy from a Dipper.* Houghton Mifflin Company, 1929.

Starting with the Big Dipper, all the more conspicuous constellations are located by means of a series of star maps.

DECKER, WILBUR F., *Home-made Telescope.* Perine Book Company, 1935.

It contains directions for making a telescope powerful enough to disclose the moons of Jupiter.

FISHER, CLYDE, *Exploring the Heavens.* T. Y. Crowell Company, 1936.

A non-technical book for beginners.

INGALLS, ALBERT G., *Amateur Telescope Making. Scientific American,* 1933.

A practical symposium on the subject.

JEANS, SIR JAMES, *The Stars on Their Courses.* The Macmillan Company, 1931.

An informal, fascinating account of the wonders of the universe as known to the astronomer, with maps and directions for locating the principal constellations and stars.

LUYTEN, WILLIAM J., *The Pageant of the Stars.* Doubleday, Doran and Company, Inc., 1929.

Tells what most of us want to know about the sun, planets, meteors, and stars.

MCKREADY, KELVIN, *Beginner's Guide to the Stars.* G. P. Putnam's Sons, 1924.

A convenient little book to use in locating the constellations.

——, *Beginner's Star Book.* G. P. Putnam's Sons, 1927.

A much larger book about the stars by the author of the previous volume. Tells how to locate the constellations but in addition has extended descriptions and stories.

OLCOTT, WILLIAM T., *Field Book of the Skies.* G. P. Putnam's Sons, 1929.

Another of Putnam's field books, excellent for those who wish to learn the stars. Well illustrated with photographs and charts.

PROCTOR, MARY, *Evenings with the Stars.* Harper and Brothers, 1925.

Each of the twelve chapters is planned as one evening's observation. By following the plan some forty constellations will be learned, with some of the important facts and interesting legends connected with each.

REED, W. MAXWELL, *The Stars for Sam.* Harcourt, Brace and Company, 1931.

A boy's book of the stars.

SERVISS, GARRETT P., *Astronomy with an Opera Glass.* D. Appleton and Company, 1901.

Tells how to locate the stars of each season, with a narrative description of what is to be seen and facts about the various constellations and stars.

——, *Round the Year with the Stars.* Harper and Brothers, 1910.

A series of charts of the sky, directions for locating the stars and constellations and something about those located.

TRAFTON, GILBERT H., *The Star Guide.* Slingerland-Comstock Company, 1927.

A series of maps of the constellations, with charts for each season and with simple explanations of how to locate the constellations.

CHAPTER XX

THE WEATHER

We humans get umbrellas out,
And, downcast from the rain we flee;
While fields and hills, uplifted, shout,
"Great King of Waters, rain on me!" [1]

— LAURA K. DALZELL

No one escapes weather. Everyone lives in it and everyone talks about weather changes. Fluctuations in weather are largely induced by variations in temperatures in different places on the earth, which in turn cause air currents in which heated air rises and cooler air falls. Winds are air currents moving toward the region of ascending masses of air, or away from regions of descending masses. If we could measure such a rising column of air, we should find it considerably lighter in weight than cooler air. In such a place the barometer would "fall" because there would not be so much pressure on the column of mercury. Correspondingly, the barometer would register somewhat higher in an area of cold air.

The typical movements can be understood by studying land and sea breezes. Land heats more quickly than water, and the air over the land becomes warmer than the air over the slower-heating water. During the day the light, warm air rises, and we have a cool breeze from the ocean coming in to take its place. At night, the land cools more quickly than the adjacent water, and the reverse takes place. If a camp is located near water where these breezes can occur, it will add greatly to the comfort of everyone.

[1] From *Orpheus' Lyre* by Laura L. Dalzell. Copyright by the Noyes-Group.

Scientific study of weather fluctuations began as long ago as the time of Aristotle with his *Meteorology* and the treatises of his pupil Theophrastus on winds and weather. Two thousand years later, the inventions of the thermometer by Galileo in 1607 and the barometer by Torricelli in 1643 made possible the advances known as modern meteorology.

WEATHER REPORTS. Weather forecasting in this country has now reached such scientific accuracy that everyone directly or indirectly relies on prognostications of the Weather Bureau. Its predictions control movements of perishable merchandise, and start ships and airplanes on their courses; it warns of storm, of flood, of sudden change in temperature, and of probable subsequent effects on agriculture.

Over two hundred "observatories" have been established in the United States, from each of which statements as to local weather conditions are sent to strategic centers twice a day. With this information daily weather maps are prepared showing the location of "highs" and "lows," with their interpretations and the probable weather indications for the next 24 hours. Not every prediction will come true for all places in the region covered. Mountain ranges and forests will sometimes deflect or obstruct winds or drain them of their anticipated moisture. Yet with all the variations, the Weather Bureau predictions are correct about 85 per cent of the time.

Copies of weather maps and forecasts can be obtained from the nearest Weather Bureau office or from the Weather Bureau at Washington, D.C. It will be interesting to see how often the forecasts are correct for your region, and also to try forecasting from a study of the maps.

TEMPERATURE. In studying the weather, we should keep in mind that the atmosphere extends more than 100 miles up from the surface of the earth, though at 24 miles its density has lessened to $\frac{1}{400}$ of that of the air close to the earth. The temperature also decreases at the rate of about one degree Fahrenheit for every 183 feet until a height of seven miles is reached. Then for a considerable distance the temperature (about 70° below zero) remains fairly constant. Gradually it approaches the absolute cold of interstellar space — approximately 459° below zero.

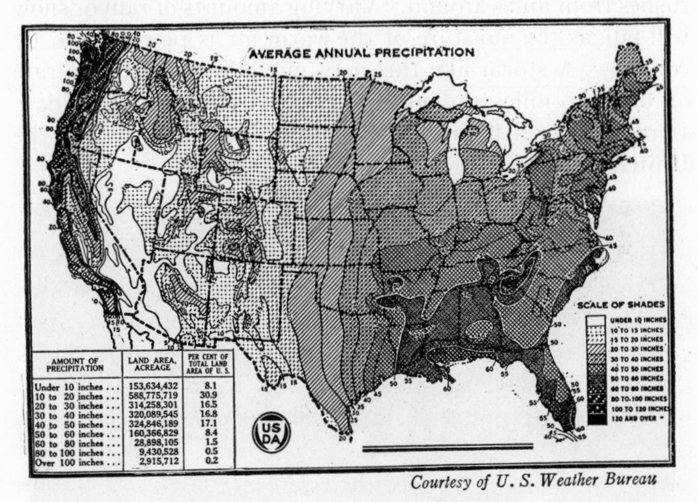

AMOUNT OF PRECIPITATION	LAND AREA, ACREAGE	PER CENT OF TOTAL LAND AREA OF U. S.
Under 10 inches . . .	153,634,432	8.1
10 to 20 inches . . .	588,775,719	30.9
20 to 30 inches . . .	314,258,301	16.5
30 to 40 inches . . .	320,089,545	16.8
40 to 50 inches . . .	324,846,189	17.1
50 to 60 inches . . .	160,366,829	8.4
60 to 80 inches . . .	28,898,105	1.5
80 to 100 inches . . .	9,430,528	0.5
Over 100 inches . . .	2,915,712	0.2

Courtesy of U. S. Weather Bureau

MAP TO SHOW ANNUAL RAINFALL

If there were no rotation of the earth, we should have warm air rising in tropical regions and then traveling, as very high currents, toward the poles. Close to the earth would be currents of cold air blowing in the opposite direction toward the tropics. Actually, however, the warm air descends near latitude 30° (the northern part of the Gulf of Mexico). South of this is an area of fairly stable weather, but north of it as far as the Arctic Ocean is a storm belt. The great blanket of air around the earth insulates us so that the terrestrial heat does not escape. With this air gone, we should freeze in a twinkling.

STORMS. A typical cyclonic storm is always an area of warm ascending air, itself whirling in a direction opposite to the hands of a clock in the northern hemisphere, and moving forward across the country in a general northeasterly direction. Such a storm is always a center of decreased pressure, a "low," into which the surrounding air rushes from miles around. Varying amounts of rain or snow will fall, as the moisture of the warm air is precipitated by cooling. A storm like this may move forward at the rate of 30 or 40 miles an hour, or it may lag to five miles a day. It may cover a township or it may spread over half the United States.

Courtesy of F. Ellerman, Mt. Wilson Observatory, Cal.

CIRRUS CLOUDS

Clearing weather comes when conditions are reversed and a great mass of cool air, an "anti-cyclone," dominates and neutralizes the cyclonic storm, so that the surface winds finally shift to the west or northwest. This produces clear and cool weather.

Sometimes we experience a local disturbance known as a thunderstorm. Usually this soon passes, though it may be one of the phases of a prolonged cyclonic storm. The fiercest storm in the United States is the tornado. This is a twisting funnel of concentrated fury, whose easterly path, though lasting only a few minutes, is strewn with destruction.

Courtesy of U. S. Weather Bureau

STRATUS CLOUDS

CLOUDS. Storms are always accompanied by clouds. Indeed, storms would be impossible without clouds, though clouds can be present without resultant storms. Clouds are made up largely of condensed moisture, together with particles of dust and smoke. When the warm, moist air rises, sooner or later it will be cooled below its saturation point and its moisture will be condensed and become visible as a cloud. Dust particles aid in the precipitation of such water vapor. Clouds may be adjacent to the surface of the earth, usually as fog, or they may be stealing along in ghostly wisps, suspended as high as eight miles.

In mountain regions, the mixing of warm air with cool air currents or the blowing of such currents against the sides of mountains may cause fogs or clouds. Similarly the contact with the icebergs, Arctic Ocean currents, or cooler land or water, may precipitate a fog or young cloud. One of the most interesting characteristics of mountain lakes and streams is the morning mist, a phenomenon which rewards the early riser who later will see it disseminated by the sun or wind. Such a mist may begin to form over lowlands or over water during the evening.

Photograph by Paul B. Mann

MORNING MIST ABOVE A STREAM

There are three typical cloud forms: the *cirrus* (feathery), the *stratus* (in layers), and the *cumulus* (in piles). Three other secondary forms are combinations known as *cirro-stratus*, *strato-cumulus*, and *cirro-cumulus*. The *nimbus* (rain cloud) is a storm cloud formed from any heavily saturated cloud.

Cirrus clouds are delicate, fleecy masses resembling feathers. They form what is sometimes called "mackerel sky." These clouds are from five to eight miles high with their moisture always frozen.

Stratus clouds are narrow bands lying parallel to the horizon. They are formed from low fogs.

Cumulus clouds are huge, white, rounded masses with flat bases. They are usually from one to two miles high.

Nimbus are rain- or snow-producing clouds. Sometimes when dark they are called "thunder heads." They are relatively low and generally without definite character.

Cirro-stratus are very delicate clouds, comprising a sort of haze or with hair-like strands. They form the halos sometimes seen around the sun or moon.

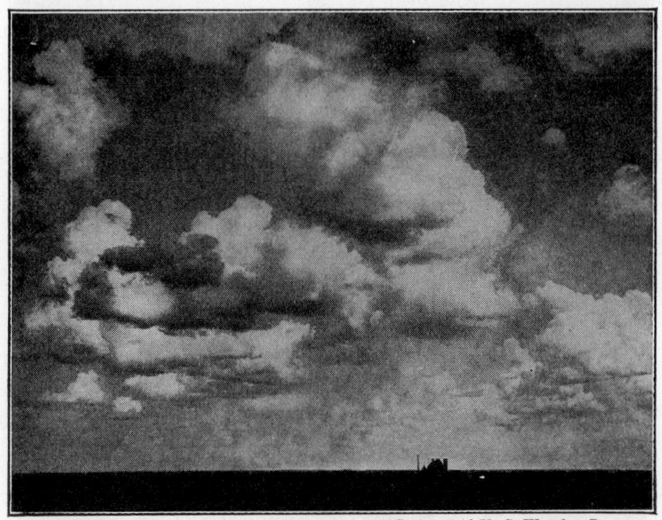

Courtesy of U. S. Weather Bureau

CUMULUS CLOUDS

Strato-cumulus are masses of more or less dark clouds, smaller than cumulus, and usually somewhat extended in form.

Cirro-cumulus resemble cirrus clouds, but are in connected masses. They are always at very high altitudes.

SCIENCE VS. SUPERSTITION. Although there are many superstitions about the weather, there are certain phenomena by the correct interpretation of which we may approximate scientific weather foretelling.

Courtesy of U. S. Weather Bureau

CIRRO-STRATUS CLOUDS

Courtesy of F. Ellerman, Mt. Wilson Observatory, Cal.

STRATO-CUMULUS CLOUDS

Courtesy of U. S. Weather Bureau

CIRRO-CUMULUS CLOUDS

Stormy weather is usually indicated by:

1. Falling barometer
2. Cirrus clouds, hazy sky
3. Lack of dew at night
4. Rising temperature
5. Smoke rising with difficulty
6. Increase in humidity
7. Halo around the moon

Fair weather is indicated by:

1. Rising barometer
2. Skies cloudless or with cumulus clouds
3. Gentle winds, especially from the west
4. Dew at night
5. Morning fog

Some superstitions relating to the weather are:

1. The weather changes with the phase of the moon.
2. Equinoctial storms are due at the spring and fall equinoxes.
3. Fur-bearing animals produce longer and thicker fur before a severe winter.
4. "Red at night, sailors' delight;
   Red in the morning, travelers take warning."

There is some truth in the latter jingle as there is also in the fisherman's statement:

"Wind in the south, blows the bait in the fish's mouth.
Wind in the north, the wise fisherman goes not forth.
Wind in the west, is the time the fishing is best.
Wind in the east, is not good for man or beast."

FINDING OUT HOW FAST STORMS MOVE. (*Note.* Enough weather maps for three or four successive days should be procured so that each one in the group may have a set.)

1. Arrange weather maps according to dates. On each series mark the center of each "low" with a certain color and the center of each "high" with another color.

2. Note the changing position of the "lows" and "highs" on successive days; now draw a line, in the color used in marking the "lows" on the last map, to show the path of each "low" from the first known position. Similarly, use the color marking "highs" to draw a line from the first known position of the "highs" to their position on the last map.

3. What was the general direction of the "lows" and the "highs"?

4. Use the scale of miles given on a similar map of the United States and determine how many miles each "low" and each "high" moved in one day and in three or four days. Divide this total by the number of days con-

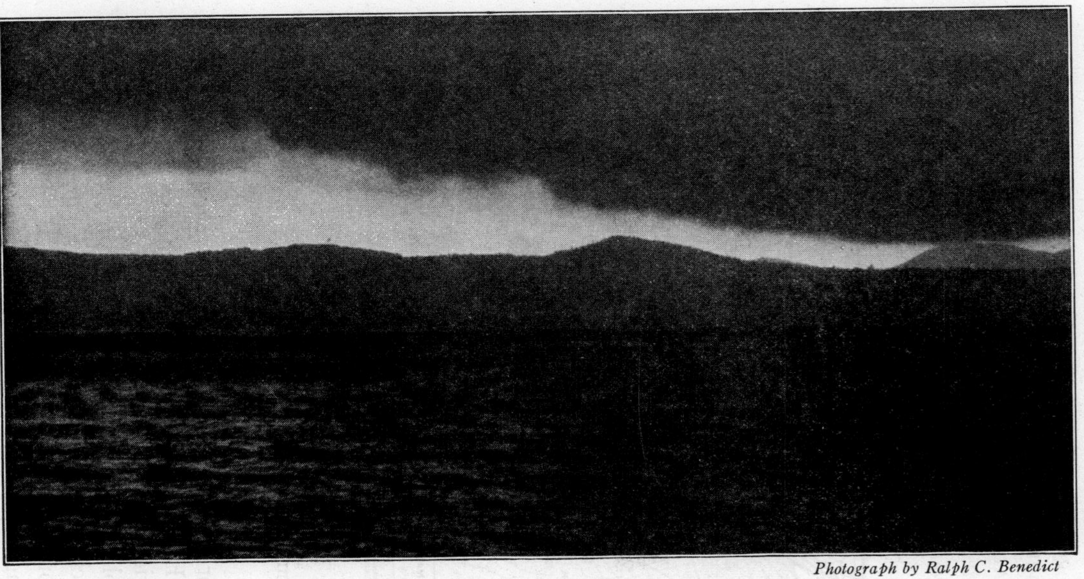

Photograph by Ralph C. Benedict

NIMBUS CLOUDS OVER LAKE GEORGE

The approach of such a blanket of dark clouds shuts out so much light that chickens may go to roost in the impression that night is approaching.

cerned to get the average speed per day or per hour. Can you compute a weekly velocity?

General Information. There are often two kinds of curved lines on a weather map. Those in heavy black are called *isobars* (equal pressure) and measure atmospheric pressure. At the end of each isobar is a number, either

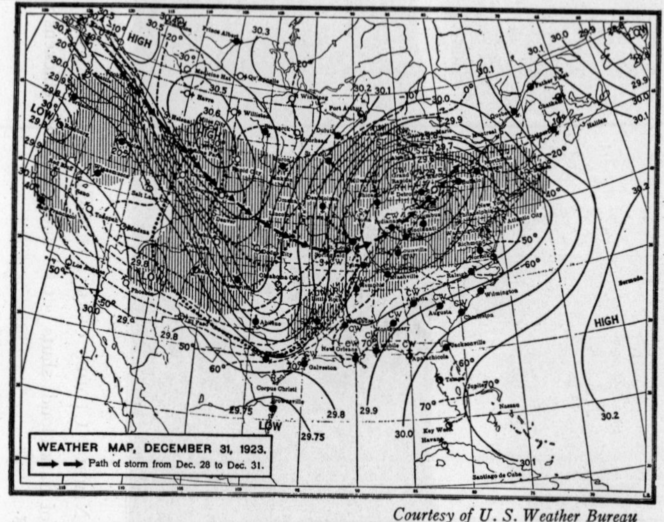

Courtesy of U. S. Weather Bureau

Weather Map

The storm path is a special feature not shown on ordinary weather maps.

29 with or without a decimal, or 30 with or without a decimal. Each isobar is drawn through places of the same atmospheric pressure. An isobar of 30.1, for instance, connects places in all of which the barometer would stand at 30.1 inches at the time the map was made. Will the isobars around a "low" register higher or lower than those surrounding a "high"? Why?

The faint dotted lines sometimes shown are *isotherms*

(equal temperature). Each isotherm passes through regions where the temperature is the same. At the ends of each isotherm is a figure which gives the temperature indicated by that isotherm. On most maps, there are no isotherms shown, but instead the temperature is given in small figures beside the arrows that indicate the direction of the wind. Clear circles at the base of these arrows show fair weather, black circles clouds, while the letters R or S inside the circles show rain or snow, respectively.

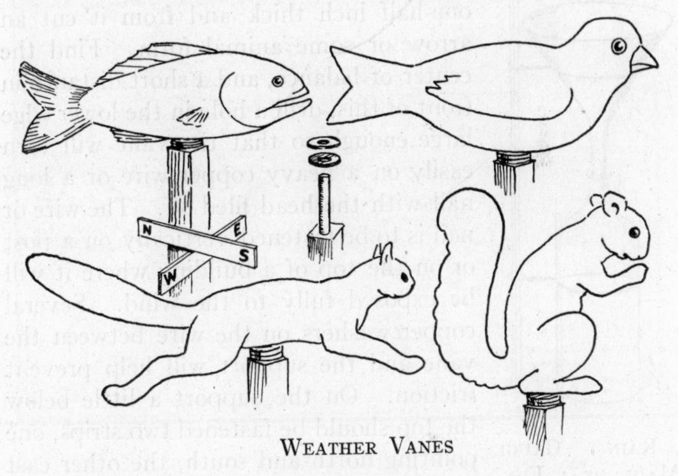

WEATHER VANES

INTERPRETATIVE QUESTIONS ON WEATHER MAPS

1. Find the isobars of the highest and lowest air pressure. Is there more than one isobar having the same figure? How do you account for this?

2. Find the region of lowest air pressure. What word is printed in the center of these isobars?

What variations in air pressure do the isobars reveal in passing from a "low" to a "high"?

3. In what direction is the wind blowing east of a "low," north of a "low," west of a "low," south of a

"low"? Give the same sort of information for winds about a "high." Give the probable relative temperature of each wind, with reasons.

EQUIPPING THE WEATHER STATION. At camp or school, a thermometer, weather vane, and rain gauge are necessary and, in addition, a barometer is desirable. The thermometer must be purchased, but the weather vane and rain gauge may be made. For the vane use a piece of wood from one-fourth to one-half inch thick and from it cut an arrow or some animal form. Find the center of balance, and a short distance in front of this, drill a hole in the lower edge large enough so that the vane will turn easily on a heavy copper wire or a long nail with the head filed off. The wire or nail is to be fastened vertically on a post or on the top of a building where it will be exposed fully to the wind. Several copper washers on the wire between the vane and the support will help prevent friction. On the support a little below the top should be fastened two strips, one pointing north and south, the other east and west — the north point being plainly marked either by an arrowhead or by colored paint. The compass should be used to place these strips accurately. The weather vane should be painted to preserve it and keep it from warping. Bright colors make it more attractive.

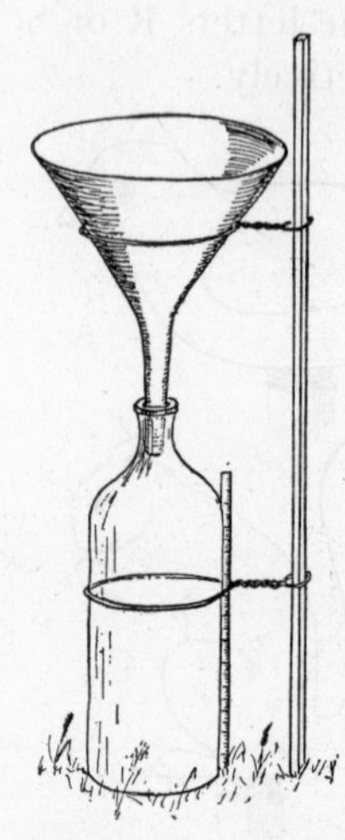

RAIN GAUGE MADE OF A FUNNEL AND BOTTLE

The rain gauge can be made from a large tin funnel and a glass cylinder or slender bottle and a ruler. The funnel is placed in the top of the cylinder and the apparatus is set up in some open space attached to a stake to keep it from falling or blowing over; or it can be set up on a flat porch or cabin roof. The rainfall can be determined by measuring the height of water in the cylinder and dividing by the square of the figure obtained by dividing the width of the funnel at the top by the width of the cylinder inside. For example, if the funnel is six inches across the top and the cylinder two inches wide, we divide six by two. The quotient, three, squared gives nine. The height of the water collected in this apparatus will be nine times the actual rainfall. The thermometer should be on the north side of a post or tree about five feet from the ground.

Observations should be made every day at the same time in the early morning and late afternoon. In making the records, use the following symbols:

Winds, none — o; faint — F; moderate — M; strong — S.

Clouds, Cirrus — Ci; stratus — St; cumulus — Cu; nimbus — Ni; cirro-stratus — CS; strato-cumulus — SC; cirro-cumulus — CC.

DAILY WEATHER OBSERVATIONS

The following chart is suggested as a form for the record of observations for one week. Successive observations for one month can be assembled by pasting weekly charts on a large sheet of paper.

	Date	*Hour*	*Temperature*	*Barometer*	*Wind Direction*	*Velocity*	*Clouds*	*Fog*	*Dew*	*Rain*	*Remarks*
Sun.											
Mon.											
Tues.											
Wed.											
Thurs.											
Fri.											
Sat.											
Summary for Week											

BIBLIOGRAPHY

BROOKS, CHARLES F., *Why the Weather?* Harcourt, Brace and Company, 1924.

Readable accounts of the factors that make up weather, conditions in the different seasons, and some notes on making weather observations.

FREE, E. E., and HOKE, TRAVIS, *Weather*. Robert M. McBride and Company, 1928.

An attempt to tell all that we ordinarily want to know about the weather and its relation to man's comfort, health, and business.

HUMPHREYS, W. J., *Fogs and Clouds*. The Williams and Wilkins Company, Inc., 1926.

A small book telling how fogs and clouds are formed and their relation to weather. A large number of beautiful cloud photographs make it possible to identify clouds.

——, *Weather Proverbs and Paradoxes*. The Williams and Wilkins Company, Inc., 1923.

A collection of proverbs and paradoxes with their explanations. Most of the illustrations are the same as in the preceding.

LONGSTRETH, T. MORRIS, *Reading the Weather*. The Macmillan Company, 1925.

Practical suggestions for campers and others who are much in the out of doors. How to use the barometer, how to forecast without instruments, etc.

MCADIE, A. G., *Man and Weather*. Harvard University Press, 1926.

The importance of weather to man in war and peace; how clouds are formed; how the weather is studied and forecast.

——, *Wind and Weather*. The Macmillan Company, 1922.

A convenient little book telling chiefly of the relation of winds to the weather and how forecasts are made.

MANN, PAUL B., *How to Know the Clouds, How to Tell the Weather*. Slingerland-Comstock Company, 1930.

A little pamphlet to fit the loose-leaf notebook. Convenient and practical.

GETTING ACQUAINTED WITH NATURE IN CAMP

Mrs. Ruth A. Nichols

"LET US BE MUCH WITH NATURE; NOT AS THEY THAT LABOR WITHOUT SEEING, THAT EMPLOY HER UNLOVED FORCES BLINDLY WITHOUT JOY."

CHAPTER XXI

THE JOY OF COLLECTING

Then we gather as we travel
Bits of moss and dirty gravel,
And we chip off little specimens of stone.
And we carry home as prizes
Funny bugs of handy sizes
Just to give the day a scientific tone.[1]

— Charles E. Carryl

Making collections is one of the usual hobbies of boys and girls, whether of postage stamps, buttons, rocks, butterflies, or of scores of other things. This instinct can be capitalized in nature work, and will lead to intimate contacts with nature, close observation to secure the best specimens, discrimination between related forms, and care in preparing them. It will also tend to make stronger mental impressions and memories of objects and places. The collection itself is something that is concrete, that can be taken home, and displayed and explained. Properly directed this activity may be one of the best methods of imparting or developing nature knowledge. The collections may be personal or may be made for a school or camp museum. Often both objects may be accomplished at the same time. Naturally the individual collection has more appeal since pride of ownership is a powerful incentive.

Objects or curios that attract momentarily but which have no real meaning do not properly constitute a collection.

[1] From *Davy and the Goblin* by Charles E. Carryl. Copyright by Houghton Mifflin Company.

Much more will be learned if one kind of thing is collected, though among the members of a class or camp different collections may be made.

LEAVES AND FLOWERS. Probably the easiest collection to begin with is one of tree leaves or leaf prints. Making a collection of this sort will not injure the trees or forest. Nature produces so many more leaves than are necessary that those taken for specimens, even if all the members of the group specialize on the one subject, can do no harm, except in the case of very young trees.

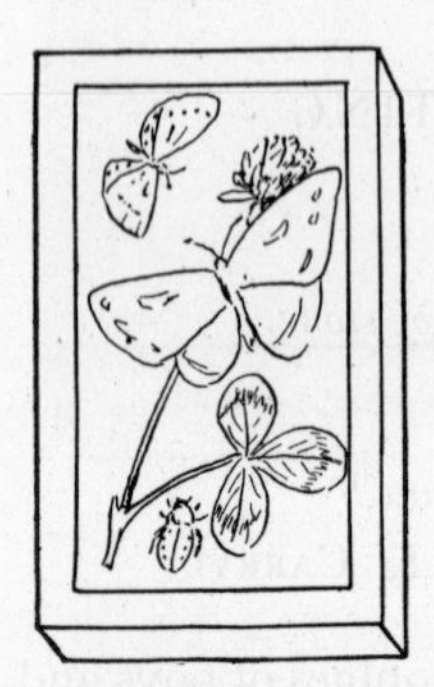

INSECTS AND CLOVER ON THE COTTON OF A RIKER MOUNT

Flower collections must be made with much more care, both with regard to conservation and in order to get good specimens. More work and more time are required. With both leaves and flowers the specimens can be kept in notebooks or on sheets of stiff paper or Bristol board.

Mounting paper may be purchased from any biological or scientific supply company, or the same kind of paper may be secured in large sheets from a wholesale paper house or from a local printer and cut by the dealer to the proper size. (Remnants from this cutting can be used for many purposes.) The size of the standard mounting paper for plants is 12 by 16½ inches. Cut to half size, 8¼ by 12, it is large enough for most specimens and is much more convenient to handle. Specimens of flowers should be mounted only one on a sheet. With leaves, several closely related forms may be mounted together. If the sheets are placed in folders of heavy paper (genus covers may be obtained from supply companies), they are easily kept and take up little room.

Photograph by G. T. Hastings

ROCK SPECIMENS MOUNTED IN PLASTER

OTHER COLLECTIONS. Collections of wood, rocks, or insects are more bulky and require boxes of some sort. Here the use of boxes of uniform size and the systematic arrangement of specimens is important if the collection is something

Photograph by G. T. Hastings

ROCK SPECIMENS IN WOODEN TRAYS

to be treasured. With each specimen there should be a label giving at least the name, place where collected, name of collector, and date. The labels should be uniformly placed with reference to the specimen — in the lower right-hand corner if mounted on cards or in notebooks; immediately below the specimens, if in boxes.

CAUTIONS. If many are making collections care is necessary, especially in the case of plants, that unusual or uncommon forms are not exterminated. The ideals of conservation may well be developed in this connection. Gather nothing from the road or trail side where it is of interest to those who pass by. Never gather a plant unless there are numerous specimens — at least ten is a good rule. Do not take plants up by their roots. Gather none that you do not actually use.

NATURE EMBLEMS FROM SEA PINES CAMP

NATURE EMBLEMS. A special nature emblem is a valuable stimulus in nature collecting. Many camps have devised individual emblems, usually small and made of felt, to be sewn on the camp uniform. They may be purchased in quantity from any firm that makes emblems, banners, etc., or they may be made by hand from the cloth. In either case they are inexpensive. The designs may be of a leaf, a bird, a but-

NATURE EMBLEMS USED AT THE CAMPS IN BEAR MOUNTAIN PARK

terfly, etc., or they may include letters or geometric figures. The museum emblems developed by Mr. B. Talbot Hyde, "Uncle Bennie," at the Boy Scout camps around the Kanohwahke Lakes, N.Y., and adopted by all of the camps in Bear Mountain Park, furnish a good example of the value of this device in increasing interest in nature.

The list in the Appendix, pages 437–440, outlines the collections or sets of notes for which emblems are awarded in these camps. This list was worked out by the nature-lore staff of the Scout camp headquarters, to make a series of requirements that were about equal in difficulty, any one of which could be completed in a period of two weeks. The emblems used are the tulip leaf, block M, and bar of green felt with brown letters. The first or minor emblem was awarded for a single collection, the second or major emblem for four collections or their equivalent, the bar for the equivalent of two major emblems.

More than a thousand of these emblems have been awarded annually for a number of years. Wherever emblems are used, definite standards should be established, at least equal to those given.

BIBLIOGRAPHY

DENSLOW, CORNELIUS, *Making Nature Collections* (Service Library, series D, No. 3198). Boy Scouts of America, 1929.

Practical suggestions for collecting, preserving, and mounting nature material.

CHAPTER XXII

NATURE MUSEUMS AND NATURE TRAILS

THE LANGUAGE OF THE TRAILS

Every mark on the ground, every scratch on the bark of a tree, every depression made in the grass by the body of a sleeping animal, is a character of this universal language. The feather of a bird, dropped in its flight, a tuft of hair clinging to a twig or root, the cast skin of a snake lying among the stones — each has a definite piece of information (apart from the fact of its presence) to impart to one well versed in the language of the trails.[1]

— ERNEST HAROLD BAYNES

In many respects, the making of a camp museum or a school nature room is of more value than making individual collections, because it should secure the coöperation of a large proportion of campers or pupils and is of interest to the whole camp. In school the biology pupils will find such nature projects fascinating. Gathering material for the museum may well be one objective of all hikes. Boys and girls especially interested in nature work may be made curators in charge of some one division of the activity, i.e., flowers, trees, rocks, animals, etc.

In general, the specimens on display should be those gathered from the neighborhood of the camp or school. Each specimen should have a label telling what it is, where and when found, and the name of the finder. Labels are more valuable if some facts of interest are added. The labels should be of one or two standard sizes. Library

[1] From "The Language of the Trails" by Ernest Harold Baynes. Copyright by *Harper's Magazine*, December, 1905.

Courtesy of Boy Scouts of America

A NATURE MUSEUM

This table is one of two prepared after a half day's collecting at a Scout Leaders training camp.

cards, 3 by 5 inches, are satisfactory for the larger size, and may be cut in half for the smaller. Labels may be attached to the edges of boxes or shelves, or placed below or beside the

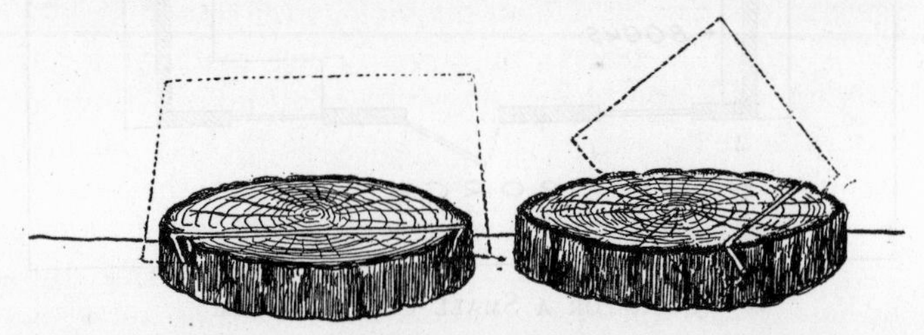

LABEL HOLDERS

specimens so as to give the best effect. A convenient holder for labels is made by cutting a disk one-half inch thick from a branch one and a half to two inches in diameter, then cutting a groove one quarter inch deep across the disk half an inch from the edge. This cut should be slightly oblique so that the label will slant backwards. Similar blocks can be prepared from lumber finished by sandpaper and stain.

LOCATION OF MUSEUM. Conditions as to the surroundings and the place available for a museum differ so much that general suggestions only can be given here. But "where there's a will, there's a way," and if the interest in nature is strong, the building up of a museum or a nature room should be possible in every camp and school.

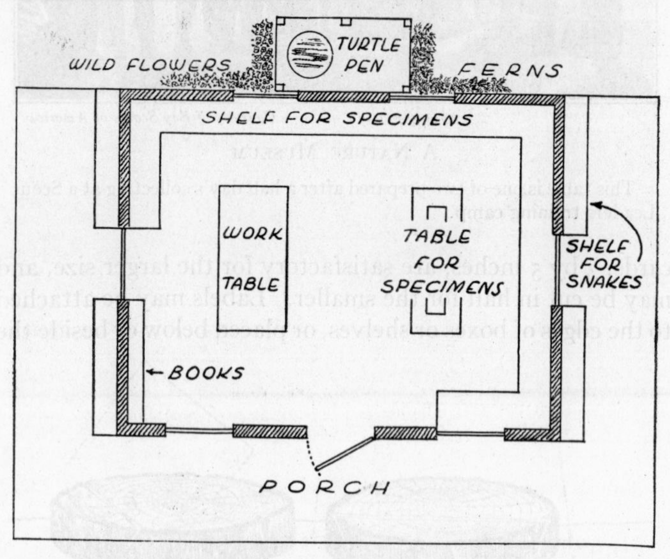

PLAN FOR A SMALL CAMP MUSEUM

In camp the museum or nature room may be a special building or room, a tent, or a corner of a recreation or mess hall. If nothing better is available, a mantel or shelf and the wall back of it can be used. In school, a corner of a laboratory or a table and adjacent wall in one corner of the biology room will serve such a purpose. Where an entire room can be devoted to a museum, a great deal more can always be accomplished, because this becomes a real headquarters. Whatever place is used will become the center for nature study accomplishments, a place where specimens can be compared and classified, where names and items of interest can be looked up and studied. Campers and students will take pride in the specimens they contribute and so help the museum to become a show place of the camp, the first place where visitors are taken.

Courtesy of Abraham Mandelstam

THE NATURE MUSEUM AT CAMP WIGWAM, HARRISON, ME.

EQUIPMENT. The necessary equipment for the average museum is slight: a few shelves, cardboard for the labels and informational bulletins, gummed labels, bottles for plants, a bulletin board, a few glass-topped boxes for insects, aquaria, small or large glass cases (Wardian) for plants or animals, and boxes or cages for reptiles and amphibians when possible. Further details regarding the construction and use of these items are given elsewhere in this book. A piece of chicken-wire meshing securely fastened behind the shelves makes a convenient place to hang specimens. For this purpose the equipment should include five or six dozen bottles of different sizes and shapes, most of which may be collected from the kitchen.

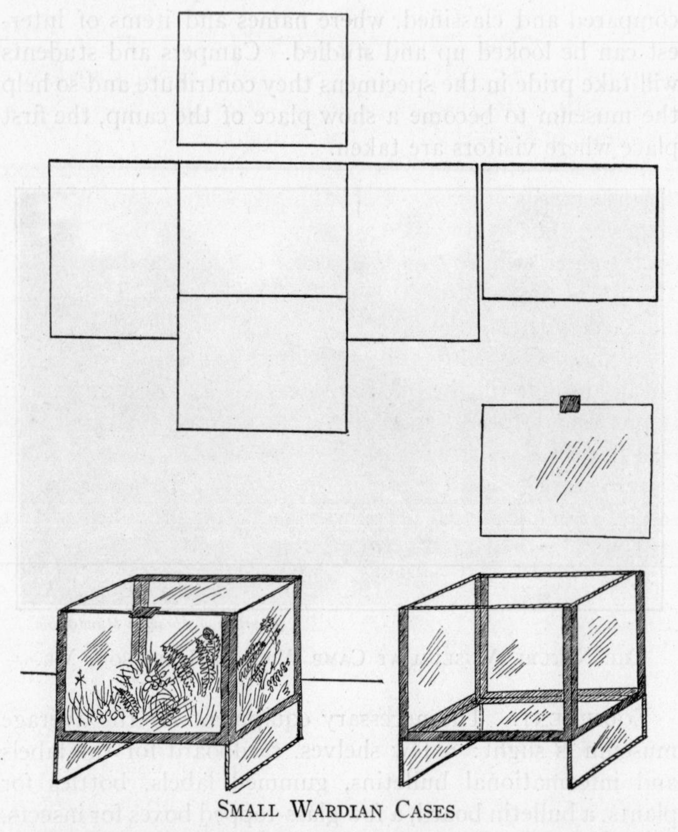

SMALL WARDIAN CASES

The rectangles above show how the glass was arranged before fastening with adhesive tape.

Small glass cases can be made for living plants or insects by using six pieces of glass of uniform size. (Old photographic negatives, 4 by 5 or 5 by 7 inches, from which the gelatin coat has been removed in hot water, are excellent as the glass is clear, thin, and evenly cut.) Old negatives can often be secured at small cost from a professional photographer, but any other glass may be used. With ordinary adhesive tape one half to one inch in width, the glasses can be put together as shown in the diagram. The sixth piece is fastened at one edge only, making a hinged cover with a small piece of adhesive on the side opposite the hinge to keep the cover from dropping in.

A larger Wardian case can be made with a shallow tin pan and five pieces of glass. For example, with a pan, 8 by 10 inches on the bottom, use two pieces of glass, 8 by 10 inches, for the ends, two, 10 by 10 inches for the sides and one piece, 8½ by 10½ inches, for the top. The sides and ends are fastened with adhesive tape into a rectangle, the pan is filled about two-thirds full of plaster of Paris, and the glass put in and left till the plaster hardens. Then the top piece is put on. Mosses, small ferns, and flowering plants do well in such a case with a minimum of care, as very little water escapes, and the air in the case is kept nearly saturated. Such cases also do very well for small frogs and snakes. Instead of plaster of Paris, sand or soil can be used in the pan though these will not hold the glass firmly.

A piece of wire fastened around the neck of a bottle, with the end bent over into a hook, makes a convenient way of hanging the bottle to netting against a wall and the same bottle may be used repeatedly. Labels may be held on the bottles by slipping rubber bands over them, or they may be fastened on with pieces of wire put through small holes near the top of the label, and twisted at the back, or again they may be hung onto the neck of the bottles by hooks made of hairpins or other thin wire. If labels are wired on, it is best to have the lower edge of the label even with the bottom of the bottle. A convenient way of obtaining wires of the proper length for fastening bottles is to cut a square of netting of such a length that as the wires are pulled out, first from one side, then from the other, they will be of the desired length to fasten around the bottle.

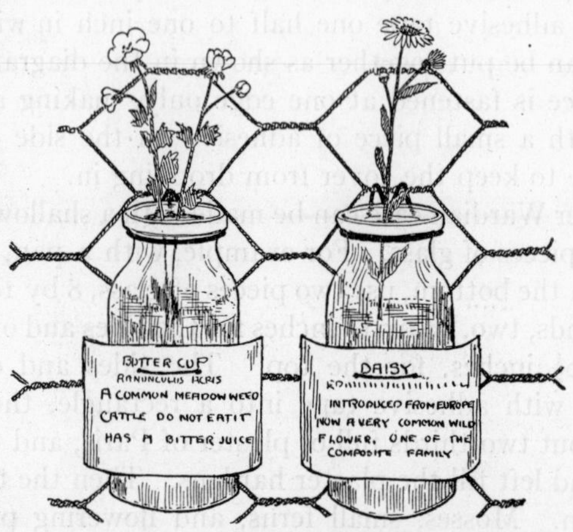
BUTTER CUP
RANUNCULUS ACRIS
A COMMON MEADOW WEED
CATTLE DO NOT EAT IT
HAS A BITTER JUICE
DAISY
INTRODUCED FROM EUROPE
NOW A VERY COMMON WILD
FLOWER. ONE OF THE
COMPOSITE FAMILY

ONE WAY OF EXHIBITING FLOWERS

There will be plenty of opportunity for help from assistants in the conduct of the museum. The assistant in charge of flowers, for instance, will see that new specimens replace old ones when wilted, that fresh water is added as needed, and that labels are written as directed. For small animals like snakes, turtles, salamanders, etc., boxes with glass or fine mesh netting fronts should be placed on shelves or on tables where they may be easily observed. (See Chapter IV.) Spread-insects may be exhibited in Riker mounts, in similar mounts made by boys and girls, in wooden boxes such as cigar boxes, or in the standard insect boxes with glass tops. Rocks and minerals may be wired in shallow boxes, or placed in trays, or arranged on shelves or tables. Charts, drawings, and pictures may be hung, or tacked to the walls or bulletin boards. Such bird and flower pictures as those published by the New York State Museum and referred to at the ends of Chapters III and XIII are excellent. If mounted on cardboard such pictures will last almost indefinitely. Charts of harmful insects, directions for fire prevention, or the conservation laws of the state can usually be procured from the State Conservation Commission or Bureaus of Entomology or Forestry.

Courtesy of Oliver P. Medsger

TRANSFERRING INSECTS FROM THE SPREADING BOARD

Aquaria may consist of simple wide-mouthed bottles or fruit jars, or they may be glass-walled tanks holding several gallons of water. They may harbor aquatic insects, fish, frogs, salamanders, or various small invertebrates. In any event they furnish unique opportunity for all observers to watch the life activities and antics of ordinarily unobservable aquatic life.

The museum should be the hub of the nature activities in the camp or school. With the right spirit actuating the nature leaders, it will not degenerate into a "dead circus" or be filled with biological antiques. Probably the major part of the exhibits should be of *living* forms found in the environment.

NATURE TRAILS. Perhaps even more important than the indoor museum is the outdoor project known as the Nature Trail. While nature trails, of a sort, have been in existence for a long time, the nature-trail idea was first popularized by Dr. Frank Lutz at the Station for the Study of Insects, located in the Bear Mountain section of the Palisades Interstate Park near Tuxedo, N. Y. This was developed under the auspices of the American Museum of Natural History, New York City, with the coöperation of the Interstate Park authorities. The Nature Trail has probably reached its highest development under Mr. William Carr, also of the American Museum, at Bear Mountain Park. The trails of Dr. Lutz and Mr. Carr are described in pamphlets published by the American Museum of Natural History. Dr. Herman C. Bumpus has also developed valuable naturalist trails in Yellowstone and other national parks.

Following the work of these pioneers, nature trails have now been adopted by hundreds of camps, and by many schools. In some cases they have been very successful; in others the campers or pupils have taken no interest in them. Why should there be such a difference?

LABELS. The answer undoubtedly lies in the way the trail was made and in the character of the labels. The trail should be planned to give as much variety as possible;

should start and end in readily accessible places, but, where possible, should include regions not regularly visited by the campers and pupils. All kinds of natural objects may be labeled: flowers, ferns, mushrooms, trees, rocks, insects, birds' nests and the like. Labels may be written on linen tags (Dennison's #3, #4, or #5; grade C light, or grade L heavy) with waterproof India ink, or they may be printed on small painted boards or pieces of sheet zinc. Some naturalists first paint the sheet zinc white, then letter it with black paint. Others print with white paint on a black or dark background. If the surface is finally given a coat or two of valspar, it will last indefinitely.

American Museum of Natural History

THE NATURE TRAIL

The labels are raised on sticks to a convenient height.

Probably for the average camp the linen labels will be entirely satisfactory. If, however, they are to be used in a region where winds prevail, it may be safer to use brass wire to fasten them. One of the authors found that even strong linen cord wore through in a few weeks on a nature trail at the seashore where breezes by day and night were constantly whipping the labels back and forth.

Whichever of the several types of labels is adopted, it should be remembered that what is on the label bears the same degree of importance to the blank label that the contents of an egg bear to its shell. A label that gives only dry, scientific terms or merely common names will not excite much interest. Contrast the interest values of "Red Cedar, Juniperus virginiana, Northeastern United States," with "This lead-pencil tree, Red Cedar, is the favorite wood for making lead pencils. It is also used for cedar chests. Smell it." If other red cedars are found on the trail, labels on them should tell something different, for example: "Can you find two kinds of leaves on this tree? Cedar leaves are always small but are different on young and old shoots," and "How did the cedar waxwing get its name? Look for the small berries on this tree. Many birds are fond of them."

The general principle back of labels for nature trails was well expressed by Dr. Lutz: "A friend somewhat versed in Natural History is taking a walk with you and calling your attention to interesting things." Labels, therefore, should be short and easily read. If there seems to be more to tell than will go on a small label, put two or three labels on a specimen. People who would be bored by a long account seem glad to read the same amount distributed over several brief labels.

With grasses or low flowers, a stick pushed into the ground beside the specimen, with the label fastened at the top, brings it to a convenient height for reading. The slim wooden rods which carpenters call dowels do nicely for this purpose. Where objects are a short distance from the trail, a string may run from the label on the trail to the near-by object.

The text of the labels might include verses of nature

poems, quotations, sentences on the work of plants or animals, statements on local geology; in fact anything which will really increase the interest. Whatever is written should be terse and graphic, with some reference, where possible, to human interests.

American Museum of Natural History

ANIMAL CAGES ON THE TRAIL

Such cages make it easy to watch squirrels, chipmunks, and woodchucks.

The trail itself should be a narrow path, with labels close enough so that one or more is always in sight ahead. It may be possible to build the cages or pens for snakes, frogs, turtles, or other animals along the nature trail. Outlines of birds, cut from thin wood and painted in correct colors, may be placed in trees, and the descriptions fastened below, or bird pictures can be mounted on boards, coated with white shellac or colorless varnish, and put up in places where birds might naturally be found, yet low enough to be seen easily.

The nature trail should become a growing, almost a living thing, with new labels put up and old ones taken down several times during the season. It should calendar the opening of new flowers as old ones wither; the development of fruits; the change in the bird's nest of eggs at the beginning of the season to the cradle for young birds, or the abandoned nest a few weeks later; the ephemeral fungi springing up after the rain; or a tiny ravine or miniature delta produced by the summer downpour.

Under some conditions, it may not be practical or feasible to change the trail frequently. But whether altered or not, it is a peculiar adjunct to nature study that ought not to be neglected.

Even urban schools, if in the outskirts of the city, and certainly all rural schools have an excellent opportunity to build and to maintain nature trails. Such trails can also be laid out in city parks if neighborhood examples of unsympathetic young *Homo sapiens* can be prevented from breaking them up.

The following are examples of labels used on different trails and give an excellent idea of labels that make a trail interesting. They are given without arrangement by topics, quite as labels would be met on a trail.

HELP TO KEEP THIS TRAIL NARROW.
GO SINGLE FILE.
KEEP ON THE PATH.

LAUREL IS RAPIDLY BEING DESTROYED BY CRIMINALS WHO BREAK IT FOR A FEW HOURS' SELFISH ENJOYMENT OF ITS FLOWERS.

A label on a twig above an old nest of the mound-building ant:

A DEAD CITY

DESERTED BY ITS FOUNDERS

THIS CITY WAS STARTED ABOUT 30 YEARS AGO BY A QUEEN ANT, *FORMICA EXSECTOIDES*, THE MOUND BUILDER.

THE WORKERS HEAPED UP STICKS AND PEBBLES IN WHAT WAS THEN AN OPEN SPOT TO CATCH THE SUN'S RAY AND KEEP THE YOUNG ANTS WARM.

THEN PLANTS GREW UP AND SHADED THE MOUND; MOSS COVERED IT; AND THE HUGE POPULATION OF THIS ONCE BUSY COLONY DIED.

This label was put at a clump of red clover.

OLD MAIDS ARE THE SUPPORT OF THE BRITISH EMPIRE

"OLD MAIDS KEEP CATS. CATS DESTROY FIELD MICE, WHICH PREY ON BUMBLEBEES' NESTS. BUMBLEBEES INSURE SEEDS TO RED CLOVER. RED CLOVER MAKES GOOD BEEF. AND GOOD BEEF MAKES BIG STRONG MEN, WHO EXTEND AND KEEP UP THE BRITISH EMPIRE." — Q. E. D.

THE GLACIER ROUNDED THE HILLTOPS AND SMOOTHED THE ROCKS THAT YOU SEE HERE. IT REMOVED HUGE BOULDERS FROM THE MOUNTAINS AND CARRIED THEM TO OTHER REGIONS. ALL THIS WAS DONE ABOUT 25,000 YEARS AGO.

HOW MANY FINGERS HAVE YOU?
THIS PLANT IS NAMED CINQUEFOIL OR "FIVE FINGER."
IT HAS FIVE LEAFLETS.

INDIANS USED THE INNER BARK OF THE BASSWOOD TREE FOR STRING OR CORD.

SOCRATES DRANK POISON HEMLOCK — BUT IT WAS NOT FROM THIS KIND OF PLANT.

A colored picture of a catbird, glued on a board and varnished, was put on a stake near a deserted nest, with this label:

THIS IS A CATBIRD WHOSE LAST YEAR'S NEST IS STILL HERE.

Another picture was of an ovenbird and its young with the following label:

IF YOU HEAR A BIRD SINGING "TEACHER, TEACHER, TEACHER, TEACHER," IT WILL BE THE OVENBIRD.
HERE IS THE OVENBIRD FEEDING ITS YOUNG.

THIS TREE HAS THE LEAVES IN PAIRS.
ASHES, MAPLES AND FLOWERING DOGWOOD HAVE OPPOSITE LEAVES.
THIS IS A NORWAY MAPLE.

DWARF SUMACH

DISTINGUISHED FROM OTHER SUMACHS BY THE WINGS ON THE LEAF STALKS BETWEEN THE LEAFLETS. NON-POISONOUS.

THE PECULIAR RIDGED BARK MAKES IT EASY TO RECOGNIZE THIS AMERICAN HORNBEAM. ALSO CALLED BLUE BEECH, WATER BEECH, AND, INCORRECTLY, IRONWOOD.

HACKBERRY

THE CLUSTERS OF SMALL TWIGS ARE "WITCHES' BROOMS," CAUSED BY A FUNGUS DISEASE LIVING INSIDE THE BRANCHES.

AMERICAN HORNBEAM

THE WOOD IS VERY HARD AND TOUGH. THE TREE IS SOMETIMES CALLED "IRONWOOD" — A NAME BELONGING TO A DIFFERENT TREE.

MANHATTAN SCHIST

THE LARGE MASSES OF MINERAL WITH SMOOTH SURFACES ARE FELDSPAR. SCHISTS ARE METAMORPHIC ROCKS, CHANGED BY HEAT AND PRESSURE FROM SOME OTHER KIND OF ROCK.

WHEN THE BARK IS PEELED OFF THE WHITE BIRCH NO NEW BARK EVER REPLACES IT.

Dr. Lutz had two trails: the Training Trail that we have described, followed by a shorter Testing Trail. On this were questions that could be answered by one who read all the labels on the first trail. If a trail of this kind is used it should be changed every week or two. Questions on this trail may be "What tree (or flower, or fungus, or rock) is this?" or "What kind of plant is this?" Or they may ask for information given on other labels, as "What trees besides the ash have opposite leaves?" "What trees on the trail have compound leaves?" "What other names has the American Hornbeam?" "For what is this shrub used by man?" Or the questions may simply call for observation, as in this label which was placed on a cut stump: "How many inches did this tree grow in its first ten years?" "Are these leaves simple or compound?" "How many needles in a bunch on this pine tree?" Campers may go over the Testing Trail and write out answers to the questions to be turned in for the counselor to score, or they may score their own papers by referring to the set of correct answers posted in the camp museum.

BIBLIOGRAPHY

Carr, William H., *Signs Along the Trail*, American Museum of Natural History, 1927.

—— *Blazing Nature Trails*, American Museum of Natural History, 1929.

—— *Trailside Family*, American Museum of Natural History, 1931.

These three pamphlets describe the second and more elaborate trail at Bear Mountain. Details of the making of the trail and incidents in its use are given.

—— *The Nature Trail Book*, Oxford University Press, 1932.

A well illustrated book, telling how to collect, preserve, and mount specimens and how to make nature trails and outdoor museums.

COOKE, EDMUND, *Nature Trails in Cleveland*, Cleveland Museum, 1930.

A pamphlet describing how nature trails are made and used in city parks.

LUTZ, FRANK E., *Nature Trails*, American Museum of Natural History, 1926.

Illustrated pamphlet on the pioneer trails in the Bear Mountain Section of Interstate Park.

CHAPTER XXIII

NATURE EXPLORATIONS

Thank God! there is always a Land of Beyond
For us who are true to the trail;
A vision to seek, a beckoning peak,
A farness that never will fail.[1]

— ROBERT W. SERVICE

A hike may be just getting over the ground, but from start to finish nature hikes are explorations.

A definite objective is worth while, but what is seen incidentally along the way is sometimes even more important. There are any number of objectives. Find as many trees as possible over a given road or trail; search for ferns, mushrooms, or flowers; hunt for rocks and minerals; visit a bog or swamp to find out what plants and animals live there; or explore some stream or shore. Early morning bird walks are discussed in Chapter IV on birds. Sometimes hikes may be made to places not previously visited by the leader, a place heard of from others, or located on a map as being of probable interest. Such a hike may be announced as an exploring trip to find the place and learn as much about it as possible. If a camp or school museum has been started, material for it can be collected, and even with no museum some specimens should be brought back to be exhibited for a few days, with a brief description of what they are and where they were found. The party should have equipment in which specimens can be carried, such as a botanical collecting can, boxes, bottles, or a knapsack.

[1] From *Rhymes of a Rolling Stone* by Robert W. Service. Copyright by Barse and Company.

Photograph by Frank E. Lutz

THE START OF THE HIKE

Following a narrow trail into the woods, with the possibility of interesting discovery any minute.

On a hike the leader should be alert to note everything of interest, and so far as possible he should encourage individual observation and get the boys and girls to call attention to trees, flowers, birds, insects, rock formations, sounds, and odors. Questions about the things seen develop more interest than simply telling about them. At times it is well to stop to make closer observation or to watch some bird or insect and see what it is doing. Two or three in the party may be appointed scribes or reporters to keep a record of what is seen and later make a report to be read or posted. If the hike is an all-day one, time may be taken after lunch to talk over what has been seen, or the leader may tell or read some nature story while the group rests. During periods of rest on the trail such games as "Twenty Questions," "I am Thinking," or other quiet games may be played. These games and other appropriate ones are described in detail in Chapter XXIV. Lecturing about nature should be as much avoided on hikes as in the classroom.

The number to be taken on a nature hike depends on the leader and the special objective, but in general small groups will see and learn more than large ones. On hikes to see birds, twelve to fifteen is a large group. In looking for trees or studying rock formations, twenty or twenty-five is not too large a group; with larger numbers some will be so far from the leader that they cannot hear or see the special things which are being pointed out. A whistle will enable the leader to call the group together when anything of especial interest has been discovered. Then the one who made the discovery can make the first announcement, while others supplement the statement if necessary.

EXPLORING A MEADOW

Grasses, weeds, insects, spiders, perhaps a small snake or a song sparrow's nest are always possibilities. The list of discoveries in a small area may equal that of a long hike.

Photograph by Paul B. Mann

OVER THE HILLS

The objective may be distant, but there is joy in every step of the way.

After a hike, a report to the whole camp or class adds to the interest in nature work. After supper in the mess hall, around the camp fire in the evening, or at breakfast time, the scribes or reporters of the trip can make a report telling a few of the things observed. A complete list of things seen and of specimens collected may be put in some convenient place where all can see them. The list may be written with crayon or ink on large sheets of wrapping paper and posted above the fireplace in mess hall or recreation room or on a bulletin board indoors or out. Or a small bulletin can be put up in the camp museum. If the small report is used it can be illustrated with pictures from the bird, tree, flower, or insect key sheets of the Slingerland-Comstock leaflets. Extra key leaflets should be kept for this purpose and the pictures cut out and colored with crayons. If lists of the kind are short, space may be available to post succeeding lists, adding to each new one only pictures of the things which may be starred as found for the first time. The cost of the leaflets is so slight that the camp or counselor can well afford half a dozen extra copies of each. A good set of colored pencils should be camp property, to be used by volunteers in making the reports. The dictionary defini-

Photograph by Paul B. Mann

EXPLORING THE BAY AT LOW TIDE

An unusual type of trip adapted to unusual conditions.

tion of *hike* is "to go with effort or laboriously," but our nature hikes should be without effort, and joyous.

BIBLIOGRAPHY

ATHEY, LILLIAN COX, *Along Nature's Trails.* American Book Company, 1936.

A little book for boys and girls telling of the insects, reptiles, birds, mammals, and plants to be found along the trails.

CAVE, E., *Boy Scout Hike Book.* Doubleday, Doran and Company, Inc., 1913.

A small book with directions as to how to hike, what to wear, what to carry, and notes on things to be looked for.

FORDYCE, C. P., *Touring Afoot.* The Macmillan Company, 1918.

Suggestions as to the kinds of outfits and equipment for hikes and trips. Camping equipment and devices.

MORTON, G. F., *Hiking and Tramping.* David McKay, 1929.

Hikes and treks with English schoolboys and scouts. The character-building effects of hiking and the joy of it. How to prepare for long hikes.

CHAPTER XXIV

NATURE GAMES AND STORIES

New stories every night they ask,
And that is not an easy task;
I have to be so many things,
The frog that croaks, the lark that sings,
The cunning fox, the frightened hen;
But just last night they stumped me, when
They wanted me to twist and squirm
And imitate an angle worm.[1]

— EDGAR A. GUEST

Teaching through play has a decided appeal to both teacher and pupil. This is especially true of summer camps where the primary purpose is recreation. There are many games that can be used for giving information about nature or for training observation, and many old games that can be given a nature trend. But games must appeal as games — there must be fun in playing them. A few games are described here; others can be found in the books referred to at the end of the chapter, and often original games can be developed. To add to the interest there can be simple prizes, such as peanuts or a bar of chocolate or bird or flower pictures. This, however, may be a dangerous precedent since it is unscientific procedure. Under some conditions points or honors might seem allowable.

Twenty Questions. This old game can be played either indoors or after lunch on a hike. Any natural object may be chosen — tree, flower, bird, insect, cloud, constellation.

[1] From "Story Telling" in *A Heap o' Livin'*, by Edgar A. Guest. Copyright by Reilly and Lee Company.

One person or a group may be selected to withdraw, while those remaining decide upon the object about which the questions are to be asked. Then the person or group that has withdrawn is summoned to return and do the questioning. Not over twenty questions may be asked, and they must be such as can be answered by *yes* or *no*. If questioning is hit-or-miss it is usually impossible to guess the object, but by beginning with some large division of nature and working down to smaller ones it is possible to guess the object in less than the twenty chances allowed. The successful individual or group helps select the next object and others do the questioning. It is well sometimes to use terms that require explanation, and thus make some instruction an essential part of the game. The following is a typical procedure:

Is the object alive? Yes.
Is it a plant? No.
Is it an invertebrate? No.
Is it warm-blooded? No.
Is it smooth-skinned? Yes. (This should mean it is an amphibian, but to make sure ask definitely.)
Is it an amphibian? Yes.
Is it shaped like a lizard? No.
Does it live most of the time on the ground? No.
Does it live most of the time in the water? No.
Does it live in trees? Yes.
Then it must be a tree frog. Right.

I Am Thinking. The leader thinks of some natural object—rock, star, bird, flower, insect—anything with which the group is somewhat familiar, and says, "I am thinking of an insect (or whatever it may be he has chosen). It has two pairs of wings. It has a mouth fitted for biting." He continues adding one characteristic after another. Each of the group can make one guess. The first person to guess the correct name becomes the leader. This is suitable to play when a group is resting on a hike or in the evening around the camp fire.

Freeze. This may also be played indoors or out. A selected group is told to do something that has a nature suggestion, such as catching a frog in the grass, stalking a woodchuck, picking a water lily from a canoe, or getting away after stepping into a yellow jacket's nest. As soon as the group is busy at the appointed task the command "Freeze!" is given. Instantly each must stop and remain motionless. When anyone moves or laughs he is out. The game is to see who can hold the position longest. The game can be prefaced by a story such as "Raggylug" by Seton Thompson or by remarks on protective coloration and the instinct of most animals to "freeze" to escape detection by enemies.

Posing. This is similar to the preceding. A small group is selected, and each member is told to pose in a position suggested by the leader — picking up a snake, smelling of a skunk cabbage flower, hunting for a bird's nest in the bushes, pointing out the Big Dipper. The rest of the group, making up the audience, votes for the winner.

Five Sense Game. This requires considerable preparation by the leader. *Sight* is tested by pointing out five things to be named — trees, flowers, birds, rocks; *sound* by listening till five nature sounds have been heard and identified — the call of a bird, the chirp of a cricket, wind in the tree tops, etc. The answers may be written down, or if sides are chosen each may appoint a representative to stay with the opposite side and record their answers. For *taste, touch,* and *smell,* one or more representatives of each side must be blindfolded. Nothing should be tasted that is not known to be harmless. Among plants of definite taste are black birch, black cherry, mints, grape tendrils, oxalis or sorrel leaves, pine and spruce leaves, water cress, wild mustard, wintergreen, spice bush, boneset. Some of these also have odors by which they may be recognized; others to be used in testing smell are flowers of many kinds, broken leaves of skunk cabbage, or twigs of ailanthus, sweet fern, hay-scented or boulder fern, yarrow, leek, and sassafras. For touch the players may be led to trees, shrubs, etc., or they may be handed leaves, stones, cones, bits of bark, berries, etc.

Spy-out-the-Land. In the fields or woods several groups may be sent out in different directions to gather information regarding the region. Each group chooses a leader. The groups separate about two hundred paces north, south, and east. After they have gone the assigned distance each group leader sends his members out fifty paces in all directions to see what they can find. When the counselor blows a whistle, after five or more minutes, each group gathers with its leader to plan its report and arrange its exhibit. After three minutes more the whistle assembles all the groups. Reports are made as to the kinds of trees, shrubs, flowers, weeds, insects, birds, stones, mosses, or any other natural objects that have been seen and can be named. Full credit will be given only where an actual specimen is brought back and correctly named. Part credit may be given for insects or birds or inaccessible objects observed, but not brought back. It may be arranged to give different credits for the different kinds of objects; for example, each bird seen and recognized, 5, each insect, 3, wild flowers, 2, trees, 1. The game can be modified to suit the particular region. In playing this game due precautions should be taken not to destroy any rare specimens by indiscriminate collecting.

Museum Collecting. (Somewhat similar to the preceding.) Our various city museums of natural history are continually sending out collecting parties to gather specimens of different sorts. So the members of the group may become collectors either individually or in groups. Before starting out, the kinds of objects to be hunted for are described and a list of points for each announced. A penalty is declared for gathering any flowers or other objects that need to be protected. On the seashore, shells of different kinds, starfish, barnacles, seaweeds, etc., may be collected and spread out for display on the beach. In the woods or fields, flowers, leaves, mosses, ferns, and stones will easily be found. Each player first selects a place to arrange his collection, then at a signal all start out to collect. After ten minutes, collecting is stopped and a few minutes are allowed for arranging the exhibits, which are then scored by the leader.

Go-get-it. An active outdoor game. While the group is resting or eating lunch, the leader wanders around picking up various objects within a radius of two or three hundred feet from the group. The objects found may be put in a box, a hat, or anything that is convenient. When fifteen or twenty have been found the group is called to attention. An object is held up and briefly described. "This is a leaf of a red maple; note the sharp angles between the lobes and the sharp teeth on the edges. This is the cup of a white oak; note that it is nearly as deep as it is broad and that the scales on the sides are in rounded knobs." At the command — "Go and get it," the group scatters to hunt for one of the same kind. The leader should have ready about twenty slips of paper, each five inches long by one inch wide, cut almost across into five equal parts, the parts numbered from 1 to 5. The first one in with the correct object gets a square numbered 5, the next the one numbered 4, and so on till five are in; then the whistle summons everyone in to start with the next object. Care should be taken not to use an object found too close to the leader, or he may be roughly jostled in the scramble for the first specimen. When all the objects have been used, the cards are counted up and the one with the highest score wins. It is well to have among the objects a few that are rather hard to find and at a distance of at least three hundred feet, though most should be nearer and in plain sight.

Match It. An indoor modification of the previous game and one which requires more preparation. The leader has collected a variety of objects, having at least eight or ten of each, such as leaves, pebbles, dry fruits or seeds, cones, etc. One of each kind is retained by the leader; the rest are scattered on the floor or tables at one end of the room. The leader stands at the opposite end of the room and calls the group around him, shows and describes one object, then sends the group to match it. Points are given as in the previous game.

Indoor Nature Trail. This may be played as an afternoon game or may be a camp contest to extend over a period of one or more days. The leader, preferably with the aid of some of the campers, brings in from twenty-five to fifty natural objects. These are arranged around some room — a mess hall, recreation hall, or whatever place is available. The objects should be numbered. They should not be placed near together, otherwise the campers will be too close to each other and will be tempted to look on each other's paper or to ask help. The campers are to go over the trail with paper and pencil, and list the number and name of each object. The lists are to be scored by the leader. If reference books are available a longer time may be given and the use of books encouraged.

Indoor Bird Hike. Pictures of birds to the number of twenty or forty are to be exposed without names or other identification. The names may be cut off from the bottom, or narrow cards may be fastened with paper clips over the names. These pictures are pinned to the walls or clipped to strings. Each has a number as in the preceding game. The campers are given a limited time to go over the trail and name as many birds as possible. The game will be made more interesting and of more value if use is made of the key sheet of birds of the Comstock series, or the Audubon Pocket Bird Collection (10 cents each from the Audubon Society).

Bird Identification. The leader may explain some of the difficulties of studying birds in the fields: the momentary flash of color as a bird disappears in the thick bushes, the distant glimpses, the bird that can be only half seen through the leaves or seen against the sky, and the frequent need of making quick identifications in bird study. He then holds up a picture of a bird for two seconds and puts it down. The players write down the names as bird after bird is shown. The time between the pictures should be varied; sometimes allow a short lapse after the names are written; sometimes snap the fingers for attention and show a picture before the last has been written down.

Kim's Game. Before playing this the story of *Kim* should be told, perhaps at camp fire some evening and the game played next day, or the story may be given just before playing. In Chapter Nine of Kipling's story we read how Lurgan Sahib had the little Hindu boy teach Kim to observe, as part of his training for the great game he was to enter. To play the game gather ten or fifteen objects — leaves, blossoms, seeds, stones, feathers, dead insects, shells. Spread them out on a table or board and cover with a cloth or paper. Have the group stand closely around, uncover the objects for thirty seconds, cover them, and have the players write a list of what they have seen. If the names of the objects are not known, descriptions will do as well. A second time the game may be varied by using more objects or by giving a shorter time to look at them. This game, often used by scouts, is especially good for training in observation.

The Mantel Game or What is it? [1] This game was origi-

[1] This game is very similar to the "Whats" used as part of the regular training at the Pennsylvania State College Nature Camp.

nated by one of the authors and has been used in camps for over ten years. It has also been adapted for use in schools. Each morning some object — a flower in a bottle of water, an insect gall, a stone, a shell, a glass case with a living insect, frog, or salamander, or any other natural ob-

Photograph by Paul B. Mann

THE MANTEL GAME

One girl is placing her answer in the box, another is using a reference book to find what the object is.

ject — is put up on one end of a mantel or shelf where the campers will have an opportunity to see it. Near by or below is a box with a slit in the top or on the side, into which a slip of paper with the name of the contestant and his or her answer may be dropped. Next day a new object is put up, while the old one goes up at the other end of the shelf with the correct name and a short description, together with a list of those who answered it correctly. The value of the game is increased if books are available in which information regarding the objects can be found. At the end of a week, or a longer period, points may be given to those with the largest number of correct answers.

Nature Treasure Hunt. Treasure hunts can be tried once or twice during the season. In the nature treasure hunt, the trail is marked by natural objects. For example, the directions may state: "Look for a group of six white birches within twenty paces. Go to them and sight to the east a large white oak. At the oak look for a boulder covered with lichens. At one side of the boulder is a small blueberry bush. Find a twig arrow and follow where it points to a sugar maple tree. From the further side of the tree look for a dogwood tree whose top has been broken over in a winter's sleet storm. From this tree go twenty paces north to an old chestnut stump. Hidden here is a note; read it and leave it where it was found. Follow the directions given." Two or three such trails may start away from camp in different directions but all meet at the stump. It is unlikely that the players will arrive at the stump simultaneously. From here on, the directions may be in the form of notes hidden under bark or stones, tied to trees, placed inside a deserted bird's nest, etc., each note giving directions where the next is to be found. The last note tells that a treasure is hidden somewhere within a definite number of paces. The treasure may be an order on the camp store, a book on nature, or whatever the leader may find convenient, but the best treasure hunts end in a camp feast of some kind in which all can join.

Nature Stories. Stories are always welcome, especially in the evening around the camp fire, when resting on the trail, after lunch on a hike, or on a rainy afternoon. The more good stories the nature counselor can tell, the better. Of course the telling of stories is only an incidental matter and must not take the place of studying nature. Stories may be read, though the effect is not so satisfactory as when they are told. If a few good stories are gone over a number of times and a few notes made to enable the counselor to recall the details, he should find no trouble in telling the stories when opportunity arises.

In the Glow of the Camp Fire

Such a setting is ideal for stories of wild animals, Indian legends, or of the experiences of explorers.

In order to tell the story well, one must first try to understand and sympathize with the animals. Next try to separate the facts on which the story is based from the fiction that may have been built up around them. In the telling be sure to emphasize the facts. Go over the story by yourself several times till the details are familiar. Make a few notes on the chief events. A series of small cards giving a few words to suggest the course of the story can be carried about and referred to without interrupting the flow of the story. If the counselor can bring two or three books of stories to camp, he can prepare new stories to tell during the season. Some may be very short and take but a few minutes in the telling, others may take much longer, but familiarity with at least a few is desirable.

BIBLIOGRAPHY

Nature Games

Palmer, E. Lawrence, *Nature Games.* Slingerland-Comstock Company, 1924.

A leafax size booklet describing a number of nature games.

Seton, Ernest Thompson, "Things to Do" in *Woodland Tales.* Doubleday, Doran and Company, Inc., 1926.

Brief accounts of games and of making various things.

Smith, Charles F., *Games and Recreational Methods for Clubs, Camps, and Scouts.* Dodd, Mead and Company, 1924.

One chapter is devoted to nature games. These have all been tried out and found to be successful.

Toplitz, E. L., *Indoor Contest Games for Groups.* Slingerland-Comstock Company, 1929.

A leafax size booklet describing games for groups.

Vinal, William Gould, "Nature Games," a reprint of the chapter in *Nature Guiding.* Slingerland-Comstock Company, 1926.

Descriptions of games for indoors and outdoors. Enough variety to suit all groups and places.

Nature Stories

Baynes, Ernest Harold, *Polaris, the Story of an Eskimo Dog.* The Macmillan Company, 1922.

This and other stories by the same author will appeal to young people, and they are accurate.

Brallier, Floyd B., *Knowing the Birds Through Stories.* Funk and Wagnalls Company, 1922.

Written for younger children, this and the other nature stories by the same author will make the birds, insects, and animals seem friends.

Burgess, Thornton, *The Bedtime Story Books.* Little, Brown and Company, 1913–1919.

A series of twenty small books of animal stories, with all the animals talking and acting like humans. They have been popular with children, and many grown-ups, for years. Also other series of stories — *The Green Forest, The Smiling Pool, Mother West Wind*, etc.

BURROUGHS, JOHN, *Wake Robin*. Houghton Mifflin Company.

Accurate observations graphically told by one of our greatest naturalists. Other books by the same author will be found of equal interest. Many editions of these nature essays have been issued.

CADY, BERTHA C., *Tami, the Story of a Chipmunk*. Slingerland-Comstock Company, 1927.

A small book giving the life history of one of our commonest small mammals.

EVARTS, HAL, *The Bald Face*. Alfred A. Knopf, 1921.

These stories, and other books by the same author, while not personifying the animals to as great an extent as many others, make the animals seem almost human and create a feeling of sympathy with them.

FABRE, JEAN HENRI, *Animal Life in Field and Garden*. Various publishers.

Various editions of this and other charming and accurate books by the same author can be found.

GIBSON, WILLIAM HAMILTON, *Eye Spy*. Harper and Bros., 1897.

Short nature narratives with beautiful drawings by the author. Other books by the same author will be found equally attractive.

HORNADAY, WILLIAM T., *Tales from Nature's Wonderland*. Charles Scribner's Sons, 1924.

Vivid stories and descriptions of animals of the past and present.

KIPLING, RUDYARD, *The Jungle Books*. Doubleday, Doran and Company, Inc., 1923.

Stories of animal life in India that have long been popular with young people.

MOSELEY, E. L., *Trees, Stars, and Birds*. World Book Company, 1919.

The fact that the book is illustrated in color by Fuertes is enough to assure its worth.

ROBERTS, C. G. D., *Kindred of the Wild*. L. C. Page and Company, 1902.

Good stories of animals, but too much personified to be really good natural history.

SETON, ERNEST THOMPSON, *Wild Animals I Have Known*. Charles Scribner's Sons, 1898.

The illustrations by the author add attractiveness to stories and accounts that are the best among their kind. Other books by the same author are equally good.

SHARP, DALLAS LORE, *Roof and Meadow.* Houghton Mifflin Company, 1901.

Like the author's other book this collection of narratives and descriptions is well written by a careful and accurate observer.

THOREAU, HENRY D., *Walden* and other books. Various publishers.

There is a choice of many editions of these classics of American natural history.

NATURE POEMS

GROVER, EDWIN O., *Animal Lover's Knapsack.* T. Y. Crowell Company, 1929.

A collection of poems about pets, domestic and wild animals, including birds and insects.

——, *Nature Lover's Knapsack.* T. Y. Crowell Company, 1927.

An excellent compilation of modern nature verse, mostly by American authors.

RICHARDS, MRS. WALDO, *High Tide.* Houghton Mifflin Company, 1916.

A collection of poems by present-day poets, many of them about trees, birds, and flowers.

VAN DYKE, HENRY, *Music and other Poems.* Charles Scribner's Sons, 1904.

This volume contains several nature poems, including "God of the Open Air," one of the finest things to read at an outdoor service. This poem can also be obtained in a small volume by itself.

WILLIAMSON, H., *Salar the Salmon.* Ryerson Press, 1935.

A charmingly written story of the life of a salmon; fiction, but scientifically accurate.

CHAPTER XXV

NATURE WORK IN THE CAMP PROGRAM

These are the things I prize
And hold of dearest worth:
Light of the sapphire skies,
Peace of the hills —
Shelter of the forests, comfort of the grass,
Music of birds, murmur of little rills,
Shadows of clouds that swiftly pass,
And, after showers
The smell of flowers
And of the good brown earth,
And best of all, along the way, friendship and mirth.[1]

— HENRY VAN DYKE

In these days of increasing emphasis on the joy and value of the out of doors, nature work in every camp should be at least coördinate with dramatics, athletics, handicraft, and games, so that every camper may enjoy it. Properly conducted it has been proved to have an appeal not equalled by any other activity. In the daily program, at least one period should be devoted to nature work, and every camper should have the opportunity for two such periods a week, with special groups spending more time. Every week should include some early morning bird hikes and some evening star study. The camp program should be flexible enough to admit special nature talks when some interesting animal, rare flower, or other specimen has been brought in. It may be a baby skunk found in the fields, a snake someone has captured, a rare orchid (plants of which should not be

[1] From "God of the Open Air" by Henry van Dyke. Copyright by Charles Scribner's Sons.

disturbed), or any one of a dozen other "finds" the arrival of which cannot be predicted but whose human-interest values are very strong and should be capitalized then and there. While every hike should be, to a certain extent, a nature hike, some can be especially planned for encouraging nature observation. Outside of the regular nature periods, opportunity should be given for volunteer work especially in the museum and camp library. All work toward winning special emblems should be individual.

IN THE EVENING. Assemblies, camp fires, or evening entertainments also give a good chance for some nature work. A nature story may be told by the counselor as the group sits around the friendly camp fire, or nature games such as "Twenty Questions," "I am Thinking," or "Freeze," may be played. The game of posing may be varied by letting one camper at a time take a pose and have the others guess what is represented. Sometimes the nature counselor may be given charge of an entire evening or of an assembly, with the program largely on nature themes. At ceremonial council fires tell stories about the trees that furnished the firewood, or tales of animals, plants, or stars. Some star study may be made part of every evening program. By taking a few minutes at a time, practical knowledge can be built up during the summer without formally designating it "astronomy." On one evening have the circumpolar constellations pointed out, and tell the stories connected with them. At the next session take the group of first-magnitude stars directly overhead — Vega, Deneb, Altair — with their constellations. Another evening the stars to the west may be observed, or again those to the south. The important constellations and their stories will furnish a season's project of this sort.

Through the coöperation of the dramatic department, it should be possible to stage a nature play, of which several are available.

ON RAINY DAYS. On rainy days, nature activities will help to nullify the monotony or the mischief which otherwise is likely to brew. One nature counselor who definitely left certain things for such days, said near the end of a season, "We have not had half enough rainy days for what I wanted to do." A dash out into the rain will secure enough leaves of a dozen kinds to occupy the entire camp with leaf printing, or pressed leaves kept on hand may be used. Collections of leaf prints of all the kinds of trees near camp may be made and brief descriptions written to make a tree book. In the book may be copied poems about trees, many of which will be found in the various anthologies in the camp library or the nature counselor's collection of books. Nature journals or notebooks can be written up on these days, nature drawings made, or large charts prepared for the museum or library. In the museum, specimens can be arranged, and labeled, live insects and animals cared for, and the exhibits leisurely examined. Modeling in clay or plasteline may include birds, flowers, animals, acorn cups or mushrooms, and jars decorated with plant forms. Have a camp contest and an exhibition of the work. Another good project is the coloring of bird, flower, and insect outlines to be kept in the nature notebooks, or used to illustrate reports of hikes or collecting trips. Specimens of rocks may be mounted on boards or in plaster, or work may be done on the herbarium. Damp weather, however, is rather unsatisfactory for the latter work as the plants by absorbing moisture are likely to curl, and the glue remains sticky. Under such conditions strips of gummed paper are much more satisfactory for mounting plants.

Short, rainy-day hikes in raincoats and boots, or in bathing suits if it is a warm rain, are especially welcome. Definite observations should be made, such as making a list of the flowers that close or bend over in the rain and of those that do not change their position; finding how grasshoppers or spiders act in the rain; seeing where the birds go; noticing the effects of the rain on the bare ground of the roadside or the sand of the shore and comparing it with the absence of such effects on the grass-covered fields or the leaf-covered forest floor. Such rainy-day hikes are a good supplement to the work done in clear weather.

ON SUNDAY. On Sunday, special emphasis can be put on nature, either in assembly where the nature counselor may give a short talk on the high spots of nature activities of the week, or in a service held under the trees or by the water. The program may include readings (by someone who *knows how*) from that great out-of-doors book, the Bible, with its imagery of the hills, lakes, springs, trees, and birds, and its stories of the farmer, fisherman, and shepherd. Take for example, the 19th Psalm or the 104th Psalm, or the 28th chapter of Job; or some of the parables — the sower, the tares, the mustard seed, the barren fig tree, the dragnet; or the only fable (Judges 9 : 8–15) — the trees choosing a king. Then there are any number of beautiful nature poems that will fit into such a service: Bryant's "The Groves were God's First Temples," van Dyke's "God of the Open Air," Holmes' "Chambered Nautilus," Kipling's "Dawn Wind." Almost any collection of poems contains some that are suitable for nature services.

BIBLIOGRAPHY

BEARD, DAN CARTER, *Outdoor Handy Book.* Charles Scribner's Sons, 1912.

Practical suggestions for young people for camping and playing in the out of doors.

CADY, BERTHA CHAPMAN, *Guides to Nature Study.* Slingerland-Comstock Company, 1929–1931.

Excellent brief notes and directions for teachers and leaders.

COMSTOCK, ANNA BOTSFORD, *Handbook of Nature Study*, 22nd edition. Comstock Publishing Company, 1911.

Over 230 teacher's stories and lessons for nature teachers in the grades by the "mother" of nature study.

PALMER, E. LAWRENCE, *Field Book of Nature Study*. Slingerland-Comstock Company, 1929.

Tables, keys, life histories, outline drawings. A great amount of information in concise form.

REIDY, MARGARET M., *Nature and Conservation Plays*. Slingerland-Comstock Company, 1928.

Three short plays, suitable for school or camp.

VINAL, WILLIAM G., *Nature Guiding*. Slingerland-Comstock Company, 1926.

Directions for nature leaders and teachers with stories drawn from the author's wide experience in camps and schools.

CHAPTER XXVI

NATURE LESSONS

Knowledge never learned of schools,
Of the wild bee's morning chase,
Of the wild flower's time and place,
Flight of fowl and habitude
Of the tenants of the wood;
How the tortoise bears his shell,
How the woodchuck digs his cell,
And the ground-mole sinks his well.[1]

— John Greenleaf Whittier

Courses in nature for young people must not overlook knowledge of adolescent psychology. Too formal a program subdues, even inhibits, spontaneity and joy of discovery. Here is a chance to arouse real interest, vital enough to remain as a point of view throughout life, and to give color and overtones to all experiences in the open. This need not become sentimentality. It is simple courtesy and homage to the poet in every boy and girl, and it will meet a response, in some cases far-reaching. Pinchot, Roosevelt, and Hornaday, somehow or by someone, were stimulated to believe in the biological cause for which each later gave so much.

What we are interested in we observe closely. Most young people do not see the trees for the woods. They have no particular feeling for individual factors; all trees seem alike, as do most plants. Few have taken the trouble to see the marvelous symmetry of a flower or to put a lens over the lacework of a mosquito's wing. Whenever

[1] From "The Barefoot Boy" by John Greenleaf Whittier. Copyright by Houghton Mifflin Company.

they attempt to tell what they see, their descriptions are likely to be inadequate as to size, color, and other characteristics and so indefinite as to be meaningless or even grotesquely erroneous. It is not that they cannot observe, but simply that not being interested they have not made their more or less lazy minds come sharply to time, to *tell the truth, nothing but the truth, and the whole truth.* What a thrill they get when they find that they are able to distinguish the separate notes in the daybreak chorus of bird songs and the separate odors in the woodland breeze!

With interest aroused, the interpretation of what they see becomes a fascinating puzzle, a sort of game where wits and patience count and where one vies with one's mates to be the first to unravel a secret. Studying cause and effect, making comparisons, forming judgments based on one's own data — every problem tackled and solved in this manner means better interpretation next time. Ability to reason is fundamental in the field. Every day will bring up questions such as the following: What animal walked in the path last night? In which direction was he going? Why did those ants move from one home to another, scurrying back and forth along a trail unmarked but of definite width and length? Why are cobwebs invisible on a dry day? Which of the past ten years have been the best seasons for growth as indicated by the bud-scale scars on the terminal twigs of certain trees? And is the same story corroborated by the ten outer rings on any recent stump? Perhaps not all questions can be answered, and the rather important qualities of humility and patience will grow thereby.

And gradually, the young naturalist will begin to have a sense of the social significance of living things. Through reading and through reflection he sees that there is a balance in nature which results from hundreds of influences and is maintained by far-reaching relationships. He will begin to have a new appreciation of the amazing interdependence of life everywhere, and the necessity of conservation of many valuable plants and animals. When he has such a point of view, you need have no fear for his outdoor good manners.

If the nature program is to have a character of its own, it will have to be organized with certain periods as the nucleus of nature activities, for each of which a nature lesson can be planned.

A REAL NATURE LESSON

"Uncle Bennie" Hyde stops a field trip of nature counselors to give a lesson.

The fact that a nature lesson is usually out of doors gives it an informal setting that ought to be one of its charms; yet swing this pendulum of freedom a little too much in this direction and informality gives place to lack of all restraint, and even marked disorder. Correlated with the freedom is the fact that in the field or wood many different and unsought stimuli impinge themselves on eyes, ears, and nose, so that it takes a high degree of tact and leadership to shunt off unimportant or undesired percepts, and keep the attention alert to worth-while phenomena. A good teacher can do this, for a skillful teacher indoors is a skillful teacher outdoors.

Study the region or objectives beforehand, and have some idea of what you are going to do. The hit-or-miss method is chaotic, it puts an extra burden on the leader, and develops frivolity and false ideas of what nature study is. Strong interest is not incompatible with self-control and restraint. In fact, campers and pupils prize that period where there is power and leadership in an atmosphere of coöperation and kindliness. But don't be *too* serious. Scientific interpretations or too formal a presentation can strangle charm and interest. An unusual question, a joke, a comprehending smile, lighten and color nature learning as they do all good teaching.

A nature lesson necessarily involves objectivity, yet there are perils in that connection which should be guarded against. Persistent self-seekers in the group may try to monopolize objects designed for common observation and investigation. If there is only one organism of a kind, unless thought is given to the method of demonstration, timid ones may not see what is intended.

Even with specimens, the leader may take so prominent a part that it might properly be called an illustrated lecture. No fault should be found with a lecture on any subject, if interesting, not too long, and given at the right time and place, but the lecture method does not come within the scope of a lesson. The goal is the development of democratic discussion, in which personal contributions are received from all, under the guidance and inspiration of the leader. Remember that it is anathema to *tell* children what they should find out for themselves — telling does not constitute teaching. Your pupils will not become naturalists because of *your* knowledge and enthusiasm. With all your sympathy you must show enough restraint to put the problem of discovery up to them. Be what your position implies: a counselor, pointing out and guiding, even leading the way, but always conscious of the inviolability of human individuality.

SEIZING THE OPPORTUNITY

The small snake serves for an object of study before being released.

Whether or not the members of the group make complete notes is a matter of choice. A record of experiences is one of the most important items in the acquisition of nature lore, yet it may be insisted upon to such an extent that the letter of the law would crowd out the spirit. It does not seem probable, however, that a good teacher would let the matter of recording degenerate to that extent. If illustrations are made, or actual specimens put in the notebook in the proper places, this book should express beauty and joyful growth in a project full of interest and value.

If young people could early get the habit of asking themselves and others the questions "Why?" and "How?" and then set about answering their queries, they would find that in some strange way they are beginning to acquire the *student mind*, which, under the constant incentive of discovery, will lead them into all sorts of new and interesting paths throughout their lives.

In order to interpret more fully the method suggested, three different types of lessons are here outlined in more or less detail.

A STUDY OF BEACH SAND

Take the group to the stony beach at the seashore or lakeside. Tell them you want each to hunt for *rounded* stones, and to bring you the stone which is most rounded. As they are brought, have them deposited in a long row, then put by them a stone with *angular* sides. Now bring up for discussion the question of whether stones have ages. That is, how old, in general, are the rounded stones compared with the sharp-edged ones? By discussion, skillfully handled, the group will see that in all probability the sharp-edged stone was broken off from another stone more recently, and that the rounded ones have been exposed longer.

What made these particular stones round? What shape would the angular stone have if the sharp edges and corners were worn away? When they see that an angular stone could become rounded by friction, ask them against what the stone would probably rub in losing its corners. They will see that it is the stones themselves rubbing together that produce the result. By observation and reflection they should see that the power is from the waves, storms, tides along the shore, or currents of water in the stream, which cause the stones to grind against a rocky bed. If the corners were worn away, they must have gone somewhere, and it is fair to look for them. Where?

Someone will realize that the sand mixed with the stones might be the very corners. Have them pick up some sand

and examine the particles through a magnifying glass. Note the different shapes and colors, particularly the colors. Then have them look at the stones of the beach to see if the colors of the sand grains are matched in the stones. They will find the same colors in both, and therefore can fairly conclude that the sand particles are "corners" of these or similar stones.

The colors in the sand grains help in identifying the kind of mineral substances in the original stones. For instance, white or colorless particles are usually quartz, rarely calcite. Quartz generally looks like glass or a piece of china. Ask them to name another color in the sand. If they mention pink tell them that it is probably feldspar. The black grains are hornblende. Sometimes green fragments can be seen. These are probably serpentine. Someone will be sure to find shiny particles — mica. Then ask the group to look for a stone which seems to combine quartz, hornblende, and feldspar, and possibly mica. When one is found, tell them this is a rock called granite, formed millions of years ago, deep in the earth, through fusion by heat of the three or four minerals just mentioned. There are different granites, because the proportions and sometimes the kinds of the component minerals vary.

This lesson might well include the drawing of a few sand grains, as seen under the lens.

LESSON ON A LIVE ANIMAL

(Suggested for a Rainy Day at Camp)

Any live animal which can be observed easily will furnish a theme for a nature lesson. The interest values should be studied in advance to make sure none is neglected or overlooked in the actual lesson.

It is important that each person in the group come in close contact with the specimen, and make personal observations by holding it or touching it, unless dangerous to handle or liable to escape. This can be done by each in turn as the lesson proceeds.

Some reference should be made at the beginning to the circumstances of the capture of the specimen, and to its local significance, if any, also its economic importance. The lesson should never be a mere cataloguing of all the structures which can be seen, just for the sake of naming them, though the faculty of observation is undoubtedly cultivated by accurate comparisons. Most structures have definite uses. If the function can be tied up with the structure, observations of parts will have dynamic meaning.

If the animal is supposed to perform in some special way or to reveal some particular thing, be sure to introduce this activity in a way calculated to produce suspense and anticipation.

If a cage or pen of proper size to keep the animal comfortable is available, or can be made, it should be kept for a few days where all will have an opportunity to watch the creature and note some of its habits.

Suppose that a frog, a field mouse, or a snake has been brought into camp and installed in a suitable terrarium or cage. The first rainy day gives an opportunity for presenting the finds and studying them more carefully.

With the leader primed by a study of references for identification, habits, life history, and relationships, the story of the capture of the specimen becomes the starting point for the discussion. By adroit questioning the difficulties of the capture can be revealed and the causes therefor found by the group through a study of the protective adaptations and activities of the animal. Some of the questions which can direct the discussion are: Is the animal easy or difficult to see in captivity? In its home environment what colors or patterns has it that would prevent its being seen easily? How does it attempt escape — by speed, hiding, fighting, or bluffing? What structural adaptations make these attempts possible? Would they be more or less effective in escaping other animals than man?

A Nature Picnic

Before and after a picnic dinner there is time to look for all sorts of things.

The group continues the study of other adaptations through closely related questions and observations. What would examination of the mouth and feet show about the feeding habits? Does the animal's form indicate its habitat? How are its five senses (if it has developed all five) adapted to its mode of life? What is known about its life history? How and when does it reproduce? Is it a nest builder? How are the young cared for? Some reference should also be made to the range or distribution of the animal — how common is it? What relatives has it? How harmful or valuable is it to us?

Watch the interest of the campers carefully and avoid too great detail with younger groups. Those most interested will wish to help care for the specimens, and also to find additional information. They should be especially encouraged to develop a nature notebook, and to help prepare charts showing observations and correlation of material.

BIRD WALK

(Somewhat as a Leader Might Talk)

This is a good day for a bird walk. Bring your field glasses and your detective instincts and let's start out.

Do you see that bird sitting over there on a post? You think it is not a bird? The glasses will settle it. It is too small for a robin, and about the size of an English sparrow — but we want more than that. There it flies! Did you catch the two white, outer tail feathers? It is the vesper sparrow. The junco also has white outer tail feathers but it is slate gray instead of brown, and it has an easily distinguishable yellow bill.

This *chip-chip-chip-chip*, which comes so monotonously from a near-by tree, betrays the chipping sparrow. You will soon see it for it is very common. Note its small size and reddish head above the black forehead. You may confuse its notes with those of the pine warbler. The latter, however, is not nearly so common and its song — if it can be called that — is more musical, a clear, sweet trill.

That little note of a descending half-interval: *tee-dee, tee-dee*, very high-pitched, comes from a feathered mite, the black-capped chickadee. He is worth his weight in gold — and more — to the country at large. Keep very quiet and see if your whistled imitation will not bring some of the group nearer. What acrobats they are, hanging even head downward to get some sequestered insect.

Over there is a small bird whose contrasting black and white streaks give him his name, black and white warbler. He searches through the branches of the tree, hardly pausing as he picks up insects from the crevices of the bark; entirely careless of gravity he proceeds in a most erratic fashion, up or down or upside down! Far more systematic is the brown creeper, which is similar in size but always ascends the tree trunk spirally, bracing himself with his tail. Reaching the branches, he drops to the base of a near-by tree and again progresses upward. There is another little bird which is more likely to travel down the tree than up. This is the nuthatch, whose nasal, penny-whistle notes are very characteristic. Still another of the typical tree-trunk birds is over yonder on the oak tree. It is a downy woodpecker. The hairy woodpecker closely resembles it but is slightly larger. Both of these energetic birds forage in one locality longer than the three preceding species. Watch the downy woodpecker until he flies to the next tree. His flight is more or less characteristic of all woodpeckers. The wings do not beat rapidly; on the contrary the downward thrusts are quite distinct, so that the bird seems to fly in a series of waves or pulsations, rising slightly at each wing beat, but with an apparent heaviness of flight. This is even more pronounced in the case of a larger woodpecker, the flicker. This same kind of flight, though more undulating, characterizes the American goldfinch, a beautiful yellow and black sparrow, popularly called the wild canary.

That bird you see flying over there on the left is a robin. You ask "How can one tell at such a distance?" It is difficult to explain, but for one thing notice that it flies steadily and on the same plane, not with the waves just referred to. Those other flying birds are grackles. In recognizing birds in the field, one must take into account a number of apparently small items. For instance, while the grackle flight is much like that of the robin, its tail is slightly longer and the side feathers of the tail are bent upward as it flies, somewhat as though the tail had been creased in the middle to make a V-shaped trough. The robin usually flies alone, whereas the grackle is more likely to be accompanied by other grackles in small flocks. Such apparently negligible characteristics are really special clews that may be the keynote in identifying birds at a distance. Another bird which novices might confuse with the grackle is the starling, distinguished, however, by the very much shorter tail and by the yellow bill, if one is near enough to note these characteristics.

Photograph by G. T. Hastings

A Bird Hike

A group from the Penn State Nature Camp listening to bird notes in the woods.

That cheering song from the old apple tree by the fence comes from the brown thrasher, a bird whose cinnamon-colored tail is even longer than that of the grackle. Its song is a bubbling series of short musical episodes, each repeated once before a new one is given. He seems to be saying: "Cheer up — cheer up; good — good; don't you do it — don't you do it; glad — glad; never sad — never sad," and so on. If you are willing to spend some time here, you may be rewarded by seeing his mate disappear under an overhanging bush, betraying the location of the nest, which will be found to be a loosely constructed affair on the ground.

Those birds darting through the air at least a hundred feet up, looking like animated black cigars, are not swallows; they are chimney swifts. What a maze of lines their flight, charted for only ten minutes, would produce! But those other birds flying lower and not quite so aimlessly are swallows. These particular swallows have white underparts and short unforked tails. They are tree swallows. There are some more of them resting on telephone wires, a habit with these birds. But there is another swallow, skimming close to the grass, whose long tail is forked and whose underparts are brownish. It is the common barn swallow.

On a dead limb of the apple tree to the left is a kingbird. See him fly away for an insect, then return. He is white underneath and has a white band across the ends of all the tail feathers, as though the tail had been dipped into whitewash. Listen to his harsh notes. The nest is probably close by in the orchard. He is the most pugnacious bird of his size, but his aversions are mostly limited to large birds like crows and hawks.

Let us cross the road and go over into the fields. Do you hear the *kong-cher-ee* from the cat-tails? That is the male red-winged blackbird. There he is — with his brilliant epaulets of crimson and buff. His much more retiring mate is grayish and streaked like most sparrows, though slightly larger than they.

See that bird flying fast and steadily. Could you get it?

That is an English sparrow. Note its business-like type of flight, always characterized by a blur of wings. There are some more of them arguing in that tree: "*chirp, chirp, chirp, chirp*"; insistent, noisy, gregarious — they are our worst feathered nuisance.

The song we hear, so melodious and associated with the fields, is that of the meadow lark. There he is, perched as usual on the most conspicuous fence post or solitary tree top he can find, and gaily singing so that all can hear: "*You can't see me-e, can't see-e me.*" Move slowly till he flies; then note the white outer feathers of the comparatively short tail. He is not so likely to face you as some other birds, so you may not get a chance to see the yellow breast with its black crescent.

A mourning dove! Listen to the whistling sound of its wings. You thought it was a hawk? It does look somewhat like one of the smaller hawks, but is a very timid bird with sad, sweet, cooing notes.

Let us turn back. We may see two or three more as we return. There is a flash of color in that second sycamore tree over there. Yes, it is the Baltimore oriole. Listen to his detached notes as though he had formed the habit of whistling to himself. That is probably the nest hanging from the outer limb of the next tree. If it is, it can hardly be called his, for his mate constructed the whole thing.

Two more birds, flying high, dark against the clouds! You are right, they are large birds, and the darker one is what you thought — the American crow, a ponderous sort of flier. The other is a tern or a gull, evidently en route from the seashore. With the glasses you ought to glimpse the tail. Forked? Then it is a tern.

That effervescent little black and orange creature darting in and out of those bushes is not a tropical bird, it is the male redstart. What an interesting song, climbing to an incisive and abrupt ending, only to be repeated again and again.

We should hear a wood peewee as we go through this last clump of pines. Let us sit down and listen. This near-by song is that of the red-eyed vireo, whose vocal talk has given him the name of the "preacher." Always a question, then a pause, then another question, then another pause with rising inflection at the end of each phrase.

There is the song we have been waiting for: the wood peewee with its plaintive notes, *pe-a-wee.*

When we summarize our trip, we find that we identified each bird by some distinguishing feature: some oddity of habit, flight, or note, or some characteristic marking. But we have gained more than a list of birds. We have enlarged our circle of friends.

BIBLIOGRAPHY

Comstock, Anna B., *Handbook of Nature Study* (23rd edition). Comstock Publishing Company, 1935.

Short lessons by a master teacher on a host of nature objects and subjects.

CHAPTER XXVII

NATURE PHOTOGRAPHY

It is always a satisfaction merely to have found a bird's nest. How much more elation then does one feel when he has secured a good photograph of the nest and eggs, then successfully outwitted the parent birds with his blind, and finally secured a permanent record of the bird's appearance and actions when oblivious to human presence.[1]

— ARTHUR A. ALLEN

Cameras are as common as robins, but most of their output is ordinary and commonplace, of mere personal interest as souvenirs. Yet it requires only a little thought and patience to learn to photograph landscapes, natural objects, and living forms and to produce pictures of artistic merit and value. Good pictures can be taken with any camera, even with the small ones with fixed focus, if care is taken in the subject, background, and the mechanical details of stop, focus, and exposure. The photographer himself is more important than any of his tools.

For best results, it is undoubtedly true that there is a desirable minimum of equipment such as a camera with a ground glass for focusing, a long bellows and interchangeable lenses for close-up work, and a tripod for time exposures. If you want to catch rapidly moving objects, a camera of the Graflex type with a large fast lens is preferred by many. The lens is the most important and costliest part of the outfit. Some lenses are fast and some are slow.

[1] From *The Book of Bird Life* by Arthur A. Allen. Copyright by D. Van Nostrand Company, Inc.

The best lenses are fast in the sense that they are so accurately ground and corrected that they give good definition with a large diaphragm opening (stop). With such an opening more light can be admitted and the exposure greatly shortened. Only the highest-priced cameras have

Photograph by Henry Knutson

CATBIRD AT THE BIRD BATH

The camera was set up and focused in advance and the shutter released by a thread when the bird alighted.

lenses which are fast. Though not essential, such an outfit, if one can afford it, will make picture-taking possible under the most adverse conditions. Ordinary hand cameras cannot be used closer than six feet and so are not successful in taking small objects such as insects, flowers, birds, tracks, etc., unless a portrait attachment is used. The attachment is a supplementary lens in a ring to fit over or inside the regular lens. It is of moderate cost, from seventy-five cents to a dollar and a quarter, depending on the size of the camera. Full directions as to its use come with it. With the attachment the camera can be placed at two and a half or three feet from the object instead of from six to eight feet, making the object appear three or four times as large in the picture as it would otherwise.

PHOTOGRAPHING WITH A GRAFLEX CAMERA ON A TRIPOD

The numerous assistants are using more background than necessary and allowing undesirable wrinkles in the cloth.

With many nature pictures where some one object is being taken in the open, best results can be secured by using the lens wide open, or with a large diaphragm opening and a short exposure. With a large stop there is little depth of focus, so that objects behind the one in focus will appear blurred in contrast to the clearer outlines of the object photographed. By using a small diaphragm opening

Photograph by G. T. Hastings

THE USE OF A SMALL DIAPHRAGM

Note the plants in the background in focus and no one thing emphasized.

the depth of focus is increased so that all objects, whether in foreground or background, will be much sharper. For general views or distant objects this is generally an advantage. For small objects or delicate structures, the small diaphragm will give better detail, but care has to be taken to avoid a sharply defined background. With a small stop a longer exposure is necessary, dependent also on the light and time of day. Mr. Oliver P. Medsger, of Jersey City High School, who furnished many of the photographs for this book, advises using a diaphragm aperture small enough to require an exposure of from one-half minute to one minute, using "thirty feet of nothing" for a background. If exposures are longer than $\frac{1}{10}$ of a second, the camera must be on a tripod or placed on some solid support where it will not be moved. If great detail is wanted it is best to take the picture where the light is not too bright and make a time exposure. Pictures taken in the shade or when the sun is under a cloud will give better results than if taken in direct

Photograph by G. T. Hastings

THE USE OF A LARGE DIAPHRAGM

The same picture as the preceding, but the background out of focus and the plants in the foreground sharp.

sunlight. Similarly the early morning or late afternoon is better for most subjects than the middle of the day. But for moving objects, good light is necessary that will allow exposures of $\frac{1}{25}$ to $\frac{1}{100}$ of a second. Correct timing of exposures depends upon experience, though exposure tables and meters have been made which should prove invaluable to amateurs. Underexposure produces a weak or "flat" picture, lacking in detail, as shown in the upper part of the

Photographs by G. T. Hastings

DIFFERENT EXPOSURES: NEGATIVES, LEFT; POSITIVES, RIGHT

illustration on page 399. Overexposure results in lack of contrast, as shown in the bottom picture, while correct exposure gives the results shown in the middle view.

All acceptable rules of general photography apply to nature pictures: proper light, sharp focusing, good composition, correct exposures, etc. With most cameras focusing means getting the proper distance. One can measure the distance by pacing if the length of a step is accurately known. For short distances, especially with the portrait attachment, it is best to measure with a tape, a string with knots tied every six inches, or a stick with feet and half feet marked.

Artistic skill or its lack will be revealed in planning the composition of the picture. There should be enough of the surroundings to show proper relationships, but not enough to distract the attention from the subject. The subject should usually be a little to one side of the center of the picture, and there should be proper background. Often a branch across the top of one corner of the picture or a plant at one side will make it more attractive. Examine the object from several points of view to select that which you think will give the best results, note the position of shadows and whether they make the subject stand out or blend into the background. For light-colored objects a dark background will give best results, such as a dark tree trunk or rock far enough back to be out of focus. Perhaps the focusing cloth or other dark material such as velvet can be hung up or spread out for a background, or the object can be placed in front of the open door of a darkened room. Such a background is almost essential for spider webs, and light-colored flowers, grasses, and other objects. If the object cannot be moved it is often possible to remove weeds, branches or other material from around it.

Bees or butterflies visiting flowers make interesting pictures but require considerable patience. Select a plant the insects are visiting frequently; set up the camera in focus on some blossom, and wait. The insects usually seem to prefer other plants, or they get on the wrong side of the blossom. If some of the neighboring plants or blossoms are removed when the camera is set up the insect has less choice and the period of waiting may be cut down.

AN UMBRELLA BLIND

From the shelter of such a blind good pictures of birds or mammals can often be secured.

The easiest bird pictures to take will probably be of nests, either with or without the parent birds. In doing this, disturb the surroundings as little as possible and avoid making a trodden path to the nest that may lead prowling animals to it. If branches interfere, tie them back rather than break them off. With special precautions you may be able to include one of the parent birds. Sometimes good pictures can be taken of birds at a feeding station or bath. If food is put on a branch or ledge till birds become accustomed to feeding there, the camera may be focused on the spot where the bird is expected, properly set, and the shutter released from a distance by means of a thread. The thread is attached to the shutter-release, then run through a screw-eye in a stake pushed in the ground below the camera and carried off to a distance where the photographer hides and waits. Pictures of chipmunks, squirrels, and other small mammals may often be secured in a similar way. Good pictures of birds and other animals are much harder to get than ordinary pictures, but the patience and care required and the skill developed make them worth while. In getting such pictures much will be learned, too, of the habits of the animals. Once started on a project of taking nature pictures, many things will be found of which to make records, and new schemes devised for securing the pictures wanted. Illustrated nature articles in magazines will give an idea of the kind of pictures that are worth while and the possibilities of getting pictures that tell stories.

Photograph by Oliver P. Medsger

A SQUIRREL VISITS THE BIRD BATH

Here again the camera was focused on the bath and the exposure made when the visitor came.

MOTION PICTURES. The taking of motion pictures is so easy and the cameras are now so cheap that some campers will undoubtedly make their own movies. The use of the popular 16 mm. film makes possible relatively inexpensive projection and separate positives can easily be made from any frame of the negative. It is not advisable to attempt to present here the technique of motion-picture taking, but it is a new and growing factor in nature photography. The manual which accompanies the machines should be carefully studied.

Developing and Printing. Part of the joy of photography is in doing one's own developing and printing. For this a dark room is essential. If possible the dark room should have a sink and running water. Formulae for

Photograph by G. T. Hastings

Lark Sparrow at Nest

By means of a thread, the exposure was made just as the mother bird arrived with a grasshopper for the nestlings hidden behind the weeds in the foreground.

making developing and fixing solutions are obtainable from any store that sells cameras and films, or better, the prepared developing and fixing powders can be obtained, ready to be dissolved. Directions for the developing come with the films or paper. A beginner who can get help from a veteran photographer will progress much faster, as there are many matters in which experience is the best guide. The fascination and interest in peering at the developing plate or film in the eerie red glow and the thrill of seeing outlines and shapes take form on the apparently untouched plate as you rock the tray gently back and forth must be felt to be realized. Then only is it *your picture!*

BIBLIOGRAPHY

ABBOTT, C. G., "How to Photograph Animals and Birds" (in *Tracks and Trails* by L. Rossell). The Macmillan Company, 1928.

One section of a book written for Boy Scouts, simple and practical.

DIMOCK, JULIAN A., *Outdoor Photography.* The Macmillan Company, 1918.

A practical little book telling about the kinds of cameras and lenses, how to make exposures, developing and printing, the composition of the picture.

NESBIT, WILLIAM, *How to Hunt With the Camera.* E. P. Dutton and Company, Inc., 1926.

A large and in some respects rather technical book, with directions for photographing all kinds of outdoor objects, trees, reptiles, birds, and game animals.

CHAPTER XXVIII

NATURE STUDY EQUIPMENT

And hark! how blithe the throstle sings!
He, too, is no mean preacher:
Come forth into the light of things,
Let Nature be your teacher.[1]

— William Wordsworth

While the nature counselor can get along with little equipment, better work can be done with a few of the following supplies. There should be a heavy pocket-knife, preferably with two blades. A pocket sharpening stone in a leather case, with one side coarse for fast cutting, the other fine for finishing, is convenient. Instead of this, a flat piece of sandstone or shale may be picked up near camp, or a stone nearly smooth can be rubbed against another, with plenty of water, till it is smooth enough to use as a whetstone.

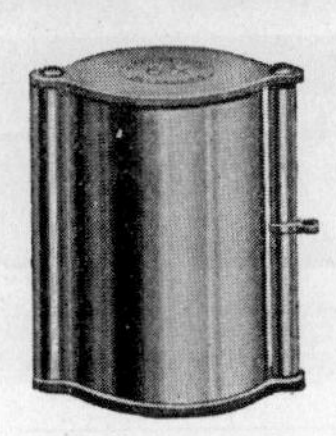

Courtesy of Spencer Lens Co.

Types of Pocket Lenses

The one at the left costs least; the one at the right, most.

Next in importance is a pocket lens, magnifying from nine to twelve diameters. For examining small flowers, wood structure, insects, and a great variety of objects, such

[1] From *The Tables Turned* by William Wordsworth.

Courtesy of Spencer Lens Co.

MOUNTED LENS

This type is valuable in the laboratory or museum.

an aid is invaluable. A good lens in nickel-plated mounting can be purchased at from two to seven dollars. The folding magnifiers known as linen markers or those in brass mounting with three legs screwed in are cheaper and do fairly well. They are not so powerful but give a larger field and longer working distance, which are valuable if higher magnification is not needed.

Courtesy of New York Biological Supply Co.

COLLECTING CAN

This is the type described here.

For bird study a pair of field glasses is highly desirable. Glasses of from three to five power provide a large field of vision and are better than those of higher power, especially where everyone in a group wants to look through them. The higher magnification brings the object optically nearer the observer, but the "field" is so limited that it is not easy to find a small moving object like a bird. Moreover it is more difficult to "hold" the object, since every tremor of the hand is likewise magnified. The minimum cost of field glasses, with a carrying case, is from six to seven dollars. Binoculars cost twenty or thirty dollars or more. If the camp can provide one or more pairs of field glasses so that on trips there may be several available, it will increase the effectiveness of bird hikes.

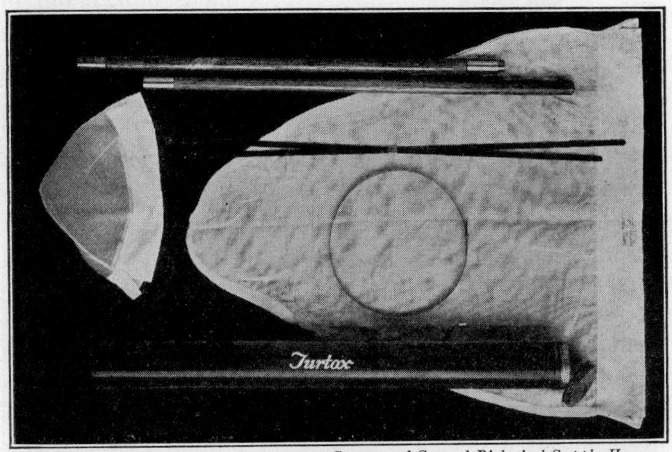

Courtesy of General Biological Supply House

A COMBINATION NET

The large net is for insects, the small one for minute water life.

A tin collecting can or vasculum should be owned by the camp. This should be of fair size, at least fifteen by seven or eight inches, as the smaller ones are not satisfactory. The door of the vasculum should open nearly the whole length and there should be a carrying strap as well as a handle. In such a can plants can be kept in good condition for several hours; if sprinkled or if a piece of damp paper is put in with them, they may be left overnight and taken out next day as fresh as when placed in the can.

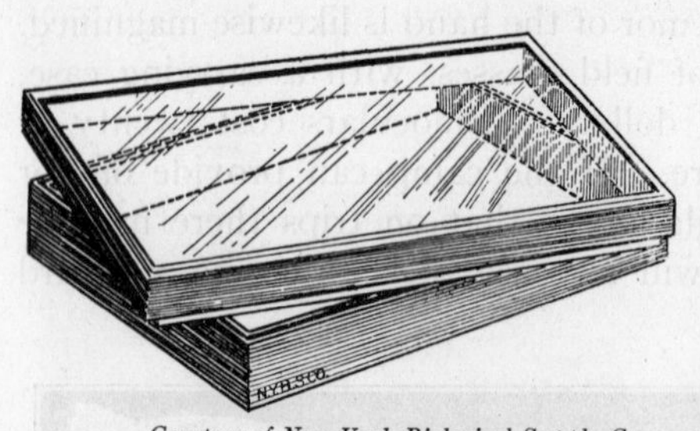

Courtesy of New York Biological Supply Co.

A GLASS-TOPPED INSECT CASE

Such an exhibition case is practically dust and moth proof.

For rocks and minerals a geological hammer with a square face and either a pointed or chisel-edged projection is useful. Specimens broken out of the rock mass may be later trimmed up with such a hammer better than with an ordinary one. There is psychological value, too, in having a tool meant for a special use.

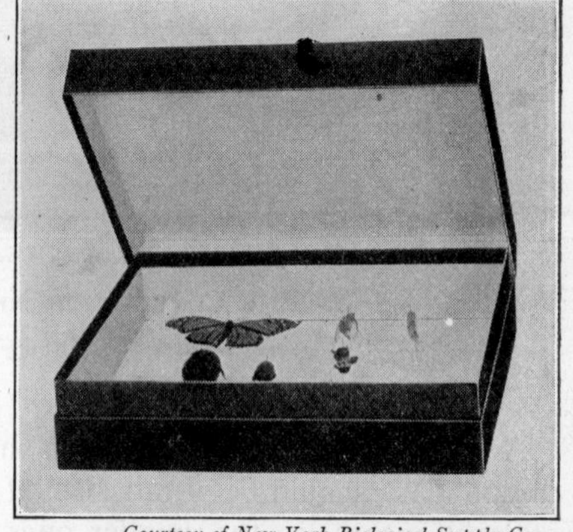

Courtesy of New York Biological Supply Co.

AN INEXPENSIVE INSECT CASE

For insects a net and a killing bottle are essential. The net may be made or purchased. If purchased it may be a cheap one at a dollar, or a more expensive one with a folding ring detachable from the handle. If collecting is to be done at a distance from camp, the folding one is convenient, but for work in or near camp it has no advantage over one with a solid ring attached permanently to the handle. Some of the nets are made with several bags of different weights to fit the one handle. In this way the naturalist has interchangeable equipment for beating bushes, dredging in the ponds or streams, or sweeping in the air. Several killing bottles of

Courtesy of General Biological Supply House

USING DIP NETS

Unexpected treasures add zest to aquatic search.

different sizes are desirable. For this purpose cyanide of potassium should be avoided. Jars made with Carbona are quite as good and safer. It takes longer to kill the insects, but Carbona is harmless to us while cyanide of potassium is deadly.

Spreading boards are inexpensive to buy, or are easily

made. Either glass-topped exhibition boxes or Riker mounts should be ready for the collected insects.

For plants a press can easily be made in camp. Newspapers do well for driers but there should be a supply of mounting paper and glue or gummed labels. Library cards and India ink are needed for museum labels and other uses. Remnants from mounting paper cut to three by five inches also make excellent labels. For the nature trail there should be linen labels.

The following is a suggested list of nature materials for camp with prices from dealers' catalogues. But prices differ with different dealers and at different times. The first list is of supplies that can be used for several years and is in the nature of permanent equipment; the second list is of materials to be used up during the season.

I. EQUIPMENT FOR NATURE WORK IN CAMP

Wide-mouthed bottles, 4 oz. 3 doz. (to hold flowers, etc.)	$6.75
Wide-mouthed bottles, 8 oz. 3 doz.	9.00
Glass-topped insect cases ($2.00 to $3.50 according to size) 2	4.00–7.00
*Riker mounts, 6½ by 8½ inches, 1 doz.	5.50
*Insect net (many kinds at various prices), a satisfactory one at	3.00
Spreading boards, 2	1.50
Plant press	2.50
Driers for press, 50	3.60
*Collecting can, about 18 × 8 × 5	5.00
Geological hammer	5.00
Field glasses	8.00
*Printing frames, 5 × 7 inches, with glass, 3	2.25
*Metal frame aquaria, 12-quarts, 2	6.00
	$62.10–65.10

II. SUPPLIES FOR NATURE WORK

Plaster of Paris, 50 lbs.	$2.50
Plasteline, 10 lbs.	2.50
Liquid glue, 1 pt.	.50
Linen labels, Dennison's No. 5, 200	2.00
Gummed labels, $1\frac{1}{2} \times 2\frac{1}{2}$ inches, 6 boxes	.90
or Botanical tape, white paper, $\frac{7}{8}$ inch by 12 yards, 2 rolls	.50
Insect pins, nos. 1 to 4, 400	2.00
Herbarium paper, $12 \times 16\frac{1}{2}$ inches, 50 sheets; or $8\frac{1}{4} \times 12$ inches, 100 sheets	3.00
Vaseline, 2 jars	.20
Candles, 2	.20
India ink, waterproof, 2 bottles	.50
Colored pencils, small boxes of 6 made up for nature work, a dozen or more boxes, each	.10
Azo paper, 5×7, 6 packages	1.20
M–Q developer, 12 tubes	.36
Acid Hypo, 1 lb.	.25
Blue-print paper in 10-yard roll, about	1.00
Carbona, 1 bottle	.25
	$17.96

If a camp can spend only twenty-five dollars, the articles starred above plus one dozen of the bottles will make a good beginning. The amount of supplies listed is rather arbitrary and would not be enough for a large camp of one hundred or more. For example, six packages or seventy-two sheets of printing paper to be used for leaf prints are suggested. If much of this work is done this will be only a beginning, but if the prints are used only for the camp museum the amount is ample. The same thing may be said of the quantity of plaster of Paris and of mounting paper. Prices, too, are merely suggestive though taken from the catalogues of regular dealers in scientific equipment. Some of the items may be secured more cheaply from local dealers. The following partial list of dealers in scientific apparatus and supplies may be helpful:

Cambridge Botanical Supply Co., Waverley, Mass. (Collecting and mounting supplies for plants.)

L. E. Knott Apparatus Co., Ames and Amherst Sts., Boston, Mass. (Bottles and other supplies.)

National Audubon Society, 1974 Broadway, New York, N. Y. (Bird pictures, field glasses.)

New York Biological Supply Co., 34 Union Square, New York, N. Y. (All equipment for nature work.)

Ward's Natural Science Establishment, 84–102 College Ave., Rochester, N. Y. (General supplies.)

Slingerland-Comstock Co., Ithaca, N. Y. (Outline drawings of and keys to birds, flowers, insects, etc.; colored pencils.)

The Fisher Scientific Co., 715 Forbes St., Pittsburgh, Pa. (General supplies.)

Michigan Biological Supply Co., 206–208 South First St., Ann Arbor, Mich. (General supplies.)

General Biological Supply House, 761–763 E. 69th Place, Chicago, Ill. (All equipment for nature work.)

Universal Scientific Co., 11 East Austin Ave., Chicago, Ill. (General supplies.)

William Welch Scientific Co., 1516 Orleans St., Chicago, Ill. (General supplies.)

APPENDICES

APPENDIX A

NAMING AND GROUPING ANIMALS AND PLANTS

A young naturalist was one day examining some South American bird skins which had just arrived at the Museum of Natural History in New York City. Picking up one, he remarked that it probably belonged to the family of flycatchers, because, though different in certain particulars, it had the slightly hooked upper bill characteristic of the flycatchers of the United States. He was right, though he had never before seen this bird. The obvious resemblance was enough to put them in the same group.

Resemblances can also be found among plants. Roses do not grow on trees, yet the flowers of the rose plant so closely resemble the flowers of apples, plums, pears, apricots, etc., that they are all considered to be members of the same family — the Rose family.

The term "family" is only one of six main groups used by scientists to classify organisms in order to understand their relationships. These groups are Phylum or Subkingdom, Class, Order, Family, Genus, and Species. The species is sometimes divided into Varieties. The largest division is the Phylum (plural, Phyla), Subkingdom, or Branch. It may help the beginner if he regards each phylum as comparable to one of the largest divisions of the country — the state. Just as the states, taken together, comprise the United States, so all the phyla considered together make up the animal kingdom and the plant kingdom respectively.

Let us consider briefly just how classification applies to the animal kingdom. For example, take the common house cat. This animal belongs to the *Phylum Chordata* (sometimes called *Vertebrata*), characterized by a bony skeleton and a spinal column. But the aquatic and scaly fish are as truly vertebrates as is the cat. So are the slippery frogs, scaly reptiles, and feathered birds. It has been found convenient to divide the vertebrates into six important groups, each called a class. (There are three other groups, relatively unimportant because their representatives are degenerate, which precede these major classes.) The fish are assigned to the class *Pisces*, the frogs to the class *Amphibia*, the reptiles to the class *Reptilia*, the birds to the class *Aves* and the cats to the class *Mammalia*. If we let the phylum correspond to the state, then the class, a subdivision of the phylum, might well correspond to one of the large divisions of the state known as the county.

But in addition to domestic cats there are wild forms like seals, tigers, otters, wolves, etc., all similar in having sharp teeth with long canines and in possessing the same food habits. Because of these characteristics they are all grouped together under the same order, the scientific name of which is *Carnivora* (flesh eaters). There are nine orders under the class *Mammalia*.

An order bears the same general relationship to its class that the township bears to the county of which it is a division. But the orders too are subdivided. The order *Carnivora*, to which the cat belongs, includes many very different flesh eaters such as bears, wolves, hyenas, lions, etc. Both the house cats and wild cats have feet with soft pads, hind feet with four toes, and claws which can be withdrawn into sheaths. The lion, tiger, jaguar, leopard, puma, etc., also possess these same characteristics and hence all these animals are placed in one group known as the cat family or *Felidae*. The order *Carnivora* includes not only the cat family but the dog, raccoon, bear, weasel, and seal families as well. If the township be considered as corresponding to an order, the separate villages of the township might well correspond to the divisions of the order known as families.

In North America, in addition to the house cat, there are two kinds of wild representatives of the cat family: wild cats and pumas. The wild cats resemble each other in having tufted ears and a short tail, while the pumas are much larger and have a long tail. Because of the essential differences between these two groups they are put into two separate divisions each called a genus (plural, genera). To the puma (also called panther) is given the genus *Felis*, which name it shares with the house cat, while to the wild cats is assigned the genus *Lynx*. In accordance with our previous comparison, the blocks in a village might correspond to these divisions called genera. The differences many times seen among members of the same genus require another grouping, namely that of species. We just referred to wild cats, of which there are at least three distinct kinds found in North America. Each of these kinds is known as a species.

The common cat belongs to the species *domesticus*, and the most common of the pumas to the species *couguar*.

In cases where species vary considerably for one reason or another it is sometimes convenient to make further subdivisions known as subspecies or varieties.

If a village block be considered as comparable to a genus the separate houses in the blocks would correspond to the divisions of a genus called species.

Biologists have agreed to use the species name preceded by the capitalized genus name, to constitute what is called the scientific name of an organism. Thus each animal and plant, no matter what its popular or common name, has a scientific name consisting of at least two words. The scientific name of your cat is *Felis domesticus*. Most of the scientific names are in Latin, and in many cases they refer to some evident characteristic of the organism. In the case of one of the three wild cats, *Lynx rufus rufus*, the Latin for the species name means "reddish" and refers to the color of the animal. Another species is *canadensis*, meaning "of Canada," the home of this animal. The third is *gigas*, meaning "giant," and refers to the size of the animal. The biological world owes a debt of thanks to Carl Linnaeus for suggesting, in 1750, this naming of animals and plants, which shortened to two or three words what before had been names so long that they were really descriptive sentences.

It is fortunate that there is an international agreement among biologists to retain the Latinized scientific name first assigned by the discoverer to a plant or an animal, without any translation whatsoever. This simplifies the study of foreign organisms. However, some of the earlier names were very poor selections, and in some cases better ones have been substituted.

As knowledge has increased, modern research workers in the classification of animals and plants (a subject called "taxonomy") have found errors in the work of earlier classifiers. Linnaeus, for instance, divided the entire animal kingdom into only six classes. Cuvier made only four divisions. Also hundreds and sometimes thousands of new forms have been discovered each year. These facts, coupled with better knowledge of relationships, have resulted in greatly increasing the number of genera and species in recent years. H. S. Pratt estimates the entire animal kingdom to consist of several millions of species, of which approximately 500,000 have been assigned scientific names.

Grouping animals and plants correctly involves knowledge not only of present-day opinions but of the now extinct and prehistoric ancestors of living forms, in order to reveal true relationships. For more than a half century after Linnaeus' publication of *Systema Naturae*, a genus was merely a convenient name under which to place species which *seemed* to have some resemblances, without particular regard to whether they were fundamentally related by common ancestry. Now we realize that correct classification depends upon a knowledge of evolution of plants and animals, involving knowledge of the changes which have taken place through the ages.

As David Starr Jordan said in his preface to *Manual of Vertebrate Animals*, 13th edition, "Classification must be more than an inventory; its basis must be genetic" [by blood relationship]. "The problems involved in a natural grouping are vastly more complex than even great morphologists like Cuvier and Agassiz had realized. . . . Genera and species are but larger and smaller twigs of a tree which we try to arrange as nearly as possible in accordance with nature's ramifications."

Frequently the same forms have been classified differently by different scientists. Sponges, for instance, were formerly thought to be plants, and volvox is even now claimed both by zoölogists and by botanists. The king crab, until recently, was classified with the lobsters and crabs. Now it is put with the spider group. Such changes may involve the learning of some new names from time to time but they reveal better understanding of structure and relationship.

While the young naturalist need not trouble himself much about the scientific names of the organisms he sees, these terms are really not so hard to remember and are so descriptive that they can be of definite assistance to him, if he will take the time to look them up. However, scientific classification of the animal and plant world is secondary to getting acquainted with the out of doors, and should never be allowed to hinder an appreciation of nature.

In order better to understand the relationships of groups of animals, scientists usually consider one-celled animals as the first or "lowest" phylum. This group — the *Protozoa* — therefore, is generally placed first among the phyla of animals because its representatives are structurally the simplest and smallest of all animals. The *Protozoa* and ten other phyla [1] — more complicated in structure — together comprise a division of animals known as invertebrates (without backbones), a designation first made by the French scientist Lamarck in 1794. There is, then, a major dividing line between invertebrates, generally considered as lower forms of animals, and the vertebrates or chordates which include the so-called "higher" animals. In the same way the simplest plants, such as the blue-green algae, bacteria and slime molds, comprise the first subkingdom of plants. These, with the mosses and ferns, are sometimes called spore plants to distinguish them from the plants that produce seeds.

Invertebrate animals have the main nerve cord extending along the ventral (opposite the back) part of the body. They never possess an internal skeleton consisting of bones, and hence except for protective shells which some possess, or a somewhat hardened covering found in others, they are for the most part soft-bodied creatures, none of which shows the structural development of the back-boned vertebrates.

To be considered a vertebrate, an animal must possess a dorsal (in the back) nerve cord, protected by a supporting sheath

[1] Authorities differ as to the exact number of phyla and of their divisions.

— the spinal column. In addition, the typical vertebrate possesses a complete internal skeleton and not more than four limbs. While in almost all adult vertebrates the spine or vertebral column is bony (in fact composed of separate bones each called a vertebra), in every vertebrate when very young (embryonic), the spine begins its existence as a cartilaginous rod. This is called the *notochord*. In one tiny animal — the lancelet — the notochord remains just such a soft, gristly rod throughout the life of the individual. And in the case of another low form — the tunicate — the notochord, while present in the young, soon degenerates and eventually disappears when the adult stage is reached. But the fact that these two marine animals have a notochord is sufficient for biologists to place them with the vertebrates. In the normal development of other typical vertebrates such as a fish, frog, snake, bird, or cat, the notochord eventually becomes segmented (consisting of joints or divisions) and bony, and is then known as the "backbone."

CLASSIFICATION OF PLANTS

A. Plants without seeds.

Phylum I. Thallophytes — Plants with no true roots, stems or leaves and with no many-celled egg cases.

- Class 1. Myxomycetes — Slime molds
- Class 2. Schizophytes — Blue-green algae and bacteria
- Class 3. Algae — Green, brown, and red seaweeds and pond scums
- Class 4. Fungi — Molds, rusts, smuts, mushrooms, etc.
- Lichens — Combinations of algae and fungi.

Phylum II. Bryophytes — Plants with many-celled egg cases, but with no bundles of fibers or ducts to carry sap.

- Class 1. Hepaticae — Liverworts
- Class 2. Musci — Mosses

Phylum III.[1] Pteridophytes — Plants with bundles of fibers and ducts to carry sap.

[1] By many authorities the Pteridophytes are divided into three or more phyla.

Class 1. Lycopodiales — Club mosses and quillworts
Class 2. Equisetales — Horsetails
Class 3. Ophioglossales — Adder's-tongue and Moon ferns
Class 4. Filicales — Ferns

B. Plants with seeds.
Phylum IV. Spermatophytes
Class 1. Gymnosperms — Cone-bearing plants (pines, spruce, etc.) and cycads and ginkgo.
Class 2. Angiosperms
Subclass 1. Monocotyledons
Subclass 2. Dicotyledons

COMPLETE CLASSIFICATION OF A COMMON FLOWER

WILD ROSE

Phylum — Spermatophyte
Class — Angiosperms
Subclass — Dicotyledons
Order — Rosaceae
Genus — Rosa
Species — caroliniana

CLASSIFICATION OF ANIMALS

A. Invertebrates

Phylum I. Protozoa — Amoeba, paramecium, vorticella, euglena: one-celled forms, mostly aquatic.

Phylum II. Porifera — Sponges, both marine and fresh-water forms: groups of cells with supporting spicules.

Phylum III. Coelenterata — Corals, sea anemones, hydroids, jellyfishes, sea fans: some plant-like; all with tentacles and sting cells.

Phylum IV. Platyhelminthes [Flatworms] — Liver fluke, planaria, tapeworm: body flattened.

Phylum V. Nemathelminthes [Threadworms] — Hair worm, trichina, vinegar eels, and other minute worms: body slender.

Phylum VI. Trochelminthes [Wheel Animalcules] — Rotifers.

Phylum VII. Bryozoa — Minute forms, mostly colonial with tentacles, such as plumatella.[1]

Phylum VIII. Annelida — Earthworms, sand worms, tube worms, leech: bodies elongated and segmented.

Phylum IX. Echinodermata — Starfishes, brittle stars, crinoids, sea urchins, and sea cucumbers: marine animals, all having spiny bodies, usually divided into five rays or divisions and bearing tube feet.

Phylum X. Arthropoda — Animals with segmented body-covering and jointed legs.

Class 1. Crustacea — Crabs, shrimps, crayfishes, prawns, barnacles: body-covering considerably hardened; five pairs of legs.

Class 2. Arachnoidea — Spiders, king crab, scorpions: four pairs of legs.

Class 3. Insecta — Insects: three pairs of legs.

Class 4. Myriapoda — Centipedes and millepedes: numerous legs.

Phylum XI. Mollusca — Clams, oysters, mussels, snails, squids, nautilus: unsegmented bodies and usually with univalve or bivalve shell.

B. Vertebrates

Phylum I. Chordata — Animals with a "backbone" or spinal column supporting a spinal cord; internal skeleton; limbs not more than four.

Subphylum 1. Urochorda — Tunicates: degenerate forms with notochord (undeveloped spinal column) present only for a time in young.

[1] Phyla IV, V, VI, and VII, together with four other similar groups, are by some authors called subphyla, and put together under the Phylum Vermes thus including all the lower worm-like animals.

Subphylum 2. Cephalochorda — Lancelet: forms in which the notochord is persistent, but no "backbone" forms.

Subphylum 3. Craniata — Vertebrata (True vertebrates).

Class 1. Cyclostomi — Hags and lampreys: cartilaginous skeleton.

Class 2. Pisces — Fishes: cold-blooded; heart with two cavities; usually with scales; fins for limbs; eggs usually very numerous.

Class 3. Amphibia — Frogs, toads, and salamanders: skin naked and mostly smooth, not scaled; external gills when young, which may or may not persist; cold-blooded; heart with three cavities; eggs numerous, usually with gelatinous coating.

Class 4. Reptilia — Lizards, snakes, turtles, crocodiles, and alligators: scaly body; digits, if present, with claws; cold-blooded; heart 3–4 chambered; eggs fewer, with leathery covering.

Class 5. Aves — Birds: the only animals with feathers and wings; warm-blooded; heart with four chambers; eggs few, with calcareous shell.

Class 6. Mammalia — Mammals: the only animals with hair; young born alive and nourished with milk; body cavity divided by a diaphragm; warm-blooded; heart with four chambers; eggs very minute.

COMPLETE CLASSIFICATION OF A COMMON VERTEBRATE

THE CAT

Phylum — Chordata
Class — Mammalia
Order — Carnivora
Family — Felidae
Genus — Felis
Species — domesticus
Variety — Angora, etc.

FAMILIES OF FLOWERING PLANTS

The following families include 60 per cent of the flowering plants of the northeastern United States as given in Gray's *Manual* and the proportion is about the same in other temperate regions.

MONOCOTYLEDONS. (One seed leaf.)

Leaves usually with parallel veins and flowers, if large enough to see, with parts in threes.

GRASS-LIKE PLANTS

Grass Family — Flowers small with neither sepals nor petals, surrounded by scales or bracts, grouped in spikelets, stem round, hollow, leaves in 2 rows on the stem. (Orchard grass, timothy, grain.)

Sedge Family — Grass-like plants, but the stems more or less triangular, solid, leaves in 3 rows on the stem. Flowers of various kinds and arrangement, but small and insignificant. (Sedge, rush.)

LILY-LIKE PLANTS

Lily Family — Flowers with 3 sepals and 3 petals, usually colored alike, six stamens, one pistil, ovary with 3 cells, stamens and petals fastened to the receptacle below the ovary (ovary superior). (Indian cucumber, cat brier, Solomon's-seal.)

Orchid Family — Flowers irregular, 3 sepals, 3 petals, one quite different from the others, forming a lip, stamens and pistil united into a column, ovary usually twisted, petals, sepals, and stamens attached to the top of the ovary (ovary inferior). (Lady's-slipper, ladies'-tresses, fringed orchid, twayblade.)

DICOTYLEDONS. (Two seed leaves.)

With netted veined leaves and flowers with the parts usually in fours or fives.

PETALS DISTINCT

Ovary superior, Flowers regular

Buttercup Family — Flowers usually regular, 3–15 sepals, usually same number of petals, many or few pistils, all attached to the receptacle. (Anemone, clematis, black snakeroot, baneberry.)

Mustard Family — Flowers with 4 sepals, 4 petals, 6 stamens (2 shorter than the other 4) 1 pistil, all parts separate. (Shepherd's-purse, watercress.)

Rose Family — Flowers usually resembling the buttercups but with 5 sepals united at base, the petals and numerous stamens attached to the base of the calyx instead of to the receptacle. (Spiraea, potentilla, raspberry, cherry.)

Flowers irregular

Legume Family — The next to the largest family of plants. Flowers with 5 sepals united, 5 petals, the upper one larger than the other, the 2 lower united on the lower edge and enclosing the 10 stamens, (9 united by their filament, one free), the one pistil forming a pod. (Clovers, vetch, false indigo, tick trefoil.)

Ovary inferior, flowers regular

Evening Primrose Family — 4 sepals united into a tube, 4 petals and 8 stamens, attached to top of calyx tube, 4 stigmas. (Willow herb, sundrops, enchanter's nightshade.) (The enchanter's nightshade has the flower parts in 2's instead of 4's with the fruits forming small sticktights.)

Parsley Family — Flowers small in flat-topped clusters, 5 petals and 5 stamens attached to top of 2-parted ovary, 2 styles, leaves often divided into many parts and the leaf stem clasping the stalk. (Queen Anne's lace, water hemlock, water parsnip.) Some of the plants of this family are poisonous.

Petals United

Flowers irregular

Mint Family — Corolla 2-lipped, 2 or 4 stamens attached to corolla, ovary deeply 4-lobed with style in center, stems more or less square, leaves opposite. (Selfheal, bergamot, skullcap.)

Figwort Family — Corolla usually 2-lipped, 4 or 2 stamens attached to corolla tube, ovary 1, two-celled. (Mullein, butter and eggs, snapdragon, turtlehead.)

Composite Family — The largest family of plants. Flowers regular or irregular in heads. Flowers very small but grouped in large heads surrounded by an involucre so that the head appears like one flower. The involucre corresponds to the calyx and the ray flowers to petals. Some, as the daisy, have ray flowers around the edge; some, as joe-pye weed or boneset, have no rays; others, like the dandelion, only ray flowers. (Aster, yarrow, goldenrod, thistle.)

BIBLIOGRAPHY

BRITTON, N. L., and BROWN, A., *Illustrated Flora of the United States and Canada.* Charles Scribner's Sons, 1913.

This three volume work describes and illustrates all of the ferns and flowering plants of the regions covered. There are full keys.

GRAY, ASA, *Manual of Botany.* American Book Company, 1908.

This is the seventh edition of the standard manual describing all the species of ferns and flowering plants of the northeastern United States.

JORDAN, DAVID STARR, *Manual of the Vertebrates.* World Book Company, 1929.

A complete but technical work with keys and descriptions.

PRATT, H. S., *A Manual of the Common Invertebrate Animals, Except Insects.* A. C. McClurg Company, 1916.

A technical reference book.

—— *A Manual of the Land and Fresh Water Vertebrates of the United States.* Blakiston's Sons and Company, 1923.

A book similar to that by Jordan, valuable as a reference but not a field book.

APPENDIX B

SOME KEYS FOR THE OUT OF DOORS

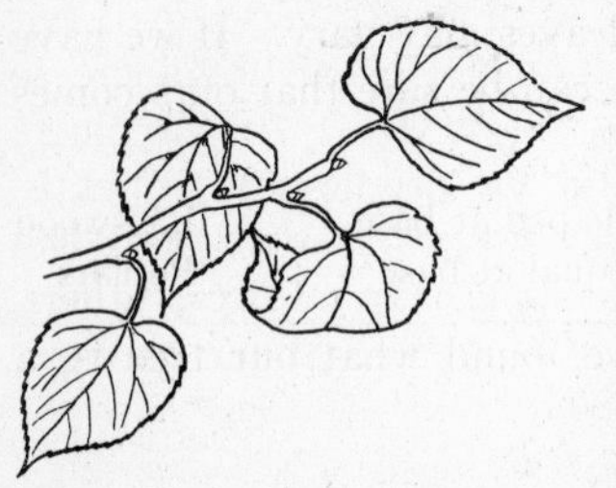

Many of the books we shall use have keys to help us learn to identify the plants or animals we find. The use of such keys is usually quite simple, but to help us get started three keys are included here, one to trees in the summer, one to trees in winter, and one to woods. Let us suppose the illustration is a twig from a tree we have found, but whose name we do not know. In the first key (on page 428) we have two statements, one of which must apply to our twig:

I. Leaves needle- or scale-like
II. Leaves broad, usually not evergreen

As our tree has broad leaves we must look under number II:

1. Leaves opposite or in 3's on the stem . . . . A.
2. Leaves alternate on the stem . . . . B.

The leaves on our twig are alternate, so we look down to B:

B. Leaves simple . . . . d.
B. Leaves compound . . . . a.

The leaves on our twig are simple, so we look under d.:

d. Margins entire . . . . e.
d. Margins not entire . . . . g.

Our leaves have toothed margins, so we choose g. and find:

g. Margins deeply cut or lobed . . . . h.
g. Margins merely toothed . . . . n.

Choosing the second we find:

n. Teeth coarse, one at the end of each lateral vein o.
n. Teeth fine, several for each main lateral vein . . . p.

The leaves we are considering are rather finely toothed:

p. Leaves very narrow, 4 or more times as long as broad . . . . Willows
p. Leaves broader . . . . r.

Of course we have to take the second of these:

r. Leaves not over $1\frac{1}{2}$ times as long as broad s.
r. Leaves about twice as long as broad..... t.

Designation of leaves according to width may be a little hard to follow, since on any twig leaves may vary. If we have chosen a typical leaf, however, we can be sure that ours comes under the first heading:

s. Leaves unequally heart-shaped at base..... Basswood
s. Not heart-shaped, sides equal at base..... Poplars

Now it is evident that we have found what our tree is, a *basswood*.

KEY TO TREES IN SUMMER

I. Leaves needle- or scale-like (mostly evergreens)

1. Leaves needle-like.......................... A.
   - A. Leaves in bundles with sheaths at base..... a.
     - a. Leaves in 5's.......................... White Pine
     - a. Leaves in 3's.......................... Pitch Pine
     - a. Leaves in 2's.......................... b.
       - b. Leaves 3 to 5 inches long............ c.
         - c. Stiff and stout..................... Austrian Pine
         - c. Not stiff, slender.................. Red or Norway Pine
       - b. Leaves $1\frac{1}{2}$ to 3 inches long........... Jersey Pine
   - A. Leaves in tufts or rosettes on older twigs.... Larch or Tamarack
   - A. Leaves singly on stem........................ a.
     - a. Leaves flat, blunt on end.................. b.
       - b. Leaves with tiny stalks.................. Hemlock
       - b. Leaves without stalks................... Balsam
     - a. Leaves four-sided, sharp-pointed......... Spruce
2. Leaves scale-like.............................. B.
   - B. Scales pointed, twigs not flattened........ Red Cedar
   - B. Scales blunt, twigs flattened............ White Cedar

II. Leaves broad, usually not evergreen

1. Leaves opposite or in 3's on the stem......... A.
   - A. Leaves in 3's............................ Catalpa

A. Leaves in 2's	a.
a. Leaves simple	b.
b. Margins entire	Dogwood
b. Margins lobed	Maples
a. Leaves compound	c.
c. Palmately compound	Horsechestnut, Buckeye
c. Pinnately compound	Ash, Box Elder
2. Leaves alternate on the stem	B.
B. Leaves simple	d.
d. Margins entire	e.
e. Leaf base broad, heart-shaped	Red Bud
e. Leaf base tapering	f.
f. Leaves 2 to 4 inches long	Sour Gum
f. Leaves 4 to 6 inches long	Cucumber tree
(NOTE: Sometimes a sassafras will be found with no lobed leaves, but it can always be recognized by the spicy flavor of the leaves and the green twigs.)	
d. Margins not entire	g.
g. Margins deeply cut or lobed	h.
h. Veins palmate	i.
i. With five sharp-pointed, deeply cut lobes	Sweet Gum
i. Square or notched at tip	Tulip Tree
h. Veins pinnate	k.
k. One or two lobes, some leaves entire	Sassafras
k. More lobes	l.
l. Lobing irregular	Mulberry
l. Lobing regular	m.
m. Lobes sharp-pointed	Oaks (Red group)
m. Lobes rounded	Oaks (White group)
g. Margins merely toothed	n.

n. Teeth coarse, one at the end of each lateral vein........................ o.

- o. Leaves slender, 3 times as long as wide........................ Chestnut
- o. Leaves not more than 2 times as long as wide.................. Beech

n. Teeth fine, several for each main lateral vein........................ p.

- p. Leaves very narrow, 4 or more times as long as broad........... Willows
- p. Leaves broader.................. r.
  - r. Leaves not over $1\frac{1}{2}$ times as long as broad.................... s.
    - s. Unequally heart-shaped at base, stem round......... Basswood
    - s. Not heart-shaped, sides equal at base, leaf stem more or less flattened.................. Poplars
  - r. Leaves about twice as long as broad........................ t.
    - t. Leaves smooth............... u.
      - u. Leaf stalk with one or two glands.................. Cherry
      - u. Leaf stalk without glands.. June Berry, Blue Beech
    - t. Leaves rough or hairy........ v.
      - v. Rough, somewhat like sandpaper.................. w.
        - w. Doubly serrate from base.............. Elm
        - w. Singly serrate from above base........... Hackberry
      - v. Soft hairy............... x.
        - x. Doubly serrate........ Birch
        - x. Singly serrate........ y.
          - y. Teeth rounded or blunt............. Red Mulberry
          - y. Teeth sharp....... Hop Hornbeam

B. Leaves compound	a.
a. Sap milky	Sumachs
a. Sap not milky	b.
b. Terminal leaflet much larger than the others	Hickories
b. Terminal leaflet little or not at all larger than others	c.
c. Leaflets rounded at tip	Locust
c. Leaflets pointed	d.
d. Leaves smooth	e.
e. Not over 7 inches long	Mountain Ash
e. Over 12 inches long	Ailanthus
d. Leaves hairy	f.
f. Terminal leaflet as large as others	Butternut
f. Terminal leaflet small or none	Black Walnut

Bud Scale
Terminal Bud
Leaf Scar
Stipule Scar
Lateral Bud
Bundle Scars

KEY TO TREES IN WINTER

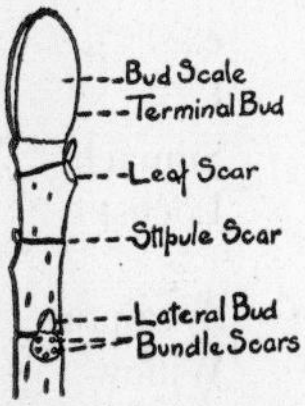

To use the key with a twig such as that illustrated, we will take the second heading "Leaves deciduous.....2." Then, in order, we choose the second 2, the second D, the second f, the second g, the first j, the first n, and the second o.

Leaves evergreen	1.
Leaves deciduous	2.
1. Leaves scale- or needle-like	A.
1. Leaves broad	B.
A. Leaves needle-like, in bundles of 2 to 5	Pines
A. Leaves growing singly	a.
a. Leaves scale-like, overlapping	b.
a. Leaves not scale-like	c.
b. Scales sharp-pointed, twigs round	Red Cedar
b. Scales blunt, twigs flattened	White Cedar
c. Leaves round or angled in cross section, on all sides of twig	Spruce
c. Leaves flat, on sides of twig	
Leaves about ½ inch long	Hemlock
Leaves about 1 inch long	Balsam

B. Leaves 4 to 11 inches long, edges rolled back.. Rhododendron
B. Leaves 3 to 4 inches long, flat.............. Laurel
2. Leaves deciduous, in pairs on opposite sides of the twigs.............. C.
2. Leaves deciduous, alternate or singly on the twigs. D.
C. Buds flat, broader than long, bundle scars forming a line.............. Ash
C. Buds longer than broad, bundle scars 3 or in 3 groups.............. d.
d. Buds large, sticky.............. Horse-chestnut
d. Buds smaller, not sticky
With 4 or more scales showing.......... Maples
With 2 scales showing.............. Flowering Dogwood
D. Buds sunk in stem, not visible, or at least no scales showing.............. e.
D. Buds with scales showing.............. f.
e. Twigs large, buds covered with hair....... Sumach
e. Twigs slender, often thorny, buds hidden... Locust
f. Buds with only one scale visible
Leaf scar encircling bud.............. Sycamore
Leaf scar not encircling bud.............. Willow
f. Buds with two or more scales.............. g.
g. Twigs with no terminal bud.............. h.
g. Twigs with terminal bud.............. j.
h. Twigs stout, leaf scar large, half around bud.............. Ailanthus
h. Twigs slender, leaf scar below bud... k.
k. Buds strictly alternate, 2 rows on twig.............. l.
k. Buds not in two rows, $\frac{2}{5}$ arrangement.............. m.
l. Bud tips pressed against stem... Hackberry
l. Bud tips out from stem....... Elm
m. Scales 2 or 3, buds red, at one side of scar.............. Basswood
m. Scales numerous
Bundle scars 3.............. Birch
Bundle scars more than 3.... Chestnut

j. Buds with one or two scales showing... n.
j. Buds with 3 or more scales showing... r.
n. Stipule scars encircling stem...... o.
n. Stipule scars not encircling stem... p.
o. Buds conical.................. Sycamore
o. Buds flattened............... Tulip Tree
p. Buds all nearly equal......... Basswood
p. Terminal bud much larger than others....................... Hickory
r. Buds several at end of twigs...... Oaks
r. Buds only 1 or 2 at end of twigs.... s.
s. Bud scales lobed at tip........ t.
s. Bud scales not lobed at tip.... u.
t. Buds yellow................ Bitternut
t. Buds brown or gray, twigs smooth.................. Butternut
t. Buds brown, twigs downy... Walnut
u. Stipule scars present....... v.
u. Stipule scars none.......... w.
v. Scars half way around stem, buds slender, sharp Beech
v. Scars less than half way around stem............ x.
x. Twigs and buds rather stout.............. Poplars
x. Twigs and buds slender
Bark wintergreen flavored.......... Black Birch
Bark bitter....... Cherry
w. Pith with cross partitions y.
w. Pith without cross partitions................. z.
y. Pith diaphragmed, chambered......... Butternut, Walnut
y. Pith diaphragmed, stuffed............ Sour Gum
z. Bundle scar 1, twigs green, aromatic...... Sassafras
z. Bundle scars more than 1............. aa.

aa. Bundle scars more than 5, in a curved line.
Buds small, bark of twigs mottled ..... Poison Sumach
(If you have handled this, wash at once in thick soap suds)
Buds large, bark not mottled... Hickories
aa. Bud scars 3 to 5 in a lunate line or ring .... bb.
bb. Leaf scars semicircular, bundle scars in a ring Sweet Gum
bb. Leaf scars narrowly lunate, scars in a line
Twigs with bitter taste Cherries
Twigs not bitter Apple, Pear

KEY TO WOODS

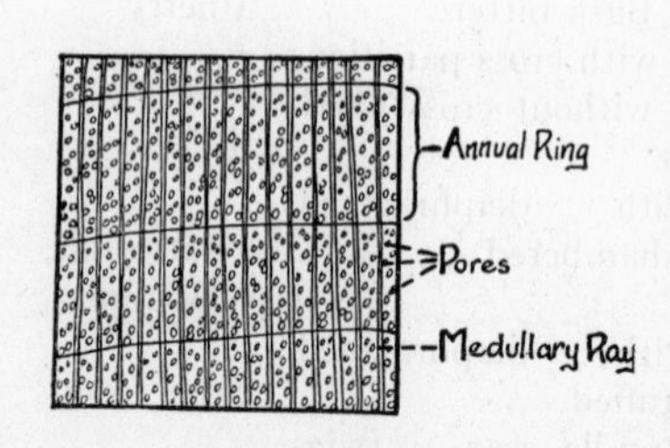

To use the key with a piece of wood such as the one illustrated in magnified cross section, we first choose "III. Diffuse Porous Woods." Then we choose the second C. The fact that spring and summer wood are of uniform density means that our wood is maple.

BASED ON CROSS SECTION

I. Non-porous (No pores visible even with a magnifier)
A. No resin ducts .... b.

b. No distinct heartwood
  Color yellowish-white.............. Fir
  Color reddish...................... Hemlock
b. Distinct heartwood
  Heartwood reddish, sapwood white.... Red Cedar
  Heartwood yellowish-brown, sapwood whitish............................ White Cedar

A. Resin ducts present...................... c.
  c. No distinct heartwood, resin ducts very small............................ Spruce
  c. Distinct heartwood..................... d.
    d. Resin ducts numerous, evenly scattered.
      Annual rings marked by fine lines...... Soft Pines
      Annual rings marked by broad dark bands........................... Hard Pines
    d. Resin ducts very few irregularly scattered.......................... Tamarack

II. Ring-porous woods (Annual rings marked by large pores in spring wood alternating with denser summer wood)
  B. Medullary rays distinct.................. e.
    e. Rays fine
      Heartwood yellowish-brown.......... Black Locust
      Heartwood red..................... Honey Locust
    e. Rays very thick...................... Oak
  B. Rays indistinct......................... f.
    f. Pores of summer wood in radial, branching lines........................... Chestnut
    f. Pores of summer wood in concentric, wavy lines............................. Elm
    f. Pores of summer wood singly or in small groups
      Summer pores minute................ Ash
      Summer pores nearly as large as those of spring.......................... Hickory

III. Diffuse Porous Woods (Pores equal or nearly equal in size and number in spring and summer wood)
  C. Rays broad and conspicuous, the widest twice as wide as the largest pores
    All the rays broad.................... Sycamore
    Some rays narrow.................... Beach

C. Rays distinct, the widest about the same as the largest pores
  Color brown or reddish-brown, spring and summer wood of uniform density........ Maples
  Color deep reddish, spring wood more porous than summer wood............... Cherry
C. Rays fine, narrower than the largest pores.. g.
  g. Pores visible without a lens........... h.
    h. Pores conspicuous, decreasing in size toward the outer edge of ring
      Heavy, heartwood chocolate-brown Black Walnut
      Light, heartwood chestnut-brown. Butternut
    h. Pores only seen on close examination
      Pores not crowded, not decreasing toward outer edge, rays distinct with a lens.......................... Birch
      Pores crowded, decreasing in size and number toward outer edge. Rays barely visible with lens...... Poplar
  g. Pores not visible without a lens........ j.
    j. Pores conspicuous with a lens
      Not crowded, nor decreasing toward outer part of ring................ Birch
      Crowded, decreasing in size and number toward outer part of ring.. Poplar, Cottonwood
    j. Pores inconspicuous with a lens..... k.
      k. Heartwood reddish-brown
        Rays distinct with a lens........ Soft Maples
        Rays not distinct.............. Sweet or Red Gum
      k. Heartwood yellowish-brown, rays distinct without a lens........... Tulip Tree
      k. Heartwood gray or creamy brown
        Rays distinct without a lens..... Basswood
        Rays not distinct without a lens.. Sour or Black Gum

APPENDIX C

MUSEUM EMBLEM REQUIREMENTS FOR BEAR MOUNTAIN PARK CAMPS

Collections may be of any of the following but the requirements given are the minimum so that a single specimen unsatisfactorily done or incorrectly named will disqualify the collection unless more than the minimum is done.

I. *Trees and Shrubs*

1. (*a*) Present pressed leaves, leaf prints of any kind, or drawings of 25 varieties of trees or shrubs.

   or (*b*) A collection of 12 kinds of wood. Specimens should be about one inch in diameter and of uniform length, cut to show the grain for half their length, with the cut surfaces carefully smoothed.

2. For each specimen there should be notes telling where it was found, the kind of soil it grows in (swampy, damp woods, hillsides, rocky soil, etc.), the average size of trees of the kind seen, and the uses of the wood of the tree.

II. *Flowers*

1. Drawings or colored outlines of 25 varieties of flowers that have been personally observed. (Comstock outlines of many of our common flowers, referred to in the Bibliography at the end of Chapter XIII, can be obtained at the camp library.)
2. For each flower there must be definite notes as to where it was seen, the size of the plant, the date it was in blossom.
3. Arrange the drawings according to habitat (all water plants together, swamp plants, meadow plants, etc.)
4. Tell the use of flowers to the plant and why flowers should not be gathered in places visited by many people.

III. *Ferns* and *Fern Allies* (Club Moss and Horsetails).

1. Drawings of the "leaves" of at least 12 kinds. If the plant has fertile and sterile "leaves" different, both should be

shown. The position and shape of fruit dots should be shown. (Originally single "leaves" were collected of each species mounted, but in the interests of conservation the collecting of ferns was stopped.)

2. Notes on each species as to where it grew, the number of "leaves" on the plant, the size of "leaves" and the date.
3. Write a description of the life history of a fern.

IV. *Fungi*, *Lichens*, and *Mosses*

1. At least 12 varieties.
   (*a*) Collection of dried mushrooms or drawings made from fresh specimens.
   or (*b*) 12 or more lichens or mosses.
2. Label and describe, giving the name, place where found, whether on living or dead plants, on trees, rocks, or in soil. Are they parasites, taking their food from living material, or saprophytes, taking food from dead organic material?
3. Fungi are as much plants as flowers or ferns are but no fungi are green. Does this have anything to do with the fact that they cannot make their own food?

V. *Amphibians* (Salamanders, Frogs, and Toads)
Reptiles (Snakes, Turtles, and Lizards)

1. Have a living collection of at least six species of one group. These must be kept with water, stones, moss, or leaves, so as not to suffer.
2. Describe the life histories of the forms collected. Tell the difference between the life histories of amphibians and of reptiles.

VI. *Insects* (Under part 1, one of the four groups a, b, c, d, to be taken)

1. A collection of twelve insects properly mounted with a label for each giving the name, date, place, and the plant on which it was found.
   (*a*) All of one order.
   (*b*) Two insects from each of the following orders: (1) bees and wasps, (2) flies, (3) beetles, (4) moths and butterflies, (5) grasshoppers, and (6) dragon flies and damsel flies.
   (*c*) A collection showing the complete life history of one insect.
   (*d*) A collection of 12 insect galls, mounted and labeled to show the plant on which found and the kind of insect causing it.

2. Make notes, telling something of the habits of the insects collected, their use or harm to man.
3. Make lists of insects
   (*a*) Harmful to crops
   (*b*) Harmful as carriers of disease
   (*c*) Useful in some way

VII. *Fish*

1. Make a collection of six species of fish caught in accordance with the State Conservation Laws in the park.
2. What are the game laws applicable to fishing in the park?
3. Name three different types of fish food and a fish using each.

VIII. *Birds*

1. Notes on 20 birds with drawings or colored outlines. (The Comstock outlines on sale at the camp library may be used.)
2. Describe the food of each species, tell whether it is of benefit to man, and give its special adaptation for getting food.
3. Extra credit will be given for bird houses, feeding stations, or bird baths constructed *and in use.*

IX. *Minerals* (Single substances of definite chemical composition)
Rocks (Composed of various minerals together)

1. Make a collection of 12 kinds of either or both combined. Label to tell what they are and where they were found. Tell which are native and which were brought by the glacier.
2. Describe the distinguishing characters of your specimens.

X. *Stars*

1. Make outline drawings of 10 constellations showing the relative magnitude of the stars, with brief notes.
2. Be able to point out the constellations to your nature counselor.

XI. *Mammals, Tracks*

1. Make plaster casts of 5 types of animal or bird tracks in the field.
2. Write notes on the habits of at least one mammal from personal observation.
3. Give the names and characteristics of at least 6 mammals found in the park.

XII. *Weather Study*

1. Keep a record for one week giving:
   (*a*) The temperature, recorded at the same time each morning, noon, and evening.
   (*b*) The wind — direction, velocity (light, moderate, hard).

(*c*) General conditions, bright, cloudy, rainy, thunderstorms.

2. Tell what clouds are and make drawings of three types.
3. What is thunder? What happens when the lightning flashes?

XIII. *Special*

Special collections with notes on any phase of nature work equal in amount and difficulty to the other collections.

Grades: Satisfactory exhibits will be graded "approved," giving the Minor Emblem, or "excellent," meaning an unusual exhibit as to the number of specimens (at least 75 per cent above the regular), originality, and care in the preparation.

Two collections rated "excellent," or *four* rated "approved" will receive the Major Emblem. These collections need not be submitted at the same time.

The Bar: After receiving the Major Emblem, a Bar may be won in *succeeding* years by submitting further exhibits sufficient to win a Major Emblem, and by giving evidence of work in instructing other campers in nature lore or in making collections.

Flowers and Ferns NOT to be collected. In the interests of conservation and in coöperation with the Park officials, flowers and ferns must not be collected and no emblem will be awarded for any such collection.

The requirements given above were adopted in 1926. Before that time collections of flowers and ferns were required. Since then there have been slight changes: collections of wood specimens are not allowed; trees, flowers, and birds must be recognized in the field in addition to the other requirements; the numbers of flowers, ferns, birds, rocks, etc., has been slightly reduced in each case; and one new topic, soil study, has been added.

INDEX

References to illustrations are in italics.